MULTIGENERATIONAL FAMILY THERAPY
David S. Freeman, DSW

SOME ADVANCE REVIEWS

Multigenerational Family Therapy

HAWORTH Marriage & the Family
Terry S. Trepper, PhD
Senior Editor

New, Recent, and Forthcoming Titles:

Christiantown, USA by Richard Stellway

Marriage and Family Therapy: A Sociocognitive Approach by Nathan Hurvitz and Roger A. Straus

Culture and Family: Problems and Therapy by Wen-Shing Tseng and Jing Hsu

Adolescents and Their Families: An Introduction to Assessment and Intervention by Mark Worden

Parents Whose Parents Were Divorced by R. Thomas Berner

The Effect of Children on Parents by Anne-Marie Ambert

Multigenerational Family Therapy by David S. Freeman

101 Family Therapy Interventions edited by Thorana Nelson and Terry S. Trepper

Therapy with Treatment Resistant Families: A Consultation-Crisis Intervention Model by William George McCown and Judith Johnson

Multigenerational Family Therapy

David S. Freeman

The Haworth Press
New York • London • Sydney

The Haworth Press, Inc., 10 Alice Street, Binghamton, NY 13904-1580
EUROSPAN/Haworth, 3 Henrietta Street, London WC2E 8LU England
ASTAM/Haworth, 162-168 Parramatta Road, Stanmore, Sydney, N.S.W. 2048 Australia

Library of Congress Cataloging-in-Publication Data

Freeman, David S.
   Multigenerational family therapy / David S. Freeman.
      p.   cm.
   Includes bibliographical references and index.
   ISBN 1-56024-125-X (alk. paper). — ISBN 1-56024-126-8 (pbk.)
   1. Family psychotherapy. I. Title.
RC488.5.F74   1991
616.89′156 — dc20   91-7953
                                                                                                                    CIP

DEDICATION

Multigenerational Family Therapy is based on over twenty years of experience with families in therapy. My own family, however, has been my greatest teacher. My wife, Virginia, has been an inspiration and steadying force in my life. Her belief in me has propelled me forward in my thinking and depth of understanding about intimacy and balance. Her love and loyalty have made it all worthwhile. My children, Amy and Dan, have taught me how each generation can teach the next love, respect, and caring.

My belief in family comes first and foremost from my original family, beginning with my dad. Throughout his years as a single parent, he always made me feel he believed in me.

This book is dedicated to him, my beloved father.

ABOUT THE AUTHOR

David S. Freeman, DSW, is Professor at the School of Social Work, University of British Columbia, Vancouver, British Columbia, Canada. In addition to teaching family therapy and family theory at the University, he maintains a private practice in Vancouver, British Columbia, and is also the clinical director of the Pacific Coast Family Therapy Training Association. The author of *Techniques of Family Therapy* (1981), and the editor of *Perspectives on Family Therapy* (1980) and *Treating Families with Special Needs* (1982), he is a charter member of the American Family Therapy Association and a clinical member of American Association for Marriage and Family Therapy. Dr. Freeman received his MSW and DSW from the University of Southern California.

CONTENTS

Senior Editor's Comments   xi
Terry S. Trepper

Foreword   xiii
Ronald W. Richardson

Preface   xvii

Chapter One: Family Therapy   1

Introduction   1
Section One: Major Principles of Family Therapy   2
Section Two: Values Underlying the Family Therapy
    Process   17
Section Three: Goals and Objectives of the Family
    Therapy Process   19

Chapter Two: Family Theory   23

Section One: The Role of Theory in Family Therapy   23
Section Two: Major Concepts Underpinning
    a Multigenerational Approach   30

**Chapter Three: The Major Systems Involved
in the Family Therapy Process**   57

Introduction   57
Section One: The Therapist's Family Emotional System   57
Section Two: The Professional Family System   64

Chapter Four: How to Begin the Family Therapy Process 69

Section One: Arranging the First Interview   69
Section Two: How to Begin the First Session   73
Section Three: How to Make the Interview Safe for All
    Family Members   75
Section Four: Beginning the Family Therapy Process
    with the Parents   78
Section Five: Family Therapy with Parents: A Case
    Illustration and Commentary   79

Chapter Five: Family Therapy with Parents and Children   **113**

Section One: How to Involve Children in the Family
Therapy Process   113
Section Two: Making It Safe for Children to Talk
to Parents: Case Illustration and Commentary   115
Section Three: Beyond the First Interview with Families:
Case Illustration and Commentary   133

Chapter Six: Family Therapy with Couples   **159**

Section One: Understanding Relationship Problems
Systemically   159
Section Two: The Functional Nature of Relationship
Problems   161
Section Three: The Role of Family-of-Origin Issues
in Relationship Problems   163
Section Four: Beginning Family Therapy with Couples:
Case Illustration and Commentary   164

Chapter Seven: Middle Phase of Family Therapy   **199**

Section One: Dynamics of Middle Phase Therapy   199
Section Two: The Process of Middle Phase Therapy   201
Section Three: The Major Practice Principles
of the Middle Phase of Therapy   203
Section Four: Involvement of the Parents of an Adult
Child in Family Therapy   211
Section Five: Family Therapy with the Adult Child
and Parents: A Case Example   214
Section Six: Ending the Middle Phase with Parents
and the Adult Child: Case Illustration and Commentary   246
Section Seven: Family Therapy with Couples — Middle
Phase: Case Illustration and Commentary   265

Chapter Eight: Family Therapy with Siblings   **287**

Section One: Why Work with Adult Siblings?   287
Section Two: Goals of Work with Siblings   288
Section Three: Problem Areas in Work with Siblings   290

Section Four: How to Make a Session Safe for Siblings 292
Section Five: Interview with Adult Siblings: Case
 Illustration and Commentary 292

Chapter Nine: Family Therapy with Individuals **317**

Section One: What Is Family Therapy with Individuals? 317
Section Two: The Problem Areas in Family Therapy
 with Individuals 319
Section Three: Major Goals of the Middle Phase of Family
 Therapy with Individuals 322
Section Four: Family Therapy with an Individual:
 Interview and Case Commentary 324

Chapter Ten: Endings **345**

Section One: The Termination Process 345
Section Two: What Does the Termination Session Look
 Like? 347
Section Three: Termination Session and Case Commentary 348

Chapter Eleven: Special Therapeutic Issues **367**

Section One: Introduction 367
Section Two: Special Issues and Dilemmas 367

Bibliography **381**

Index **391**

Senior Editor's Comments

The purpose of the Haworth Marriage and Family book program is to provide high-interest books for professionals, researchers, and students in the rapidly expanding field of family studies, with an emphasis on works that will be useful to practicing family clinicians.

I am most proud to present this outstanding book, *Multigenerational Family Therapy*, by David S. Freeman. This is the type of book students of family therapy and professionals yearn for: A step-by-step, detailed account of how to *do* therapy. Very well grounded in theory, the major strength of this book lies in its ability to precisely define the process and content of the therapy itself. It is rich with personal reflections and anecdotes from the author's many years of experience as a family therapist. Dr. Freeman includes a large number of clinical examples and verbatim transcripts of interviews to demonstrate various principles and practices, and he even includes a full length case illustration of multigenerational family therapy with an individual.

David Freeman is highly qualified to undertake the challenge of writing a work as broad in scope as *Multigenerational Family Therapy*. A professor at the University of British Columbia's School of Social Work, he has written or edited six books, including *Perspectives on Family Therapy* (1981, Butterworth); *Techniques of Family Therapy* (1981, Jason Aronson); and *Families with Special Needs* (co-edited with B. Trute, 1983, Canadian Association of Social Workers). He has also written numerous articles on family therapy and serves on a number of academic journal editorial boards. Dr. Freeman is a clinical member of the American Association for Marriage and Family Therapy and a charter member of the American Family Therapy Association. Perhaps most important, he has been a practicing family therapist for almost 25 years.

So many family therapy texts are written in a pedantic, unreadable style which then end up sitting on the bookshelf. I assure you this will not be the case with Dr. Freeman's work! *Multigenerational Family Therapy* is one of those rare books which is both intellectually stimulating and highly fun to read. From the first chapter, it is clear that this book is written by a warm, caring, and sensitive person—a person who can translate those qualities to the written page. I am certain you will find *Multigenerational Family Therapy* to be the excellent "read" that I did.

Terry S. Trepper, PhD
Senior Editor
Haworth Marriage and the Family

Foreword

This book comes as a much needed breath of fresh air and expands our vision about what is possible in family therapy. It offers us the type of wisdom that is only gained from years of experience. It provides excellent clinical examples on a wide range of therapeutic issues and an inside look into how Dr. Freeman thinks about his interventions during the therapy sessions.

Multigenerational Family Therapy is for those therapists interested in a genuine, straightforward way to practice family therapy. Dr. Freeman's framework views the family as a positive resource for its members. It demonstrates a tremendous respect for clients and their struggles to develop their sense of self within family. It illustrates why the process of deep, longlasting change is normally slow and gradual rather than quick and dramatic.

Dr. Freeman makes many significant, unique contributions to the field of family therapy in this work. I would like to highlight a few of those I consider the most outstanding.

1. First and foremost, Dr. Freeman offers us a view of the family that is respectful of all family members and that values the multigenerational family as a resource. I cannot imagine a client of Dr. Freeman's feeling unsafe or attacked, blamed, or diminished during a session. Dr. Freeman consistently frames his clients' problematic behaviors in family relationships as expressions of their anxieties, hurts, losses, and struggles to make the world a safer place. These underlying issues are what Dr. Freeman addresses in therapy.

Today much of the family therapy field is preoccupied with symptom-oriented, pathological formulations of the family and a focus on "dysfunctional families." Dr. Freeman broadens our view and helps us to understand, clearly and powerfully, how family also holds the power of healing, growth, and wisdom. Dr. Freeman is masterful at helping people tell their stories non-reactively without feeling a need to justify themselves. When they achieve this comfort they are then able to rethink their stories and explore new options.

2. Dr. Freeman's verbatims of his therapy sessions are unique in the family therapy literature. He gives us the full text of therapy sessions. In addition, he annotates the text with the thinking behind the interventions.

We are able to see the internal thinking process of a master therapist at work. This is in contrast to much of the literature which gives only five or ten minute excerpts from a session. These brief excerpts usually focus on a specific dramatic technique; they do not give us a sense of the full flow of a session and how to handle all that can happen within it.

Dr. Freeman's work provides a demystifying picture of how the beginning, middle, and end of a session look; when and how to do the transitions; the emotional traps which can easily derail a session and how to handle them; the thinking behind choosing one intervention over another as a part of the change process; and a picture of the emotional fit between the therapist and the clients, i.e., how the therapist positions self, or adjusts his or her own emotional connection with the clients in order to further the goals of the therapy.

3. Dr. Freeman affirms that change is a deeply complicated process, that it requires readiness, and that it takes time. The field of family therapy has been overwhelmed in recent years with tricky paradoxical techniques, mechanistic images of fixing cybernetic systems, structural maneuvers, relativizing constructivist formulations, and symptomatically focused quick change solutions. This book powerfully restores the sense of humanity to the field of family therapy.

4. Dr. Freeman demonstrates again and again how our clients' stories are also comprised of their parents' stories and their grandparents' stories. I don't know of any other book in the multigenerational literature which so clearly illustrates the powerful impact of this insight. Helping clients understand their stories in the context of their families' multigenerational stories seems to be an irresistible force for change.

When a client tries to understand his or her family's stories, without assuming a blaming, pathologically-focused stance, then the self of the client begins to change in the process. He or she feels more self-confident, develops more self-esteem, becomes less defensive and more relaxed and generally better able to connect with important people in his or her life. In this book we are able to see how this process unfolds over time. Dr. Freeman's work takes a new direction in family therapy by involving the parents and siblings of his adult clients. The interview in Chapter Seven with the parents of his client could well become a classic in the literature. Dr. Freeman has developed a unique approach which bridges the gap between the generations and honors the parents rather than blaming them. This approach helps the parents become resources to their adult children and improves the quality of the connection between them (again without a loss of self on either side).

5. Dr. Freeman's work has a strong theoretical basis. He shows us that nothing is more practical than a good theory. In the annotations to his

verbatims he shows us just how theory guides practice. Building on Bowenian family systems theory, Dr. Freeman creatively expands his practice of the theory. His is no standard, dry retelling of Bowen theory. Rather, he offers us a fresh approach to the theory. Sitting with him in his office, we see it come alive.

Multigenerational family therapy has at times been characterized as being concerned with "dead" history, being too rational and dispassionate and too intellectually focused. This book gives the lie to all of that. It shows how emotionally powerful this work can be (even when that is not the goal of the work) and how the therapist's own humanity joins with his clients' in their common human struggles.

6. Dr. Freeman highlights the role of the therapist and what he or she brings into the family session. He describes how our view of our families, and our relationships to them, will affect how we "treat" our clients.

Time after time as a trainer, I have seen therapists project their own family issues onto their clients and then treat those issues in the same reactive way they deal with them in their own families. Dr. Freeman shows us the pitfalls of introducing our own family issues into our clinical work.

7. Dr. Freeman's section in Chapter One on "Values Underlying the Family Therapy Process" is unique in the literature. We continue to be affected by the mistaken belief in "value free" therapy. Dr. Freeman clearly defines what he believes to be of importance and value in family work. Ultimately he seeks to honor family and the individual. He is not a therapy of "getting clients free of family," nor is it about individual clients adapting to the family. He understands that the issue we all face is how to be connected to emotionally important others and still be a self. With this book he adds to our understanding of this common human struggle.

8. Very little is written about the middle phase of family therapy. Shorter term therapies do not address the issues of this phase. But a major portion of Dr. Freeman's book is about the middle phase and the various directions it can take. His first book, *Techniques of Family Therapy*, focused primarily on first phase work. I don't think there is anything else in print that tells us so much about the nature of middle phase work, or explores it in such depth.

So I strongly commend this unique book to you. I found it truly refreshing and hugely rewarding.

Ronald W. Richardson, DMin
Author of Family Ties That Bind
and Birth Order and You

Preface

In 1981 I wrote *Techniques of Family Therapy* which represented my thinking about family theory and therapy to that point. Notwithstanding the title, it was not a book about technique; but rather, it was an attempt to clarify the theoretical underpinnings of a family therapeutic approach and to operationalize those theoretical principles into a set of practice strategies. Since writing that text, I have rethought some of the major principles about family therapy, particularly, whom to involve in family therapy and how to begin the family therapy process. Although many of the basic theoretical principles outlined in my earlier text are relevant, I have reconceptualized the process of family therapy. I have learned that it is wise to move slowly and with caution when working with families.

It was important to me to write a book that honors the family as a multigenerational unit. Over the years I have seen countless examples of how the family frames its problems in terms of its historical reality. It is unusual for a family member to talk about a problem in the present without making some reference to an experience in the past. I have come to appreciate that much of the way we behave in the present is a way of honoring some part of our history. This attempt to honor our past can block us from developing alternative responses to today's problems. This book presents a model of family therapy that can help the clinician use the past as a positive force for change.

This book is divided into eleven chapters. The first chapter defines family therapy and discusses the major theoretical assumptions that underpin a family therapy model. It also presents a definition of the multigenerational approach, including a discussion of the major values and goals that frame the family therapy process.

Chapter Two discusses the importance of family theory to family therapy. The major concepts that are the foundation of the family therapy model are outlined. Chapter Three discusses the importance of the therapist's own family to the family therapy process. It also examines potential problems arising when other professionals become involved in the family therapy enterprise.

Chapter Four through Chapter Eleven of this text guide the reader from the beginning of the family therapy process through to its termination.

They discuss therapy with various combinations of family members, including parents, parents with children, couples, siblings, adult children with their aged parents, and individuals. The importance of working with different family units cannot be overestimated. Chapter Four through Chapter Ten present examples of treatment sessions with these different family units. Each chapter contains a complete interview with a commentary. I point out to the reader the various theoretical principles that have guided my intervention. The interviews are analyzed in terms of beginning, middle, and ending strategies. Each interview focuses on helping a particular group of family members to reframe their problem, to connect with each other at a deeper level, and to understand the historical and symbolic context of issues they are dealing with in the family.

Chapter Eleven, the last chapter in this text, deals with therapeutic dilemmas and special family therapy issues.

My hope is that both the student and the experienced therapist will find this book useful. It is written not only for family therapists but also for anybody who is interested in understanding how to work with families in more depth. This book can be used to increase understanding of family behavior as well as to help the therapist understand how to make it safe for various family members when they are seen together and are trying to connect with each other on a deeper level. My underlying principle and value is that the family is a major resource system to the individual. All but the most extremely deprived families come together with some positive history. To be cut off from that history is to lose an important part of our sense of the self. The family therapy process should help people to rediscover their family history and to use it as a positive force for dealing with today's uncertainties and dilemmas.

Chapter One

Family Therapy

INTRODUCTION

A multigenerational approach to family therapy honors the family in a special way. The approach recognizes that the family can be both a resource and a problem for its members. One of the goals of the therapeutic process is to maximize the family's positive influences as a way of dealing with the problem areas.

It is critical that the family therapist understand the influence and power the family exerts over its members. Without this understanding, a therapist may unwittingly side with a family member against his or her family. The collusion is subtle but profound. It is common for a client to begin therapy by telling the therapist various stories about how rejecting, critical, and unloving his or her family is. Many therapists assume these stories are generally accurate and focus their efforts on helping the family member deal differently with his or her family. These therapists may have a view of family similar to that of their clients and may even advise that family contact should be kept at a minimum. Other therapists may encourage their clients to confront family members about the behavior they see as upsetting and destructive. These approaches, although intended to be supportive and helpful to the client, in fact, reinforce the client's preconceived assumptions about family thereby maintaining distance, a lack of family connection, and a sense of loss.

Multigenerational family therapy emphasizes the importance of family connections in people's lives. Therapists employing this framework encourage their clients to work on family relationships. Ordinarily, people enter therapy feeling quite ambivalent about their families. If the therapist shares this ambivalence, he or she will feel discomfort about involving the family and avoid this potentially positive resource. My model of family therapy views the family as a powerful ongoing influence in its members' lives. My approach may involve seeing aged parents, adult siblings, and other important family members as well as the more traditional parents and children.

This introductory chapter describes the major family therapy principles that underlie a multigenerational approach to family therapy. When a therapist involves several generations in the therapeutic process, he or she embarks upon a radical approach to problem solving. This chapter provides a framework for that approach.

SECTION ONE:
MAJOR PRINCIPLES OF FAMILY THERAPY

Principle One: A family member's problem is contributed to and reinforced by the other family members' response to it.

All family therapy models endorse this basic principle. However, there continues to be an active debate about which came first, the problem or the "response." My position is that it does not matter. By the time the family is seen by a therapist, the problem has existed for so long that it has become part of the way in which the family functions.

The family therapist's task is to understand the functional nature of the problem and how the family reinforces it as a way of problem solving. When an individual family member experiences difficulty, either physically, socially, or psychologically, the family system has to respond to him or her in some way. This response will set up certain family behavioral patterns that may influence behavior after the original problem is gone. Family members who define a particular individual as having a problem will do so in relation to their view of themselves as "healthy." Perceived dysfunctional behavior in one family member may contribute to another family member's feelings of adequacy. And so, certain responses, once set in motion, may become part of a permanent behavior pattern.

In a session that I once had with two parents and their three adolescent children, the father told me that his wife usually jumped in to break up any conflict between him and his older adolescent daughters. When I asked him how that affected the way he dealt with his daughters he answered that he knew he could count on his wife to rescue him if he became too angry. He went on to explain that knowing this allowed him to indulge his anger and, at times, actually get angrier than he felt initially. When I asked his daughters what they had learned about their father from their conflicts, they answered that they had discovered their father was not as safe as their mother because his temper got out of control. In fact, the mother's rescuing the father contributed to the father's unsafe appearance to the daughters and added to the distance that developed between father and daughters. The family members had not recognized the reciprocal nature of their behaviors.

Whatever the nature of the problem, it is up to the practitioner to take a holistic view of the family and resist zeroing in on the identified problem. The immediate concern of the family is often not the major underlying problem. The important issue is how the problem has affected the relationship network within the family.

Principle Two: Change will not be sustained in a family unless the most powerful members of the family are willing to sustain it.

It is an important system's principle that change occurs from top to bottom. If a child tries to change his or her behavior towards a parent without a corresponding change from the parent, within a short period of time, the child will revert to the old familiar behavior. However, if the parental unit is able to sustain a change in their behavior towards a child, eventually the child will behave differently.

The general principle is when one member in the family system changes and remains involved with the entire system, the other members will be unable to maintain their old behavior. The question for the therapist to determine is which members of the family have the greatest potential for change. In many families, the child acts out as a way of connecting with his or her family. It is futile to try to get such a child to change without the cooperation of the parents. A more effective approach is to help the parents understand how their reaction to the child encourages this behavior. The family therapist must analyze the family system to discover the functional nature of the problem and the reciprocal roles the family members play with the problem. The next objective is to determine which unit within the family has the greatest potential for change. In my opinion, the parental unit is the most powerful one in the family. When a therapist helps the parents respond to a child's behavior in new ways, the child will modify the behavior and a new family structure will develop.

A simple experiment will help the reader understand how difficult and risky it is to do something differently in one's family. Think about some traditional behavior that your family counts on you to continue exhibiting. Then stop behaving in this manner and examine the reactions. The usual response by family members is anger, hurt, and criticism. In turn, the one who has changed becomes anxious about the reaction that his or her new behavior has brought about. He or she quickly discovers that by resuming the old behavior his or her own anxiety and the anxiety of family members can be reduced. This exercise illustrates how difficult it is for a family member to change his or her customary way of taking care of other family members.

Principle Three: Functional families maintain a balance between individual autonomy issues and family solidarity concerns.

When assessing a family, it is important to evaluate how it is able to balance the individual needs and expectations of its members and the solidarity concerns of the group. Often parents enter family therapy with the hope that the therapist will work toward greater solidarity in the family; and in effect, bring the family members together in a closer, more involved way.

Adolescents and young adult children tend to resist coming into family therapy because they are apprehensive about becoming more involved in family issues. Adolescents are in the process of moving away from the family. Even the term family therapy increases their anxieties about their ability to eventually emancipate from the family. The family therapist, therefore, has a unique balancing act to perform. He or she has to address the parents' concern for greater togetherness while also communicating to the adolescents that their needs for greater autonomy and separateness from the family are understood and supported.

In most functional families, individual autonomy is not a major concern. Family members are able to respect each other's differences while at the same time feeling connected as a group. When there is a dysfunctional member within the family, whether a parent or a child, this balance becomes threatened. Some of the family becomes overinvolved with the dysfunctional member and others are more on the periphery. Usually when there is a concern about one family member, the ability of the family to maintain a balance between individual needs and group concerns is lost. The anxiety is too high and the preoccupation with the dysfunctional member too great to maintain the balance. The involvement of helping professionals usually reinforces the imbalance with its focus on the dysfunctional member. The responsibility of the family therapist is to realign the family boundaries.

The family with an alcoholic parent provides an example of family imbalance. The common pattern is for the nonalcoholic parent to be preoccupied with helping the alcoholic partner give up his alcoholism. During periods of sobriety, the children will tend to feel great anxiety about when the alcoholic parent will start drinking again and throw the family back into chaos. A great deal of thinking, talking, and feeling is directed towards the alcoholic and his drinking.[1] The drinking behavior controls the family. Families function for years maintaining this anxiety. Everyone is cheated because of the preoccupation with the alcoholic. Individual needs of the children are considered secondary concerns and the individual needs of the nonalcoholic parent are seen as less important than taking care of the alcoholic member. When the alcoholic partner ceases to drink, it also creates anxieties within the family because the members have not learned how to function as a family without the familiar preoccupation.

Whenever there is a family problem, it in some way undermines the ability of the family to be able to give attention to the individual needs of its members. One of the therapist's task is to help the family support the individual growth and development of its members and in the case of children to help them leave the family while at the same time feel connected and supported by it.

Principle Four: The family therapy session must be safe for all members and respect individual differences.

Principles three and four are interconnected. One of the ways in which the family therapist operationalizes principle three is by the way he or she relates to the family members in the sessions. It is up to the family therapist to make all the sessions safe for each family member. Family members are worried that they will be scapegoated, held responsible for the problem, focused on excessively, invalidated, etc. It is a great relief to family members to leave the first session feeling respected and understood and to have had the opportunity to explain their view of the world to the rest of the family. One can understand the anger, ambivalence, and silences of family members as stemming from the anxieties that have been described. The job of the family therapist is to join with each family member around his or her concerns and to help to make it safe for them. I routinely ask family members questions that focus on how they have learned to make it safe for themselves, both in the family and in the world at large.

In addition to providing a safe environment, the therapist must be respectful of the individual differences within the family. The therapist must guard against trying to get family members to perform and/or behave in ways that make the therapist feel comfortable. Some family members may choose to be silent, some may choose to tell their concerns through stories and humor while others may choose to be angry for a while, etc. All the behaviors that family members exhibit during the early phase of family therapy are representative of the way they cope and make it safe for themselves. When they realize that the family therapist is not going to judge them, control them, and/or evaluate them, they will begin to relax and involve themselves in a positive way in the process.

The therapist plays an active role in keeping the sessions safe. He or she must foresee the reactions by family members that would tend to invalidate what another family member is saying. For example, when a child tells his or her story and describes reality as he or she perceives it, it is essential that the family therapist does not permit the parents to criticize or invalidate the child's story. Allowing parental criticism is a common error of therapists. When a therapist asks a family member to comment on what another member has just said, the member frequently responds with criticism and verbally attacks the other family member. When this happens, the therapist has allowed the session to get out of control. He or she has set up a situation in which one family member has undermined and invalidated what another family member has said. It is essential that the family therapist prevent that from happening. The therapist must give the family members an opportunity to say things through him or her to other family members without the statements stirring up anger, criticism, or hostility. Being heard without being criticized is a powerful experience for a family member. The degree to which the therapist is able to prevent family members from reacting to each other with hurt or anger determines the degree of safety experienced by family members in the session.

Principle Five: The family therapy session must offer the family members an opportunity to experience each other differently.

In the early stages of the family therapy process, the family tries to duplicate their "at home" behaviors in the therapist's office. Family members are both hopeful and anxious about the therapist being wise enough to prevent this duplication of experience. Family members desire change yet are frightened by it. They will resist it. Behavior that is unpleasant and makes one sad and/or unhappy is nonetheless familiar. Coping mechanisms for dealing with the behavior have been developed. Change that prevents us from reacting in the familiar way will force us to develop a different understanding of ourselves. Many people find this frightening.

When a family therapist offers family members an opportunity to experience each other differently, the members become hopeful that they will be able to achieve something new and more meaningful. Simultaneously, their anxiety levels go up. In the beginning phases of family therapy, the family members will start expressing more of their concerns as they become more comfortable. They will feel relieved and hopeful during the session. However, when they return home and react to each other in the old predictable ways, they begin to feel defeated. They will return to therapy saying that they feel discouraged because they have not been able to react differently with each other outside of the family therapist's office. The challenge to the family therapist at this point is to ask questions that will help the family members identify what the loss for them would be if they were to respond differently to each other. Inexperienced family therapists commonly get discouraged at this point and question their abilities and/or think family therapy is not working.

The therapist must continually help the family members understand that their old responses stem from ambivalence and anxiety rather than dysfunction and illness and that gradually change will occur.

The skilled therapist offers the family members hope that they can connect with each other in a more positive way and learn about each other while these new connections are occurring. The behavior of the wife in a couple I once worked with illustrates the struggles that we can have about changing. For several months I had been encouraging the wife to bring her mother into a session. She eventually agreed to do this. However, when the session arrived she appeared without her mother. When I asked her why her mother was not there, she answered she did not really want her mother to come to the sessions. I then asked her what the loss would be for her if I met her mother. Her answer was that she had spent a lifetime learning how to deal with her mother and that this allowed her to maintain a comfortable distance from her. If a session with her mother challenged the view she had of her mother, she would lose this comfortable distance. The risk of having to give up her old story about her mother created tremendous anxiety and prevented her, at least at that point, from connecting with her mother differently.

There is no question that it is risky for family members to see each other differently. Once you see someone differently from the old familiar pattern you have to reevaluate your own behavior towards that person. You cannot hold the other person solely responsible for what is going on between the two of you. The ultimate challenge for the family therapist in all this is to shake up old patterns and remain calm in the face of the family's ambivalence when the therapist is successful in doing so.

Principle Six: The family therapist must control the process during the session.

When conducting a therapy session, the experienced therapist is continually focusing on the process and is avoiding becoming caught up in the content. Families will often present a story and then try to get the therapist to say who is right or wrong. It is, of course, impossible to figure out a story. If you as a therapist can be convinced that one member's view of the story is correct, then you have entered the triangle and everyone in the family, as well as yourself, becomes the loser.

When looking at the process, therapists should be alert to how individual members within the family use conflict to maintain emotional distance. There are two major types of conflict: (1) non-productive conflict, which maintains relationships the way they are; and (2) functional conflict, which involves the renegotiation and reorganization of relationships.

As discussed earlier, when one family member changes, other members can become uncomfortable and conflict can occur. The way in which the family deals with conflict, rather than the conflict itself, is critical to its functioning. The therapist will want to note which members of the family are most comfortable with change and how they are positioning themselves within the family to deal with that change. The therapist will also want to note what other family members are doing in response to that change. It is not the issue (content) which is important, but how it is dealt with (process).

The family will try with all its might to get the therapist to take a side on content issues. When family members become anxious, they almost always revert to content issues. When a therapist gets hooked into content, it is usually because it has to do with an issue in his or her own life. Later in this text, I will deal with the issue of unfinished business and how it affects the therapeutic process. The success of the therapist in understanding content issues as symbols of struggles and unresolved losses will be determined by the degree to which the therapist has worked through his or her own past losses and struggles.

A popular joke highlights the importance of process over content. A famous rabbi in Russia was well known for his astuteness and ability to resolve marital conflicts. A couple with serious marital conflicts went to see him. When they entered the rabbi's office, they found him there with his rabbinic student. The rabbi asked the husband why he came to see him. The husband responded by telling him many terrible things about his wife. When he finished, the rabbi said, "You're right." Then the rabbi asked the wife why she came to see him. The wife proceeded to tell the rabbi many terrible things about her husband. When she finished the rabbi said, "You're right." At this point, the rabbinic student was very confused and said, "But Rabbi, how can the husband be right on the one hand and the wife right on the other hand?" The rabbi reflected for a moment, stroked his beard and said, "You know something; You're right, too."[2]

Principle Seven: The family must own its change and take responsibility for its outcome.

In a family system's approach, the experts are the family members. The goal of the therapist is to help the family develop its own way of discovering how it wants to move from point A to point B. One of the therapist's jobs is to encourage family members to assume the expert role. The initial expectation of the family is that the therapist will provide the answers. This expectation presents one of the first challenges to the therapist. Consequently, there may be an initial struggle between the therapist and the family about who will do what. If the therapist takes responsibility for the solution to the problems, then he or she must also take responsibility for the outcome. If the therapy works, it is because he or she is a great therapist. If it fails, it is because he or she is inadequate. In either case, the family does not assume responsibility for resolving its problems.

One of the most powerful experiences family members can have in therapy is to discover that they have their own effective ideas about how to resolve their dilemmas. The therapist's initial task, then, is to encourage the family to find its own solutions. Typically, when families enter therapy, it is because they have been ineffective in resolving their problems. Often their view of the picture exacerbates the situation and impedes their finding better solutions. Therefore, one of the first tasks in family therapy is to redefine the problems. In accomplishing this task, the therapist must help the family understand how its problems affect the entire family. This process helps the family members gain a broader, more sophisticated definition of themselves as a system. As this occurs, they will also develop a new set of ideas about how they want to resolve their dilemmas. As the therapist focuses on the family's ideas, the members will begin to see themselves as experts in dealing with their problems.

The course of therapy with the "M" couple illustrates the importance of this dynamic. During the course of therapy the couple decided to separate. Mrs. M decided to continue in therapy to work on some self-issues. One of her major concerns was doing things alone, which was the basic reason she had remained so long in an unsatisfying relationship. She found it difficult to go to movies alone, go out to dinner alone, travel alone, etc. One day she came in and announced ecstatically that she had gone to a movie alone and had found it an enjoyable experience. I responded by challenging her as to why she wanted to do this alone. At this point, she became angry and asked if this was not what we had been working toward all this time. I replied I didn't know. I asked if this was something that she thought was good for her and stated that I was not sure myself. She told me with tremendous energy and conviction that this was the best thing for her and that she needed to do this. I could not convince her otherwise. I took a rather contrary position with her because I wanted her to "own" the change rather than do something to please me. I did not want her to think about my advice as a way of making it safe for her to go out alone. When she tried to talk me out of my lack of enthusiasm for her activity, it reinforced within her the idea that she was the mistress of her fate. It is important for family members to own their outcome and not do something to please their therapist.

In addition to the seven general principles described on the preceding pages, there are several specific principles that underlie a multigenerational approach to family therapy. Both sets of principles dovetail and when taken together form a holistic approach to family therapy.

The following principles represent the most significant themes discussed throughout this text. They are evident in both the basic theory and the practice components of the model.

Principle Eight: The family is a multigenerational emotional system.

Relationship patterns are passed on from generation to generation. One needs to look at multigenerational patterns to understand current family patterns.

Parents will bring lessons from their own families-of-origin and try to put them into practice in their new family-of-procreation. A family has a minimum of three family influences, the husband's family-of-origin, the wife's family-of-origin, and the synthesis of the two families in the nuclear family. The success with which the differences, as well as the similarities, are integrated by the couple will determine the overall balance of the new family unit. Many people assume that when they marry they start with a clean slate and will evolve a unique family unit. The family that the couple develops is indeed unique; however, it has been greatly influenced by the emotional lessons and experiences each person has brought into the family.

It is helpful in understanding how we operate in our families to look back at least three generations. It is not enough to understand just our parents and siblings. The way our parents organized our family and responded to us as children should be understood in terms of their experiences in their own families. Often a family therapist assesses a family by asking the parents to talk about their experiences in their own families. He or she will ask about what happened between various family members in the extended family, that is, what were the losses, how were emotional needs met, who was the most involved, who was the most distant, etc. This information, though important, does not reach back far enough in helping us understand family structure, function, and development.

Our parents' behavior toward us was, to a significant degree, determined by their parents' behavior toward them. If our parents experienced separation, divorce, or significant loss in their own families, these experiences would have had a profound impact on how they dealt with their family-of-procreation. If we do not understand our parents' experiences in their own families, we will not fully appreciate how their struggles and losses have shaped their behaviors and feelings toward us. A multigenerational approach provides a different framework for understanding why certain reactions, decisions, and positions are taken in a family.

On one occasion when I was asking a highly conflictual couple about their families-of-origin, the husband told me his father had never really told him much about himself. He grew up seeing his father as being in the background, not really involved in the family and somewhat unimportant in his life. He described his mother as being more central to the family. He adopted the general notion in the family that his father did not care much about the family. I encouraged the husband to learn more about his father. He discovered that his father was an orphan who had been deserted by his extended family and had raised himself from the age of thirteen. When the husband told me this story, he interrupted himself and said, "You know, I never considered my father an orphan. I never thought of him as a little boy who did not have a family." This new idea about his father led to him viewing his father's separateness from the family differently. He stopped seeing it as a sign of lack of love and caring and began to understand it as a manifestation of his father's early sense of loss and isolation from his own family.

It is helpful to family members to understand that current concerns have historical significance and, in turn, implications for future generations.

Principle Nine: People's relationships are shaped by their family stories.

One way to change family behavior is to help the family modify its emotional stories about its history. Everyone has stories about his or her experiences with family.[3] Most people think that their stories are accurate accounts of what happened. In truth, many of the stories that we carry in our heads are symbolic of losses and/or important emotional events that have shaped our thinking about ourselves, our family, and the world around us. These stories are often used to maintain safe distance in relationships.[4] If we felt hurt, rejected, abused, misunderstood, or invalidated in our family, we will be cautious about duplicating the experiences underlying these feelings in our adult life. One of our hopes when we marry or form close relationships is that our new partner will either make up for our past losses or replicate the safe, positive experiences we had in our families. When our partner's behaviors remind us in any way of hurtful memories or when our partner disappoints us by not making us feel okay, we take a defensive stance. This stance is a familiar reaction that allows us to feel emotionally safe.

In order for change to occur in relationships and/or families, we have to rethink the basic stories that we carry in our heads about ourselves and our family. When we feel that our family experiences occurred because we were not lovable, then we will continually look to others to make us feel worthwhile. Paradoxically, we will also be more likely to perceive others' behaviour towards us as confirmation of our feelings of inadequacy.

One of the major objectives of a multigenerational approach is to help people rethink their family stories. One must recognize, however, that many of us are not prepared to give up the stories that we have developed about ourselves and our family. These stories allow us to maintain a safe distance in relationships. We know how to function with these stories intact. If we give up these stories then we have to alter our style and way of relating.

Principle Ten: Significant change in the extended family influences the functioning of the nuclear family.

To understand the family problem, we have to understand the family's developmental history. There is an intimate connection between the nuclear family and the extended family. The nuclear family is commonly described as the family-of-procreation, the biological mother and father raising biological children. One can extend the definition of the nuclear family to include stepparents, stepchildren, and adopted children, but basically, the nuclear family is a small unit of parents and children. The extended family includes grandparents, uncles, aunts, in-laws, cousins, etc. Most people are not aware of how they are influenced by extended family changes. The death of a parent, illness of a sibling, the break up of a marriage within the extended family, the death of a cousin, etc., are all changes that can have a profound impact on the nuclear family.

When one assesses the family on a multigenerational basis and charts all the major events, one begins to perceive a relationship between the timing of problems and developmental shifts within the family. It is not unusual, for example, for the death of a parent to produce marital problems for an adult child. Similarly, the divorce of parents after thirty or forty years of marriage can threaten the sense of family solidarity among the adult children in the family. Not just the behavior but the response of the extended family to major developmental events in the nuclear family has a tremendous impact on the nuclear family.

The meaning a family attributes to its problems is often based on its previous experiences with that type of problem. Couples often view a problem as stemming from the husband's side of the family or the wife's side of the family. It is not unusual for a couple to fight over which side of the family was responsible for producing a particular problem in a child. Our view of a problem and the labels that we give to it are to a large degree determined by our previous family experiences of that problem. Professionals in turn also contribute to the labeling process. It is a powerful event when the professional definition of a problem coincides with the family member's personal definition of a problem. When this occurs, the label becomes firmly embedded in the family's mythology.

In my practice I ask numerous questions about the timing and context of family problems. For example, I will ask: (1) what losses have occurred in previous generations, (2) have there been any major developmental changes coinciding with the problem, (3) what was going on in the family prior to the problem occurring, (4) what have the family members learned from the family in their attempts to cope with this type of problem, (5) how do the anxiety levels of the two parents compare, and (6) how do the parents understand these differences? When the family addresses these questions, they begin to see how change in a nuclear family may be connected to events in the extended family. They also begin to get a sense of how their previous experiences with a particular problem influences their current perception of the problem.

Principle Eleven: We are never totally free of our family involvements.

Family relationships extend beyond space and time, life and death. By involving members of the extended family in the course of therapy, we bring in new energy and information, which in turn helps broaden and deepen family understanding. We occasionally see people who believe they can escape their family ties. Some individuals on the West Coast feel that the Rocky Mountains have separated and freed them from their family on the East Coast. What they learn, of course, is that family issues and relationships follow us wherever we go.

Some people attempt to suppress any thoughts of their family and avoid seeing them for years at a time. However, they fill the vacuum by looking for replacements. They try to construct a new family based on what was not finished within the old family. When their new relationships begin to feel like and/or to remind them of the old issues, they quickly revert to the behavioral patterns that were played out when they were still in contact with their family.

One cannot, by distance, work through old family issues. One must deal with them at the source if one is going to be truly free of difficult issues. During the course of therapy, it is crucial to involve available extended family members. It is always a powerful experience to participate in a session in which aged parents, siblings, or other important relatives tell their stories. The later chapters in this text contain general examples of interviews with different family constellations. In various ways, they illustrate that we cannot, by sheer willpower and distance, make peace with our family members. The most solid way for us to accomplish this is to reposition ourselves in the present with family members so that we understand their stories from a new perspective.

It is well known that the more solid the parent/child relationship the less devastating the parent's death is for the child. Many children who have conflictual relationships with their parents maintain the fantasy that one day their parents will understand and accept them and all will be fair. When that parent dies, the anger, the rage and the sense of betrayal increases. They feel that once again the parent has cheated them out of the relationship. Working with adult children prior to a catastrophic loss is a form of prevention. Helping them make peace with these relationships will result in fewer regrets when the parent does die.

Principle Twelve: Children emerge from the family-of-origin with a certain degree of unfinished emotional business.

We all have unfinished business. Unfinished business affects our choice of partners, the type of family structure we create, and the expectations we have of our mates and children. The premise underlying unfinished business is that children take on their parents' anxieties, vulnerabilities, and fears. It is difficult for children to separate their own emotional experiences from those of their parents. When a parent reacts to a child out of anxiety, neediness, or fear, the child will to some degree act out those feelings for the parent.

One of the most dramatic examples of unfinished business is seen in second generation survivors of the holocaust. Numerous studies indicate that the second generation assumes the same fears, anxieties, and phobias of their parents. Many of these children have not been told about their parents' experiences in World War II concentration camps. Nevertheless, they exhibit similar behavioral patterns to those of their parents.[5]

Unfinished business is present in all families. The critical factor is the degree of unfinished business that an individual carries from one generation to the next. There is a certain amount of deprivation built into all family life. The extent of the deprivation one experiences in the family is the main determinant of how much unfinished business one carries into the next generation. Unfinished business does not go away. It is something we need to work on and to understand so that that part of ourselves does not interfere with our relationships with others.

Principle Thirteen: Relationship problems are a reflection of unfinished business and not an indication of a lack of commitment, caring, or love. One cannot give emotionally to others what one has not received from the family-of-origin.

This principle underscores the importance of reframing relationship problems as family-of-origin issues. One of the more compelling reasons for forming a relationship is to feel special. Most people want to be admired, liked, and needed. Those relationships that produce these feelings are the ones we cherish the most. When someone is asked what he or she needs from another to make the relationship work, the answer usually focuses either on what the individual did not receive from his or her family or on what he or she wants to duplicate from his or her family.

There are two major issues that get played out in most relationships: One either moves into a relationship as a way of making up for one's losses or as a way of replicating one's own family experiences.

Relationships based on finding someone to make us feel whole and right are formed out of mutual need. The focus is more on what one needs than on what one can give. There is a high degree of reactivity in these relationships. The parties quickly become disappointed and negative towards each other. Of course the more a person feels unloved and/or unlovable, the greater the neediness he or she brings into a relationship.

The second major type of relationship is one that is based on the couple's desire to duplicate experiences that they have had in their own families. These types of relationships have their own sets of difficulties. These difficulties come to the fore when one partner is not able to behave in a way that fulfills the other partner's expectations. When one emerges from a family-of-origin feeling special and cared for in a certain way and has a mate who is not able to reproduce these feelings, disappointment and disillusionment will set in. In summary, most of us look for someone to make up for previous losses or to take care of us in a special way. When we do not find this we feel let down. This feeling leads us to take a defensive, distancing stance in the relationship and relationship problems will occur.

Principle Fourteen: The basic North American family structure is extended.

It is a myth to think that the basic family structure is nuclear. Most people are powerfully involved with their extended family members, although the look of the involvement has changed over time. The current notion of extended family is no longer based on how many people live under the same roof.

Our definition of family structure is significant because it influences whom we see as important and whom we include in family treatment. For many years, North Americans have popularly viewed the family as a two-generational unit. The work of Parsons and Bales[6] has influenced this view. Their studies indicate that the nuclear family is the most viable, flexible family system in an advanced industrial society. Parsons and Bales describe the nuclear family system as a family of parents and children lacking strong ties to extended kin. In a moment's notice, these families can move where the labor market demands its presence. Since Parsons and Bales's work was first published, many articles have appeared reiterating their view that the extended family is dead and that the nuclear family is the major family structure in North America. This view has become so accepted that family units with close and significant ties to extended families are at times seen as dysfunctional and inappropriate. Although the initial work by Parsons and Bales is over thirty-five years old, the prevailing attitude continues to be that the more functional family structure is a small nuclear family unit. This attitude obscures the importance of the extended family.

The critical question is not whether we call the family nuclear or extended. What we should be looking at are the roles various family members in the nuclear and extended family constellation play to facilitate and/or handicap the family unit. If we limit our concept of family structure to two generations, we ask fewer or no questions about extended family and can miss discovering the natural resources that are available to family units.

The importance of the extended family is not its physical proximity but rather its emotional impact. A few of the questions that I commonly ask to get a sense of the role extended family members play in the life of a nuclear family are as follows:

1. Who are the most important people in your life?
2. Who can get you upset most quickly?
3. Who do you turn to first for help?
4. Which family members do you spend the most time talking about?

5. Who has had the strongest impact on your own development?
6. What relationship in the family do you have the most regrets about?
7. If changing one relationship in your life would help you feel better about yourself, what relationship would that be?

SECTION TWO:
VALUES UNDERLYING
THE FAMILY THERAPY PROCESS

It is important that the family therapy model be guided by clearly articulated values. Values are the "oughts" or "shoulds" of behavior. They set the parameters of acceptability and prevent us from experimenting with families in harmful or unethical ways. The therapist's intervention must always honor the family's sense of itself as a positive unit. Therapy should never undermine the solidarity of the family. As previously discussed, one of the major tasks of the family is to help its individual members grow, develop, and leave while at the same time fostering the need for continuity, connection, and belonging. When a family therapist enters the family, his or her challenge is to address both of these opposing developmental goals. On the one hand, the parents will want the therapist to support their needs for family solidarity. On the other hand, the adolescent children will want permission to begin to move away from the family, their concerns being with issues of autonomy.

The therapist must be aware of his or her own values and refrain from superimposing them on the family. The therapist's job is to learn about the family culture, its values, its goals, and its vision. The therapeutic strategies and expectations must be based on that knowledge. Each family has a unique value system based on the values that each parent has brought into the relationship as well as the values of the children. The children's values are, in turn, influenced by school and peers and may be in conflict with the parental value system. In actuality, a family has several value systems which may be competing with each other. The fact that issues arise from a conflict in values is not always addressed. Often value differences are not even discussed, yet these differences get acted out around incidents and problems. Understanding the family's values will allow the therapist to see when conflict arises from different belief systems. The skilled therapist will ask questions that allow each family member to articulate his or her value system and how he or she developed it over time.

Honoring the family's value system allows the family to own its outcome. The therapist should not impose solutions on the family or assume that he or she knows best how the family should function. There is no hard data about what makes a family functional. We are guided by our hunches, hypotheses, myths, and values. This makes it all the more prudent to take a research stance concerning families and to allow the family members to teach each other and the therapist about how they have learned to get the job of living done.

The value system of the family therapist should be open enough to allow the family a greater range of differences. The therapist must guard against preconceived ideas about what does or does not work for the family. At the same time, the therapist must have a bottom line about what is permissible, or basically unacceptable, in terms of family behavior. Families cannot change or risk talking about important matters when there is a threat to the members' safety. The family therapist has the responsibility of making it clear to families that when there is any suspicion of violence or abuse that the family members' safety must be guaranteed or the family therapy process cannot proceed.

To be effective, the family therapist must not be involved in secrets nor should he or she collude with or align with certain family members against other family members. The family therapist must honor his or her commitment to all the members of the family, those present as well as those in the background. The underlying goal of the family therapist is to help family members at all levels connect in a deeper way. It is important that the family therapist be a positive force in a family's life. The therapist accomplishes this by serving as an impetus to the family as it rediscovers its basic wisdom.

A school counselor raised an interesting value dilemma during one of my recent consultations. It covered a family that consisted of a biological mother, her lesbian lover, and two adolescent children. One of the children was acting out at school which initiated referral to the school counselor. The counselor was in a quandry about whether he should invite the mother's lesbian partner into the family sessions. He was not sure if the partner was truly a member of the family. Clearly, our own attitudes about what constitutes a family will determine whom we invite into the sessions. As it developed, the children in this family saw the mother's partner as an important caretaker and family member. It is critical that the therapist honor the family's definition about who is family. When we block the family's definition then we become part of the problem.

Other value dilemmas commonly experienced by therapists arise from their views of "proper" lifestyle and "appropriate" parents. An example of a value stand that is presented as fact can be seen in the following quote:

There are also three generation families, which are more typical of lower social economic groups and lower middle income groups. In such multi-generational families, where there are grandparents and parents, parents and children, the question many times becomes who is parenting what child?[7]

The inference here is that families that use extended family members for child care exhibit more confusion about parenting. This value bias would interfere with an open-minded approach to assessing the family and the way it uses its natural resources.

SECTION THREE:
GOALS AND OBJECTIVES
OF THE FAMILY THERAPY PROCESS

The therapist must have clear, concise goals and objectives for the family therapy process. Goal-setting for a system like the family is complex and involves four major levels. Each individual has personal goals and hopes; the family unit has its expectations as well. The community at large has goals, particularly when a family member is having difficulties outside the home, at school, at work, etc. The therapist's goals and expectations comprise the fourth level.

To facilitate goal-setting at the various levels, it is helpful for the therapist to communicate his interest in helping the whole family as well as its individual members.

As mentioned previously, the two major developmental goals of the family are: (1) to help its individual members be competent and independent, and (2) to maintain and foster commitments to the family as a whole. One of the major successes of family living is to learn how to be part of a group while at the same time be separate from that group. Many families have difficulty achieving this balance. They may emphasize family solidarity to the point that individual members must relinquish their autonomy. Alternatively, they may emphasize autonomy to the point that there is no family commitment whatsoever. Difficulties in balancing the two poles of individual autonomy and family solidarity underlie many of the problems experienced by families.

When a family first enters therapy, symptom relief is one of its major goals. Symptom relief is the elimination or alleviation of a problem that has been attributed to one of the family members.

It is unusual for a family to begin therapy with the understanding that family change is desirable. The usual complaint centers on one member.

For example, Johnny is misbehaving and the family cannot control him or dad is drinking and is disruptive to the family. The task of the family therapist is to help the family develop broader goals. The therapist must help the family expand its perception of the problem from an individual focus to a group interactional level. It is enlightening for the therapist to ask each family member to explain how he or she sees the problem. This process quite quickly illustrates how subjective our perceptions are. It also provides an opportunity for each member to express related difficulties and to thereby bring additional goals into focus.

Another aspect of goal-setting is developing short-term and long-term goals. The therapist should be setting goals for each session as well as long-term goals. For example, one of the major goals for the initial session is to create a safe environment for the family in which no one feels solely responsible for the family experience. Simultaneously, the therapist is developing goals for the long-range therapeutic endeavor. The long-term goals will encompass significant behavioral change within the family. However, if the therapist is unable to accomplish the initial short-term goal of providing a nonthreatening environment, the achievement of long-term goals will be severely limited.

The major long-term goals of family therapy are to help the family to:

1. Reframe the problem from an individual concern to a family focus.
2. Improve the ability to deal with and accept differences.
3. Improve individual and family problem-solving abilities.
4. Decrease the need to use scapegoats.
5. Develop an intra-observational capacity of its own internal function.
6. Improve autonomy and individuation.
7. Develop a balance between individual autonomy and family solidarity.
8. Expand the boundary of the family to include important extended family members as resources for the family.
9. Work through its unfinished business.
10. Become its own resident expert.

ENDNOTES

1. Stanton, Duncan and Thomas Todd & Associates. 1982, *The Family Therapy of Drug Abuse and Addiction*, New York: Guilford Press.
2. Freeman, David. 1981, *Techniques of Family Therapy*, p. 99. New York: Aronson.
3. Stone, Elizabeth. 1989, *Black Sheep and Kissing Cousins*, New York: Penguin Books.

4. *Ibid.*, pp. 21-24.

5. Bergmann, Martin and Milton Jucovy (eds.). 1982, *Generations of the Holocaust*, New York: Basic Books.

6. Parsons, T. and R.F. Bales. 1955, *Family Socialization and Interaction Process*, Glencoe, Illinois: Free Press.

7. Pillari, Vimala. 1988, *Human Behavior in the Social Environment*, Pacific Grove, CA: Brooks/Cole Pub. Company, p. 252.

8. Freeman, David. 1981, *Techniques of Family Therapy*, p. 99. New York: Aronson.

Chapter Two

Family Theory

SECTION ONE:
THE ROLE OF THEORY IN FAMILY THERAPY

The practice of therapy must be based on clear conceptual thinking. The therapist needs to have a theoretical framework that will guide his or her practice without diminishing the intuitive or artistic aspects of that practice. The theoretical foundation brings perspective to the behaviors families exhibit. A strong theoretical base will help dispel the confusion and anxiety that is commonly experienced by a therapist in the midst of a demanding family session.

The therapist's theoretical framework should be based on a well-developed set of concepts that help explain systems behavior. These concepts serve as a cognitive map of group behavior and bring order to what may initially appear to be chaos in multidimensional family behavior. The concepts facilitate the formation of diagnostic impressions, which in turn, will serve as guides for structuring therapeutic strategies. Our conceptual map must be a broad one that will help us to perceive the widest range of behaviors. Family systems concepts will provide a broad understanding about behaviors and will help us to categorize these behaviors in meaningful ways. Other concepts can be limiting and can serve as blinders that pigeonhole our perceptions.

Family therapy is guided by theoretical concepts that relate to several different systems levels. Psychoanalytic theory, humanistic theory, and learning theory promote our understanding of how the individual functions in the world. These theories help to explain the family's influence on the individual as well as the individual's influence on the family. This orientation highlights the fact that from the moment of birth a child is temperamentally different from all the other members of his or her family. Thomas, defines temperament as "the behavioral style of the individual child — the how rather than the what (abilities and content) or why (motivations) of behavior. Temperament is a phenomenologic term used to describe the characteristic tempo, rhythmicity, adaptability, energy expenditure, mood, and focus of attention of a child, independently of the content of any specific behavior."[1] As therapists, we take temperamental differences into account to understand how an individual's uniqueness influences family behavior. Personal characteristics, such as temperament, physical appearance and intellectual capacity as well as the timing of the birth of a child in the developmental life of the family are all important variables affecting the family. This book will not discuss the psychiatric and behavioral theories concerning individual behavior other than to note it is important for a family therapist to be familiar with them. A family therapist focuses on the whole system but should at no time lose sight of the individual.[2]

We require one set of theoretical concepts to explain the family as a system and another set to understand the family's community. We may conceptualize the family as being positioned between individual needs on the one hand, and environmental and community expectations on the other. The family must help its members to achieve their individual needs while at the same time satisfying and responding effectively to the expectations of the community. It is helpful for family therapists to have an understanding of the community resources available to families and, at times, to influence what is happening in the community, particularly the school community. Families often request therapy because a child is having difficulty in school. The family might have entered therapy unwillingly at the recommendation of the school. At times a family will complain the school is not supportive of their child or has unrealistic expectations of the child. In these situations, the families will tend to view the school as hostile and judgmental rather than as a resource.

When evaluating the family, the therapist may discover that, in fact, the family has been doing a good job with its members but that its way of educating their children is in conflict with the school system. Quite often this is the case with native-Indian families whose value systems and ways of communicating are quite different from those of the non-native community. Typically schools will try to help the native children become more like non-native children. The therapist who understands how community expectations add to familial problems will work with the school system to help it to become more sensitive to the needs of the family. Quite a different approach would be utilized if the therapist agreed with the school system that it was the "problem child" who needed the help. The important idea underlying this discussion is that the therapist should have a working knowledge of how the systems that the family depends on in the community influence the family. These systems may serve as resources for the family, making the family's job easier or as barriers, adding to the family's difficulties.

Diagram 1 illustrates the five systems levels affecting family behavior.[3] The first and smallest unit is the individual. Understanding at this level is based on intrapsychic theories. The second and third levels represent the nuclear and extended families. Intervention here is based on family theory. The fourth and fifth levels represent neighbors, friends and peers, and the community at large. Intervention at this level is based on community organization theory.

When a therapist has a solid grounding in these five theoretical areas he or she can move between and within any one of these systems levels to produce change. At times an individual needs direct work, particularly when his family is not available to him. At other times the most important intervention takes place in the community. Most often, the family is the preferred unit for producing change.

It is important for the therapist to employ a set of theoretical assumptions to guide his or her interventions in all five system levels. The basic assumptions guiding family practice are as follows:*

Assumption One: The family as a whole is greater than the sum of its parts.

This assumption suggests that what a family produces as a group cannot be understood by understanding family members separately. Many therapists have found that when a member is seen outside of the family context, he appears quite different. When all family members are seen together, their behaviors are influenced by the emotional processes going on within the group at the time. However, when one member is taken out of the group, even the most bizarrely functioning member, his or her behavior and performance become significantly different. It is important for the family therapist to meet the entire family. Old myths and stereotyped ideas about how an individual functions can be thrown into question when the whole family gets together. When one or more family members are absent, it becomes more difficult to question ideas family members have about those who are not present.

---

*The following five assumptions were previously described in Freeman, David, 1981, *Techniques of Family Therapy*, New York: Aronson. pgs. 18-27.

DIAGRAM 1. Five Interconnecting Systems

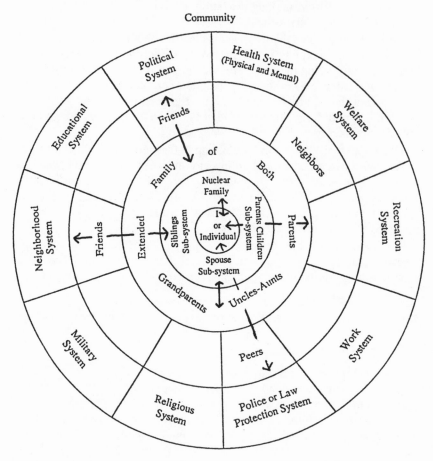

Assumption Two: If you change one part of the family system you change the whole family.

This assumption stresses that change in one part of a system affects the rest of the system. For instance, if one member of the family refuses to play old games, that is, to maintain old patterns of behavior, but remains in contact with the family, the family has to adjust to this change. Unfortunately, that person often distances from the family and has little or no interaction with other family members. Hence, a void is created. This void has to be filled, but the chances are that it will be filled by someone else playing the distanced member's role, especially if that role is important to the family. The scapegoat process illustrates this point: If one member of the family is scapegoated to maintain emotional calm or distance among family members, it is likely that another member of the family will become the scapegoat when the first person refuses to maintain that position.

Therapists who have worked in psychiatric hospitals are familiar with the scapegoat process. When a member of the family is hospitalized, it is usually because his or her behavior has become too disruptive to the family. Within a short time, most hospitalized individuals appear much less disturbed. Emotional distance from one's family or community can change disturbed behavior quickly. However, soon after the person is returned to the family and community, the old behavior returns. The revolving door syndrome that exists in many of our psychiatric hospitals is, in part, a result of this process. Unless the family changes with the individual, they will tend to put pressure on this individual to resume the familiar behavior patterns to maintain the old balance. However, if the family can be involved and can learn how the new behavior is in the best interest of the whole family, they will learn how to accommodate this behavior and appreciate the benefits of doing so.

Assumption Three: Family systems become more complex and organized over time.

This assumption stresses that families are complicated systems that grow and develop over time. With the increase of information, resources, and additional members, the family has to adjust, grow, and adapt. The family must be perceived as an open system experiencing dynamic tension that constantly helps it to expand both its functions and its structure. General systems theory has emphasized that a universal characteristic of living systems is a tendency toward complexity. "Biological wholes achieve higher stages of organization in contrast to physical wholes, in which organization appears to result from the union of pre-existing elements."[4]

This assumption cautions us that it is wise to take the position that one never knows for sure just how a particular family functions or what its structure will be at a given time. Each family changes from moment to moment. Every day brings new information, energy, and dilemmas to the family. The family's method of dealing with these variables will in turn affect its overall functioning.

The family as a whole continually negotiates between its internal and external needs and wants and its resources and demands. The active negotiation between the internal and external components of a family will determine its eventual course of action. Each time that the family comes together, a slightly different course of action is triggered. It is therefore impossible to predict from one moment to the next how a particular family will react to a given stimulus. Accordingly, the preferred therapeutic stance is to learn about a family by continually questioning family members about their decisions and how they make them. The therapist who assumes that he or she knows what is going on within the family is, in fact, closing off an opportunity for learning. This is true not only for the therapist but also for the family. As the family learns more about itself, its options, and how it has changed over time, so does the therapist.

Therapy is an ongoing learning process between the family and the therapist. The better the questions the therapist asks the family, the more opportunity the family will have to learn about itself. In contrast, the more statements the therapist makes to the family to explain their functioning, the less the family will learn about itself. It is up to the therapist to help the family to realize that it is always changing and that change itself is natural. The favored therapeutic position is to become a researcher for the family to help it to learn more about itself.

Assumption Four: The family is open, changing, goal directive and adaptive.

The family has resources within itself to deal with both internal and external stresses. One of the goals in work with families is to identify the resources within the family so that the family can help itself. This goal is directly related to Assumption Three. One should not view the family solely as a reactive system that fends off change, but rather as a proactive system that has the potential for finding its own answers and developing its own strategies to meet its needs.

Most family literature depicts families as primarily closed systems with few inner resources to deal with their problems.[5] This view is somewhat accurate for those families experiencing extreme stress and anxiety. However, most families are not so immobilized. With appropriate intervention they can tap internal resources for dealing with their difficulties. Drawing on the family's resources highlights and reinforces the family's positive growth potential. It can be safely assumed that a family that has been together over time has learned something about how to manage its affairs. This assumption directs the therapist's role in relation to the family. In addition to asking the family about its problems, disappointments, and failures, the therapist should also focus on what has worked, what has gone well, and what the family members see as their strengths and resources.

Basically, families try to get the job of living done in the best way they know how. They have ideas of what works well and what does not. When one supposes that families are adaptive and goal-directed, then the therapist looks to the family's strengths and the other resources that can be called into action from the family gestalt. This approach is similar to social network therapy in which the therapist involves many members of the family gestalt to revitalize the family system.[6]

Assumption Five: Individual dysfunction is a reflection of an active emotional system.

When an individual member within a family experiences any type of difficulty the family system must respond to it in some way. This response will set in motion certain family behavioral patterns that may influence behavior even after the original problem is solved. A family member is seen as a problem in relation to those in the family who are seen as healthy. It follows that dysfunctional behavior serves a certain role within a family. The behavior occurs as part of reciprocal processes between family members.

In one family I worked with, the mother was the mediator. All family members believed that without the mother's mediating there would be nothing but fighting. For her part, the mother expressed her wish to stop playing a role which caused her great stress and discomfort. What was not clear to the family was the reciprocal needs these roles served: The mother felt responsible and in control, and the other family members were free to take no responsibility for their behavior.

There is a complex interplay of roles in response to any problem. For example, when a family has a diabetic member, the need to control the diabetes can have a powerful effect on the total structuring of the family. When the diabetic is a child, issues arise around who will give the child his medicine, who will be responsible for his diet, who will make the medical appointments, and who will generally be the most concerned and anxious about keeping the diabetes under control. When one parent is responsible for maintaining the diabetic child, then a special relationship develops between this parent and the child, occasionally to the exclusion of other family members.

Whenever a family member has a problem, the possibility arises that other members will develop a structure that causes two or more individuals to be overinvolved with each other to the exclusion of others. When this occurs, the immediate concern of the family may not be the major underlying problem, but rather how the family is dealing with the problem. A parallel issue is how the relationship changes when the problem no longer exists.

In summary, each one of the preceding theoretical assumptions strongly influences how the therapist practices. They determine whom to see, when to see them, and how to proceed in the therapeutic hour. They provide a framework for understanding the family's behavior. They discourage the therapist from relying on his or her own feelings about the family's interactions and feelings, which are an unreliable guide at best since they are rarely the same as the family's feelings about itself.

It is important for the therapist to utilize a theoretical framework that gives meaning to behaviors that might otherwise appear as discrete or bizarre. A theoretical framework helps the therapist formulate questions and strategies for intervening in a family system in a logical, consistent manner.

SECTION TWO:
MAJOR CONCEPTS UNDERPINNING
A MULTIGENERATIONAL APPROACH

Our theoretical understanding of family behavior requires that we view the family as a structural, functional, and developmental system. Structurally the family is made up of a number of subsystems, such as parent/child, husband/wife, brother/sister, grandparent/grandchild, etc. We can no longer say families begin when people decide to marry. Nowadays a family begins when two people decide to form a common household. An increasing number of people are choosing to live together. We also have an increasing number of remarried parents who bring children from earlier marriages to the new relationship. Current statistics indicate that only 35% of North American families are comprised of the biological mother and biological father raising biological children.[7] In these changing times, it is wise for the therapist to ask the caretakers in the family for their own personal definition of family. It is also important to understand that an individual's personal emotional definition of family may be quite different from the family structure in which he or she is currently living. The therapist must separate the emotional components of the definition from the current structural definition of family.

The functional workings of a family are closely interconnected with the family's structural development. The way the family chooses to organize its life will influence how it chooses to relate within its intrafamilial systems and to its extrafamilial systems. There are two aspects to family function: (1) the actual functional responsibilities delegated to the family by its environment, and (2) the behavioral phenomena or processes that occur within the family and move it into action.

The major functions assigned to the family by society are as follows: the meeting of survival needs; the protection, care, education, and rearing of children; the creation of a physical, emotional, social, economic setting that nurtures the development of individual family members; the nurturing of affectionate bonds within the family that will help each member become a contributing member of the family and community; and the responsibility for the social control of its individuals.

Over the last hundred years, the function of the family has changed dramatically in our society. At one time the family's major function was an economic one, with the family preparing its members for economic survival. With the advance of the industrial revolution, technology, and various social welfare institutions, the family has moved away from a predominantly economic function toward a more affectional or emotional function. Today the family's major responsibility is to prepare its members for coping with society emotionally and socially, rather than economically.[8]

Family relationships are the most powerful influences on how children relate to others in the family and to the outside world. Sibling relationships usually mirror the relationship between parent and child, and husband and wife in the family. When the husband and wife relationship is supportive, respectful, and caring and, in turn, each parent is fair, loving, and consistent with all the children, the siblings will have a solid, loving, supportive relationship with each other. On the other hand, when the parents in the family are disrespectful, hostile, and abusive toward each other and their children, the children will act out these behaviors with each other and their relationships will be primarily adversarial.

It is now generally recognized that a child's peer group and school also play a powerful role in his or her socialization. However, the child will continue to use the family as his or her major frame of reference for understanding what goes on outside the family unit.

A systems perspective requires that the family therapist be cognizant of the individual developmental stage of each family member as well as the developmental stage of the family as a unit. Ideally, the individual's developmental stage and the family's developmental stage will be mutually supportive. Unfortunately, this does not always occur.

As an example, consider the teen-age mother. We know the adolescent years are a time when individuals want to experiment and test authority in their search to discover who they are. However, the adolescent who is responsible for taking care of another human being must put personal desires aside while meeting the dependency needs of the child. Adolescence is a time of ambivalence. The teen-ager moves back and forth between wanting to be cared for and wanting to be independent. It is a tremendously reactive period. When an adolescent must meet the responsibilities of a caretaker, developmental conflict is inevitable.

The family unit, like the individual, goes through various developmental stages, beginning with the creation of the spouse subsystem and working toward the development of a family with the birth of children. In the early years, a family's development will center around the caretaking, nurturing, and dependency roles. When the children start school, the letting-go stage will begin. As the emancipation of the children continues, the parents will begin to reassess their individual goals and desires. By the time the children leave home, the parents will have come to terms with being a couple rather than being caretakers. Ideally, this process will be gradual and will allow the family as a unit to prepare itself for the different needs and expectations that it will encounter overtime. However, many parents will delay preparing for these changes, most commonly by devoting themselves primarily to caretaking responsibilities to the exclusion of other roles. Life events may also interfere with the ideal developmental process. Separation, divorce, remarriage, illness, and death all have a significant impact on the family's developmental growth. A series of developmental and situational losses may throw the family off balance and change the developmental life cycle of the family. We then see dysfunction in the family as a unit.

The following theoretical concepts help us understand the family as a multigenerational emotional system. Each concept has structural, functional, and developmental aspects. The concepts dovetail with each other and when taken together provide a theoretical framework for understanding the family as a complex socio-emotional system.

Genogram/Multigenerational Perspective

As discussed previously, the family is a complex multigenerational system. The family must be seen in the context of the extended family and the community as a whole. It can also be seen as the middle system, situated between the internal needs and expectations of its members on the one hand and societal demands on the other. The most powerful subsystem within a family is usually the parental unit. The parents bring important lessons from their own families that they try to put into operation in their new family. Here we see a blending of three family influences: the husband's family-of-origin, the wife's family-of-origin, and the synthesis of these two. The success with which the differences, as well as the similarities, are integrated in the new unit will determine the overall balance of the family.

One of the best methods of achieving a multigenerational perspective is by preparing a multigenerational map or genogram. The genogram provides a quick survey of the structure, function, and development of the family field. It provides a multigenerational perspective of the family, thereby allowing for the understanding of the problem in an historical perspective. When the therapist solicits information for the genogram from the parents, they are provided with an opportunity to review their history in a neutral, nonjudgmental setting and to gain new information about each other and themselves. *Genograms in Family Assessment* by McGoldrick and Gerson is an excellent book on how to construct the genogram.[9] Reproduced below is an illustration of a typical genogram.

The genogram in Diagram 2 presents a dynamic changing picture of the family. A therapist never completes a genogram with the family. As the couple/parents become more comfortable with the therapist, they will provide additional information for the genogram. Even those people who are presented as family in the first session may change over time in therapy. The more anxious the family member, the more reactive and guarded he or she will be in sharing information about the family.

This latter point was dramatically illustrated by a woman I saw in family therapy. This woman presented herself as being extremely anxious and unable to cope with fairly mundane matters. She described her family-of-origin as being normal and average. She indicated she was the last-born of four daughters. Nothing in her family history struck her as eventful. She described her parents as loving. Being the last-born child in the family she felt special and said that there was not much conflict between herself and her siblings. It seemed rather strange that this woman would have such an extreme anxiety reaction when her children reached their mid-teens. No one in the family could understand why she seemed so disturbed. Nuclear family life appeared uneventful. During the sixth session with this couple, the woman told me that she had forgotten to mention that her parents had had a son when she was eleven-years-old. I asked her what she saw as the significance of this event. Her reply was that she was the last-born daughter and the princess of the family, but when the prince was born there was no further need for a princess and she began to feel invisible. She was so furious at her brother that she felt she had eliminated him from her memory. When I asked her if she saw a connection between her brother's birth and her two daughters reaching their teen years, she said that she did. She

Diagram 2. Example of a Multigenerational Genogram

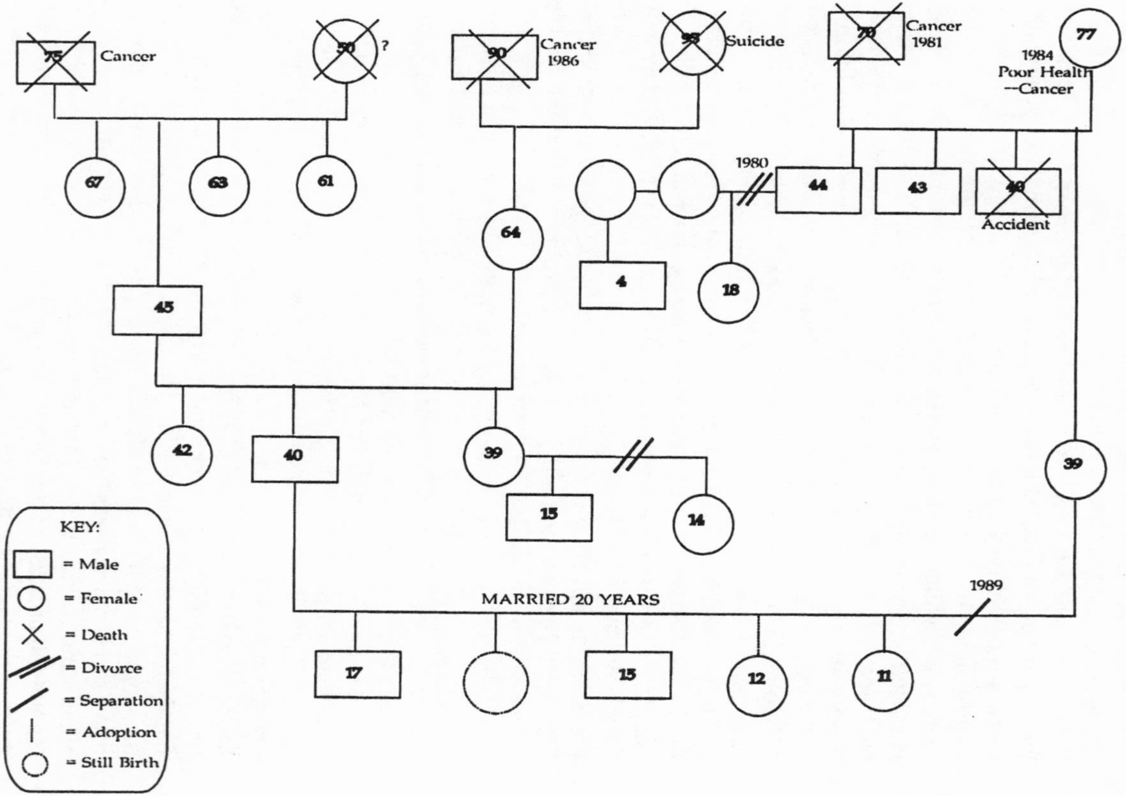

had been quite involved with her daughters until just recently when they had begun to make moves away from the home. They were currently more involved with their friends and school than they were with her. The mother said that she had begun to feel the same sense of loss that she had felt when her brother was born. One could then understand her anxiety reaction as stemming from her need to bring the family back together to make it safe for herself.

In constructing the genogram, it is important to obtain a history of developmental changes within the family such as births, deaths, accidents, moves, dates family members left home, marriages, illnesses, etc. Every significant developmental change will have an impact on each member of the family and a potential for adding to unfinished business. The genogram provides an instrument for understanding how the family evolves over time.

People's experiences in their family-of-origin influence the expectations that they have for their own children and determine how they structure the sibling roles of their children. The family-of-origin provides the individual with a certain kind of relationship with his or her siblings and a particular role in the family based on the sibling position. As a parent, the individual will either try to duplicate the structure that he or she experienced as a child or try to improve upon it.

To understand the family's structural organization, we have to understand how the family members deal with the various sibling positions in the family, such as the role of the oldest child in the family as compared to the youngest. By taking a multigenerational perspective, the therapist gains a better sense of why certain problems are emerging in the family-of-procreation. One finds that the more problems that existed in the family-of-origin, the more unfinished business there will be in the family-of-procreation. The degree of unfinished business will depend on which members of the family-of-origin were central to the difficulties in the family. When one child is the center of concern in a family, the other children may not be as emotionally entangled and consequently may be able to develop with minimal stress. By taking a multigenerational reading, the therapist can determine which family member was of central concern in the family-of-origin.

A multigenerational perspective also provides the family therapist with an indication of the emotional level at which the parents functioned in their families-of-origin. It is not uncommon to find that the father and mother have quite different concerns regarding family behavior. Many of these concerns are based less on what is going on in the present family than on the unfinished business from their families-of-origin. It is there-fore crucial to understand how the parents' families were structured. The genogram provides for this knowledge in a systematic way.

The genogram is usually constructed during the first interview. After the parents have presented their view of the problem, the therapist sug-gests that it would be helpful to put the problem in an historical perspec-tive. This suggestion begins to redefine the problem and provides the first opportunity to connect with the parents as individuals as well as parents.

In summary, the genogram or multigenerational perspective of each parent assists the therapist in the following ways:

1. It allows the therapist to understand the parents as emotional people in their own right.
2. It gives the therapist an idea of how the parents' history influences their view of themselves in the world.
3. It helps the therapist develop hypotheses about why a particular problem is affecting the family at a particular time.
4. It begins to identify multigenerational themes that are being played out in the present.
5. It allows the therapist to form a solid connection with each parent.
6. It helps the parent feel understood and accepted for his or her unique history.

Clients often complain that therapists offer advice and suggestions too quickly without really knowing who they are and what their history is. A genogram helps avoid this pitfall.

Unfinished Business

Unfinished business is the carrying and transmitting of unresolved emo-tional issues from one generation to the next. This concept is based on a multigenerational perspective. As young children, we do not understand that our parents' reactions to us are based more on their own experiences in their families-of-origin than what is going on with us. We all, to some degree, have incorporated our parents' values, attitudes, and emotional issues. Our parents cannot, without great effort, give to us what they did not receive from their own parents or a significant substitute. The unfin-ished business of one generation is projected into the next generation and forms the basis for that generation's emotional issues. This process is a complicated one. Most of us do not truly appreciate its power to affect major decision-making.

Not all children are equally affected by their parents' unfinished business. Sibling position, timing of birth, the relationship between the parents, the physical well-being of extended family members, job pressures, and the general health of parents and other family members all influence the degree to which any one child will become the central focus of a parent's unfinished business. The only child is more likely to inherit his or her parents' unfinished business by virtue of the simple fact that the parents are unable to spread their issues out among more children. If the parents are able to confine their conflict and neediness to the husband/wife relationship, there will also be less unfinished business projected onto the children. On the other hand, if something about the child, such as temperament and/or timing of birth, reminds the parent of an unresolved issue from his or her own family-of-origin, that child will be more vulnerable to the parent's unfinished business.

Unfinished business is present in all families. One cannot come out of a family without a certain degree of unfinished business. What is important is the degree of unfinished business that a person carries from one generation to the next. A certain degree of deprivation, anxiety, and loss is built into family life. The degree to which these experiences are played out in our families is the main determinant of the amount of unfinished business that we will carry into the next generation. Unfinished business does not go away. It is not something that one can run away from or ignore. It is a dynamic that each of us has to work on throughout life. A major goal in family therapy is to help the family members gain a better understanding of their own unfinished business. Instead of reacting to this unfinished business, it should be used as a way of understanding one's own issues with more depth and sensitivity.

Another form of unfinished business is the process by which parents project certain characteristics, both positive and negative, onto their children. Different children remind parents of different issues in their lives. When the issues make the parents anxious, they try to change the child's behavior to lesson their anxiety. When the child's behavior brings back pleasing memories of the family, it is reinforced. It is the parents' responsibility to distinguish the child's uniqueness from the parents' emotional history. The parents' need for their children to succeed in the world is connected with their own issues from their families-of-origin. Ideally a parent will not be overly excited about a child's successes or overly dismayed about a child's failures. Instead, the parent should see the child's experiences as learning opportunities for him or her. Many children become confused because they do not understand their parents' reactions to their behavior. The projection process can be an extremely burdensome process for the child. It can invalidate the child's own experience in the world and undermine his or her relationship with the parents, thereby contributing to significant unfinished business in adult life.

Developing a Sense of Self

The concept of self is developmental. It includes the process of differentiation of self over time from primary caretakers. Differentiation describes a person's ability to define the self as a separate entity. The process begins at birth and continues throughout the life cycle. Over time an individual moves from a state of relative undifferentiation to progressive differentiation.

Birth begins the differentiation process. For a period of time, children rely completely on the parents and family for security and identification. From birth to approximately two years of age, children are unable to distinguish or differentiate themselves from their environment or caretakers. This stage coincides with Erickson's stage of trust.[10] When the environment is secure, supportive, and consistent, children will move from personalizing events as a reflection of themselves, towards separating themselves out from what is happening around them. As this process occurs, children move toward an identification of their selves that is separate from their caretakers and immediate environment. The more insecure, inconsistent, or rejecting the environment, the more difficult this task becomes.

Development of an individual's sense of self is a continual process that moves from undifferentiation or fusion with one's environment toward increasing differentiation or uniqueness and an identification of oneself as being separate from one's environment. Infants are unable to distinguish themselves from their parents or caretakers. Their senses of self or ego boundaries are very much interconnected and fused with their caretakers. In their beginning attempts to be different from their environment, children behave in ways that are in opposition to their caretakers' wishes. This form of opposition, or reactivity, represents an attempt to become separate from the parents. There are two major periods of reactivity in child development: (1) age two to approximately five, and (2) age thirteen to approximately nineteen. During these periods, many parents feel that they have "problem children." The children are seen as obstinate, argumentative, and more importantly, different from their parents. Unless the parents can understand some of their child's behavior as an attempt to differentiate himself or herself from the immediate environment, they will identify any reactive moves as symptoms of emotional problems. The parent who resists a child's attempts at differentiation will either prolong the child's struggle to find himself or herself or will stifle the child so much that the child will give up all attempts to become an independent entity. The latter response is the much more serious problem.

The child who continues the struggle to be unique has the ability to come to terms with who he or she is in relationship to the family. The child who gives up the struggle loses the ability to develop a clear sense of his or her own identity. Adolescents with no sense of self have trouble in adulthood becoming goal-oriented, competent, and nonreactive individuals.

In adult relationships where ego boundaries overlap, one finds a significant degree of personalization. Individuals who have difficulty identifying themselves as separate from others will tend to use others as a way of defining themselves. In their relationships, they exert considerable pressure on the other to be like, to agree with, and to support their view of themselves. Any attempt by others to be different, to take a different stand, or to see the world in different terms presents a crisis and throws the relationship into emotional turmoil. When the other partner maintains a different stance and refuses to give it up to support the relationship, then the reactive partner has to find some means to reduce his or her tension, either by finding another relationship that is supportive of these emotional needs or by making some differentiation moves that will define the relationship at a higher level.

Emotionally, differentiated individuals are able to behave in a proactive manner by defining who they are, what they want, what they think, what their goals are, and what they are prepared to work on, in ways that are minimally influenced by others. Granted, all of us maintain some concern about what others think and are influenced to some degree by others. However, the more differentiated the individual is, the less his or her thinking is dominated by approval of other people. On the other hand, the undifferentiated or fused individual is more reactive and is strongly affected by what others feel and think. Considerable emotional energy will be spent worrying about what others think and he or she will be predominantly controlled by need for approval from others. Very few decisions by these individuals are made independently of outside forces.

These two emotional stances, proaction and reaction, should be viewed as opposite ends of a continuum. When an individual is feeling calm, in control, and confident, he or she will behave in a more proactive or self-oriented way. However, when an individual feels anxious, threatened, or emotionally shaky, the sense of self is impaired and the individual is generally reactive in his or her behavior. This continuum is in fact punctuated by three general self-stances.

The first stance is the proactive stance that represents the ideal of being in control of the self with minimal concern about the approval of others. The second stance is the reactive or pseudoself stance. This stance involves a person taking a stand in reaction to another's demands as a way to demonstrate competence to a significant other. This stance is not truly differentiated because the other retains some control over the self's decision; however, there is an attempt to be different from the significant other. The third stance is the fused-reactive state in which the individual is unable to take a stance separate from the other. Most of the individual's emotional energy goes into being liked and approved of by the significant other.

These three self-stances are developmental. The third stance, the fused-reactive self, is seen most often in the first years of life and in the pre-teen years. The second stance, the reactive or pseudoself, is in evidence in adolescence when developmental tasks focus on proving competence in the environment. When these two stances are "traveled successfully" the individual will move on to higher degrees of self. It is important to remember that differentiation of self continues throughout life. The task is never complete.

When an individual leaves the nuclear family, one's sense of self will guide his or her choice of friends and spouse. Individuals usually marry people at the same level of emotional health. If someone leaves the family-of-origin feeling shaky and unsecure, he or she will look for a relationship that will help him or her feel more secure. It is likely that this individual will find someone who needs to support and to make another person feel good as a way for that person to feel good. This dynamic is illustrated when partners are asked what initially attracted them to each other.

I remember one husband telling me he was attracted to his wife because she always made him feel good. She laughed at his jokes and made him feel wise, witty, and competent. The wife reported that what she liked about her husband was that he really seemed to need her, that he made her feel good, secure, and wanted. Later in the marriage, they became disappointed in each other. The husband wanted his wife to continue to flatter him and make him feel good. The wife was disappointed that her husband was not more secure and competent. She resented what she saw as his pressure on her to carry the show.

Relationships most often solidify when a couple discovers they can fulfill each other's needs and emotional expectations. However, these needs and expectations change as the relationship progresses. Most often, one person will change more quickly than the other. When this occurs, the relationship begins to suffer because one or the other sees the partner differently.

Changing needs and expectations are actually moves toward differentiation. However, unequal rates of self change within a relationship often cause a crisis. The one who resists change will attempt to undermine or sabotage the other's progress. It is crucial that a therapist recognize this process because it is often the impetus for the couple's decision to enter therapy. When the therapist perceives this sort of situation his or her best approach is to support the individual who is making self-moves. This individual, in addition to wanting things to be different for the self, will also display a degree of understanding for the other who is finding these moves threatening to the relationship.

When one member of a relationship is working on the self, there is a good likelihood that the relationship will end unless the other partner eventually makes corresponding moves. In my experience, when only one member is actively working on the self he or she may leave the relationship and become involved in other relationships at a higher emotional level. The member of the couple who remains more or less emotionally untouched, except for a state of anxiety, will tend to get involved with someone at the same level of reactivity. To break out of this pattern, it is important to work with the husband and wife together.

Fusion/Emotional Triangle

The tendency toward fusion is a significant dynamic in family relationships. Fusion occurs when two or more people join forces to agree on a shared view of reality in order to deal with some external threat or internal discomfort. It is a reactive mechanism to reduce anxiety.

As was pointed out in the previous section, fusing with a powerful other, such as a parent, when one is very young is a functional, developmental process. However, as we mature this reactive behavior becomes increasingly dysfunctional. Mature adults should be able to introduce and to be comfortable with a degree of variety in the family. When there is a threat or crisis in the family, the more ideas and options there are for responding to that crisis, the better. If one has to give up one's "differences" in order to reduce other family members' anxiety, the ability to problem solve is retarded. The more functional the family the greater its ability to deal with "differences." The less functional the family, the more the pressure for sameness exists. Highly anxious individuals with poorly defined selves tend to experience different points of view and/or different approaches to a problem as criticisms of themselves.

One of the most common ways people fuse is through the use of the emotional triangle. Bowen provides the clearest definition of how triangles operate:

The basic building block of any emotional system is the triangle. When emotional tension in a two person system exceeds a certain level, it triangles the third person, permitting the tension to shift about within the triangle. Any two in the original triangle can add a new triangle. An emotional system is composed of a series of interlocking triangles. The emotional tension system can shift to any of the old pre-established circuits. It is a clinical fact that the original two person system will resolve itself automatically when contained within three person systems, when one of them remains emotionally detached.[11]

When we talk about the development of a sense of self, we must consider the concept of the emotional triangle. The more emotionally fused two people are, the more likely they are to operate in emotional triangles. One way for an individual to avoid working on the self or examining his own part in a relationship is by triangulation. Triangulation provides the opportunity to stabilize one's emotional feelings about others by talking to a third person. The more anxiety there is in a dyadic relationship, the more likely one or both will move out of the relationship by involving himself or herself with another individual to reduce the tension level. The individual may be a therapist, friend, another family member, a subject, an object, or even a pet.

A student of mine volunteered a story about her family which illustrates how pets can be part of our triangles. In her family, the mother and children arrived home at the end of the day before the father. Their habit was to wait in the living room until the father arrived. Upon the father's arrival he would join the family in the living room and proceed to talk to the family dog. On the basis of what he said to the dog, they gained a sense of how he felt about his day and they approached him accordingly. After finishing her story the student said that this system worked very well for her family. When I asked her how the children and mother told the father about important events in their day, she explained that they followed the same procedure and talked to him through their dog. The student explained this procedure very matter of factly as though this was a usual way for a family to behave. Nobody in the family experienced any stress over this form of communication.

We find that the more fused the relationship, the more important it is for the individuals to maintain the relationship for their emotional survival. In these relationships, the triangle is the best way to reduce anxiety. It allows the couple to avoid focusing on anything that might throw the relationship into question. One can both triangle out of the relationship by talking about it with someone else and triangle within the relationship by talking about anything but the relationship. Discussions about politics, religion, television, or other people's problems can all be ways to avoid dealing with what is going on with self, the partner, and the relationship.

It is important to realize that the triangle serves as a stabilizing influence by helping to maintain the status quo in a relationship. It is a way of maintaining calm. The higher the anxiety, the more likely that people will talk in triangles. The lower the anxiety, the safer it is to talk about self. When I am teaching people about this concept, I often suggest that they try an experiment with their families. The experiment involves starting a conversation with just one member of the family while in the presence of other family members. The conversation can be about something that is going on with the self, with the other person, or between the two of them. Invariably, the student will find that someone else in the room will interject an issue or deflect the attention from the two of them onto himself or herself. The student or the person he or she is talking with will change the subject to reduce the anxiety.

One of the primary goals of family work is to help family members become more objective about what is going on around them. Individuals are unable to understand events in their lives when they are overly involved with or take on excessive responsibility for what is occurring within the family. One of the goals of therapy is to help family members see how feelings affect thinking. When feelings take over, distortion and fantasy increase.

To gain a better understanding of how this distortion and fantasy operate, the following experiment might be tried with your own family. Ask family members to recall an event which was important to you. This event can be a positive or negative one as long as several family members were involved in one way or another. Have the family members write down their memories of the event and then compare the reports. Their perceptions of what occurred will be significantly different. Some will feel the event was positive, others may think it was unpleasant, and some may not even remember the event. Your perception of how family members felt about the event may be very different from their actual reactions. You may discover that you do not know your family as well as you thought you did. The more conflictual a family, the more likelihood there is for distortions, misconceptions, and false assumptions to develop about family members. The more emotional the family, the more the feelings take over to color events with a personal perspective.

The more fused people are with each other, the more their feelings predominate. When anxiety is high and feelings are controlling thinking, the message sent is often not the message received. When a person is experiencing a very high state of anxiety that threatens his or her emotional survival, he or she is incapable of hearing what is being said without coloring it to suit his or her feelings. As an individual gains better control of the self and feels more confident, thinking or logical processes will become more evident. It is also important to realize that people who intellectualize their feelings and appear to deny them are probably in truth over-feeling. The more frightened one is of feelings getting out of control, the more likely one is to keep those feelings under wraps. This is a situation of feelings controlling the self rather than the other way around. In contrast, people who feel capable of handling their own feelings will be freer to feel any way they choose. One can see that the safer the environment the therapist is able to create during the session, the more comfortable and receptive the family will be about processing new information.

Alliances

Alliances are any connections between two or more people for mutual emotional support. Various types of alliances, such as diadic alliances, triadic alliances, intrafamilial alliances, and extrafamilial alliances develop in the family environment from the moment that it is created. The structure of the family encourages three main alliances: spouse, sibling, and parent/child. Husband and wives have alliances with each other apart from their relationships with their children, the children have alliances with each other separate from their parents, and each parent has an alliance with each child.

Alliances can serve useful purposes within the family. An alliance permits one to talk to another about a concern or idea that could not be easily shared with others. An alliance makes one feel that he or she belongs and is accepted by another. On the other hand, alliances can be maladaptive. Collusions, coalitions, or triangulations are all maladaptive alliances. These maladaptive alliances can cause family members to turn against each other as a way of coping with discomfort in relationships. In contrast, adaptive alliances help family members to learn about different aspects of themselves. Family members also form extrafamilial alliances that are important in shaping their sense of self. Mentors, special teachers, parents of friends, coaches, older adults, etc., may all be important partners in alliances. Ideally, individuals learn positively about themselves from both familial and extrafamilial experiences.

The importance of extrafamilial alliances was illustrated by a couple I saw recently. The husband was physically violent towards the wife. The wife was in a transition house at the beginning of therapy. The husband told me how he was brutalized by his father. One day, when he was sitting on the porch with his girlfriend, his father came home and became so enraged at seeing him sitting there that he began to beat him up. The mother heard the noise, came out of the house to observe what was going on, and then did nothing. My client felt alone and helpless. When I asked him if there was anyone there for him, he went on to tell me about a special teacher who made all the difference in the world. The teacher believed in him and was a source of support and caring. The husband felt that he would not have been able to survive in his family without this teacher. Although this young man at times loses his temper and strikes out at others, there is a part of him that desperately wants to connect more intimately with others. It is as though there are two warring parts within him, the part that arose out of the abuse and neglect from his mother and father and the part that was nurtured by the caring and respect from his teacher.

When engaging a family in therapy, the therapist will try to form functional alliances with the family members. It is the job of the therapist to connect with individual family members as well as the family as a whole. A shaky self will have the strongest need for support and validation from the therapist. When a therapist questions the story of a person who is struggling with his concept of self, these questions will be experienced as criticism. Accordingly, at times it will be necessary for the therapist to form a functional alliance with a family member so that he or she feels understood and supported in spite of the fact that his or her story may contain a fair degree of distortion.

I worked with a family in which the wife was very shaky and defensive. Whenever her husband spoke she would jump in to clarify his statement and to point out the error of his ways. My immediate goal was to get her to trust me to the point that she could allow her husband to tell his story without worrying about my siding with him. The wife's story had to be supported before I could even begin to ask questions that raised doubts about her view of events.

The timing of questions about the self is important. If the questions are raised too early, defensive and reactive individuals will stop therapy because they feel criticized and undermined. If the alliance process continues on too long, the therapist forms a dysfunctional triangle with the individual and becomes part of the problem. The art of therapy is to know when to back away from the alliance and encourage the individual to question his reality.

Communication

Communication is the lifeline of the family. All that goes on in the family, the legends, secrets, distortions, roles, goals, and values are conveyed through each family's pattern of communication. Each family develops a unique way of communicating among its members. Any outsider will have difficulty understanding the subtleties of the family's patterns of communication. However, the family therapist must pay attention to several aspects of the family's communication, such as how the family exchanges important information, which family members act as interpreters of family behavior, what words and concepts they choose to use, etc. Once the therapist has learned the family communication style, he or she needs to plug into that style rather than expect the family to adapt to the therapist's style. One way to accomplish this is to have each family member define the important terms or concepts he or she uses during the interview. When a family member uses words such as love, hate, sad, or lonely, it would be helpful to ask this person what these words mean to him or her. In this way everyone learns the unique meaning a particular family member attaches to important emotional words.

The communication network of a family provides information about the roles various family members play in the family. The way family members choose to express themselves is indicative of their values and what they consider important. The family members responsible for explaining family experiences have usually been chosen for this role in observance of the family power structure. It is important that the therapist recognize the power structure that parallels the family communication structure.

Often the family member who is the family interpreter is the most anxious member of the family. It can be risky to allow this anxious member to define the level of family functioning. This member will be more likely to describe the family problem in terms based on his or her own family-of-origin issues or on the anxieties he or she has about the family. It is critical that the family therapist invite each family member to define what he or she sees as the family concerns. It is rare that there is general concensus about what the family problem is.

Often one of the major concerns of the less anxious family members is that the overinvolved member is more anxious than need be about the family problem. This view can lead to a reframing of the problem from the original problem to the response of certain family members to that problem. The therapist must be careful not to take too literally the most anxious member's definition of the problem. Otherwise, he or she may collude with that family member and become part of the family problem.

Overfunction/Underfunction Reciprocity

Relationships have to achieve balance in one way or another. The stronger the sense of self, the less a person will require another to provide emotional support. The weaker the self, the greater the tendency to enter into fused relationships. Fused relationships operate primarily in emotional triangles and set in motion an overfunction-underfunction reciprocity process. One member is usually perceived as more adequate than the other in a fused relationship. The adequacy of one is balanced by the inadequacy of the other. An understanding of this concept is critical to work with families.

If one gets involved with the more inadequate or underfunctioning member of a family without recognizing that underfunctioning is sustained by another's overfunctioning, there is limited possibility for change in the system. If a therapist proposes to work with an individual, rather than the family unit, he or she would be well advised to work with the overfunctioner in the family. The overfunctioner is invariably more anxious and has more difficulty giving up the overfunctioning role than the underfunctioner has in becoming more productive. A clinical example of this dynamic follows:

A father consulted me about his eight-year-old son. The father described his son as incorrigible. He complained his son would not listen to him, did not seem to pay attention, and did not respond to his questions. During the session, it became clear to me that the father responded to my questions in three or less seconds. In contrast, the son required at least eight seconds to respond. When the son took longer than three seconds to answer, his father became enraged and would yell at his son, demanding to know why he was not paying attention. He would then turn to me and say, "You see what I have to put up with?" When this occurred, the son would get flustered and would require even more time before he could formulate an answer.

Who has the problem in this relationship? The father or the son? Who do you think you can change in a relationship like this? The son temperamentally needs more time to formulate a response. Change in this interaction will occur when the father is able to change his thinking and reduce his anxiety to a level where he is comfortable giving his son more time to respond.

Typically the overfunctioner overfunctions at about the same rate that the underfunctioner underfunctions. In order for the overfunctioner to decrease his overfunctioning, the underfunctioner has to function at a higher level. Often the overfunctioner will try to stop overfunctioning; however, at the first sign that the underfunctioner is not improving, the overfunctioner, being the more anxious one, will begin to overfunction again. It follows that in all families where there is a dysfunctional member there are also more functional members. These more functional members may lock the underfunctioner into his or her role so that he or she has very little room to function better.

Timing, when and how things should be done in a family, is a significant variable in the overfunction/underfunction process. Family members may have different time frames for certain activities, decisions, or behaviors. When time frames are significantly different, one member may be seen as lazier, less thoughtful or conscientious, etc., than another.

Another form of overfunctional/underfunctional reciprocal process seen in relationships is the pursuer/distancer dynamic. In many couples one member actively pursues the other member to change. The pursuer usually wants the distancer to be more involved. The more he or she pursues, the more the distancer moves away. Often therapists will collude with the pursuer in pursuing the distancer.

In my opinion, many therapists are naturally pursuers and are not aware how counterproductive it is to join with the pursuer to get the distancer more involved. I have discovered that each partner in the pursuer/distancer relationship has difficulty with closeness and intimacy. At some level, the pursuer counts on the distancer to distance in order to make it safe for the pursuer to be involved in the relationship. They only enter therapy when the distancing or the pursuing is so great that the anxiety becomes intolerable. Once the more comfortable pursuer/distancer relationship is reestablished, they usually want to terminate therapy.

It is important for the therapist to recognize that the pursuer and distancer function at the same emotional level. Commonly, when the pursuer stops pursuing, the distancer will begin to pursue. Usually therapy begins with the pursuer wanting the distancer to be more involved. After a number of sessions it is usual for the distancer to say that he or she wants the relationship to succeed and now sees that he or she should not have been distancing. As soon as the former distancer assumes a new position, the former pursuer will say something to the effect that it is too late, and the distancer cannot be trusted anymore. Now it is the former distancer's turn to try to convince the former pursuer that in fact it is not too late and the roles have been reversed.

The stance the therapist should take in a pursuer/distancer scenario is to encourage the distancer to distance by asking how he or she has learned that distancing makes it safe. Similarly, the therapist should ask the pursuer how he or she can change his or her thinking about the relationship so that the anxiety can be reduced and, therefore, the need for the distancer to be different can also be diminished. As the pursuer slows down and the distancer begins to talk about the coping mechanism that he or she has brought into the relationship, a different picture emerges.

Intimacy

The capacity for intimacy should be viewed developmentally. At various points in our lives intimacy takes on different forms. Early attachment is the precursor to intimacy. As children, we are more attached to our parents than we are intimate with them. This is developmentally appropriate. In a family, the child's major needs are to be taken care of, to be protected, and to be helped to grow and mature. It is, to some degree, inappropriate for parents to be intimate with their children, and to share certain thoughts, fears, concerns, and worries with them. Developmentally the child is not able to hear the parents' anxieties, fears, and worries separately from his or her own need to be taken care of, protected, and helped to move beyond family attachments. The child first attaches to the parent dependently and over time works through that attachment to become more intimate with other people who are at the same developmental level. The ability to be intimate with another adult is partially determined by how well we have worked through our original attachment and separation issues with our parents.

Bowlby's early work on attachment and separation is classic in its description of the harmful effects of early separation or extreme attachment to and dependency by the child on his or her parents. His research illustrates the connection between the child's ability to grow and develop over time and the way the child has worked through the separation and attachment issues with his or her own parents.[12]

Once the child leaves his or her family-of-origin the type of intimacy he or she needs changes and continues to change over time. Our relationships in our twenties and how we position ourselves in them are quite different from our relationships in our thirties, forties, fifties, and later in life. In my opinion, true intimacy is a mid-life task which begins in the thirties. The first thirty years of life are a training period for the ability to be truly intimate with another.

I define intimacy as the ability to share important aspects of oneself in a relationship without needing another to behave in a certain way to make it safe. In order to be intimate, one has to let go of outcome; in other words, needing another to be different in order to make it safe to talk about oneself. Many people will say that they can be intimate as long as others will accept and understand them. In fact, their ability to be intimate is dependent on how others behave. This difficulty in intimacy usually stems from an individual's family-of-origin where he or she has learned that talking about certain subjects or behaving in certain ways will result in criticism or a withdrawal of love. The individual becomes very cautious about how he or she presents himself or herself to the world.

It is a long process to acquire the security that will allow an individual to function without the need for outside validation and/or the fear of intimacy.

Letting go of our need to be validated by others is a developmental principle. Before we can let go of this need, we do have to be validated by significant others. Lerner defined intimacy as follows:

> Intimacy means that we can be who we are in a relationship, and allow the other person to do the same. "Being who we are" requires that we can talk openly about things that are important to us, that we take a clear position on where we stand on important emotional issues, and that we clarify the limits of what is acceptable and tolerable to us in a relationship. "Allowing the other person to do the same" means that we can stay emotionally connected to that other party who thinks, feels, and believes differently, without needing to change, convince or fix the other.
>
> An intimate relationship is one in which neither party silences, sacrifices, or betrays the self and each party expresses strength and vulnerability, weakness and competence in a balanced way.[13]

One of the primary jobs of the family is to validate the child's basic sense of worth. This procedure is the foundation upon which the child tests the world. When a child leaves the family feeling shaky and unloved, it will be very difficult for him or her to share himself or herself and risk feeling intimate. These individuals with shaky selves are cautious in relationships and preoccupied with being judged and accepted. They seek validation in relationships and rarely, if ever, find it. They have tremendous difficulties being intimate in the way I have defined it.

There are also some developmental differences between how men and women enter relationships and develop intimacy. A fair amount has been written about the different ways men and women position themselves in families and their different expectations for family life. Carter and McGoldrick discuss how differences between men and women can interfere with family life.[14] However, not much has been written about how men and women differ developmentally in their quest for intimacy. Notwithstanding the feminist movement and the heightened awareness and changes it has brought, we know that boys and girls for the most part have different experiences in family. Boys are encouraged to be more aggressive, to use themselves physically, to be competitive, and to hide their feelings. Girls are encouraged to express their feelings, show their vulnerability, and be caretakers. A great deal of research has indicated that girls are verbal at an earlier age than boys and boys become physically active at an earlier age.[15] Male/female differences are evident throughout the life cycle and may lead to problems in how men and women relate to each other as couples and as parents in the family. My belief is that many relationship problems occur not for lack of love, caring, or commitment but because of the different orientations men and women bring into a relationship. How couples define these differences is often a greater barrier to intimacy than the differences themselves.

Men in young adulthood and into their early thirties show caring through performance. Work accomplishment, material possessions, business successes, and career improvements are all indicative to many men that they are successful in the world and are taking care of their families. Women, including women with successful careers outside the home, view relationships as primary to their satisfaction in the world. Having a family, being emotionally connected with another, taking care of and being available to others are all important indicators to women that they have meaningful involvements in the world. Both sets of behaviors are important and ideally should complement each other. Unfortunately, for some couples these differences become battlegrounds. Men commonly feel whatever they do is not enough; women often feel unappreciated and diminished by their partners. These themes are encountered over and over again.

The degree to which these differences become a problem is related to the experiences the partners had in their families-of-origin. The man with an excessive need to prove himself or the woman who is overly concerned with being adequate are both acting out early losses and struggles. These differences interfere with the couple's ability to be intimate and have a profound impact on how the family operates as a unit. Unless understood, these differences can undermine the cohesiveness of the family and interfere with how well the parents connect with the needs of their children and each other.

Loyalty and Debts

Loyalty is an emotional commitment to be faithful to one's ideals, beliefs, and/or history. Most people are fiercely loyal to their original families. One way their loyalty is shown is in their attempts to honor their families by adhering to certain values, making certain life decisions, joining a certain profession and/or organization, living in certain parts of the community, etc. Loyalty has been underestimated as a major factor in decision-making. How well couples understand each other's loyalty ties to their original families will influence their sense of connection with each other.

Our sense of indebtedness to our families is another way our loyalty shows itself. In addition to wanting to take care of our parents and remain responsible members of our families, we want to pay our parents back for what they have done for us. Most people are not aware how often they make decisions out of loyalty to their families. Second generation survivors of the holocaust provide numerous examples of how loyalty and indebtedness influence major life decisions.

A young physician consulted me because she was feeling depressed and anxious about her life. She had moved across the country to put distance between herself and her parents whom she felt placed oppressive demands on her. Both her parents were survivors of the holocaust. Her mother had lost her entire family except for one sister. Her father had lost a number of family members. My client was the older of two children, with a brother three years her junior. She complained of feeling sad about moving away and deserting her parents but felt suffocated by their neediness when she was with them. She felt conflicted and guilty about not being close enough to her parents to take care of them. She reported that it took her two weeks to recover from a visit home. She would develop insomnia, have trouble eating, and at times have suicidal thoughts. Although she was functioning adequately in her profession, she was unable to maintain meaningful relationships, particularly with men. She wanted a family but was fearful that she would never be able to be intimate with a man.

This young woman was living in an apartment and had been unable to buy any furniture for it. She spent hours going to furniture stores trying to pick out the right couch. She was at a loss to understand her trouble in this area. In response to questions about what the purchase of a couch meant to her, she came to realize that furnishing her apartment represented a decision to remain on the West Coast. To her, this decision represented disloyalty to her parents and a rejection of their losses.

It is important and revealing to ask people how they honor or are loyal to their parents. The degree to which debts and loyalty issues influence their decision-making is determined by how well they have been able to make peace with their parents. Helping couples understand how their own parents dealt with loyalty and debt issues in their relationships with their families can be tremendously helpful in providing couples with a clear sense of the loyalty issues they carry into their new families.

Loss and Mourning

It is impossible to emerge from a family without experiencing some degree of loss. How well the individual has made peace with these losses will determine how freely he or she is able to move on in his or her life. Every family has to deal with loss, separation, and death and many different forms of disappointment. As parents get older, they have to deal with their own losses, such as their parents' and siblings' failing health and deaths and the failures that they experience in their careers, relationships, and dreams. Many parents try to hide their sadness and losses from their children. However, part of the family's task is to teach its members to learn and grow from loss. Family members who mourn together feel connected with each other. To observe a parent grieving, expressing sorrow, and then recovering can be a hopeful and encouraging experience for the child.

At various times, everyone mourns the loss of family. Therapy should address how family members deal with or will deal with family losses, including death. We know that the more connected and solid the relationship a child has with the parent the fewer regrets the child will have when that parent dies. In spite of the loss, he or she is more at peace with the relationship. The more conflictual and cut off the relationship is between parent and child, the harder the death will be on the child. Couples who understand the other's sadness, losses, and disappointments are less likely to misinterpret the other's reactions. They will understand that much of one's anxiety is connected to sadness about the loss of special people in one's life.

Balance

To function well, families must be in balance. Balance means that each subsystem is able to meet its own special needs without undermining the needs of another subsystem or the family as a whole. It is a complex task to keep all the relationships in balance.

Each subsystem needs to be attended to, nourished, and given sufficient time to meet its needs. Many husbands and wives will make their relationship issues secondary to their parental concerns. Some parents interfere with the sibling relationships between their children. In other families, the individual may feel he or she has to give up his or her autonomy to meet the needs of the family. In some families, one parent is overinvolved with a child to the exclusion of the other parent. These examples point to potential problems for the healthy development of the individual family members.

Each family has to develop its own system for achieving balance. The balancing of individual autonomy with family solidarity and togetherness is a unique challenge for families. Developmental differences will affect the family's approach to this task. For example, parents of adolescents may try to maximize family togetherness knowing that their children will soon be leaving home. The teen-agers, on the other hand, will want to spend more time away from the family and with their peers as they seek to establish their separate identities. How well the family is able to balance these and other opposing developmental issues will be a major determinant of successful family functioning.

ENDNOTES

1. Thomas, Alexander, Stella Chess, and Herbert Birch (1968) *Temperament and Behaviour Disorders in Children*, p. 4, New York: University Press.

2. See for example: Bloom-Feshbach, Jonathan and Bloom-Feshbach, Sally (1987), *The Psychology of Separation and Loss*, San Francisco: Jossey-Bass, Pub.

3. See for example: Skolnick, Arlene (1987), *The Intimate Environment: Exploring Marriage and the Family*, Boston: Little, Brown and Company; and Bennis, Warren G., Kenneth Benne, Robert Chin, and Kenneth Corey (1987), *The Planning of Change*, New York: Holt, Rinehart and Winston.

4. Gray, William, Frederick Duhl, and Nicholas Rizzo (eds.) (1969), *General Systems Theory and Psychiatry*, p. 14, Boston: Little, Brown.

5. See for example: Nichols, Michael (1984), *Family Therapy, Concepts and Methods*, New York: Gardner Press; and Hoffman, Lynn (1981), *Foundations of Family Therapy: A Conceptual Framework for Systems Change*, New York: Basic Books.

6. Speck, Ross V. and Carolyn L. Attneave (1973), *Family Networks*, New York: Pantheon Books.

7. Carter, Betty and Monica McGoldrick (1988), "Overview: The Changing Family Life Cycle — A Framework for Family Therapy" in *The Changing Family Life Cycle: A Framework for Family Therapy*, pp. 11-13, New York: Gardner Press.

8. *Ibid.*, pp. 3-28.

9. McGoldrick, Monica and Randy Gerson (1985), *Genograms in Family Assessment*, New York: Norton & Company.

10. Erikson, Eric (1964) *Childhood and Society*, 2nd ed., New York: W.W. Norton.

11. Bowen, Murray (1978), *Family Therapy in Clinical Practice*, New York: Jason Aronson, p. 306.

12. Bowlby, John (1969), *Attachment and Loss, Vol. I: Attachment*, New York: Basic Books; and (1973), *Attachment and Loss, Vol. II: Separation, Anxiety and Anger*, New York, Basic Books.

13. Lerner, Harriet Goldhor (1989), *The Dance of Intimacy*, p.3, New York: Harper & Row.

14. McGoldrick, Monica (1988) "Women and The Family Life Cycle" in Carter, Betty and Monica McGoldrick, *The Changing Life Cycles: A Framework for Family Therapy*, pp. 31-68, New York: Gardner Press.

15. *Ibid*.

Chapter Three

The Major Systems Involved in the Family Therapy Process

INTRODUCTION

Most therapists consider the nuclear family to be the major system involved in family therapy. Little has been written on the other major systems that impact on the family therapy process. Of course, the family therapist's primary responsibility is to provide therapeutic services to the families that he or she sees. However, it is crucial to understand that there are two other powerful emotional systems that affect the family therapy process.

These systems are: (1) the therapist's own family emotional system, and (2) other professional systems, both those to which the therapist belongs and those involved in the family's life.

This chapter will focus on the therapist's personal family system and the professional family system. In order for family therapy to be productive, these two systems must be in balance and under the control of the therapist. The therapist must be aware of his or her own issues and realize the power other professionals can have in the life of the family.

SECTION ONE: THE THERAPIST'S FAMILY EMOTIONAL SYSTEM

When working with families, therapists are guided by their own definitions and understanding of how families should function. There is a tendency for therapists to believe that they are experts on how families should look and behave. They, like everyone else, come out of their families-of-origin with strong feelings about what to avoid and seek in family relationships. When therapists have not come to terms with these feelings and expectations, they are likely to attempt to mold other people's families so that they either resemble or are quite different from their own. Therapists are likely to identify with one or more family members as being healthy and view the others as dysfunctional. They will often unwittingly bring their unfinished business into the clinical situation. Therapists who left their families-of-origin reactively, with a strong need to put distance between themselves and their families, and those who were overfunctioners in their families-of-origin, who, in effect, took responsibility for their families, will be the ones who have special problems in guiding the family therapy process.

Therapists who were overfunctioners often feel comfortable taking responsibility for the functioning of their clients. This overfunctioning is not helpful for the family. One of the major goals in family work is to encourage the family to become its own expert. The therapist's job is to encourage family members to help each other become more adequate, resourceful individuals. The more the therapist overfunctions, the less likely the family will be to develop its own internal resources. The anxious therapist who feels he or she must act to save the family actually interferes with the family's ability to grow and change during a family crisis.

The therapists who have distanced themselves from their own families-of-origin are less likely to see the wisdom of helping family members reconnect with their lost families. It is a general rule that we will involve ourselves with others in ways that make sense to us and fit with our emotional sense of reality. The therapist who is cut off from his or her own family and believes that this is a healthy position to take when there are difficulties will collude with family members to maintain their isolation from their families. It is difficult for a therapist to excite a family about the potential of reconnecting and repositioning with their families-of-origin when the therapist has had difficulty accomplishing this in his or her own family-of-origin. The therapist will have trouble helping a family move further than he or she has been able to go in his or her own life. It is difficult for such a therapist to frame helpful questions about family connection, loyalty issues, losses, etc. This therapist is more likely to back away from themes that make him or her anxious or uncomfortable. The following examples illustrate how therapists can collude with families when their own issues coincide with the family's issues.

1. A therapist at a therapeutic group home began his presentation of a case by saying that he did not think the approach of focusing on process rather than on content would work with the family that he was presenting. He went on to say that no matter what approach he took, the family always came back to the subject of eating. They would fight about eating or argue about food during the entire session. He was unable to move them away

from the content issue of food. The therapist was certain that this focus had nothing to do with him, but rather that the family was unusually stuck on this content issue. The therapist had videotaped a session which he had observed on his own several times in an unsuccessful attempt to figure out what part he played in the family's becoming stuck in this particular content area. We proceeded to watch the tape together.

The session involved the mother, the father, and their three children. The mother appeared particularly happy at the beginning of the session. She was smiling and told the therapist that she had accomplished something with the family that she had been attempting to do for a long time. She had managed to get the family to go to a restaurant together. She indicated that she had always wanted her family to be able to have a nice dinner together in a restaurant. After she finished telling the therapist how important this occasion was for her, the therapist looked straight at her and inquired, "What did you eat?" In response, the mother reviewed the dinners that each family member had had. Before she finished, the other family members jumped in to say that her recall of what they had eaten was wrong. Throughout the rest of the session the family fought about what they had eaten in the restaurant.

It was interesting that the therapist did not even hear himself ask the mother the content question about what the family had to eat. He first became aware that he had asked the question when I asked him what was the reason for asking this particular question. He was surprised at himself for asking such a concrete question. I asked him what got stirred up in him when the mother reported her feeling of accomplishment about taking the family out to dinner. He replied he knew it was a significant opening and he became very anxious about making the session a profound experience for the family. His anxiety about making something happen for the family resulted in his falling back on a content issue. This focus reduced his anxiety but reinforced the family's "stuckness." This process is not uncommon. When a therapist becomes anxious, the tendency is to revert to the teaching mode and/or to make statements to the family to reduce his or her own anxiety. The therapist is then behaving like the family that uses statements about others, scapegoating, and a preoccupation with content to deal with its problems. The job of the therapist is to understand the process underlying the family's content issues. When the therapist becomes anxious along with the family, there is little hope that the family will be able to have a different experience. It is critical that the therapist be the master of the process. The only way he or she can accomplish this is by understanding content issues differently from the way the family is experiencing these issues.

2. The second example arises from a consultation with a group of school counselors. During the consultation, I was stressing the importance of involving both parents in two-parent families. Several counselors commented on how difficult it was to involve the fathers in therapy. I suggested that they approach the fathers on the basis of what the fathers have to offer in terms of helping the counselors understand what is going on in the family. They should avoid giving either parent the impression he or she is being blamed for the children's problems. During a follow-up session with the group, one of the counselors said that she had managed to get the whole family to attend the first session but that the father had refused to continue after this session. She acknowledged that it made sense to involve both fathers and mothers but that this case proved the point that fathers are difficult to involve in counseling. She had taped the session and reviewed it to see what part she had played in the father's refusal to return. She had concluded that she had not done anything to discourage his involvement.

We watched the tape together, and it was immediately apparent that the seating arrangement was quite unusual. The counselor had arranged the chairs so that her back was to the father. Whenever the father made a statement or asked a question, she turned her head slightly towards him, responded as briefly as possible and then returned to the mother and children. As the session continued, the father became increasingly agitated. By the end of the session, the father declared this was getting the family nowhere and stormed out.

When I asked the counselor why she had arranged the seating as she did, she replied that she had not been aware that she had placed the father behind her. I asked her if she had any particular feelings about this father that might have influenced such a seating arrangement. After giving it some thought, she acknowledged that this father reminded her of her own father. Her father was a senior executive of an aero-dynamics firm. She had always felt intimidated by her father whom she experienced as unaccepting and critical. In fact, she had moved far away from home in order to put a safe distance between her and her father. When she heard me talk about how important it was to bring fathers into sessions, she felt it was something she should do. However, she knew this father was a senior executive of a major forestry company. Meeting him face-to-face, she immediately felt anxious and intimidated, much as she had with her own father. In talking about it, she realized the only way she knew how to make it safe for herself was to turn her back on this father and avoid any involvement with him.

An interesting aspect of this case is the interplay between the therapist's ambivalence and the parent's ambivalence. Parents often feel that the need for family therapy is a reflection of their failures and they blame themselves for the difficulties in the family. They are ambivalent about attending the sessions. A part of them wants the therapist to help them while another part wants to defeat the therapist to prove that the problem is not a family problem but something unique about the child and/or the school or community. When the therapist shares the parents' ambivalence the parents will use his or her behavior to justify distancing from the therapy process to reinforce their denial of their part in the problem. They will view the therapist as inadequate and will project their problem onto other systems.

The therapist's role is to recognize the parents' ambivalence and to use it to connect at a deeper level with the parents' concerns, anxieties, and fears. In order for the therapist to be effective with a family, he or she has to assume what I refer to as the "Involved/Detached I" position. This position requires that the therapist be emotionally involved with the family, and yet, keep part of his mind out of the emotional involvement and in an observational stance. When therapists are so emotionally involved in the family that they lose their detachment, they are unable to recognize the symbolism behind the family content issues. On the other hand, if they maintain too much distance from the family and its issues, they will not have a sense of the family's pain and anxiety and will not be able to connect with the family at a deeper level. These therapists will communicate to the family that they are not hearing them or understanding their issues.

The Detached I position allows therapists to be emotionally involved with the family, yet apart from that involvement, so that they can experience the family in a way that allows them to understand the family's dilemma differently from the way in which it is being presented. In order to sustain the Detached I position, therapists need: (1) to reduce their anxieties about being with the family, (2) to be free of ambivalence about seeing the entire family, (3) to be free of agendas for the family, (4) to avoid feeling responsible for the outcome of the process, (5) to avoid taking on the family's problem as their own, (6) to be able to recognize that the family has its own resources and strengths, and (7) to identify with the healthiest members of the family system.

Another helpful approach for therapists in the family therapy process is to maximize and turn into the family's advantage, their own limitations. The particular life experiences, issues, and losses of the family will be different from those that the therapist has experienced. It is important for the therapist to understand that he or she enters the family therapy process with significant limitations and shortcomings. The therapist's job is to maximize his or her limitations. He or she should not attempt to appear knowledgeable about everything that a family is talking about, and instead should turn this lack of knowledge into an asset. It can be very helpful for the therapist to tell a family that he or she has not had a particular experience, and is having difficulty understanding what that experience is like for a family member. This approach allows the family member to become the teacher about this experience which in turn leads to the family member understanding that experience differently. As one family member is teaching, the other family members also learn what that experience has been like for him or her.

One of the most difficult tasks for the beginning therapist is to master using a lack of knowledge as an asset. University and other professional training programs emphasize what one does know. In my opinion, this approach is counter-productive in teaching people how to become therapists. We should be helping people become comfortable with what they do not know. When the therapist maximizes what he or she does not know, the family members begin to emerge as experts on themselves. When they define their own experiences, they have to reevaluate the meaning of those experiences for themselves. If a therapist pretends to know things that he or she does not know, he or she sabotages the possibility of the family having experiences with each other which will allow them to connect at a deeper level around their members' unique wisdom in the world.

In order for the therapist to feel comfortable with his own or her inadequacies, the therapist must feel pretty solid about himself or herself. The therapist cannot use the family as a source for his or her own validation. He or she must feel solid enough to feel comfortable appearing ignorant. In order to achieve this level of comfort, the therapist must make peace with the issues of validation arising from his or her family-of-origin.

An example of how difficult this process is was illustrated by one of my graduate students. Prior to the Christmas break, he told me he was looking forward to visiting his parents back east. He was eager to apply all he had learned about repositioning and being non-reactive over the Christmas holidays. Off he went, with my wondering what he had heard and what he would try with his family. We spoke on his return and he reported that his resolve lasted three seconds. When his parents greeted him at the airport, he was smoking a cigarette. The first thing his mother said was, "I see you are still smoking." He immediately exploded, saying he was an adult and if he wanted to smoke it was his business. He said that he felt like lighting up three cigarettes simultaneously. He was unable to take a different stance. He was unable to thank his mother for being a mother or to say to her that it was nice to be home and have someone take care of him. This alternative approach would have allowed him to use his mother's anxiety about his smoking as a way of connecting with her. Instead, he had to defend himself against his mother to prove that he was an adult.

This amusing example shows how quickly we become reactive when we return home. Although we may think we are fully-mature adults, when we go home, we discover the old reactive issues are just dormant and are waiting to bubble to the surface. Our parents' ability to stir us up in ways no one else can is one of the gifts that they give us. When you want an accurate reading on how reactive you can be, if possible, go home for a few days. This same experience can help the therapist to understand the areas in which he or she is most vulnerable in the family therapy process.

Family therapy can trigger many old historical issues for the therapist. It can be much safer for the therapist to work with individuals. Individuals rarely stir up the therapist in ways that families do. Many professionals have consulted me about how they have lost their objectivity when they have met with an entire family. They find that the family stories often remind them very much of their own issues and that it is extremely difficult for them to stay detached and neutral. The process becomes even more complicated when it is suggested to them that they turn their limitations and shortcomings into strengths when working with families. The family therapist cannot expect the family to validate his or her competence as a therapist. He or she must already have answered the questions: "Am I good enough?" and "Am I adequate enough?" These questions cannot be answered in the family therapy process. The family will exert considerable energy trying to defeat the therapist. This ambivalence on their part presents the greatest challenge to the therapist.

When the therapist is truly able to let go of the need for the family to validate him or her, the family's need to defeat the therapy can be used as a way to connect with the family. The same principle applies to the therapist's involvement with his or her own family. The therapist's parents may respond to him or her in a way which infantilizes him or her. When this occurs, the therapist should avoid being defensive, being critical of the parents, or distancing from them. The therapist needs to understand the parents' anxieties behind their behavior and recognize that the parents' statements are actually about their own issues and not about him or her. The degree to which the therapist can achieve this nonreactive understanding with his or her own parents will determine how well he or she will be able to achieve it with other adults. This is the basic principle underlying the importance of the therapist's working through his or her own unfinished business so that the therapist can connect with families in therapy in a more profound way.

This process is an ongoing one with the therapist improving over time and with practice. It presents special challenges to young therapists who tend to have more unresolved issues with their own families. These therapists are more likely to move too quickly, to be too critical and too anxious, to take sides, to focus on content, and generally, to involve themselves inappropriately with the family. It is one of the reasons why young therapists and other inexperienced therapists require consultation and support in their work. It is important for them to have someone available to them who can ask them the questions that they are not asking themselves.

Family therapy offers a unique opportunity for therapists to work on their own unfinished business. I believe these issues never go away. However, the therapist who is able to look at his or her emotional involvements with a critical and observant eye is less likely to indulge the reactive parts of himself or herself in the therapy process.

SECTION TWO:
THE PROFESSIONAL FAMILY SYSTEM

It is unusual to see a family in therapy that has not had some history of professional involvement. Unfortunately, very few professionals review this history of professional help with the family. Therapists also tend to overlook the involvement of informal helpers, such as friends, neighbors, confidantes, etc. Both groups of helpers influence the way the family is currently dealing with their issues. Often it will take several sessions before a family can talk about its problems without simply repeating what has been told to them by other helpers.

In addition, during therapy the family may continue its involvement with other informal and formal helpers as a way to reduce anxiety. In order for the family therapist to be helpful, he or she must have a thorough knowledge of the former and current helpers involved in the life of the family. If one of the family members has an important confidante ouside the family, he or she may involve himself or herself with the confidante as a way of distancing from family intimacy. Unless the therapist is aware of this dynamic, he or she will not be able to help that family member use the family therapy process in an effective way. I have discovered that one must ask the family specifically who they use as helpers. Families tend not to volunteer this information. A story illustrates this point:

> I was working with a family in which the parents, the grandfather, and the children were all present during the session. After about four sessions, very little change had occurred. I have discovered that when things seem to stay the same or when family members do not seem invested in the family therapy process there are usually one or more important people missing from the sessions.
>
> I decided to start the next session by asking if all the important family members the family used as resources were present. The father replied that he had not mentioned that his grandfather, the children's great-grandfather, was still living in the home. When I asked him what role his grandfather played in the family he answered, that, in fact, he played an important part in the family. He went on to explain that following each session the entire family sat around the great-grandfather's bed and told him what had gone on in the session. I asked how the great-grandfather responded and was informed that he told the family what to do about what was going on within the family. The father at no time saw this exchange as part of the problem, but instead, he saw it as part of the solution. Although the talks with the great-grandfather were comforting and reduced the family's anxiety, they also served to reinforce the old familiar ways of dealing with family problems and made it difficult for real change to occur.

Generally, the family members will only tell the therapist what they feel he or she needs to know to understand the problem as they define the problem for themselves. It does not occur to them to discuss the other resources that they draw upon. Confidantes, other therapists, lovers, friends, and extended family members are frequently sought out by families' members. Although these people will not necessarily help family members resolve the problem, they help to reduce their discomfort about what is going on within the family. It is important to know who the family uses to reduce family anxiety. It is also important to remember that these family helpers respond to the family on the basis of their own unfinished business and vested interests. They rarely maintain a Detached I position, as the therapist attempts to do.

An example of how the professional family can interfere with the process of engaging a couple in therapy follows:

A young couple, whom I will call "John and Alice," consulted me because they were ambivalent about whether or not to marry each other. They had been living together for four years. They were hopeful that therapy would help them sort out whether they were suited to each other or not.

During the first session, John mentioned in passing that he was seeing a psychiatrist at the University Student Health Center. He then proceeded to tell me about the problems that he was having in the relationship. After he finished, Alice described her problems in the relationship and mentioned as an aside that she was seeing a psychologist.

After hearing their stories, I said that I was confused as to why they were starting yet another therapy process. They both replied that it was not confusing to them at all. They were each seeing their individual therapists for their own emotional difficulties and had decided to come to see me for their relationship problems. I explained to them that as long as they were discussing their problems with other therapists they were unlikely to have the energy or desire to discuss these issues together in our sessions and that there was little chance they would be able to use our sessions to understand each other differently.

When a family member goes outside of the family to deal with a problem, he or she distances from the family. The family therapist offers the family the opportunity to deal with problems in a way that will allow them to deepen their connections with each other. The therapist will not be able to accomplish this goal if various family members go outside the family to resolve their problems.

The majority of people that I see in therapy have had previous involvement with helpers or are involved with other helpers at the time of their initial contact with me. One of the more important beginning steps to take with families is to help them make a decision about where they are going to focus their energies in terms of working on their problems. If they decide to continue with other helpers, it is usually best not to begin another therapy. Additional therapy, rather than making their problem better, will be more apt to confuse matters. Although concurrent therapies are not productive, there are various concrete services that other professionals have to perform for the families, such as occupational therapy, physical therapy, medication, etc. When these multiple services are required, it is helpful for the family therapist to meet with the other professionals so there will be a concensus about their roles with the family.

It is a basic principle of family therapy that anxiety increases when the family begins to change. Often certain family members are more anxious about change than others and will involve other professionals for the purpose of ventilating their anxiety. When these other professionals are not supportive of the family therapy process, they collude with the anxious family member and sometimes advise that the therapy may not be appropriate for the family. The family therapist can prevent this undermining of the process if he or she meets with these other professionals and explains to them what reactions they might anticipate from the family. The other professionals can be most helpful when they encourage the family members to bring their concerns and anxieties to the family therapy session. It is appropriate for them, with the consent of the family member, to advise the family therapist when a family member has approached him or her with his or her concerns. When a family therapist is able to coordinate help in this way the opportunity for the family to change is greatly facilitated.

Another professional system that can influence the course of therapy is the intraprofessional system to which the therapist belongs, that is, his or her professional colleagues, and for some, his or her agency. Family members, particularly during the early stages of family work, continually pressure the therapist to form alliances and triangles and to take positions. It is difficult to practice good family work in isolation. It is helpful for practitioners to have colleagues with whom they can discuss their work and who can assist them in remaining objective. Having a colleague view videotapes of family work is a helpful technique, particularly for identifying when the therapist has become overinvolved in the family dynamics. The therapist who has support from his or her colleagues will be likely to increase creativity and competence in family work. On the other hand, the therapist who works in a hostile environment has to direct a great deal of energy into defending his or her practice. This stance makes it difficult for the therapist to summon the necessary energy for quality family work.

Family therapy requires a tremendous expenditure of energy on the part of the therapist just to separate himself or herself from the family process. For therapists who work in agencies, the actual physical setup can be either a source of support or a hindrance to the family work. Ideally, the interviewing room should be similar to a living room and should not contain a desk separating the therapist from the family. The family members should be able to sit comfortably in a circle, and there should be no distractions from the other offices.

A well-equipped agency will have videotape equipment and one-way mirrors so colleagues can observe each other's work. Therapists should reserve a few hours each month for consultation with peers and more experienced therapists. The therapist who is able to discuss the emotional issues that have been stirred up for him or her when doing family work will be able to accelerate the learning process and increase his or her effectiveness with families.

The best stance for the therapist to assume is that of a researcher/ scholar/therapist. If he or she can view family work as a way of learning about the human dilemma, then the work will inspire him or her to a more creative therapeutic involvement. Our families are our best teachers. The therapist must strive to hear the stories of the family without a preconceived judgments so that he or she can become wiser and more expansive in formulating ideas about how people get the job of living done.

Chapter Four

How to Begin
the Family Therapy Process

The first important decision the therapist makes is deciding who should attend the first session. The family member who first contacts the therapist usually defines the problem on the telephone. The caller will have his or her own ideas about who should be seen. How the caller defines the problem will influence who he or she thinks needs the therapy, that is, the acting out child, the non-communicative spouse, etc. It is up to the therapist to ask some general exploratory questions of the caller in order to make a decision about who to see in the first session.

How we define the problem has important implications for how we try to resolve the problem. If the therapist accepts the caller's definition of the problem at face value, then the therapist will probably agree with the caller's opinion about who should come into therapy. On the other hand, when the therapist makes his or her own decision about who should be seen, the therapist begins to challenge and redefine the family's definition of the problem. It is important to ensure that the most powerful, key members of the family are present at the first session. The therapist needs to connect with them and develop a relationship with them before change can occur.

There are numerous pitfalls associated with focusing on the child as the problem. This focus makes it difficult for the therapist to understand the parents' own emotional systems. The parents will use the children to camouflage their own self-issues. The children will cooperate by behaving in a way that keeps the focus on them. When this occurs, the families behave in the family therapy sessions as they do in the home. The therapist can change this pattern by starting with the adults in the family. Focusing on the adults is a gentle way of beginning to redefine the problem away from the children while forming a solid relationship with the parents. The therapist must be mindful of the principle that parents who do not trust and do not feel connected with the therapist will continually fight to maintain their definition of the problem. If they feel undermined by the therapist, they will quickly terminate therapy and seek out a more compliant, accepting therapist.

Engaging the parents is the most important initial step in the therapeutic process. By developing a strong, positive relationship with the parental subsystem, the therapist will set the stage for helping the entire family redefine and restructure itself as a system. The therapist, in arranging the first session, should try to help the parents to understand the wisdom of meeting without the children to discuss their concerns about the family. The therapist should use these initial contacts as an opportunity to help the parents to understand that he or she will support their position in the family, while at the same time using therapeutic influences to redefine the family as a behavioral unit.

As mentioned previously, the therapist's first contact with a family member is usually by telephone. During this call, the therapist should ask questions about family composition and should be able to identify which family members are most intimately involved in the concerns expressed by the caller. The following telephone conversation provides an example of which areas to cover in the initial telephone contact.

Caller (Mother): We are having problems with our thirteen-year-old son. He is not getting along at school, and we are not able to manage him at all.
Therapist: Can you tell me a little bit about your concerns?
Caller: Well, he has been expelled from two schools and now the newest school is threatening to expel him. He is involved with a very bad crowd, and my husband and myself are just not able to control him.
Therapist: Can you tell me who else is in the family?
Caller: We have three other children besides Peter.
Therapist: What are their ages and sexes?
Caller: Our youngest, John, is nine and he is doing well. No problem with him whatsoever. Our daughter, Joan, is eleven and she is also doing well at school. She is the opposite of our son Peter. The oldest in the family is Sam, who is seventeen. He spends more time out of the home than in the home. We don't have any concerns about him at all. Our major concern is with Peter. Peter is also getting into a lot of difficulties with his brothers and sister.
Therapist: What about your husband?
Caller: He is so upset about what is going on in the family that whenever

he tries to deal with it he just yells. The reason I am calling you is because he is so distraught about the whole thing. He just doesn't want to get involved anymore.

Therapist: Have you ever seen anyone else about the problems that you are having? Is there anyone else currently working with the family?

Caller: We have been involved with the school and the school counselor and we have seen a child psychiatrist for Peter, but none of these things seem to have helped. Actually, things have gotten worse over the past couple of years. We can't understand why, of all the children, Peter is the one who is causing such trouble.

Therapist: Who has been seen in the family by these various helpers?

Caller: My husband and I have both been involved. We have tried not to involve the other children. My husband is so upset that he refuses to talk to anyone else. We have sent Peter to counselors and to a psychiatrist, but he refuses to go anymore. He says he doesn't have any problems.

Therapist: How about the school counselor?

Caller: My husband talked to the school counselors. They told him that if we couldn't control Peter more effectively, they would expel him from school. They weren't helpful.

Therapist: Has the family ever been seen together to talk about some of their concerns?

Caller: No, never. I don't know why we would want to do that. We are not having any trouble with the other children.

Therapist: Well, for the first session why don't you and your husband come in together and meet me. This will give me a chance to talk to both of you about what you see happening within the family. After this session we can make a decision about who should be involved. How would that be?

Caller: I think that would be a good idea. However, my husband has been so upset and pessimistic that it may be hard to get him to come in.

Therapist: Well, I can understand that. However, you should mention to him that it would be helpful to me if he shared with me some of his experiences with those other agencies and professionals. And if both of you fill me in on the experiences of the family, we can then make a decision together about how to proceed.

Caller: That sounds like a good idea.

This conversation illustrates the common situation in which one family member seeks help for another family member. By arranging to see both parents without the child, the therapist begins to help the caller redefine the problem. The therapist could have proposed that the entire family attend the first interview, but decided instead to give the parents an opportunity to feel comfortable with the therapist before exposing their children to a stranger. In the long run, the therapist will be able to provide more support to the entire family if he or she has the confidence of the family organizers, the parents. Once this confidence is established, the parents will be more open to the therapist's suggestion that all the family members be seen together.

Most parents experience considerable anxiety about their "problem child." They feel guilty and responsible about the problems within the family. Consequently, it is understandable that they may resist the idea of involving the entire family in therapy. The parents are often concerned that the involvement of an outsider will only serve to undermine their efforts. When the therapist meets with the parents alone, these concerns should be addressed and allayed so that they will become more willing to allow the therapist to enter into the family.

In summary, the therapist should obtain certain basic information about the family before making a decision about who should attend the first interview, or, in some cases, before making a decision about whether to become involved at all. The following checklist outlines the information which should be elicited in the initial telephone call:

1. Age and sex of each family member and other people in home.
2. History of previous therapy.
3. Identify which family member is most anxious or overinvolved in the expressed problem.
4. Identify which family members are peripherally involved.
5. History of the problem.
6. Determine who is willing to attend therapy session.
7. Find out if certain family members have left home. If so, find out when and where they now live.
8. Determine parents' present employment status, their schedules, and their availability for sessions.
9. Ask about recent changes in family structure, such as birth, separation, remarriage, death.
10. When there has been a remarriage or divorce, determine the nature of the involvement of the absent parent and possible stepparent as well as their involvement with the rest of the family.

A therapist will often receive a referral from an agency or family doctor. The referral source will have a personal view of the problem and may even suggest who should be involved in therapy. Therapists occasionally accept a referral at face value and begin working with the family on the basis of the information given. However, the information provided on referral rarely reflects the strengths and resources of the family. The referring source may have been involved with just one family member or may have accepted the family's definition of the problem. It is unusual for the referring agent to have an understanding of how the family operates as a system. It is essential for the therapist to make independent judgments about the families who have contacted him or her.

When a therapist begins to see a family, four major areas need to be assessed: (1) the spousal relationship, (2) the parent/child relationships, (3) the sibling relationships, and (4) the parents as individuals. When assessing the individual parent, the therapist should examine what each parent brings into the family from his or her family-of-origin, such as a personal value system, personal expectations, and the expectations that originated in the family-of-origin. This assessment provides a multi-generational perspective as well as an analysis of what is going on within and between various subsystems of the family. It also provides the therapist with a general idea of how the family is operating as a system.

SECTION TWO:
HOW TO BEGIN THE FIRST SESSION

When the parents attend the first session, it is helpful for the therapist to begin by asking them a neutral question. I often start with general questions such as, "I'd like to get a sense from each of you about how you understand being here today." If the original caller was particularly anxious on the telephone, I will modify my approach by pointing out that I have already talked to one of them and would now like to hear from the other person about how he or she understands being here.

It is useful for the therapist to set up the first interview himself or herself. The therapist begins to develop hypotheses about the family based on how the caller has presented the problem to him or her. When that person appears overly involved with the issues in the family, the therapist should avoid starting the first session with that person. By not focusing on this person, the therapist does not allow him or her to dominate the initial part of the interview with his or her anxiety. By directing the attention to the noncaller, the therapist makes a major therapeutic maneuver. The under-involved person is brought center stage, and the overinvolved, anxious one is put on the sidelines.

When the therapist begins, he or she does not define the problem for the family. Even since the initial telephone call many things may have changed. It is also common for the less anxious parent to present the problem somewhat differently from the more anxious parent.

Although it is the therapist's responsibility to reframe the problem, over time the parents should be given the opportunity to explain the problem to the therapist in their own way. It is unwise for the therapist to overtly challenge the parents' definition of the problem. How they define the problem can help the therapist develop hypotheses about how the family is operating emotionally. Their definition can also be seen as a metaphor for their unfinished business.

There are two basic types of questions that the therapist can pose about the problem: (1) direct questions about content that will elicit information about the problem and its meaning for each person and how it shapes, affects, and/or dominates the family member's life; and (2) questions that deal with process and help the therapist and the parents to understand the functional nature of the problem. These questions address such issues as to how the problem has produced a structure in the family that allows the family members to stay connected. When the therapist focuses just on content the problem serves as part of a triangle in which the parents stick to content as a way of distancing from their own pain, anxiety, and sadness.

The therapist can begin to reframe the problem by taking a developmental history of the family. It is helpful to put the problem into some sort of historical perspective. To do this, it is necessary to take the family back in time before they had the problem. What was different about the family prior to the development of this particular problem? What were the parents like as people before they became a couple? The genogram discussed in Chapter Two is a useful tool for obtaining a developmental history of the family.

In summary, the goals of the first session are:

1. To develop a positive relationship with the adults in the family.
2. To understand the problem in an historical, developmental context.
3. To begin to reframe the problem from a relationship problem, an individual problem within a child or adult to a family systems concern that involves all members of a family.
4. To help the adults begin to identify their emotional themes from their families-of-origin and to begin to see how these influence the way they define and deal with the problem.
5. To constructing a Genogram which identifies the key family members who are involved in the family problem and should be involved in therapy to move beyond the problem.

6. To develop hypotheses about the symbolism underlying the problem and to formulate ideas about how to use the family as a resource system.

SECTION THREE:
HOW TO MAKE THE INTERVIEW SAFE
FOR ALL FAMILY MEMBERS

The therapist has a responsibility to help make the first session a positive, safe, and profound experience for the parents/couple. To accomplish this, he or she must stay in control of the process at all times. The therapist should always remember that the stories and content issues that people bring into therapy are more of an indication about where they are stuck rather than a reflection of their situation. The therapist who tries to figure out the rightness or wrongness of someone's emotional story will quickly discover the futility of that exercise. No amount of persuasion has ever convinced a person in a relationship to agree to the other person's version of a story. The wise therapist will see that the important aspect of a person's story is how it reflects on the person's need to maintain a safe distance from another. Whether or not the story happened as related is not significant.

Each person will struggle to hold on to his or her content issues as a way of staying emotionally safe. The therapist understands that a content serves a purpose. How family members use that content, what meaning they place on it, and how they develop particular content issues all help the therapist understand the degree of unfinished business of the various family members. The therapist needs to float above the content. If the therapist is involved in what is going on between family members, they may be deprived of experiencing the situation differently. Most people can find friends, confidantes, and colleagues who will buy into their content stories and take their side. What family members need from a therapist is someone who can stay detached from the content and ask the questions that no one else has asked. For example, when a wife says that her husband is never available, does not seem to care for her, and is never around, the therapist should not ask the wife more about her husband's behavior. The therapist should ask the wife questions about what she needs, such as: how she knows when she gets what she needs; how does she protect herself when she feels her needs are not being met; when her needs are met, what is different about her? The therapist should avoid the temptation to ask the wife questions about what the husband does or does not do for her. The therapist who asks questions about the husband becomes part of a dysfunctional triangle, two people talking about a third person.

The effective therapist avoids dysfunctional alliances and/or collusions with members of the family. The therapist does not become party to secrets or get involved in relationships with one member of the family to the exclusion of other members. It is essential that the therapist work with all the adults in the family. When one adult is seen and the other adult is on the outside, the solidarity and basic foundation of the family is undermined. The parents should feel the therapist is connected with both of them, understands the struggles of each of them, and is not taking sides with either of them.

Couples will commonly try to get the therapist to take one side or the other. They will approach the therapist in the same ways that they approach other people in the world. From the beginning, the adults in the family will put pressure on the therapist to play a familiar role with them. The therapist's unique challenge is to avoid these collusions and dysfunctional alliances and yet connect with both of the adults in a meaningful way.

The therapist is detached, but involved. The therapist must be able to watch himself or herself work with the family and should not become so involved in the emotional issues that his or her detachment is lost. If the therapist takes sides, feels angry, feels overly elated about the progress of the family, needs to makes things different for the family, or takes responsibility for the outcome, he or she has lost this detachment and, usually, loses effectiveness as well. The therapist must know where his or her responsibilities end and the family's begin. The therapist should resist basing his or her sense of confidence on the success of the family and should not be overly concerned when family members are unable to behave differently or overly pleased when they are able to change. A therapist should stay detached and should be able to ask each family member what meaning has been attached to the therapist's attempts to make things different. When a family member complains that things are not going well, the therapist should ask what has been learned, what has has been tried in order to make things different, what the loss would be if change did occur and things were different, etc. If the parents come to a session saying things are better, similar types of questions should be asked. The important point to remember is that adults have to own their own change. They cannot change for the therapist, nor should the therapist need the family to change in order to feel successful.

The questions the therapist asks the adult family members are self-questions, that is, questions a person answers by describing what is happening for the self rather than what he or she wants from others. The importance of self-questions will be discussed in more detail in subsequent chapters. The important point to remember at this time is that the therapist must avoid entering into dysfunctional triangles between the family members. When a family member talks about others, the job of the therapist is to ask that person more about the self. The therapist then avoids focusing on the safer agenda of how to make others different.

When people enter therapy, they are ambivalent about the process. Although they want things to be different, they are frightened of change. We have all developed our personal stories or views of the world to explain why things are happening in a certain way. We use these stories to keep things emotionally safe for ourselves. Although we may want change, we are reluctant to give up our stories about others. When a therapist challenges a person's stories, the person reacts by holding on to these stories more firmly than ever. The therapist should not try to convince the family member to give up his or her stories. Rather, the therapist should ask what would be lost if the stories were given up. When a person talks about what would be lost by making things different, rather than about what would be gained, he or she is more likely to give up fighting against change.

Prior to the end of the first session the therapist should help the parental couple connect the past with the present. It is essential that the therapist not leave the person in the past. Although the therapist has taken a developmental history, this should be related to the current situation. In the absence of this connection, the parents will think that they have just given information to the therapist so that their lives can be figured out. They will not see themselves as being connected with that information in the here and now.

The first session with a new couple or family has four distinct stages. The first, and most reactive stage, is the presenting of the problem. During this phase, each person will try to convince the therapist of the correctness of his or her own definition of the problem. The second phase focuses on the historical themes. The third phase begins the reframing of the problem, with the therapist gently challenging the definition of the problem by giving it an historical perspective. Charting a genogram and obtaining a developmental history of each member will help to start a reframing of the problem. The fourth phase is the integrating of the session and the contracting for ongoing therapy. This phase ties together the session for the family so that the members understand what course the therapy will take and why history is so important to the present.

SECTION FOUR:
BEGINNING THE FAMILY THERAPY PROCESS
WITH THE PARENTS

It is a challenge for a therapist to meet with the entire family and to make it a safe and meaningful experience for everyone. I have discovered that one of the most effective ways to proceed with a family with children is by beginning with the adults. Whoever is assuming the parenting or caretaking roles should meet with the therapist first. It is important for the therapist to form a solid, trusting relationship with these parental figures.

The parents should know from the beginning that the therapist will ultimately help them connect in a positive way with the family. The parents must feel confident that their therapist has the skill and wisdom to see through their stories, issues, struggles, and fights and understands that the family wants to find a way to stay connected and caring with each other. The way in which the therapist deals with the parents' content issues will form the basis for the parents' initial judgment of therapy and their comfort with him or her. Sometimes it is necessary to have several sessions with the parents before the children are involved. Although the children may not be involved, it is crucial to meet with all the parental figures from the beginning. When a parent is omitted, the therapist runs the risk of undermining the integrity of the family as a unit. He or she also sends the message that other important family members could be left out. The therapist must make it clear that he or she is committed to the whole family, and will not take sides or get lost in their struggles. The therapist must bring safety to the family by remaining apart from their issues and reframing their struggles from negative to positive.

When a therapist begins with the parents, he or she develops an initial hypothesis about how this family lost its way and an understanding of the fact that the problem has historical roots. Most parents are basically loving and caring but have been unable to achieve their goals because of issues in their own lives. These unresolved issues interfere with their ability to deal with their children in ways that are separate from their own emotional histories. When the therapist asks the parents questions about what they bring into the family, a new learning process is established. As the parents begin to learn about themselves and each other, they begin to see that the problem does not lie within an individual family member but is far more complex. Each of the parents brings into the family themes, needs, and anxieties that get played out between all the family members. As this family complexity is revealed, hope and purpose begin to emerge. There is hope for change and a sense of purpose that there is a forum where painful, difficult issues can be discussed in a positive, connecting way.

After the therapist has developed a solid connection with the parents and they are no longer worried that he or she will take sides or undermine them, it is then possible to involve the rest of the family in the sessions.

SECTION FIVE:
FAMILY THERAPY WITH PARENTS:
A CASE ILLUSTRATION AND COMMENTARY

The following session is an initial interview with parents who consulted me because of concerns about their eighteen-year-old daughter whom they considered seriously disturbed. The daughter was in foster care, and the first session included the parents and the foster mother. The session illustrates how this family moved from the reactive phase, in which they are blaming their child for most of their misery, to the second stage, in which they begin to examine the historical themes that they brought from their own families-of-origin. The middle phase of the session illustrates the beginning redefinition of the problem and consequent discussion about who should attend the session as the problem takes on a different meaning. The session concludes with the contracting with the parents about how the therapy should unfold over time.

The R family was referred by the foster mother. She called me because she felt she was overinvolved with the family and needed some help to change her role. She described various difficulties that she was having with the foster child. She felt that she had a good relationship with the parents and had very little contact with the other child in the family, a nineteen-year-old son. She indicated that the foster child was the biological child of the parents, but that the nineteen-year-old son had been adopted at birth. I suggested that she have one of the parents call me to set up the first session.

It would be a mistake to have the referring person set up the interview for the family. These arrangements should be made by a family member and the therapist. The therapist can learn so much about the family during his or her initial contact. The commitment of the family to the process is heightened when the contract for the first session is made between a family member and the therapist.

It was the mother who called to arrange the first session. I explained that I would like to see her with her husband and the foster mother, Joan, to gain a fuller understanding of what was happening in the family. We could then decide who else to bring in. She was quite anxious and wanted to know why I would not see their daughter with them. She felt her daughter would be very upset about being excluded and would feel uncomfortable if I saw the three of them without her. I explained that it was important for her and her husband to have a chance to get to know me and decide if I were the right person to involve in the family. I also told her she could reassure the daughter that whatever was discussed in the session would be discussed again when she was present. I realized from talking with the mother that she was extremely anxious and quite involved with the difficulties that she perceived her daughter as having. I decided I would start the first session with the father.

The session began with my asking Mr. R how he understood being there that day. The session continued as follows:

Mr. R: We have two children, a nineteen-year-old son who will be twenty next month, and who is adopted. Sue is our daughter. She is eighteen. She will be nineteen in February. There is a year and a half between them.
Dr. F: Your son's name?
Mr. R: John. John was identified as learning disabled in Grade 4.
Mrs. R: Actually he had speech difficulties.
Mr. R: Yeah, that's right.
Mrs. R: It was at age 4. It was speech therapy at age 4. So there was a problem right away, dyslexia.
Mr. R: From Grade 4 to Grade 12, we invested substantially in him — emotionally, physically, financially, every other way. He's a very easygoing guy, very friendly, very popular, very athletic, very good looking, very tall. Sue has always felt that she was at the low end of the totem pole. She didn't have the advantages of her older brother, didn't have the attention of her older brother. She does not have an easy-going personality. She has a difficult personality, which we noticed at birth. John, when he was two-and-a-half-months old, was just easy-going, happy-go-lucky. He loved everybody. Sue came into the world crying and worrying.

Sue was a difficult child right from birth. Even though the adoptive son, John, had learning difficulties from the beginning, the parents framed him as the healthier, easier child. As is evident in the rest of this interview, the parents continually saw their daughter as a challenge in their lives. They viewed her behavior as uncontrollable and unpredictable. On the other hand, they saw their son's handicap as manageable.

At the time of the first interview, they continued to see their son as a person who was making a good adjustment in the world and their daughter as having considerable difficulty. One of the major reframes for this family will be to encourage them to see how both children play equally important parts in the functioning of the family. If the parents were left to their definition of the problem, they would omit their son entirely and focus all the family tension on Sue. If the therapist had accepted that focus he would have colluded with the parents and would simply have reinforced the family's stuckness. As the excerpt indicated, Mrs. R often interjected and offered information in reaction to the husband's responses. This behavior is usually a sign of anxiety. The anxious parent has difficulty listening to the other parent's story and will often clarify or add information. The therapist should be aware of the anxiety but not encourage that type of involvement in the therapy process.

It is usually most helpful for the therapist to avoid responding to the anxious parent's interruptions. If the therapist continues to focus attention on the other parent, over time the anxiety will begin to diminish. In contrast, if the therapist encourages the anxious member to jump in by redirecting the attention to him or her, then the therapist colludes with the overanxious member to keep the other family member on the sidelines.

Mrs. R: There was a difficult pregnancy involved. I had surgery at three-months gestation and thought that she would be handicapped. We were thrilled to death that she was normal. In fact, I was told throughout with the whole pregnancy not to get excited about this baby. I mean, this baby may have two heads, or it might be whatever because of the intervention procedures that they did. Well, I went through this, and I spent nine months thinking I was going to lose this child. So it was a miracle, actually. We were overjoyed when she was quote "exceedingly normal and healthy." So you know, it was a rough beginning, I think, for her. She did keep us up nights, but we were told it was just neurological, that she would outgrow the need to wake up at three in the morning. We tried everything, like um . . .
Mr. R: She would wake up in the middle of night screaming her head off. And would refuse to be comforted by anything that we did. She has always been very determined, very independent, very creative, very intelligent . . .
Mrs. R: Very intelligent.
Mr. R: Things went along, reasonably OK. She started to have trouble in elementary school in her middle years. Started to get into conflicts with a couple of teachers and some of her classmates. We thought, well, this is not the situation for her. In particular, one teacher she was not getting along with, we thought was a bit of a jerk. He was just not handling her in the right way. So we said, well, maybe she needs a different environment, different atmosphere. We knew of an alternative elementary school where

Joan (the foster mother) is the head teacher. It's Joan's school. Sue went there for the last two years of elementary school, and following a bit of a difficult transition, she had just a wonderful two-year period. Blossomed!

Mrs. R: She was friendly at home, quiet, pleasant, happy.

Mr. R: And really began to establish her own identity, began to express ... Well, she always had her own identity, that was never a problem, but began to express herself creatively. She got into writing, poetry, acting, and was just very pleased with how that went.

Mrs. R: Blossomed!

Mr. R: And we got to know Joan. It was a parent participation model, so we both got involved in the school, with the school. Joan has been a friend of Sue's, and of ours . . .

Mrs. R: Believe me.

Mr. R: And has helped us at various times throughout the difficulties we've had.

Mrs. R: Crises.

Mr. R: Since Sue left elementary school. She went from there to a regular high school. The first year, she had a difficult time fitting in with the big high school.

Mrs. R: Twelve hundred kids.

Mr. R: But towards the end of the year, it looked like she was beginning to make the adjustment. She went away to summer camp, met a group of girls there. They became an instant group. Then she went back to school, and the whole thing began to unravel. She began to fight with people, get in trouble with the teachers, skip classes . . .

Mrs. R: Yes.

Mr. R: Run around with this group of girls. Started to get into trouble. We were frantic. She eventually had skipped so much school that it was clear that she just wasn't going to do anything at that school. She just wasn't going to go. So finally, we said, OK, maybe it was a mistake to put her in the regular school so how about an alternative high school. She started going to Alternative School, she was emotionally and physically exhausted when she started that experience. She started to make a transition, but it was difficult. Then one of the girl friends in her group also dropped out of the school and started to go to the Alternative School. In fact, I don't think any of the girls in that group ever have finished school.

Mrs. R: Yes, all five of them.

Mr. R: They all screwed up in various ways. It was quite an interesting group of people. Again it looked like in the spring of the year, Sue was starting to make the adjustment. Then her girlfriend started working the street downtown and Sue went down initially to protect her, take care of her . . .

Mrs. R: To save her.

Mr. R: Got sucked into the downtown street scene, started skipping school, spending all hours downtown. We asked Joan to become involved, working with us with a problem-solving method, because that's a large part of how the school is run. It's one of the things Joan does, so she agreed to help my family work out some issues. We did work out a lot of things. We did not deal with any of the downtown thing. She just said "I refuse. It's the only place I feel comfortable. They accept me blah, blah, blah." I mean, the usual thing that kids say when they get sucked into that scene. We had determined that that was the most dangerous place in the area for a teenage girl and we decided we would do something rather drastic to try to break her from that.

So one day when she went downtown against our wishes, as I had previously arranged, Jean and I moved out of our house. And Joan and her son, and a foster, not a foster child, a foster young woman, sort of, moved in. And Joan said to Sue . . .

Mrs. R: We switched houses.

Mr. R: Said, "I'm going to stay here. I'm not here to take care of you. I'm not here to take care of the house, cook, or clean, or shop, or watch. But I'm just here to be your friend and to make sure the house doesn't burn down because your parents can't deal with you anymore."

So Sue was touched. She held out for two weeks and then asked to get together. We worked out an arrangement where she wouldn't go to the downtown street scene.

Joan: That was the first one.

Mr. R: Yeah, I know there's lots. However, by that time she'd blown her school year. Since then, she has refused to go back to school. She has worked intermittently. She has been extremely difficult to live with. I think she last worked at the end of '86.

Mrs. R: As a sales clerk.

Mr. R: And lost her job.

Mrs. R: No Christmas, she was laid off.

Mr. R: She said, "If only I could live by myself, if I could find a job." So we set her up in a room, in a bedroom in a house with a group of other people. She did find a job, that fell apart the end of the year. Then she decided that she couldn't stand living in that house. She wanted to live with somebody else. We moved her into that place, paid all the expenses hoping that she would get a job. She refused to get a job, refused to get training, refused to do anything, and just spiralled out. There were some

blow ups, and physical confrontations, and all kinds of hassles. And difficulties, which we'll eventually get into. It got to the point where she was
living in her own apartment. We were paying all the expenses and she was
just turning her toes to the wall.

Mrs. R: Seventh of the month . . .

Mr. R: Sleeping all day, running all night. Eventually we came to realize
that what we were doing wasn't working and, in fact, was probably hurting her. So we started to cut her off. She then went on Welfare. She then
agreed with Joan's help to go into the psychiatric unit of General Hospital.
She was there for three weeks when they kicked her out because she was
simply not participating in the program. She wanted things done her way.
She said, "I want this, this, and this." She said, "I want a therapist who
will dig into my background and find out all the terrible things that were
done to me." That's not the way they operate. They want to deal with the
here and now. So after three weeks, they asked her to leave because there
was no progress being made. So then, Joan agreed to take her into her
place for a week to see if they could start to work things out. And the deal
now is the end of August, Sue will have to find her own place. She is on
Welfare, she's working with a Social Service worker, and she's working
with Joan. A condition of Joan's involvement at this point is that we and
Sue not really interact because part of the problem has been this sort of
dependency hook and guilt hook. And Sue has been using that as a reason,
just simply not to confront the consequences of her own actions.

Dr. F: (Turning to Mrs R) Do you have anything to add to this story?

Mrs. R: Yes. I think that was very succinct. It left out some of the color
which I would have put in. You know she's got a lot of creativity, and I
think she's a very intelligent person. I think she has been very manipulative, but we've been part of that because we haven't understood how to
get her unraveled from that. So part of our problem has been saying no.
She's very strong. So saying no to her is not easy. I haven't found it easy.
And I don't think you have either?

Mr. R: No.

Mrs. R: Maybe because of our own upbringings, or how we were brought
up. Models that we have in front of us. So the color I would add there is
that there is a context of this person, and it's not just the facts. And also, I
would add that Joan is a very unusual person. I mean, you are not going to
meet very many people like Joan in your life. I think we are very privileged to know her. And it's been amazing how she has been able to keep
Sue's trust through all of this. And I would say that Sue doesn't trust
anybody else right now, period.

To this point in the interview the parents have chronicled the problems
that they have experienced with Sue. If the therapist permitted this to go

on, the parents could use up the entire session talking about their problems with Sue. However, the mother gave the therapist an opening to begin to reframe the problem when she said, "Maybe because of our own upbringings or how we were brought up." When she framed her concerns about her daughter this way, she gave the therapist permission to ask the parents about their own families and what they brought into their new family from the past.

If the therapist listens carefully, he or she will find that most parents will relate a present problem to past concerns. The therapist does not have to ask questions about extended family out of context. Rather, the therapist needs to ask the parents to expand on their own family-of-origin experiences when they give the therapist an opening. Occasionally parents are so preoccupied with concerns about a child that they do not frame their experiences in any way on their own pasts. When this occurs, it is helpful for the therapist to stop the parents' recital and to tell them that it would be helpful to obtain a broader sense of what is occurring in the family by looking back at least one generation to see how the parents experienced their families. The therapist may explain to the parents that an understanding of their own experiences will help to better understand what is going on in their current family. I have seldom encountered a parent who resented or was confused about this type of question. Most parents understand that their reactions come from somewhere. When the therapist explores this area in a nonaccusatory, nonjudgmental way, most parents are willing to provide information about their pasts.

The family therapist does not ask questions about the past for the purpose of assessing or diagnosing the parents. The therapist opens up these areas to begin the gentle process of reframing the problem away from the "identified patient." The therapist intervenes in a subtle way to help each parent begin to understand in a deeper way that his or her reactivity towards the child is based not just on the child's behavior but also on his or her family history. It is not helpful for the therapist to state this principle overtly. However, by the nature of the therapist's curiosity and by the direction of the questions, the therapist will lead the parents to think about their part in the family dynamics somewhat differently.

Returning to the R family, we see that the therapist took advantage of the opening that the mother provided to ask each parent about their own families.

Dr. F: Before we spend some more time on Sue and Joan, I would like to ask you a few questions about what you said a moment ago, more about the family, what types of families you've come from. I'd like to get a fuller sense of who everybody is and put it into context. Then we can take it from there. Mrs. R, how old are you?

Mrs. R: I'm forty-five.

Dr. F: What type of work do you do?

Mrs. R: I'm a personnel manager. I've been at that job now for three years, but I had been a nurse for a long time. I've worked for several organizations.

Dr. F: How about your hours, what type of hours?

Mrs. R: Daytime, Monday to Friday, nine to five is supposed to be what they are. I do have work I have to do in the evenings because of the client load that we carry and the amount of talking to clients on the phone on the weekends.

Dr. F: You say this has been over the last three years?

Mrs. R: For the last three years, but I was always involved in this type of work.

Dr. F: So you've done this for many years.

Mrs. R: Yes, and I worked also as a nurse at a hospital and a social service agency. And I managed a social service agency.

Dr. F: And how long have you been married?

Mrs. R: Twenty . . . is it three, now?

Mr. R: Twenty-three years.

Mrs. R: Twenty-three years. In June, it will be twenty-three.

Dr. F: How many pregnancies have you had?

Mrs. R: Sue is the only one.

Dr. F: And the timing of that one?

Mrs. R: We had difficulty getting pregnant. I guess that would be the correct way of putting it. So she was a much desired child. We adopted John, our first child. And then . . .

Mr. R: Our plan was always sort of to have one child and then adopt.

Dr. F: That was your plan?

Mrs. R: Yes, that was our plan.

Mr. R: So what we did was just reverse it, sort of. First adopt, and then we'll work on the other one at leisure. Of course . . .

Mrs. R: Of course it happened like nothing. Brian was a student back East at the time. He was doing his masters. So it was quite an adventure to live in a basement suite and suddenly go from no children to two children eighteen months apart. It was like having twins.

Dr. F: So only one pregnancy. You stopped at that.

Mrs. R: Yes, we discovered, in retrospect, that it was really a good idea to keep it to two.

Dr. F: And that was a difficult pregnancy right from the beginning. You were anxious about it.

Mrs. R: Yes, it was.

Mr. R: One other factor, in addition to the surgery at two months or so, or whenever it was, the doctors a few weeks after that said you were threatening to miscarry.

Mrs. R: Oh, yes. It wasn't fun.

Mr. R: So that was also a burden that was carried up until the eighth or ninth month. We then got to a doctor back West. The guy took a look at her and told her, "No, you're not going to miscarry." It was just that her surgical scars had never completely healed. That's all it was.

Mrs. R: Oh, it was fun to have somebody that was bright enough to figure that out.

Mr. R: But she carried that. A big burden.

Mrs. R: So it was wonderful. It was a real relief. But I think I had a bit of a postpartum depression because there was such a build-up to this and it was like, huh. I can remember the first two or three months and Brian was busy with his degree, doing his masters, doing his thesis and, you know, I'm working also.

Dr. F: You didn't stop?

Mrs. R: Well, I did work in the emergency ward. I used to do the hiring for this hospital. I was in personnel for a hospital and did all the hiring of nursing staff, but I had to stop that because it didn't fit in with the children. So I switched over and worked in the emergency ward, as admitting nurse on the four to midnight shift so that Brian could look after John in the daytime. No, the reverse, I looked after John in the daytime . . .

Mr. R: You worked at night, and then I was home.

Mrs. R: That's right, I know that we had an arrangement.

Dr. F: Well, Mrs. R, how large a family did you come from?

Mrs. R: Just two.

Dr. F: And who would be the first-born?

Mrs. R: I am.

Dr. F: And then?

Mrs. R: My brother is eight years later. So it's like almost two families in a sense.

Dr. F: He would be?

Mrs. R: Thirty-five now, is he? Well, subtract. Hey, Joan, you know math, you were?

Mr. R: Forty-five minus eight is thirty-seven.

Mrs. R: Thirty-seven. My goodness, how time flies.

Dr. F: What is his first name?

Mrs. R: Bob.

Dr. F: Is he married?

Mrs. R: No.

Dr. F: Never been married?

Mrs. R: No.

Dr. F: Where does he live?

Mrs. R: He's in a suite on the east side. He works in a nightclub. He's so rebellious; my brother is rebellious.

Dr. F: Does he live alone?

Mrs. R: With women from time to time, depending on who is coming in and out.

Dr. F: Now your mother is how old?

Mrs. R: My mother, she is sixty-seven.

Dr. F: And how is her health?

Mrs. R: It's been really delicate. Before my dad died, she had seven tumors removed in the bowel and she has a jaw problem. She has agoraphobia, which is a serious problem.

Dr. F: How does that fall onto you?

Mrs. R: She won't go on a holiday. She will go out with me; I can take her out to dinner. She will go to church and home, walking the same pattern. But she will not do anything fun, adventurous. She is a recluse. Basically, she does not see her friends, no friends. I mean, not one person she sees.

Dr. F: You can get her to do something like go out?

Mrs. R: Oh, I can.

Mr. R: Provided it's not too far away, and not too long.

Dr. F: But no one else can?

Mrs. R: On her birthday she left at nine o'clock because she got tired of the people there and she said she had to go home right away.

Dr. F: How long has this been going on?

Mrs. R: It started before Dad died. I think it was beginning, I could say maybe ten years before my dad died. So I can't say it's just the death of my father. He died seven years ago.

Dr. F: How old was he?

Mrs. R: He was only sixty-four. Heart attack.

Dr. F: Did he have a history of heart trouble?

Mrs. R: Diabetes.

Dr. F: Was that his first heart attack, the one he died from?

Mrs. R: No. It was the diabetes that complicated it. He would have survived the heart attack if it hadn't been for the diabetes.

Mr. R: He was a very dynamic, high-profile guy around which the family . . .

Mrs. R: Successful . . .

Mr. R: Around which the family revolved. And when her world was removed she just sort of . . .

Mrs. R: He was sort of the sun. He was a very vivacious, outgoing, but also very dominant person in terms of expectations. And that would affect me. He had very high standards for me, and I felt the pressures of that. I dealt with that though. I really feel comfortable with them now. But when I was younger, I can remember being very resentful of those standards. And I remember being sort of protective of my mother, feeling that she was somehow always doing his bidding, looking after him. But then I discovered after my dad died that really she was just as powerful as he was. It was amazing. I had always thought of my mother as a very weak person or as a person who was my supporter, who was very gentle. But then I found out what my father had to put up with. I think she had strength through weakness. Which is the opposite.

Dr. F: When did you become aware of that?

We have reached a very important point in the interview. Mrs. R has begun to talk about several major changes and losses in the family. Many of these losses occurred around the same time that Sue began to act out at home and in the community. The parents date Sue's serious decline as starting around age eleven. The parents do not connect the loss of Sue's maternal grandfather and the other major changes that occurred around that time with the increased acting-out behavior of their daughter.

When the therapist asks questions about the timing of developmental changes in the family without suggesting that there is a direct connection between one family event and another, the therapist allows the parents the opportunity to begin to think about these connections without feeling pressured. It is a mistake for the therapist to point out these connections because the parents will usually experience this as blame. The more helpful approach is for the therapist to take a chronology of major developmental shifts and to ask each parent what changes they perceived in the family around these transitional points.

As the reader will see when reading the transcript of the children's reactions to the losses of this period, the connections are obvious. However, at this point in the interview the therapist has confined himself to gently questioning the mother about how major life events have affected her and has tried to arouse her curiosity about how these events also affected her children. It is important to note that the husband has not jumped in much to help his wife out. It appears that he is a bit less anxious than his wife and is able to listen to her story without needing to make it safe for the two of them. Mrs. R seems to have taken on the responsibility of caring for her mother and taking on her mother's sadness about the loss of her husband. Future interviews make it apparent that a common theme for Mrs. R is to feel responsible for what is going on around her and to become quite anxious when family members appear to be in any sort of distress.

Mrs. R's comment that her mother ". . . had strength through weakness . . ." is an important one to build upon. One of the lessons learned in families is how to get attention, reduce anxiety, deal with one's neediness, protect oneself from being vulnerable. A child learns to deal with these strong emotional issues by observing how the parents deal with their relationships and with the children's concerns. A parent will often react to a child without giving much thought to why he or she responds to an issue in a particular way. When a therapist asks a parent about how he or she learned to deal with a concern in a certain way, it stimulates the parent into thinking about his or her own family and the more powerful emotional lessons that they have learned. As parents become more aware of the themes that they carry from one generation to the next they begin the slow process of changing their behaviors.

As the interview continues, the mother discusses how her father's death affected her and her family and refers to some of the major changes that occurred in the family around this issue. This information is helpful to the therapist in his formulation of hypotheses about why Sue began to experience difficulties when she did. There is usually a connection between a child's acting-out behavior and a major family event that upset the family balance.

Mrs. R: After my dad died, we moved in. My mother said she was helpless, and she could not cope on her own. I felt that it was probably true at that point, and so we made a decision to rent our own house. It was to be a three-month trial period to see if we could cope. It was a disaster. My mother began drinking quite heavily. She would wait for me to cook the dinner because she wasn't sure about what I would like for dinner. And I'd be working all day, of course. And Sue was with us. And Sue was subject to that too.

Dr. F: How old would Sue be at that point?

Mrs. R: Sue's eighteen, so seven years ago. Eleven. And she loved her grandmother. Very close to her grandmother, thinks her grandmother is perfection. So I think she was annoyed with me because I was having trouble with Grandma. And I never had trouble with Grandma up until I lived with her after being an adult. I found that I had grown. And I had changed, and I couldn't go back. She's a clean alcoholic. I mean, she was rushing around; she'd be cleaning everything. We're fine now. We're back to caring and loving and supporting each other again, but we had a little blow-up. One day I was dragging groceries in from the car. And she just sat there and said, you know, and I got a little annoyed. I just thought you're not doing anything, aaaaa help me. So anyway we made this decision to leave, but we worked it out. Sue may have also had some pain around that.

Dr. F: What impact did that have on John, do you know, at this period in time?

Mrs. R: John was away at school. This is a really complicated story because he has dyslexia. It's a school that costs about $50,000, for the two years of schooling.

Mr. R: Well, we got him through elementary school. We really didn't want to throw him into a high school.

Dr. F: This was a joint decision?

Mrs. R: Oh, yes. In fact, I was pushing it more.

Mr. R: We checked all the high schools, and all the support programs and services. We're looking at a Grade 9 drop out here, and a terribly frustrated, damaged guy if he goes through the experience. And we've got to do something. We were then dealing with Dr. L. He told us about this school, and we said that sounds like the place. So we sold the house.

Mrs. R: The one that we had just moved out of to move in with my mother.

Mr. R: And took the equity out, and sent him to his school. Excellent school!

Mrs. R: Wonderful.

Mr. R: He did very well.

Mrs. R: Loved it.

Mr. R: Loved it, and it's too bad he couldn't have stayed there.

Dr. F: This was 198—?

Mrs. R: This was the same year my dad died, 1980-81.

Dr. F: Let me just see if I have 1980-81 straight, because really it sounds like it was an interesting year.

Mrs. R: Yes, it was.

The therapist has now highlighted the major changes for the family. He has directed attention to the significance of the period from 1980-81 in the life of the family. He has asked the mother to review the major changes to illustrate that this period was a transitional one for the family and possibly the beginning of a period of high anxiety. The therapist does not point this out directly. Instead he chooses to ask the mother again to explain these major events on the assumption that it will lead her to rethink the events and reassess their impact on the family. If the therapist tries to point out the significance of the events prematurely, both parents will likely become anxious and defensive and respond by arguing with him. If the therapist's questions increase the parents' anxiety, the power of the questions will be lost.

Once a family member becomes defensive, he or she stops thinking about the question and begins to put his or her energy into defending his or her position in the world. The member will begin to justify how he or she has dealt with an issue, rather than to evaluate what the emotional costs of that issue have been. The skillful therapist takes the family member to the brink of a defensive, anxious response, and then retreats. The therapist must stay alert to the first sign of a defensive, reactive response. If the therapist has a personal agenda for the parents or tries to move too quickly with them, the therapist will lose the opportunity to help them think about his or her questions in a new way. The therapist should always remember that the family member's public response is different from his or her private thoughts. One does not reveal one's private thoughts often. However, even "acceptable" public answers that are given to provocative questions can still stir up important private thoughts. The family member who is not made to feel defensive will reflect on these private thoughts, and over time, will begin to talk about his or her history differently. The therapist must believe in the value of this process because its results only become apparent over time. Eventually, the therapist will see that the same questions asked at a later date in the process will elicit different responses.

The interview continues with more questions about the period from 1980-81.

Dr. F: Your dad died in 1980?

Mrs. R: Yes.

Dr. F: Suddenly. You weren't prepared for this one?

Mrs. R: No. We thought my mom was going to die because she had the tumors. He was stressed because of her surgery. Instead of her dying, which is what we thought might happen, he did.

Dr. F: You were more prepared for your mother to die?

Mrs. R: Because we had this huge build up about all this stuff.

Dr. F: You moved into your mother's home?

Mrs. R: It was her home. We rented out ours.

Dr. F: All four of you?

Mrs. R: No, John didn't. It was just three of us.

Mr. R: John was away at school.

Dr. F: So John went to school just prior to your dad's death or just after?

Mrs. R: Just after.

Dr. F: A week after, a month after?

Mrs. R: It was September.

Mr. R: He died in May.

Mrs. R: John went to school in September.

Dr. F: So there were two big changes in that year, and you moved into your mother's home. You stayed in that home for how long?

Mrs. R: It was only a couple of months.

Dr. F: And then you moved out of that home?

Mrs. R: Back to our old house.

Mr. R: We moved into our old house and then sold it.

Mrs. R: We sold it because it had dry rot and termites.

Mr. R: We also needed the money to pay for the school for John. I don't know how many stress points that adds up to but . . .

Dr. F: A lot.

Mr. R: That is a lot.

Dr. F: We'll come back to that year later, but I really want to ask you a bit about your family. Are any of your grandparents alive?

Mrs. R: Oh, not now.

Dr. F: OK. When did your dad's father die?

Mrs. R: My dad's father died right after dad's death, wasn't it?

Mr. R: No. We were in Edmonton when your grandmother died.

Mrs. R: No, that was Nanna. Nanna died when I was seven months pregnant.

Dr. F: That was your dad's mother?

Mrs. R: My dad's mum died in, I've got that one down. Sue was born in 1969, so she died in December, 1968. Nanna.

Dr. F: And your granddad, do you remember?

Mrs. R: That's a little vaguer. Somewhere in the early to mid-70s.

Dr. F: You don't have it clear in your mind.

Mrs. R: Not really.

Dr. F: When your mother's father died, what year was that?

Mrs. R: I never met him. I did meet him once. I was four years of age, and he died shortly after. I don't remember.

Dr. F: What about your mother's mother?

Mrs. R: She died when my mother was only 17.

Dr. F: So the major grandparents for you would have been on your dad's side?

Mrs. R: Yes.

Dr. F: And your children got to know?

Mrs. R: Neither one of them.

Dr. F: They didn't get to know your father's father?

Mrs. R: No, just as babies. They were really tiny, and they wouldn't have any memories. I had a really close relationship with my grandparents, by the way.

Dr. F: They were important people to you?

Mrs. R: Yes. They took me away for summer holidays, took trips to everywhere. I would go away for three months with them.

Dr. F: Your brother too?

Mrs. R: Just me. Because he was eight years younger.

Dr. F: So these are two important people in your family.

Mrs. R: Yes.

Dr. F: Were there aunts, uncles, cousins?

Mrs. R: They all lived back East. So virtually my father was the one that went out West, young man. You know, sort of the wild thing to do.

Dr. F: So his parents stayed near, did they?

Mrs. R: They came out West because he pushed and shoved them to, and then they said they wanted to go to Florida. Actually they ended up going to Florida and commuting back East for a few years before they died. But he had them for a few years out here. He bought them a house, and so they came.

Dr. F: A rather small family.

Mrs. R: Very nuclear.

Dr. F: Your mother's family, now, would be you and your children.

Mrs. R: She has a sister at the moment who is dying in Seattle.

Dr. F: How old is the sister?

Mrs. R: The sister is seventy-two. She is an ex-Mother Superior.

Dr. F: An ex-nun?

Mrs. R: And so was my mother.

Dr. F: Your mother is an ex-nun?

Mrs. R: Tradition.

Dr. F: So all these ex-nuns.

Mrs. R: Well, Mother Superior is a big one up there. And she left, created rebellion.

The therapist has now obtained an overview of the mother's family which highlighted the major developmental changes. The therapist shifted the focus from the "identified problem child" to major events in the mother's family. It is important that he now give equal time to the husband's family.

It is crucial that the therapist be connected with both parents' stories. When the therapist becomes overly intrigued and/or anxious about one parent's story to the neglect of the other, the less involved parent is likely to discontinue therapy or undermine the process. The therapist must carefully orchestrate the time. He or she must know when it is appropriate to focus on the "identified patient," when it is time to back away from the "identified patient," when it is important to call attention to other family members, and when it is necessary to give balance to other's stories. All of which must occur within the allotted time frame.

At this point in the interview, the therapist directs his attention to the father and begins by asking him some basic questions about himself and his family.

Dr. F: Well, Mr. R how old are you?

Mr. R: Forty-six.

Dr. F: And what kind of work do you do?

Mr. R: I'm the manager of a firm.

Dr. F: And, in terms of time commitment and responsibility, what does that take?

Mr. R: All the time. I started that work in November. Prior to that I was working for five years in the city on a redevelopment project, which was a reasonably demanding job. However, really, since September, when I taught part of a semester at college, I have just been swamped adjusting to the new job. It's not going very well. In addition to the family crisis, we've just been hit with a union certification by an employee who I think is probably not capable of doing the job. I think we'll probably have to terminate her, and with the union involved, it's going to be a long, heavy mess. And I'm in trouble with my board anyway. So I've been under a huge burden since last September. Things are beginning to look up, and I'm feeling reasonably up that it'll work out. But I went through a real slump. I started the job physically and emotionally exhausted and went through a real slump.

Dr. F: What was behind this big change in your career?

Mr. R: The project in the city was, and is, a success. I worked myself out of a job. I had become very established in the city and had established a lot of credibility with the local community, business community, City Hall, etc. And so I was a natural to take this job, which is basically the economic development manager for the city, although it's not working for the city. So occupationally, career wise, I had a real peak last summer when I was coming to the end of this job and I was seen as a big success. And, at the same time, our family situation was becoming rather aggressive.

Dr. F: The job you had, the one you worked yourself out of, how time-consuming was that?

Mr. R: It was pretty time-consuming, but not really as much as the one I've got now.

Mrs. R: Well, it was quality time-consuming as opposed to negative time-consuming.

Mr. R: I didn't work, I would go to meetings and meetings. Twice a week. I didn't do a lot of office work at home. I did some, but not a whole lot. But starting with September, I've been working most nights . . .

Dr. F: A real increase.

Mr. R: And weekends.

The therapist has spent a few minutes getting an overview of the father's work situation. Does he work in the evenings? Does he do shift work? Does he have long hours? It is important to get an overview of each person's job commitment and involvement. However, if he stays too long on this subject, he will not learn about the more important aspects of the father's life. The therapist will want to obtain a sense of the type of family the father has come from and learn about some of the losses that he has experienced from his family-of-origin. After spending just enough time with the father to get an appreciation of his work world, the therapist shifts the focus to his extended family.

Dr. F: How large a family do you come from?

Mr. R: I'm in the middle of three sons.

Dr. F: So you have an older brother and a younger brother. And how old is the first-born?

Mr. R: There is a year and a half apart, between us. I will be forty-seven next month, so Bill has had his birthday. He's forty-nine and Joe is forty-five.

Dr. F: Is Bill married?

Mr. R: He is in the stages of getting a divorce.

Dr. F: Is he separated?

Mr. R: Yes.

Dr. F: How many children does Bill have?

Mr. R: Two.

Dr. F: Can you tell me their sexes and ages?

Mr. R: Karen is seventeen and Paul is eighteen.

Mrs. R: Paul's at first year university.

Mr. R: Nineteen I guess.

Dr. F: Is he involved or getting involved with other women? What does the separation involve?

Mr. R: The separation occurred because his wife's, well she . . .

Dr. F: She made the move?

Mrs. R: She's from England, culturally . . .

Mr. R: My brother fought it and was most reluctant to accept it. It was not his idea at all.

Dr. F: This started when?

Mr. R: Oh, gosh, I think . . .

Mrs. R: It's been going on for quite a while.

Mr. R: Yes, you're right. It would be about five years because she went back to England to be with her grandfather and to help her mother run the business. She stayed there, and for a period of time, their children, one was in one country and the other was in another for a year, and then they'd switch. Then a year ago, she came back and now the two kids are living with Bill. But I guess she moved back because the back and forth was not working. So his son will be going into his second year at university.

Mrs. R: He's doing great.

Mr. R: A fine young man. The daughter is going into her last year in high school at the school that . . .

Mrs. R: Sue dropped out of.

Dr. F: Do they connect with each other, see each other?

Mr. R: No. Well, they know each other, but they were never at school at the same.

Dr. F: And Joe. Is he married?

Mr. R: No.

Dr. F: Has he ever been married?

Mr. R: No, never been married.

Dr. F: And where does he live?

Mr. R: He lives in the city in an apartment.

Dr. F: Alone?

Mr. R: Yes. Occasionally he has lived with women.

Mrs. R: Lives with women, on and off.

Mr. R: He's not the sort that lives with people very well.

Mrs. R: Lasts for about six months.

Dr. F: A little bit like your brother.

Mrs. R: Actually they're identical. In that sense they're very much alike.

Dr. F: How about your mother, how old is she?

Mr. R: She is eighty-two.

Dr. F: Her health?

Mr. R: Excellent.

Mrs. R: She's going to outlive both of us. She's a legend.

Mr. R: She's incredible. She bought a new car last fall, and she's looking to go to China this fall. She's a tutor. She lives by her tutoring. She also teaches.

Mrs. R: It's for learning disabled children.

Mr. R: Anyway she works three mornings a week, volunteers in this special school. She's very active in the world of drama, she's a make-up artist.

Mrs. R: She wins awards, and she's . . .

Dr. F: A little bit different from your wife's mother.

Mr. R: Just a bit. She's a going concern, go-getting.

Mrs. R: Sort of like my father, if I had to describe him.

Mr. R: She was a substitute teacher.

Mrs. R: And she's tough too.

Joan: And she's little too.

Mr. R: She used to arm wrestle the guys.

Mrs. R: If she had discipline problems.

Mr. R: If some guy in Grade 9 was acting up, she'd arm wrestle him.

Mrs. R: And win, every time, and they'd have to lose.

Mr. R: Well because she had shorter arms.

Dr. F: Tell me about your dad.

Mr. R: He was a business executive, had his own company.

Dr. F: And he's dead?

Mr. R: He died. He committed suicide in 1960. When I was 19.

Dr. F: He was how old?

Mr. R: He was fifty-six.

Dr. F: What is the story behind this suicide?

Mr. R: He died suddenly, obviously. For a year after his death, I was told that it was a heart attack, which I accepted. A year later, my mother and my older brother informed me that he had committed suicide, and they gave me a copy of his letter. So I had adjusted to his death, or was in the process of adjusting to his death, and then I had to get into the fact that it was suicide. I only partially understood it, until my brother Bill and I went for dinner with a business associate of my father's who had been very close to Dad, personally as well as professionally. And he just talked about what had happened. And that kind of filled in the blanks. And so, I think I understand all that.

Dr. F: How do you understand that? What sense have you made out of it?

Mr. R: His whole meaning was tied up in his job. His whole reason for living, his whole sense of being was tied up in this job. He had been very successful in business and well respected. But his whole style of working was very personal, got to know his clients very well, and he was very comfortable with a kind of low key approach to business. And the field began to change, began to go to high-tech and high-pressure, and that was just not his style. So even though it was his company, even though he had a partner, he began to feel that the business world, his world, was passing him by and he was no longer able to keep up with it. Also, he was very much a driven guy. I remember him working long hours, coming home late at night, working on the weekends, going into the office on Saturdays. So he was a workaholic. He had trouble releasing stress. He used to go away on holidays by himself up to the Interior to a certain place without my mother. He was a periodic, heavy drinker, I don't know whether he was an alcoholic, but he certainly had periods where he would drink excessively. At one point, he was going to two different chiropractors. So he was trying to do something to relieve the burden of stress and could never accomplish that. And then it got to the point in his life where, I guess, the one thing he really felt competent in was removed from him, was slipping away from him. The company brought in a hot-shot executive from New York because they recognized that they had to modernize. And his friend, the business associate, tells of one time when Dad brought a proposal he had put together, in the kind of folksy way that he did these things, and this guy from New York just blew it away. He said, "It's ridiculous. It's crazy. You've got to do this, this and this. This stuff, it's not going to work anymore." And that really clobbered him.

Dr. F: Do you remember the story about why your mother and brother waited a year to tell you that your dad committed suicide?

Mr. R: Because they felt that I was so closely identified with him. I was the one in the family that was closest to him — physically, and emotionally, and intellectually. They felt I couldn't take it.

Dr. F: What lesson did finding out this way teach you about family?

Mr. R: I was ambivalent about it. On the one hand, I felt maybe I'm glad I didn't know. Maybe the grief that I would have had to have borne would have been much worse. On the other hand, the other part of me said I had a right to know. So I really . . .

Dr. F: Had mixed feelings. How did your brother find out?

Mr. R: He found out the same time. I remember sitting down, in fact, I just recalled seeing us sitting down in the living room, the four of us, and Mum telling us. Joe's reaction was, I mean, I started to cry, and Joe's reaction was, "I knew something was wrong. I knew something was up." He was going through his difficult teen years when my dad died. I don't recall him mourning. My brother Bill and I took it pretty hard, but Joe was very shallow.

Dr. F: So Bill knew right away.

Mr. R: Yes.

Dr. F: You and Joe learned a year later.

Mr. R: Well, Dad had typed this letter and had made multi-carbons and he'd gone in the office and put it on everybody's desk, so . . .

Dr. F: He wanted people to know.

Mr. R: Oh, yes, that was the whole idea. He had one letter for the office and one letter for my mum. He had typed it all out. It was very carefully planned. He had planned this for some time, and he had waited until his sons were in their late teens, sort of getting ready to move on.

Dr. F: Did your mum remarry?

Mr. R: No.

Dr. F: Were your grandparents involved in your upbringing?

Mr. R: My mother's parents were dead by the time she was thirteen. My dad's father was dead long before. I never knew him. To compensate for that my grandmother lived to 103.

Dr. F: So your major grandparent was your father's mother. What year did she die?

Mrs. R: After we were married. I think it was the second year after we were married. Probably '65, '66.

Mr. R: '65, '66.

Dr. F: So your parents were actually quite a bit older than Jean's parents in age. But you two are very close in age.

The therapist has now obtained an overview of the father's family and has discovered some major losses in his family. The discussion about the suicide, its meaning, and how the mother and the older brother dealt with it are all very important themes to consider. As therapy continues with this family, one of the major issues that will emerge is the parents' concern that Sue might be suicidal. In a subsequent session with the children, Sue raised the subject of her father's reaction to her whenever she mentioned suicide. It is easy to hypothesize that the father would be terrified that one of his children might commit suicide. Any hint that the children might consider this would be a trigger point for the father.

The degree to which the father has been able to talk about suicide with his children and share a bit about his history will determine how well he will be able to normalize this issue for the children. The therapist discovers over time that there has been considerable secrecy around the grandfather's suicide. The father kept it a secret from his wife for a period of time. They both kept it a secret, to some degree, from their children. Secrecy is a major theme in the family. The father's response to my questions about how he understood his mother's decision to keep the father's suicide a secret is very revealing. He speculated that his mother thought that he was most like his father and that the knowledge might harm him. This attempt at ill-guided protectionism is carried from one generation to the next. Although it is meant as a positive caretaking device it, in fact, hinders family members from connecting with each other.

The therapist deals with this delicate issue with care. In response to the therapist's general questions, the father will reflect on the impact these events may have had on him and his family. Again, the therapist does not try to make connections between these events and the current family issues. If the therapist rushed these connections, it is highly likely that the father would have become reactive and defensive and would have blocked any new thinking about these life events.

At the end of the session, the therapist decides to move away from extended family issues. There are only a few minutes left, and the therapist wants to bring the past into the present and tie it together in some way that gives direction for the future. The therapist still has to bring the two children into the story and also make some connection with the foster mother. He decides to start by asking questions about the son rather than the daughter. If he began this phase of the first session by focusing on the daughter, the family's anxiety would return. By directing attention to the son and by asking about how he fits into the family, the therapist again shifts the focus away from the identified problem.

To this point the therapist has moved the couple from their most reactive phase, in which they discussed their concerns about their daughter, to the gentle reframing phase, in which they discussed their own families and the themes they brought into their marriage and family-of-procreation. Now that the therapist has been able to accomplish some reframing, he attempts to bring the children back into focus, but in a somewhat different form. The job of the therapist at this point is to give the parents the opportunity to talk about their two children, but with less anxiety and concern. The parents' responses give the therapist an indication of both how stuck they are in their preoccupation with the daughter, and how able they are to begin to use their thinking about their own families as a guide for reflecting on their children somewhat differently. At the conclusion of the session, the therapist does some contracting about how to proceed from that point on.

Dr. F: Now before I ask Joan a few questions, I want to find out about John, and how he fits into the whole picture here, and what involvement he has with his sister. So maybe we can start with you, Mrs. R, in putting him into this family.

Mrs. R: John dominated the family, I suppose, for the first ten years of his life because of his disability, and I think that Sue felt that strongly. So that has put John really in the picture because there was a great deal of concern, a great deal of time spent, especially when we didn't understand what was wrong. And hours with teachers after class, hours. I became active in the Association for Children and Adults with Learning Disabilities. We gave just everything in the community to figure out how to help this child. And I was very slow.

Dr. F: You say "we." Was it fairly equal?

Mrs. R: Brian also. I initiated it, and then you came very well along. I think you had some concern about labeling and I did too. In fact, the school system is against labeling. But as it turned out, it was the best thing when we finally had a label because then we could deal with it. So the labeling actually has proved to be not so serious as we thought it would be.

Dr. F: So a lot of your time and energy was devoted to John's problem?

Mrs. R: And Sue was chugging along quite nicely. Actually, maybe she wasn't. Maybe I was so distracted I couldn't see. I'm not clear. All I know is I don't remember having really difficult times with her. I mean we had the average things, the normal kind of discipline problems that one would expect from any child. But I do remember a few winces, but the trouble at school that I had was so much less. In other words, when I had to go and listen to a teacher talk about Sue, it was so minor compared to when I . . . it's like, it was hard for me. I thought that was good if it was only a few things. So I would go, and listen, and think, oh well, she's doing really quite well. So maybe there was a distraction.

I knew she was strong-willed but then we were both strong-willed. Brian is, and so am I. And then I had a father who was, and you had a mother who was. I don't think I was overwhelmingly surprised.

Dr. F: What did you observe happen in the relationship between John and Sue?

Mrs. R: I observed that we had to curtail John because of his strength. I remember they would have arguments, and I would have to sit on John and say, "No you can't hit your sister. She is smaller than you are." In fact, I probably overdid that. There were times maybe when I should have let him have at her, as I now understand later. But I was very protective of Sue. In other words, John is 6'5". He's a giant. He doesn't resemble us.

He's another kind of person all together, physically. So I remember having to really get John into sports. John was very athletic so his whole thing was to achieve in sports.

Dr. F: When did you tell John he was adopted?

Mrs. R: Right away. Well, as soon as he was able to talk.

Dr. F: And Sue, when did she know?

Mrs. R: Right away. He was just part of our family. Sue, one time we knew we were in real trouble, it was a cute story. We moved into a new neighborhood, and Sue went and told the whole neighborhood that she was adopted.

Mr. R: We knew then we oversold.

Mrs. R: Yes. We oversold the idea. So we were in trouble. It was like, whoops, adoption is great, but you know, you can also overdo it.

Dr. F: How many years was John away from the family?

Mrs. R: He was only away for two years.

In this part of the interview the therapist tried to focus on the son's role in the family. The mother talked about her son in terms of his impact on the daughter. She sees him as being somewhat different from the rest of the family and indicated in some ways her daughter needed protection from him. The therapist introduced the issue of adoption and asked when the son and daughter were told that he was adopted. The questions serve as a way to make the adoption issue a normal part of the family reality. One of the more important areas the therapist asks about is John's leaving the family home. The therapist's objective is to help the parents recognize the importance of involving John in ongoing sessions. If the therapist does not characterize John as a central person in the family, the parents will use their anxiety about their daughter to exclude him from the sessions. It is evident from the discussion about John that he is an important family member and excluding him from the sessions would undermine the goal of family integrity and connection. At this point, the therapist turns his attention to the father and asks him some specific questions about his son. It is important to ensure that both parents are given the opportunity to talk about the children's involvement in the family.

Dr. F: Mr. R, let me ask you this question about John. How much involvement does he have with what's going on with Sue now?

Mr. R: OK. Just to go back a bit. John got a lot of attention because of his disability and also his abilities. He was tall, handsome, athletic, easygoing, warm, so he was getting a lot of positive attention. And negative attention too, to Sue's detriment. In fact, when John was away at private school we thought, well, that's good because now Sue will be kind of one . . .

Mrs. R: Center front . . .

Mr. R: A single child, and that would be good for her. How does John fit in?

Dr. F: Now?

Mr. R: Now. He thinks that his parents are a bunch of idiots.

Mrs. R: For the way we raised Sue. Not him of course.

Mr. R: He does not understand Sue at all. He doesn't understand why she behaves that way. And she doesn't understand why he behaves the way he does. But he is really highly critical of us. He says, "She has led you around for years. She has manipulated you. You should have clamped down on her, and she's an idiot, and . . ."

Mrs. R: And he's not going to raise his children that way.

Mr. R: Oh, yes, he knows exactly what not to do now.

Mrs. R: Good.

Mr. R: He sees himself as having to carry this burden of this screwed-up family . . .

Mrs. R: It's embarrassing.

Mr. R: Screwed-up sister and incompetent, wimpy parents.

Mrs. R: But he also loves us, now come on . . .

Mr. R: Yes, he does. And we love him. And he knows that. Now, the relationship between the two of them is quite peculiar because they are very critical of each other. Yet, underneath, there is a concern. There is an affection.

Mrs. R: I think so.

Dr. F: Caring?

Mr. R: Yes, there really is. And I'm convinced when they are adults . . .

Mrs. R: They will work it out.

Mr. R: That they will get along. There was one incident where Sue was driving our car, and one of the idiots that she was tied up with was apparently using it to make nonprescriptive, pharmaceutical deliveries. He was transporting drugs around. Apparently he was a real bad actor, and John found out about it and says to me, "If that guy hurts Sue, I'll kill him." That to me revealed something about how he felt about her.

Mrs. R: He's also army. Maybe we should tell that. He's in the militia so his brain is . . .

Dr. F: He's at home now?

Mr. R: Yes. Now, going back to the earlier relationship. He was always bigger than she was, obviously. But up until a certain age she dominated him. She was just tougher than he was. And she could out talk him. And she could outwill him.

Mrs. R: Her tongue, yes.

Mr. R: And that was terribly frustrating for him because he just could not defend himself against her. We have rolled over in our mind the possibility of something sexual between them, some kind of sexual abuse. To me, emotionally, that doesn't match up because she has never been submissive to him.

Mrs. R: I can't imagine her being submissive to him.

Mr. R: Now, there was one point when she was thirteen, or fourteen, and she was bugging him, and bugging him, and bugging him, and he finally lost his temper and beat her up. Just burst.

Mrs. R: That was the first time.

Mr. R: That was the first time I think he had ever really . . .

Mrs. R: She decided that Kraft Dinner wasn't good for him and kept throwing his Kraft Dinner in the garbage. And he put up with it and finally just said, "NO!"

Mr. R: So we jumped on that and said, "John, you can never do that again. Obviously you can't live in the house if you are going to do that kind of thing." And we told him he had to give up a ghettoblaster to her and couldn't drive the car. And he accepted that because he knew that the tables had been turned and that Sue would never bully him again. Sue was heartbroken, just completely heartbroken. My sense is that she also knew she had lost another victim, and that was a real sense of loss.

Mrs. R: And she demanded to be taken to the hospital, and she wanted to charge John . . .

Joan: I wouldn't call it heartbroken. Sorry to butt in. Furious is what I was thinking.

Mrs. R: Yeah, furious, thanks. And then she demanded to be examined. So we took her to the hospital so she could get . . .

The therapist has continued to focus on John's involvement in the family and hopes the parents will view as reasonable his request to see the whole family. However, prior to introducing this idea, the therapist asks about what other types of help the family has sought and who has been involved in these efforts. The parents' response to these questions will give the therapist an indication of how difficult it will be to get the whole family to come in together.

Dr. F: Let me ask you one other question before I turn to Joan about all the help you've gotten, all the different people you've involved. We won't have time this morning for me to find out all the different ways you've gone about doing this, but have you ever had anybody sit down with all four of you together?

Mrs. R: Only once, and that was years and years ago.

Mr. R: We tried once, and it just didn't go anywhere. I should tell you two other incidents. There was an incident in our house that occurred July, August last year, when Sue had taken John's credit card. We had taken the gas card away from her because she was just running up a few bills and we gave her all the gas allowance. She got John's card. I said, " Sue you must give the card back. You are not allowed to have it." She said "I won't." I said, "In that case you can't drive the car." I went out and dismantled the car. She came in at two o'clock in the morning when we we were asleep and demanded that I put the car to rights so she could drive it, and I said no.

Mrs. R: Screaming over our bed.

Mr. R: And so she's screaming away at us in our bedroom and I say, "Sue it's our bedroom, get out of our bedroom." She said, "NO, you must get that car right. I'm just going to stand here. You must do that." And I lost my temper and got physical with her, pushed her around. And then I went into the bedroom and closed the door. She went into the kitchen and got a knife and started going around the house cutting up furniture and parts of the house and stabbing the door where I was at. And . . .

Mrs. R: I'm still not through that one . . .

Mr. R: And eventually I confronted her, and decided she wasn't going to stab me and took the knife away from her. But that was a big deal. And another time when she was living on her own, living with these people, I took her out somewhere, took her back to drop her off at the house. We got into an argument; she refused to get out of the car. I had to go back to work so I said, "Sue, if you want to stay in the car and go back to the city with me that's up to you but I've got to go." So she refused to let me drive the car. She was pulling the car and punching me, and I also lost my temper. Got out of the car, pulled her out of the car, physically, and then drove off. So, those were the two physical incidents.

Mrs. R: Apparently the police were called at that instance because she found some neighbor in the community and screamed, "My father did this to me." Then you went to see a lawyer just to make sure that all of your own story . . . The police said she had six months to follow up if she was going to take it to court, and it wasn't followed up on.

This is an important part of the interview. The parents have demonstrated their anxiety by upping the ante. They have told the therapist even more complicated, stressful problems about their daughter in an attempt to get the therapist hooked into their major concern of adjusting her behavior.

The therapist's challenge is to resist reacting to the parents' anxiety and to avoid directly challenging their understanding of the problem. He must hear their anxiety as conveyed through their stories yet not comment on the stories. The therapist should continue to move in the direction he thinks most fruitful for the family.

The therapist has heard the increased complaints and concerns from the parents but chooses not to respond to them. Instead, he involves Joan by asking why she thought family therapy might be indicated. This deflection is a safe way of avoiding an old battle with the parents while at the same time sustaining the focus on the whole family.

Dr. F: (Turning to Joan) Now, you made this request for family therapy. What did you hope would happen by my being involved with the family?
Joan: Well, I hoped that you could help the four of them sort out what I see as a sort of power problem. Where some very powerful people are screwing each other up and really seem to care for each other tremendously.
Dr. F: Four powerful people.
Joan: I don't know about John. I don't have a strong feeling about John. Three powerful people certainly.
Dr. F: You haven't been involved with John at all?
Joan: Well, you asked Brian about other people helping. I did do weekly problem-solving with just the three of them a lot of the time, but we did pull John in occasionally. He simply was agreeable. Sue was very, very hard to problem-solve with but John would hold out a bit for certain things he wanted. But mainly, he was very agreeable. So I don't know him very well.
Mr. R: He is strength through weakness. He is very passive, very dig-in-his-heels in a very passive way.
Dr. F: Now, Joan, tell me your role in the family. What did you do? How did you get involved?
Joan: I generally respond to people who phone me in a panic and do what I would consider emergency measures until I can get somebody who can do it better than I can. I never trained in any of this kind of thing. Now with the school, we do problem-solving. And so I have built up a fair skill in problem-solving, but it is not therapeutic. It is simply to work out workable solutions. So when Mr. and Mrs. R first called, I said I would come, and Sue was used to problem-solving and would see if we could

problem-solve a way out of what appeared to be a rather mechanical problem.

As time went on, it seemed to be more than just a mechanical problem. When I moved into the house, it was because I didn't know what else to do. We were really stumped. Sue would, correct me if I'm wrong because my memory is not good on these things, but as far as I remember, Sue would not go to any kind of counseling, would not accept anybody saying anything to her. I was one of the few people that could say to her, "Stop." Now she is a very powerful girl. Just the other day, we were in the social service's waiting room, and I had my car parked in a zone that was going to be cleared out. I was sort of hoping that we could get in before I would have to go move my car. She marched up to the desk and demanded to get in right away, something, personally, I never would have had the nerve to do. She has this very strong assumption that she has a lot of rights. I stayed involved because I was unable to think of anyone. We tried different people. We tried psychologists, and psychiatrists, and all kinds of things. The reason I moved in was because she was insisting on being on the street, and it seemed to us after considerable discussion that she could get hooked on drugs and prostitution and that she would in fact go down the tubes. So it was a desperation move.

I've been working with kids and families for thirty years and I never get involved unless someone is desperate and they beg me to. I try to not get involved in cases where I can't do any good or I don't see any hope. But with Mr. and Mrs. R and Sue, I see tremendous potential for Sue.

Dr. F: Now if we continue these sessions, how would you see your role?

Joan: Well, I always see myself as easing out as quickly as I possibly can. However, on the personal level, I'm very intrigued with what you're doing. I'm really interested, happy to sit in on a session just for my own use. But I don't particularly want to be any more than friends of Mr. and Mrs. R, and a friend of Sue.

Dr. F: Well, Sue is where now?

Joan: She is staying with me.

Dr. F: And the plan is for her to stay with you?

Joan: Until she can get an apartment or whatever.

Dr. F: So you'd be willing to meet with John and with the rest of the family if we did that? (Turning to parents) That's OK with you to keep Joan involved?

Mrs. R: Oh, yes, yes.

Dr. F: Because I think that's important.

Mrs. R: Actually I think that would help. I think Sue without Joan, I think that it would be very tricky to keep her motivated.

Mr. R: Yes, even if it was useful to make the transition, if this is going to be an ongoing situation, until she has made the connection and the link.

The therapist has now brought Joan into the session. Prior to the session he had instructed the foster mother to come as an observer, to let the parents tell their story, and not clarify any of the parents' information. However, it was important to involve the foster mother prior to the end of the session. Her participation is vital to the success of the therapy. When a crucial support person is left out, it can easily undermine the family therapy process. Joan had the benefit of listening to the parents telling their story. She did not interrupt to defend herself or to explain her position in the family. At the end of the session, the therapist asked her what she had learned about the family from her own involvement. From her response, he learned about her role in the family and her areas of reactivity. He also gained an idea of how positive a support she would be for the family. He wants to ensure that the foster mother feels supported and understood by him and that her goals and hopes for the family will be addressed in the family therapy process. If the foster mother felt she was not a part of the process, she might unwittingly undermine the objectives of the therapy. As indicated by her comments, Joan, in some ways, reinforces the parents' perceptions of Sue.

The session continues with the therapist addressing the issue of involving John.

Dr. F: I will say that I wouldn't want to see Sue without John. I wouldn't want to have any session with Sue unless John was also present. I think that is very important.
Mrs. R: OK. She was very angry that John will be included.
Dr. F: But we can't. . . .
Mrs. R: No, I'm just saying that probably shows that there is an importance in him being here.
Dr. F: That's very important.
Mrs. R: Yes.
Mr. R: And John was very angry that he would have to come. He's started saying, "You screwed her up. Don't involve me."

In this short interchange, the therapist has established the importance of involving John in any sessions with the children. There is some ambivalence and anxiety about including the son, but the therapist consistently reinforces the need to see the entire family. Once this principle is established, he begins to talk to the parents about the role that he would like them to play when the children attend the session.

Dr. F: Now, there is something that I want to ask the two of you to do. Should we decide to have John and Sue here next week, I would like to be able to talk to the two of them without either one of you, any of you, clarifying any point, even though it might sound totally outrageous to you.

Mrs. R: No, I think that's more than fair.

Joan: He means things that they say might be totally outrageous. You may know it's totally the opposite.

Mr. R: In other words, we observe but say nothing.

Dr. F: That's right. I used to start family therapy with the whole family, but I've learned that because these issues are so hot it's a struggle to have parents just listen to their children. They want to clarify something. So I think often its prudent to meet the parents first to make sure that I'm the right person for the family and that you feel confident before I meet the children that I'm not going to collude with anybody. But I think that it's very important that the four of you always work together in whatever is going to evolve. And the children have to meet me, but I think that it's better that they meet me with you being here.

Often after the therapist has advised the parents as to how he would like them to behave during the whole family session, their anxieties will increase. As will be seen in the transcript below, the parents begin to tell the family therapist about the potential suicidal behavior of their daughter. These types of stories present the ultimate challenge for the therapist. He can continue his attempts to redefine the situation or can be drawn into focusing on the potential suicide of the child. This issue is further complicated in this family by the father's own issues around suicidal behavior. The father discusses the potential suicide of his daughter in an offhanded way; however, his nonverbal communication shows considerable distress about this whole area. The therapist does not have enough information to assess whether the daughter is actually suicidal. He asks one of the more reliable information givers, the foster mother, her opinion about this concern. Joan, who is a bit more detached from the family emotions, reassures the family and the therapist that suicide is not a concern and that she is not worried about it. She bolsters her position by revealing that she has experienced a suicidal grandparent and does not take this issue lightly. On the basis of this information, the therapist proceeds with his plan to see the whole family. He will begin the next session with the children telling their stories in the presence of their parents, but without interruption, as a way to connect more intimately with them.

The concluding moments of this session test the therapist's commitment to his model and his understanding of the role of anxiety. Without these, he could have easily colluded with the parents and focused on the identified problem child.

Many parents will increase their efforts to convince the therapist of the rightness of their view by describing the worst family scenarios. The therapist must always remember that his or her efforts to reframe the problem will create a fairly high degree of anxiety. The parents' anxiety usually manifests itself in the form of increased complaints about each other's behavior and/or another family member. The therapist listens carefully to the complaints, both to understand the role anxiety is playing and to try to assess the severity of various problems. When there is a realistic concern about suicidal behavior, the therapist may have to modify his or her approach and deal with the seriousness of that possibility. However, many times when suicide is mentioned, it is not the major concern, but rather, an expression of the extreme anxiety the parents are experiencing at the idea of rethinking their concept of how the family operates.

The session concludes as follows:

Mr. R: That's important because Sue, particularly, being quite paranoid now, is really afraid that we are going to, because we're so clever and articulate and believable, just sort of twist you around and . . .

Mrs. R: We should probably say that she called us at 2:30 this morning and said that she was going to kill herself and she's back at her apartment to clean it out. Brian, you better tell it because . . .

Mr. R: Well, a number of months ago, we started thinking, clearly, this isn't working. And Sue had been very successful at manipulating us through threats, "I'm going to go down on the street, and I'm going to become a prostitute. I'm going to sell drugs. I'm going to kill myself." At a certain point, we just said we cannot respond to the threats, so we stopped responding to the threats. I think that was an important step. But anyway, she tried again last night, about 2:30 in the morning.

Mrs. R: It's been quiet for about three weeks actually. It's been lovely.

Mr. R: Well, because Joan made the very positive move of saying, "You guys don't deal with these others except through me." And that was very important, and a very wise one, but when your daughter calls at 2:30 in the morning and in a very groggy, slurry way says she is going to kill herself. . . . I stayed on the phone and listened for about an hour and tried to talk to her until I felt that if she had taken an overdose she would be worse off than she had been at the beginning of the conversation. When she got a bit angry she became much more articulate, and then she told me that she had only taken one sleeping pill and that she was thinking about killing herself but hadn't made the decision. So I said, "Well, when you decide phone me and let me know." And then . . .

Mrs. R: She agreed to that, and we found that she's alive this morning because I telephoned to check.

Dr. F: (To Joan) Is this a concern of yours?

Joan: Suicide? Well, it had been because my tiny bit of knowledge about suicide is that you always take it seriously. And the fact that her grandfather committed suicide. My own grandfather committed suicide and I've never considered suicide so I'm not too done over by that, but I'm afraid of that. But seeing Sue over the last three weeks, my guess, my strong guess is manipulative rather than real. She has a strong will to live and whenever she has nothing to do with her parents she thrives . . .

Dr. F: OK. We're going to have to stop here. I will see everybody next week.

This case example illustrated a first interview with parents who identified their child as the problem. The therapist guided the family through the four phases of the first interview. In the first phase the parents told the therapist their story about the problem. The second phase focused on the parents' historical themes and how they may be played out in the nuclear family. In the third phase, the therapist began to reframe the problem and pinpointed the timing of major family events. In the fourth and final phase, the therapist contracted with the parents about how to proceed with the family therapy process. By the conclusion of the first interview the parents should have a clear sense of how the therapy will proceed and the therapist should have formed some hypotheses to guide his questioning and intervention.

Chapter Five

Family Therapy
with Parents and Children

SECTION ONE:
HOW TO INVOLVE CHILDREN
IN THE FAMILY THERAPY PROCESS

This chapter focuses on the involvement of the children in the family therapy process. Prior to their involvement the therapist should have concentrated on establishing a firm, solid relationship with each parent in the hopes of creating an environment in which the children can talk and the parents can listen in different ways. For this set of circumstances to occur, the therapist must ensure that the children feel safe and comfortable throughout the process. Many children will resist coming to family therapy sessions out of the fear that they will be blamed for or pulled into the family struggles. Even the term family therapy creates anxiety in many children. The term implies togetherness and solidarity. Many adolescents and young-adult children are in the process of reducing their involvement with their families. So when their parents invite them to attend the sessions, they are reluctant because they feel that they are not a part of the problem and/or they do not want to become involved in the problem.

The family therapist needs to make it clear to the parents that the first session with the children will take the form of the children telling their story to the parents through the therapist. The parents' role is to sit back and listen. They must refrain from imposing their point of view, correcting, or justifying their behavior. It is essential that the parents feel that the therapist is respectful and supportive of their vision for the family. If the parents lack this confidence in the therapist, they will see him or her as siding with the children and will not feel comfortable with this process. In contrast, when the therapist has established a solid relationship with the parents, they will realize that this approach is used to connect the family and they will be more supportive and curious about what the children have to say.

One of the difficulties family members experience in their own homes is listening to each other's concerns without becoming reactive, defensive, hurt, or angry. It is difficult for two people in the home environment to have an intimate conversation without other family members jumping in and taking sides or otherwise distracting the two people to reduce the intensity and anxiety. When the therapist blocks the parents' reacting to their children, he or she is changing this pattern by creating a new experience for the family. In this approach, the therapist directs the questions at particular family members and does not allow family members to react to each other. Instead, they are encouraged to talk about themselves through the therapist to other family members. The procedure allows the family members to be intimate with each other through the therapist. If this structured approach is loosened up too soon, the family will react in their old familiar, defensive, angry ways. These old patterns are consistent with the way the family members function at home. Playing out these patterns in the session is not therapeutic for the family and will discourage family members rather than give them hope. The therapist offers hope through this structure that family members can have different experiences with each other. When family members can talk about themselves in the presence of the others in their family through the safety of the structure that the therapist has established they can have different experiences with each other. The questions that the therapist asks the children are directed towards helping them to explain themselves to other family members. Special attention should be paid to all the children and they should be given the opportunity to talk about issues that concern them in the family, outside the family, between siblings, and between their parents, as well as their own desires for how they want the family to develop over time. As the children realize they will not be evaluated, judged, or criticized they will begin to relax and expand upon their views of the family. When this occurs there will generally be an increase in hope and enthusiasm displayed in the session and the family will begin to become more connected.

The following case examples are of the second and third interviews with the "R" family. The first interview, during which the therapist developed a solid relationship with the parents, was presented in Chapter Four. Both children were present for the second and third interviews. The second interview was highly structured and provided the opportunity for the children to talk about their concerns and struggles. In the third session the therapist loosened up a bit on the structure and gave the parents, as well as the children, an opportunity to voice some of their concerns about family issues. These two sessions illustrate how quickly the family members can begin to be more connected once the parents' anxiety about being judged has been reduced and their curiosity about what their children are thinking has been aroused.

SECTION TWO:
MAKING IT SAFE FOR CHILDREN
TO TALK TO PARENTS:
CASE ILLUSTRATION AND COMMENTARY

The therapist begins the second interview with the "R" family by asking Sue how she understands being at the session. He asks this question to learn what the parents may have told the child about the session. The children's fantasy about what will occur in the session will govern their initial behavior. The therapist wants to ensure that no family member is labeled as the problem and that the session does not start on the basis of the parents' initial definition of the problem. It is important for the children to tell the therapist about their concerns and how they define the problem. The session begins as follows:

Dr. F: (To Sue) What is your understanding about being here today?
Sue: About being here. Um, that depends.
Dr. F: I'm asking why you are here with your family and with me.
Sue: Because we are having problems.
Dr. F: Is that how you understand this? What problems?
Sue: With the family.
Dr. F: You define it for me.
Sue: It's really hard to define it, correctly. It is our problem. It is the problem of how we relate to each other. That's the main problem. And, a couple of things.
Dr. F: Have you been in sessions like this before?
Sue: No.

Sue has explained to the therapist that she understands her being at the session as having to do with family problems. Although she has trouble defining what the problems are, it is important to note that she does not blame herself for the problems. The therapist goes on to explain to Sue and John that he is interested in hearing from both of them about their family situation.

Dr. F: So this is your first time. You know that I met with Joan and your mother and dad last week. I asked them to sit back and listen this week because I wanted a chance to meet with you and hear from each one of you what has been happening in the family. I think that each of your perspectives are really important. Just so I can get a sense of who you would call family, who would you identify as family?

The therapist has explained briefly what he would like from Sue and John. The opening question about whom they identify as family is an important one. It begins to reframe the problem away from a single member and helps broaden the definition of who constitutes family. Usually the children's definition of family is slightly different from their parents'. The therapist is continually looking for additional family members who might be included in the ongoing family therapy process. The children's definition of family gives the therapist an idea of the role that grandparents, uncles, aunts, godparents, and other significant persons have played in the family. The therapist is hoping to discover family members who are resources to the family and who may be brought into the therapy process to expand the family sense of purpose and connection.

Sue: Family. Family you are born in or family of feeling?
Dr. F: Feeling. As being emotionally available to you.
Sue: Emotionally available to me. I've only got my grandma.
Dr. F: Anyone else?
Sue: Within the family, like . . . no everyone's pretty well out of reach. I don't have too much in me of family around here. I have a lot of people back East.
Dr. F: How about your mother's brother? Any involvement with him?
Sue: We don't have any kind of relationship.
Dr. F: You wouldn't consider him an emotional support, someone who is available?
Sue: He's not, no.
Dr. F: And your dad's older brother, Uncle Bill. What about him?
Sue: He's Uncle Bill.
Dr. F: Somebody you would see as family?
Sue: Uncle Bill. He's family, but if there was a problem I wouldn't call him. It's just not very reasonable. I wouldn't call him.
Dr. F: You wouldn't call him.
Sue: No. We're a Christmas, Thanksgiving and Easter family.
Dr. F: And his children, your cousins, how about them?
Sue: Um, no. We probably have cousin-type relationships.
Dr. F: How about your grandma, your mom's mom?
Sue: Well, she kinda got thrown into the situation as the family mediator we could find at the time. I adore her all the time, and sometimes when

things were just getting a little too silly for words, I'd phone her up and
then she'd phone up. That's her place within this, but that might. . . .
Dr. F: She's helped over time?
Sue: She's done what she can. She does what she can. She listens to me,
you know. Sometimes she yells back at me, but most of the time, she is
real kind to me and understanding. So I really appreciate that.
Dr. F: Do you have a different relationship with her than with your mom?
Sue: Very different.
Dr. F: What's different about what you have with your grandma?

The therapist has taken Sue through the various extended family members to try to determine the emotional connection that she has with each of
them. He has asked Sue to describe the differences between her relationship with her mother and her maternal grandmother. Responses to questions such as these can be very revealing. Occasionally children form
closer bonds with a grandparent than they have been able to form with a
parent. Parents have mixed reactions to these relationships. Some parents
are happy that the grandparents can give emotional support to the grandchild; others are conflicted that their child is receiving more emotional
support from the grandparents than they themselves have received. The
role of grandparents in family development is always significant. The loss
of a grandparent can have a ripple effect throughout the nuclear family. As
becomes apparent in the interview with the "R" family, the death of the
grandfather significantly changed the way the family operated. This issue
is raised in this session and takes on special meaning in the third session.

Sue: Well, grandmothers can have granddaughters and that's how it
works. Moms can have daughters which is a different situation all together.
Dr. F: Give me an example that will help me understand the difference.
Sue: The difference between being a granddaughter and being a daughter?
Dr. F: Yes. How does it work?
Sue: I don't know how it works. Like I see her as my grandmother not her
mother, but she was her mother first. I see her as my grandmother and
detached from the situation, detached from them. OK, and sometimes
being in it, but always over on the side. It's hard to describe the relationship between any of the three of us right now cause it's not very good.
Dr. F: The three of you? You mean the three of you or your grandmother
too?
Sue: No. I just mean my parents and me.
Dr. F: Well, how about your dad's mom. What type of relationship do
you have with her?

Sue: I don't know. She's really a great person, very interesting . . .

Dr. F: Is she available to you in a way that's different from your mom's mom? Do you have a different relationship with her?

Sue: Well, it wasn't until recently that, um. At first it was like, when we were kids, like she is very down to earth and a very honest person . . . She said "When you're kids, you're kids. You're just grandchildren. You don't really have any personality." And, um, she says, "Well, now I'm starting to consider you one of my friends," which is really nice considering I like her too.

Dr. F: When did that happen, when she said that to you?

Sue: We saw each other a couple of times when I was in the hospital. And when we went out for dinner one night, we had a really good talk.

Dr. F: This was recent?

Sue: Yup, two or three weeks ago.

Dr. F: You heard her say that she sees you more as a friend?

Sue: Yeah, she's very open. I tend to look at the problem from about four or five different angles. I often don't really talk about the other three angles. I'm looking at the problem from, usually one or two of the angles. I just decided to throw a few of my weird theories into it, and she talked to me about it. You know, she made sense out of it for me. And she understood, which I found interesting. She understood cause my theories can get very bizzare. She understood.

Dr. F: That's interesting. She heard it. She listened to it. She didn't judge it.

Sue: No. No, she doesn't. I mean, she's not overwhelmingly sympathetic or anything, and that's good. She just doesn't say anything.

Dr. F: So you see her as being more available to you as time goes on. You're able to talk to her more than you might have say a couple of years ago.

Sue: Oh, yeah, definitely. Well, things were different then. You know, I mean, John and I just had no brains.

Dr. F: Sue. Your mom's father died in 1980. Do you remember him? You would have been about eleven years old. What sort of relationship did you have with him?

Sue: Major granddaughter/grandfather type relationship. I was still quite young, but basically he was the center of my life. I adored him. I still to this day respect him, and I respect few men. And, um, I miss him, a lot.

What Sue says about the death of her grandfather is very important. The timing is significant. She began to exhibit difficulties within the family at age eleven shortly after the time her grandfather died. The grandfather was obviously a special person in her life. The therapist now wonders what other changes occurred in the family around this crucial time. The loss of a grandfather for Sue was, of course, the loss of a father for Sue's mother and the loss of a husband for Sue's grandmother. As will be seen as the interview continues, these losses changed the relationship between these women. The death of the grandfather was a profound loss to the family.

Often a family is not aware of the impact that the death of an extended family member has had on its members. Individual family members may be so caught up in their own loss and grief that they may not see how the loss is affecting the rest of the family. When they do see other family members showing sadness, anger, and concern, it is not uncommon for them to feel resentful. Clearly, a family can lose its way after the death of a grandparent, sibling, or other important extended family members.

The therapist stays with the subject of the death of the grandfather, which gives Sue an opportunity to explain to her parents how great a loss his death was for her.

Dr. F: It was a super special relationship then?
Sue: I think so. I don't know whether he thought so, but I always thought, like, I was very close to him.
Dr. F: Would he have been the person you felt the closest to back then?
Sue: The closest?
Dr. F: Yes, the closest family member.
Sue: I didn't really block everything out then. People weren't put into groups. He was my grandfather, just Baba and Gramps. I've always adored Baba, and I've always loved Gramps.
Dr. F: So they were very special?
Sue: Yeah.
Dr. F: When he died, what changed?

By the wording of this last question, the therapist has emphasized that the family changed after the grandfather died. He did not ask whether things changed or if Sue noticed a change. It is not a yes or no question but one that requires Sue to think about process. It assumes and emphasizes that change has occurred. The interview continues with Sue's description of the changes.

Sue: Baba did.
Dr. F: How did she change?
Sue: She became another person. She became not who she was. She was angry. She was always quite angry. She seemed to reject us . . .

Dr. F: Do you remember it quite well?

Sue: What I remember is all the stuff being tagged, and the things that were sold . . .

Dr. F: Things that belonged to your grandfather were sold?

Sue: He had a lot of antiques. He collected antiques. Some of them she kept. Some of them went to me. Some of them went to the family.

Dr. F: Some special things to remind you of your grandfather?

Sue: Yeah.

Dr. F: What changed with your mom when your grandfather died? What did you notice was different about your mom?

Sue: I'm not sure.

Dr. F: Did anything change between you and your mom, after your granddad died?

Sue: Probably.

Dr. F: Can you think about it? Can you see it around that time?

Sue: I don't know how I see it around that time. But I'm sure that when the situation changed, if anything, it probably would have happened then.

Dr. F: Sue, tell me in your memory, if you go back through all your memory, when did things start changing in your family and not go so well? When was that?

Sue: I really have no idea. I know, I mean, we can narrow it down to when my headaches and stomach aches and other problems started.

Dr. F: What year was that?

Sue: I was in Grade 5 when I started getting the headaches.

Dr. F: Grade 5 would be what year?

Sue: I don't know.

Dr. F: How old were you in Grade 5?

Sue: Eleven, about eleven.

Dr. F: You had some physical symptoms, headaches, stomach aches, that sort of thing.

Sue: I got those before anything else started, I believe, where I was coming home from school and having these horrible raging headaches.

Dr. F: Let me see if we can just tack this down as precisely as possible. Did it happen before your grandfather died or after your grandfather died, the headaches? As you remember?

The therapist is taking a chronology of family change around an important event/loss in the family. His purpose is to heighten the awareness of the family about this event. His questions do not stem from a need to be precise but from a desire to emphasize to the family members in a non-threatening way that they should become aware of how various family members were affected by this event. This approach is a safe, nonconfrontive way to call attention to a highly charged period in the family's life. It will not increase defensiveness or anxiety in the family members but it will allow them in the privacy of their own minds to rethink where they were, how they were feeling, how they reacted, and what was different about them and other family members. This is an important procedure that does not place blame on anybody for what happened. It allows each family member to rethink an important family event and possibly at a later date to reconnect with other family members around that event. It is hoped that this approach will allow for the sadness and loss to be felt rather than the anger and hurt that may have been experienced by family members misunderstanding each other at the time of the loss.

Sue: What month did he die?
Mrs. R: May 9, 1980.
Dr. F: 1980.
Sue: Well that depended on whether I was going into Grade 5 during that summer or not?
Dr. F: It's hard to remember the exact timing of his death and the beginning of the headaches, stomach aches?
Sue: Yeah, I can't remember.
Dr. F: But it was close. It was within a year.
Sue: Well, it was probably pretty close.
Dr. F: Let's go back prior to that, prior to Grade 5. What do you remember about the family and how things were.
Sue: There was a lot of movement.
Dr. F: A lot of movement. What was the average stay in a house?
Sue: I think we stayed the longest in the house in the city. About five years or so. We were there the longest.
Dr. F: How much time was there in between the moves? A year? Two years?
Sue: I'm not really sure how soon we moved out of our house on Main Street into, we moved on Elm first. That was our first house . . .
Dr. F: Do you remember a lot of movement, a lot of house changing?
Sue: Yup.
Dr. F: What type of nature do you have Sue? Would changes, like changing houses, be something to be excited about or something to dread?
Sue: It was commonplace when I was younger, and you didn't think about it.
Dr. F: New friends?
Sue: Not very much, not any more than going to school.

Dr. F: What were you told about the moves?

Sue: Only that we were moving.

Dr. F: Did your dad sit you down? Did both of them sit you down? Did you find out pretty much at the time that it was taking place?

Sue: Well, you'd find out when things started getting wrapped in newspaper and stuff like that, just seeing things like that . . .

Dr. F: You never remember your mother sitting down and explaining what was going to happen?

Sue: About our moving?

Dr. F: Yeah.

Sue: I can't remember as far back as that really. Maybe in the city, maybe they told me about the city.

Dr. F: Did your mom and dad tell you together, or your mom or your dad tell you alone? How would it work?

Sue: I can't remember that far back.

Dr. F: Did they tell you together, or would you and John be together, or would they tell each of you separately?

Sue: No, they probably told each of us separately.

Dr. F: I'm just wondering how you would find out important information about things that were changing or happening in the family like your grandfather's death. How did you find out about that?

Sue: Um, probably when he went to the hospital.

Dr. F: Do you remember the scene? Do you remember them telling you that?

Sue: I was young.

Dr. F: Did you cry together?

Sue: No.

Dr. F: How do you know that?

Sue: I don't remember.

Dr. F: Did you talk to your mom about it?

Sue: No.

Dr. F: Ever?

Sue: Not really.

Dr. F: So when things began to change in the family, the sense I get is around 1980, fifth grade, you were not doing as well, physically. Catch me up now on what happened. That was 1980, and now it is 1987. What happened during these last seven years?

The therapist is now moving from the past to the last several years in Sue's life. It is necessary to get a sense of the recent past and what the changes are as perceived by the child, remembering that the parents complaints about Sue center on the last few years. Many parents do not understand how their child's current behavior is influenced by past events. The therapist continues by encouraging Sue to explain what has gone on at school, at work, and with friends; in other words, the life she has devel-. oped outside of the family. It is important for therapists to ask the adolescent or the young adult children about the moves that they have begun to make outside the family. In this way, an opportunity has been created for the child to feel that the family understands both his or her feelings about the family and his or her goals and aspirations outside the family.

Sue: I wish it never happened. I remember I went to school. My first year there was kind of rough. I didn't know anybody. I hadn't gotten in with a group yet. In my second year, I got in with a big group. It was one of my best years, I think, in Grade 7. And then I went to Leland 'cause I was hanging out with Ruby, who was a friend from the past who had reappeared at school, who was in the in group. And I couldn't stand any of them. So then I met this girl, we used to go to St. Mary's church, Leslie. And she introduced me to her friends that are a year older than me — Helen, and Jane and her. And we all started to hang out together. And we spent a lot of time together. And they all got in trouble. We all got into trouble, just teenage things, you know, all the time. I stayed at Leland until, I wasn't sure if I was going to get into Grade 9 or not, but then I ended up somewhere in the year of Grade 9 in alternative school. I can't remember how it happened, but my friend Jody, she also went there. She left Leland and came there. That was OK. Then I just wanted to leave school altogether, decided that wasn't for me . . .
Dr. F: You'd be how old now, when you decided to leave school?
Sue: Sixteen. And after that I worked as a receptionist, after that I worked . . .
Dr. F: Paid?
Sue: Yeah, as a receptionist. Somewhere in there I was a busperson, but not long. I worked as a nanny, worked at a clothing store, worked so many other places . . .
Dr. F: You did all those jobs, all those different jobs over the last couple of years since you quit school.
Sue: Yes.
Dr. F: That was a pretty important decision that you made to quit school, to go that way. How did you let your dad and your mom know that you made this decision? Let's say your dad, how did you tell your dad?
Sue: I'm not sure if they knew beforehand. Now that I think about it I don't think they knew beforehand. They may have, I'm not sure. They may have got it from the school board, or maybe I told them. Because I remember the day I left school I had just decided that day to leave, and they were having a meeting and I went in, and they talked to me and I told them. They didn't have too much to do with the decision.

Dr. F: When you made this decision, you had to make a decision in your own head about how much of it you wanted to explain to your dad, how much of it you wanted to explain to your mother directly.

Sue: I would probably just have told them that I quit school, and they knew how it was.

Dr. F: I still want to get a sense of what happens for you when you try to explain to your mom and your dad . . .

Sue: There are certain things that they're pretty good about and certain other things I do, such as my quitting school. They may have freaked out but they didn't freak out in front of me. They may have been really angry about it, but they wouldn't have been angry about it in front of me. It's only recently, the past couple of years, where that comes out. Where they jab at me about that, about not having an education, about why don't I go back to school. But at the time, I don't believe they were. I probably wouldn't allow it. You know, I made a decision and that was it. And there probably wasn't a huge fight. I mean, there were other things that they reacted to, you know, quite seriously, but I don't think that was one of them. I think it was basically the decision had been made and I was the one who made it. I don't know how they were feeling about it. I don't remember any fights. I don't remember anybody freaking out to any great extent.

Dr. F: Something you still haven't talked with your mom and dad about in any detail?

Sue: About quitting school?

Dr. F: Your decision to quit school?

Sue: My decision?

Dr. F: Yes.

Sue: No, the decision had been made. I don't think we ever sat down and discussed the fact of whether I would or would not leave school.

Dr. F: How do you decide, Sue, what to tell your mom and dad and what not to tell them?

The therapist has asked Sue to explain her thinking process about how she screens out information. The answer to the question is not important. What is important is the recognition that there is a screening process through which she consciously decides what is safe to talk about and what should be kept hidden. The question makes public a private process. The child will not usually provide a clear answer. However, the question helps the family to recognize that this process exists and that it can be changed when the family members feel safe and solid enough to risk talking more about self. The interview continues.

Sue: Well, I had my own pride. I usually told them just about anything. I was not secretive at any time, although they may believe I may have been. There was a lot of speculation at certain points through my life. What I have been doing, what I haven't been doing, and all that. They know what went on. I mean, whether they chose to listen, is what I felt the problem is whether they choose to understand what was going on. But there was rarely anything of importance kept from them. I wouldn't go to them and discuss leaving school. I wouldn't sit down with them and say to them, "Hey, Mom and Dad, how do you feel about me leaving school?" Cause I felt at that time, it is my life and I will do exactly what I please. If I don't want to be in school and I don't think it's doing me any good, I'm not going to work hard. I had my decision, and I had my reasons all worked out. At the time, I felt they had no right to say anything about it. That's just how it was working at that time and probably still is.

The therapist has now concluded his questioning of Sue. He has made a positive connection with her. She has been able to speak openly through him to other members of the family without raising any defensive reactions on their part. They appear to be attentive and involved with her story.

The therapist now shifts his attention to John. John is seen by the family as somewhat of an outsider who does not get involved in family issues. He tells his own story about how he handles family conflict by emotionally exiting from the family. In this phase of the interview, John is being given the opportunity to address the same areas of concern Sue has just discussed. John is now asked to give his own definition of family. It is important that each family member knows the others' definition of family. The therapist addresses John:

Dr. F: John, I want to get a sense from you about two things. One is what you understood this to be about, the purpose of this session. Let's start with that one.
John: OK, um, I just wanted to find out. I have to say I wasn't too pleased.
Dr. F: What about it weren't you pleased about?
John: I just figure it's their problem. I never really got into it, except for once. I just said, "You guys work it out. Leave me out of it."
Dr. F: You see it as being between your sister and your mom and your dad, and not you. Well, that has to do with my second question. Your sister described you as being peripheral, on the sidelines to what is going on here.
John: Yeah. I just stay back and watch them.

Dr. F: Do you see yourself that way? On the sidelines of this family?
John: Yeah. I guess sometimes I do.
Dr. F: Sometimes you don't?
John: Well, I guess when I have my own problems, I like to feel just as much in the family as everyone else. I usually just hang back, and I'm not around much, not lately, except for . . .
Dr. F: Well, I find that the one who is the least intimately involved or intensely involved probably has the clearest sense of what is going on. So tell me what's going on here.

This last statement is a major reframe by the therapist. John has identified himself as being on the sidelines of the family. The therapist has responded by observing that his detachment gives him a clearer idea of family behavior. John responds to this comment with a slight smile. The therapist has accomplished two tasks by reframing John's being on the outside as a way of being on the inside. He has recognized that John is affected by the family and has pointed out to the family that any family member who can stay on the outside of conflict may be able to perceive it differently. This powerful message is hard to convey to family members in the beginning phase of therapy without appearing to be critical of their way of handling issues. John has given the therapist an opportunity to introduce this principle of emotional behavior without preaching or criticizing. The interview continues . . .

John: Well . . . (smile)
Dr. F: Do you know Joan?
John: Yes. I know Joan.
Dr. F: OK. What's going on?
John: Well, I just see Sue trying to do what she wants, and my parents trying to have her do what they want her to do. And sometimes they don't listen, and sometimes she doesn't listen. And they both want things done their way, and so it gets into a really big squabble. And, really, neither one wins. It used to be that Sue won, and that's, I guess, lately, sort of changing.
Dr. F: You say "they," your mom and your dad. Are they a team? Are they a unit or is there any difference between Mom and Dad?
John: I think sometimes they disagreed on what was happening . . .
Dr. F: Between the two of them?
John: Between the two of them, but when it came to them against her, it was . . .
Dr. F: Two to one.
John: Yeah, but she still won. So, it's two against one.

Dr. F: What do you mean by winning?
John: Well, free judgment, but there is a reason for it. Sue wanted the car and wanted money for whatever, and they didn't want to do it. Then a big argument would start, and she would get it.
Dr. F: How have you managed to stay out of this one?
John: I would go in my room and turn my music up. I just didn't really think that it was any of my business, really.
Dr. F: Did this happen over time?
John: Basically it started right off. I was away. I was away at school when it first started, and then it just kept on happening when I came home.
Dr. F: What year were you away at school?
John: Thirteen, 1980.
Dr. F: 1980 again. 1980 keeps popping up in everything.
John: That was 80-82.
Dr. F: 1980?
John: So I missed most of it.
Dr. F: I asked Sue a question about the family, and I want to ask you the same question. I am confused about how small or how large this family is. When you define family for yourself, who is family for you? Who do you include?

John has given the therapist an overview of his observations of the family. He has put his sister Sue in the middle of the family conflict. In some ways, he is aligned with his parents against his sister. He confirms that he exits when the emotional intensity is too high. The therapist notes the distance that exists between the brother and the sister and the alliance that exists between the parents and the son. In order for any significant change to occur within the family, the brother/sister relationship will have to be reinforced and strengthened and John will have to sever his alliance with his parents and form separate relationships with each one of them. He will also have to see his sister separately from her conflict with the parents. When the therapist asks John about his own definition of family, it provides a way to gently approach the topic of the importance of his sister in his life.

John: I include everybody.
Dr. F: Who is everybody?
John: Mom and Dad, my sister, grandparents.
Dr. F: Anyone else?
John: Uncles and aunts, cousins.
Dr. F: And who would you be the closest to? Not here, but uncles and aunts, grandparents, cousins. Who would you be the closest to?

John: I really can't say. I guess I'm distant with a lot of people.

Dr. F: Would that be more of the way you are, more of a theme for you?

John: Yeah, I guess I like to keep quite a distance.

Dr. F: How involved have you been with your grandmothers?

John: Not really.

Dr. F: As involved as Sue? Less involved?

John: When I think about Sue, I guess, maybe less.

Dr. F: Less involved than she is?

John: I don't know how involved she is, but it would probably be less. I think she's more involved with them than I am.

Dr. F: Were you involved with your grandfather, your mom's dad at all?

John: Yeah.

Dr. F: You were away when he died?

John: No, I was still here.

Dr. F: Do you remember the changes that occurred in the family after he died?

John: The whole family? Well, my mom's mom, I think she became a little more quiet. You know going out and seeing people, going to church, uh . . .

Dr. F: How about your mom, what changed in her?

John: Well, I guess she just felt a little worried about her mother.

Dr. F: How did your sister change?

John: I don't know. I think she was pretty, well, normal when I was home. Nothing to notice any change.

Dr. F: How did she feel about your learning disorder? I'm just curious. What impact, John, do you think it had on your sister?

John: That I went away to school? I think she was jealous. I think it bothered her that my parents were spending all the money on me and not really keeping any to spend on her. I think she wanted to go away to school. I think it's just so she could compete, that she would get the same treatment I was.

Dr. F: So she could feel as special?

John: Yeah.

Dr. F: 'Cause it made you special?

John: It didn't make me special. I didn't think it made me special. I had a learning disorder, and that was it.

Dr. F: You didn't feel like it made you special, different?

John: It made me happy.

Dr. F: Did you talk with your sister before you went away to school? Sit down with her, tell her that this was going to happen?

John: No.

John has answered the question about who is family in an interesting fashion, by saying he includes everybody. When the therapist reviews who everybody is, he discovers that John left the family to go away to school around the same time as the grandfather's death. He was away from home during a time of crucial family change. We have learned that the family lost the son as well as the grandfather. The therapist begins to ask John about how the loss of the grandfather affected him. John left home soon after the grandfather died and in some ways was not as affected by the loss as his was sister. When he returned home two years later, it was to a family that had felt the impact of his absence and his grandfather's death. The therapist has now begun to work on the brother/sister relationship. When he asked John about whether he talked to his sister about leaving for school, it was not to elicit information about the past, but rather to expand John's thinking about how to deal with his sister in the present and the future. This question is more to illustrate how brothers and sisters should deal with changes in each other's lives.

The therapist continues by spending a few minutes working directly on the sibling relationship. Each sibling is given an opportunity to talk about how he or she would like the relationship to work. It is important to remember when doing family therapy that all the various subsystems within the family should be in balance. Over time the therapy will focus on the husband/wife relationship, the parent/child relationships and the sibling relationships. It is a major goal in family therapy to help the siblings feel connected with each other and to free them from any obligation to act out the parent/child conflict in their relationship.

Dr. F: Sue, what do you think about the question I asked John? What impact did his learning disorder have on you?

Sue: It is speculation that it did?

Dr. F: Yes. At this point, I have to make some speculations.

Sue: I don't remember the time too well. I don't know. One day he was here, the next day he wasn't.

Dr. F: It felt that way? One day he was here, the next day he wasn't?

Sue: Well, I didn't know anything about it, anything about the school. They dropped him off at school, and then he . . .

Dr. F: You went to school in September 1980, and you were gone for two years?

John: One year in the school in New York and one year prep.

Dr. F: Was there any time then when you were close to your sister?

John: I don't really remember, but probably.

Dr. F: What would you say, Sue? Was there a time when you felt close to John?

Sue: When we were very young. But we moved a lot, so I guess we were more playing buddies, things like that. Once I started socializing in school and he started socializing in school, that was the end of that.

Dr. F: It changed. I'm just so conscious of time. I have some other people coming in, but I want to ask you all about your own vision of family. You have four grown people here. You don't really have anybody who needs to be taken care of anymore. I think it would be important in terms of my involvement, or lack of involvement, with all of you to deal with that one question. Sue, give me an answer to that one. What vision do you have for the family? It's potential?

Sue: My fantasy of the perfect family, or how I feel about them right now?

Dr. F: What you want for yourself in terms of family.

The therapist is concluding the interview. He does this by asking each child to talk about his or her hopes for the family. The therapist is trying to end the session on a note of optimism. Each child has a fantasy about what makes up a good family. It can be difficult for a child to talk about this ideal to the parents without sounding critical or hostile. By asking the question in general terms, the therapist has given each child an opportunity to say what he or she would like to see in the family without having to defend himself or herself from the parents' reactions. Sue describes what she would like to see in the family:

Sue: In terms of family. What's realistic, or what I want?

Dr. F: What you want.

Sue: Well, it's hard for me to describe it. In terms of reality, my ideal of a loving, caring, supporting, wonderful little family who all sit around the hearth together and drink tea, I mean, that's not realistic, and that will never happen. In this family, the most I can hope for is that things go a little smoother or we can find a way not to affect each other in the way that we have been. That's what I hope for. I don't hope sitting around the hearth drinking tea or being buddies with these people. I just hope that things can go easier.

Dr. F: What would that look like? What would be an example of things going smoother? Think of a scenario that could happen.

Sue: I don't believe that I would come to them for support of some sort. Emotional support of some sort. As I'm working out my financial situation right now, the only thing that would be left would be to resolve what has happened in the past already and regaining some kind of civil footing.

So at least when we're in the same room together, it wouldn't feel like we hate each other. But I don't expect miracles or that we're all going to sit around loving or adoring each other or anything like that, cause that's not going to happen with these people. Just for things to make a little more sense, make sure everyone knows what is going on.

Dr. F: You have to put some effort into making that happen?

Sue: Me? They don't know, but I have in my own way. But it hasn't been very . . .

Dr. F: Let me change the question. You will continue putting some effort into making that happen?

Sue: I will do. If a year and a half ago, or six months ago, I had dropped the situation completely sometimes I think things would be better. But my problem is I have to go and try and make them understand. I have to go back and try and make them understand what's happening in my life. It doesn't happen obviously, but each time I try.

Dr. F: But you try?

Sue: I believe I do. And I don't know why I try. I honestly don't, because things have happened that none of us like. I don't want to talk about it, but I will still try. I'll be angry, very angry, and resentful, very, but I'll still try.

The question about the child's vision for the family is more important than the answer. The act of asking the question sends the message that this is an important subject to think about. What the question stirs up in family members is far more critical than the public answers. Over time, and upon further reflection, the answers will change. The therapist will return to these questions later in the therapy process when the reactivity and the anxiety are reduced. At this point, he is laying the ground work for ongoing work with the family. The children's answers to the question reveal their sadness, their sense of loss, their hope, their anxiety. The therapist does not find it necessary to comment on the child's vision but he ensures that it is heard by all family members. The interview continues with the therapist asking John the same questions.

Dr. F: What about you, John? What would your vision be?

John: I guess a family that gets along and trusts each other; can communicate to each other; is able to go out and do things together; able to sit down and talk openly.

Dr. F: How much effort would you put into that work?

John: I guess, if I thought it would happen, I would put a lot of effort into it. But I think we're, as a family, we've grown as far apart as a family can be.

Dr. F: Oh, no, I've seen families farther apart than you. I guess it feels pretty far apart to you.

John: Yeah, and a lot of time, I just prefer to be somewhere else.

Dr. F: Because of that feeling?

John: Yeah.

Dr. F: Not because of desire, but because of that feeling?

John: And then, if I can be elsewhere, I will be elsewhere.

Dr. F: But I think that it's an interesting distinction. It's more your frustration about it not being different that gets you to put your energy elsewhere. Do you say that to yourself?

The therapist has just attempted another major reframe. John has indicated that when things are not going well he prefers to exit. The family has interpreted his exiting as being uninvolved and/or uncaring. The therapist frames his exiting as a sign of caring and the only response that John knows for dealing with so much caring. The next time John responds to the family tension by leaving, the family will begin to understand his behavior differently from how they have viewed it in the past.

Prior to the interview concluding the therapist asks the parents about their vision for the family. The question is a safe one in that it elicits the parents' own views, but not their reactions to what the children have said. Their response give the therapist an idea of how reactive they have been to their children's stories and whether these stories have modified their sense of family. The therapist learns that the parents have been able to hear their children without feeling angry or hurt.

Dr. F: (Turning first to Mr. R) Is your vision for the family different from your children's?

Mr. R: I guess my vision is to get out of the child rearing. I feel that I've done as much as I can in that area, for better or for worse, for good or for ill, and there's not a great deal of major benefit under the category of child rearing at this point because I think the time is past. And I'd like to move ahead to a more adult relationship in the family. I think that in time we are going to have a good relationship as members of the same family.

Dr. F: That is your vision. (Turning to Mrs. R) What would be your vision?

Mrs. R: A combination of the two. I would like to have an adult relationship with my children as I have with my own mother, which is so enjoyable. But at the same time I would like to have tea by the fireplace.

Dr. F: You're not going to give up that dream.

Mrs. R: I don't want to do that.

The therapist involves the foster mother, Joan. He wants to learn how she has heard the family stories and what it has stirred up in her.

Dr. F: Joan, what's it like being here for you?
Joan: I'm getting quite teary. I don't know what kind of an answer you want.
Dr. F: I don't know what kind of an answer I want either.
Joan: I have a beautiful relationship with my own parents and my own children, who I love and treasure, and I think that this family has the potential to have it. And I would love for them to have it. I didn't always have it with my parents. I went into therapy, personal therapy rather than family therapy. And so I treasure it, I suppose all the more because I really had to work for it.

The therapist concludes the session by seeking a commitment from each family member and Joan for ongoing sessions.

Dr. F: Sue, is it important to have Joan here?
Sue: Very.
Dr. F: If we continue to have sessions here, would you want Joan to join us.
Sue: Yeah, I really would.
Dr. F: Is that OK with you?
Joan: Yes.
Dr. F: This is a good beginning. Let me ask each of you if you are willing to come back as a family?
Sue: Yes.
John: OK.
Mr. R: Good idea.
Mrs. R: That's fine.

SECTION THREE:
BEYOND THE FIRST INTERVIEW WITH FAMILIES:
CASE ILLUSTRATION AND COMMENTARY

Once the therapist has established a solid relationship with the parents and children, he or she can begin to move into more sensitive areas with the family. At this stage in the process the therapist's major objective is to help the family members talk about the family losses, sadness, and anxiety that have damaged their connections with each other.

The following session is a later interview with the same "R" family. It deals with two highly charged issues of loss.

The therapist now loosens the structure in which the children spoke through him to their parents and asks questions of each family member. This process fosters an appreciation among the family members of how the family history has affected each one of them.

After a brief opening, the therapist encourages the father to tell his story about his discovery of his father's suicide. It is important for Sue to understand that her father's reaction to her threats of suicide stem from the loss of his own father and not from a lack of caring for her. The children are encouraged to talk about how their lives changed when their maternal grandfather died. It becomes evident that this loss was catastrophic for the family and, in fact, is still taking its toll. The interview is important in that the family members are able to talk about sensitive, traumatic events together in a safe, supportive, and caring way. The therapist remains in control of the process as the parents continue to be somewhat reactive about the family difficulties.

The shift from the reactive phase to the proactive phase of therapy is quite dramatic. In the reactive phase, the parents remain defensive and anxious about what their children are saying. In the proactive phase, they become more curious about their own history and less anxious and judgmental about their children's behavior and choices. At this point in the treatment, the "R" family is just beginning to move from the reactive phase into the middle phase of therapy. The therapist continues to employ the structure of having each family member talk through him about his or her concerns and sadness.

The therapist opens this session by asking the parents what changes have occurred since the last interview. The father mentions the sale of the family home and a possible job loss. Moving as a way to deal with developmental changes is a well-established theme in this family.

Dr. F: What changes have there been for you? I remember the last time you were here there were all kinds of things happening.

Mrs. R: Well, we moved into a new apartment. We purchased a condominium and we're now rapidly getting settled. But, I'm feeling tired today because it's been quite a long stretch of activity. And Brian, you want to talk about your job situation.

Dr. F: What happened there?

Mr. R: Well, it's still dangling. But I believe that tonight a decision will be made. And the likeliest outcome is that I have either no job, or possibly the best I can hope for is half-time, or part time of some kind.

Dr. F: We ran short of time last time, but I wanted to ask you about the implications for you if the worst happened and there were no job. What would all that mean?

Mr. R: Well, we have simplified our lives by making the move from the house — physically, financially, emotionally. But if there is no job there, then I'm in the process of redoing my resume, and I'll just have to apply for unemployment insurance and go look for work. I'm not entirely sure where the next job is coming from, but I'll just have to start beating the bushes, doing the kinds of things that Jean teaches at her workshops for people who are looking for work.

Mrs. R: I am useless with my own family in that regard, I might add. I'm very good at helping strangers, but I have not been that successful with my own family. But I guess that's . . .

Mr. R: Well, there's too much at stake.

Dr. F: What's at stake?

Mr. R: Well, I'm going back to my family experience. My mother was a teacher and a tutor, and she was never able to teach her own children. And I think that's the same kind of phenomenon. There's just too much emotional investment in your spouse, or your child, and you can't be balanced and detached. You're sort of right there in the middle.

Dr. F: Brian, I've been thinking about the very first session when you were talking about your father. Have you told your children the story about your father?

The therapist has just opened up the sensitive area of Mr. R's father's suicide. He has asked the question so that the father can talk to him as a way of being intimate with his children about this significant loss. It becomes clear that the family has not previously heard this powerful story from the father. Each family member has a different piece of information about the suicide. The therapist's questions give the father the opportunity to explain an important part of his own history while simultaneously reassuring his children that he is not considering suicide, even though his work circumstances are not dissimilar to those previously encountered by his father. As Mr. R explains how he understood his father's death, the family's anxiety about his self-doubts decreases. The interview continues as follows:

Mr. R: What story?

Dr. F: About how your dad died?

Mr. R: I don't know. Do you know how my dad died?

John: He's told me.

Mr. R: Well, it's not something that's talked about a lot in the family, but I'll tell you what my understanding of it was. He died suddenly. He had

had sort of minor heart problems, but he just went like that. And it wasn't until a year afterwards that I was told he'd committed suicide. He had got himself into a box where he saw only one job and one career for him, advertising. And when it was apparent that he could no longer succeed in that, he had nothing to fall back on. He felt that his life was over. He was completely wrong, because there were other things he could have done. But emotionally, he felt that there was no point in him continuing. And he was the kind of guy that built up pressure, and built up pressure, and built up pressure, and had really no way to release it. He was a workaholic. And he tried. He would go through periods where he would drink very heavily, and then go through periods where he would go to a chiropractor four times a week, and then he would go on a holiday. He was always looking for something just to relieve the pressure of his advertising career and made what I thought was an incorrect decision. But that's the way it was. That happened when I was nineteen.

John: I thought your dad died when you were fourteen.

Sue: I thought it was fifteen.

John: There we go.

Mrs. R: I actually met Brian a couple of years after that and we married and you didn't tell me until we had been married for approximately three years.

Dr. F: That story.

Mrs. R: That's right.

John: Keeping secrets, Dad. We don't like that.

Dr. F: I was wondering, Brian, what lesson you learned from your family on how they handled your father's suicide?

Mr. R: Well, I was curious why my mother decided that I should not be told for a year. And it was my mother's feeling that since I resembled him more than my other two brothers, physically and intellectually, that I might identify with him. My own feeling of myself is that I have not. I have other ways to go, other options, other alternatives. And I have ways to deal with pressure, so that I don't see myself as ending up at the point that he was.

Dr. F: In some ways you see yourself as different from Dad. What would be some of the major differences?

Mr. R: Well, he felt he was an old-time advertising man and had been very successful and very well-regarded. But the advertising field was passing him by and passing by his old style of doing business and doing folksy kind of campaigns and a lot of personal contact with your client. In the 1960s, it was getting into high-pressure, media campaigns, push, push, push, lots of dollars, lots at stake. And it was his company and he was losing control of it and felt that he could no longer compete, no longer keep up, and no longer produce under pressure, which he had always prided himself on being able to do. It got to that point. So my difference is, and I wish that I could have said this to him, get out of the game. Get out of that business. Find a job in marketing or sales or other kinds of advertising, or public relations. All of which he could have done. But he felt that there was just one thing. He was the owner/manager of the company, and if he couldn't be that, then he could not see any future for him.

Dr. F: When you found out that he committed suicide, what got stirred up in you?

Mr. R: I felt angry at the circumstance that led to that and felt sorry that I couldn't have helped him. If I had known the trouble that he was in, I felt that I would have taken some action.

Dr. F: He didn't let the family in on that? You or your older brother. Do you think he let him in?

Mr. R: No. Oh, about his decision to kill himself?

Dr. F: About how hopeless he felt about the whole thing?

Mr. R: No, I don't think anyone knew.

Dr. F: He didn't use the family more as a resource?

Here the therapist has encouraged Mr. R to discuss his father's death in some detail. His asking the question about the father using the family as a resource was a form of prescription. This therapeutic strategy involves making a suggestion by formulating it as a question. Here, the therapist has suggested that Mr. R consider using his own family as a resource. As Mr. R continues talking about his father's behavior and its impact on him, he will be more likely to consider his role in his own family and how he may want to change it. Prescriptions are powerful suggestions that allow the family member to consider doing things differently by posing questions that imply that there are other ways of doing something. The interview continues:

Mr. R: No, he didn't. He didn't.

Dr. F: He didn't let you be there for him.

Mr. R: No, he didn't. He kept it to himself. I think Mom knew after the fact. I mean, you recognize these things after they happen. You say, "I should have known what was happening." But, he was a workaholic. He worked all the time. We were rarely together for dinner.

Dr. F: I asked you that question about whether he let you in because I was wondering if the way you use your family is similar or different from the way your dad used the family?

Mr. R: I talk to Jean about my triumphs and tragedies; and successes and failures.

Dr. F: More than you think your dad did with your mom?

Mr. R: I think probably yes. Because if he had communicated to her just how troubled he was, I think she would have done something. I have not communicated particularly with John or Sue about those kinds of things.

John: Mom takes care of that.

Dr. F: Yes, I'm puzzled about that because you know from the other side what that was like, being the son, and being left out. Now, as the dad, how do you make these decisions?

Mr. R: I have some degree of social and emotional support and I also feel that tomorrow is always a new day. There's always something that can be done or something that can be worked out. There are no dead ends.

Dr. F: So you're saying that you'd have to be desperate before you would turn to your kids?

Mr. R: No, before I would kill myself.

Dr. F: Oh, yes, before you'd kill yourself.

John: If you kill yourself Dad, I'm not going to talk to you anymore.

Dr. F: Your children are about the age that you and your brothers were when your father killed himself.

Mr. R: Yeah, about that age.

Dr. F: Is what you've tried to do with John and Sue that different from what your father did with you?

Mr. R: I think that John and Sue are more aware of my situation than my brothers and I were of my father's situation. I think we had no idea of the trouble he was in.

Dr. F: Now, is that because of you telling them, or because they got it from a different source?

Mr. R: I think there has probably been more general discussion around the house than there ever was in my house then.

Dr. F: Are there any other differences that you try to create? Your not having a sister, does this affect how you try to deal with Sue, for example?

The therapist is now encouraging the father to think about his role in his own family. He wants him to consider what lessons he learned in his family-of-origin and how they affected his behavior in his family-of-procreation. The therapist is also beginning to ask him to differentiate between how he deals with his son and his daughter. He is trying to help the father think about the differing needs of his children.

At this point, it is not important how the father answers the questions but the therapist wants to stimulate his thinking about the meaning of the question and the role he wants to play with his children. The therapist is encouraging Mr. R to honor his father by thinking about how he can use what he learned from him as a positive force for dealing with his own children. The interview continues along these lines.

Mr. R: You mean as far as where I'm at and what's happening to me in my life?
Dr. F: Yes. Neither of you had a sister.
Mr. R: Yes, I deal with them differently. I'm just trying to figure out how I do that in relation to communicating what's going on in my life. I know I will from time to time say, "This is what's going on right now." I don't go into great detail, but I have said, "Well, this is what's happening," or "It looks like my job may be changing," or "My job is coming to an end, and I'm not sure what's coming after that."
Dr. F: But would you protect them from your anxieties or your fears, your worries, your doubts, that sort of thing? Would you protect, say, Sue more than John, or John more than Sue? How would that go?
Mr. R: I don't think so.
Dr. F: You don't think there is a difference?
Mr. R: No. I deal with them differently. In fact, in the last couple of years I think I have made some comments to them as part of helping them understand what the real world is like. That there are problems . . .
Dr. F: Not what the real world is like, what you are struggling with here?
Mr. R: Yes, but if I tell them there is this difficulty in my life, that will help them understand that's part of living. But I haven't sort of sat down and said, "Let me share with you where I am," physically, emotionally, any other way.

The therapist has now gone as far as he can on the issue of how the father may want to be different with his son and his daughter. He has encouraged the father to be more analytical about his role as a parent. The father has begun to get defensive and has started to talk about his need to be parental towards them rather than the possibility of having a person-to-person relationship with them. The therapist avoids the father's defensiveness by shifting focus to the children. It is important for each of the children to have an opportunity, through the therapist, to let their father know how they have experienced him in the family. The therapist will ask them in some depth how they have tried to connect with their father. He will also ask about the suicide of the grandfather and the meaning that they attached to it. The interview continues with the focus on the children:

Dr. F: You haven't done that. Sue, have you gotten the message from your dad that you should be careful about what you ask him about himself?

Sue: OK, always in the house their problems were their problems and it was between those two. I don't think there was a space for either of us to get in. And I feel like the pieces of information that they did give us were pieces of information to either use as guilt or use as a tool. OK, coming from both of them, Mum does it more dramatically, Dad does it more subtly, but that's the way I felt, those pieces of information that were coming to us or at least me. It wasn't like, "Hey, I need you. I need you in my life. I think that you have talented abilities that will help me." I don't know if people actually go to their children for that. I don't know. But it wasn't that sort of stuff I was getting . . .

Dr. F: So it was more they were trying to teach you something, or shape you up in some way, instruction . . .

Sue: Yeah, they were used as tools.

Dr. F: Did that make it hard for you to talk to your dad or ask him things about himself beyond that stuff?

Sue: It's hard to see when the focus was on me or John, and those are the times we remember. When I started doing my thing, suddenly, it was just all the time. I mean, I've always felt they don't trust me. They don't trust whatever I've picked up through all the wonderful mistakes I've made. And I couldn't be supportive to either one of them. I couldn't say, "Hey, you know I'm here," because it's just I know that they don't feel it. I probably could, but I know that they don't feel like this could be a support person in my life.

Here the therapist is encouraging the daughter to explain matters to him as a way of helping her tell her parents what she needs in order to feel supported, understood, and competent in the family. Sue is quite articulate and able to state how certain behaviors make her feel invalidated and undermined in the family. She does not distinguish between her mother and father. This is a not uncommon practice for children in the family. They talk about their parents as if they were fused together into one personality. It is important for the therapist to differentiate between the two. The therapist should ask the children to explain the differences between Mom and Dad and should discourage references to them as a unit. One of the goals in the family therapy process is to help the children and parents have separate relationships with each other.

Dr. F: Back to the "they." Do you think it's equal between Mum and Dad, or maybe different, with one a bit more than the other?

Sue: I was going to say before they've always been sort of a united front, so I'm not sure exactly.

Dr. F: Have you been able to separate them a bit more?

Sue: Oh, yeah. I separate them as personalities. But when it comes to parenting and stuff, it's like, you know . . .
Dr. F: Hearing this story today about your grandfather, have you heard it before?
Sue: No, I mean information kind of trickles through but . . .
Dr. F: What did that stir up for you?
Sue: Me with my own problems relating to suicide. Dad cannot, I've always felt Dad, maybe having known that information, that he can't handle it at all. And though he's a quieter storm than Mum is, even in Mum's hysteria about things I felt, I don't know what I felt. But there is a difference there in how they both deal with that particular issue in my life. It was a pretty big deal for a while there.

With the encouragement of the therapist, the daughter begins to differentiate a bit more between her mother and father. She also begins to talk about her own suicidal thoughts. She makes a beginning connection between her grandfather's suicide and her father's reaction to her suicidal thoughts. As the sessions continue, Sue comes to understand some of her father's reactions to her behavior stem from his own anxieties around his father's suicide and are not a sign of a lack of caring or concern for her anxieties and struggles. The therapist continues with Sue:

Dr. F: If you had known earlier about your grandfather, how would you have dealt with your father differently around this?
Sue: See, I don't feel like I was given the story. I mean, the thing is, it's not talked about in our family. I mean, it threatens Dad a lot. They never really put the trust in me to actually take a piece of information like that and let it guide my hand or guide the way I dealt with them, because nothing guides the way we all deal with each other. I mean, any piece of information, any emotional instability, it doesn't matter. It's how you're feeling and what you're thinking right now that's coming out. It doesn't matter what is going on.
Dr. F: So in some ways if your dad had told you about it, it would have been a sign of respect and confidence?
Sue: Perhaps. It's hard to say if it would have changed anything. But maybe it would have been a sign of, yeah, I think you are OK enough to give you this and know that you're not going to, you know. . . .
Dr. F: Kill yourself with it.
Sue: Well, or betray him with it. Well, that's exactly what killing myself would be.
Dr. F: Interesting.

This is an important part of the interview. Sue has said clearly that if she had known about her grandfather's suicide she would not have betrayed her father with that information. She acknowledges that killing herself would have been a form of betraying him. Sue is making a powerful statement about her loyalty and commitment to her father.

Mr. R: There is a point here and that is that there are things that you maybe tell your teenage kids or deal with them in a way that you would not with younger ones.

Dr. F: Yes. This is true.

Mr. R: And Sue was, I think thirteen when the troubles started and up until . . .

Sue: That's when they legally started.

Mr. R: . . . quite recently we lived with that. This whole conflict and concern. And where was she going. And what was happening. And where would it all end. And so there was about five years of that. And I think that . . .

Dr. F: Got off track.

Mr. R: Well, I don't know how different the relationship would have been without it. It would have been different in some respect.

Mr. R has interrupted and indicated his anxiety by his defensive response. His interruption is a sign of his discomfort about what Sue has been saying. Commonly, when a parent's own anxiety or sadness has been stirred up, he or she responds with defensive, critical comments. It is important for the therapist to block these comments so that the parent's anxiety will not undermine what the children have tried to say to the family about their own sadness, concerns, or loyalty issues. If the therapist permits the parent to act out his or her own anxiety about the child's story, then the session may get out of control, thereby indicating to the family that it is not safe to talk about sad, emotional, or painful issues. Here the therapist permits the father to make a few comments and then stops him in a gentle way by shifting the focus to the son. This is a natural refocusing of the family tension and is an important therapeutic maneuver. The therapist has stopped the father from acting out his anxiety and avoids focusing on the daughter, whose pattern is to take care of her father by acting out his anxiety. Instead, the therapist turns to the son, who has been on the sidelines for most of the interview, and gives him an opportunity to reflect on the impact of the grandfather's death for him.

Dr. F: John, there are a few questions I want to ask you. Let me start by going back to what I asked Sue about feeling comfortable about asking Dad about stuff in terms of his own life. How was that for you?

John: Well, I knew about his dad committing suicide. The only part I did not know was that he was nineteen, I always thought he was fourteen.

Dr. F: Did you know he heard the story differently a year before he was told the truth?

John: I didn't know the reasons why he committed suicide. I heard that he died of a heart attack, and then as I grew older, I eventually heard from Dad that he committed suicide, I didn't bother to ask why, how, what did he do, was it long, was it short. No, I didn't ask the details. Things like that, asking people about their lives, it's not really, I don't really do it. It's not a big thing on my list. Frankly, I don't really care.

Dr. F: Not part of your nature, eh?

John: No, whatever they did, they did. It's up to them. And with most people I meet . . .

Dr. F: You are that way.

John: Yeah, I don't bother. People always ask me, what has happened to me in my past, and . . .

Dr. F: So it isn't like you got the message from Dad that he wanted hands off on these things.

John: Well, I don't think it really had to be put across to me that it was hands off. I don't know if I got the idea or not, but I wouldn't have asked.

After allowing the son to talk about his early history, the therapist shifts the focus to another important developmental change in the life of the family. The son went away to school during a critical period in the family's life. Several major losses occurred in the family around the same time. The maternal grandfather died, the family left the family home to live with the maternal grandmother, and the son left home to attend a special school for children with learning disabilities. It was during this period that the daughter began to exhibit serious emotional problems. The therapist begins to encourage the children to articulate how that period affected them and changed their roles and relationships within the family. Many times families experience profound developmental changes and losses without recognizing the toll that these losses take on various family members. When the family members talk about these events, they begin to recognize that some of their current problems were set in motion by past events. This historical perspective helps the family reframe some of their problems. The therapist continues with John:

Dr. F: There's something I've wanted to ask you for a while now, and your Dad just reminded me of this when he mentioned Sue was thirteen. There was a time when you went away to school?
John: Yeah, I was away when she was eleven.
Dr. F: And that was around the period when your grandfather died?
John: It was a little before that. I was home for that.
Dr. F: So there were three quite dramatic things that happened in the family. Grandpa died. You went away. The family changed houses.
John: A few things. I missed them all.
Dr. F: What was it like for you to leave the family at that time?
John: I had a great time. The only time, sorry to say this guys . . .
Sue: No home, with three hundred dollar tennis rackets.
John: The only hard part about it was when I went away to school for the first time, and it got to a few weeks before the Christmas vacation. That was the first time I'd been away from home, and I got a little homesick. Before that, like when they first dropped me off at the school, I was the happiest guy in the world. I was like, bye guys, see you later. And after Christmas, when I went back, I wasn't homesick and I enjoyed myself. I liked it.
Dr. F: How did you say goodbye to Sue?

The purpose of this question is to encourage the siblings to work on their relationship. Asking siblings such questions as how they say goodbye to each other, what their worries are about each other, how they try to stay involved with each other are all prescriptions. These questions are not so much directed at what they did in the past as they are suggestions for what they can do in the future.

John: Same way I said goodbye to them. Bye.
Sue: In the back of the car . . .
Dr. F: How long a period was there between the time you knew you were leaving and the time you actually left?
John: I knew for one year for sure.
Dr. F: That you were going to do this?
John: I didn't know anything about the second year until later on in that year.
Dr. F: And you didn't really spend time talking to your sister about your not being around for her.
John: I never was. No, I didn't.

Dr. F: Sue, let me ask you a question about that period because it seems that it has been identified as a turning point. What was the loss for you having your brother leave?

Sue: Not having him around.

Dr. F: What changed for you?

Sue: I don't think it affected me very deeply. I don't think it affected him very deeply. There was lots of stuff . . .

Dr. F: Did you think he deserted you?

The therapist has now introduced the desertion theme, which is a major theme in this family. There have been a series of desertions including the paternal grandfather's suicide, the parents' moves during crises, the death of the maternal grandfather, the son's leaving home, etc. The daughter quickly picks up on the desertion theme. The labeling of some of these losses as desertion frees up the parents to talk about them in a more positive way. Helping family members see how they needed each other to help soften these losses, offers them an opportunity to reconnect in the present rather than feel alone and misunderstood because of the way these events were dealt with in the past. The interview continues on the desertion theme:

Sue: Deserted me?

Dr. F: Left you behind?

Sue: I don't think I was too concerned about it. Well, I don't know, I mean, there was a whole thing of desertion in my life anyways, everyone on the list but . . .

John: I was the first one.

Sue: You were the first one. There was a whole bunch of stuff preceding that because at that point we were going back East and live in a center. And then I was in the new house, or was it the old house, and somebody went away for a week, and I was just with Mom. And then Mom went away for a while and I was just with Dad. And then there was lots of stuff preceding that so I don't know what that has to do with anything. And then the trip, and the wedding, and all of this. I mean, I remember noticing he was gone only when we were still back East. He wasn't at the wedding with us and a couple of other things.

Dr. F: Which wedding was this?

Sue: Helen, my Aunt Helen's wedding, I don't know how they relate to me but they had a good time. I don't know. I don't know. There was a noted change in the fact that there wasn't an extra body hanging around the house, but as we keep professing, John and I aren't close, weren't close. We josh around now, but I don't know if I felt deserted. I don't know that.

Dr. F: Let me ask you another question about that time. When your grandfather died, what was different?

The therapist shifts the focus to another developmental loss — the death of the maternal grandfather. Sue begins to share her pain and sadness about what happened to the family after the grandfather died. The parents had not been aware of what the grandfather's death meant to the children. The grandfather's death becomes a metaphor for loss in the family. As the children discuss what happened to the family after the grandfather died, it becomes apparent that the family truly lost its way. The mother tried to become her own mother's husband and felt torn between the needs of her children and the needs of her mother. (These issues are discussed in later interviews.) As the children talk about the death of their grandfather, they also mention how he made Christmas come alive. This discussion leads to the understanding that the children's current avoidance of Christmas festivities is based on their sadness about their lost family and not on a lack of caring for their parents. It was a revelation to the parents to hear their children talk about how Christmas reminded them of their lost grandfather and the joy that Christmas had represented when he was alive. The interview continues with Sue responding to the question about what was different when the grandfather died:

Sue: Everybody was freaking out. I remember we moved in with my grandmother for a month. Were you there? (to John)

John: Oh, no, I was . . .

Sue: That's right. You weren't there.

John: I missed all those moves actually.

Sue: Well, we moved from our house to the city to Grandma's house and then to the suburbs. It was all real weird. It was weird seeing Baba without Gramps. I did not understand. I knew I didn't understand what happened. There was a scene in the limo on the way to the funeral. I remember very clearly, and I just didn't understand.

Dr. F: Describe the scene you remember. What happened?

Sue: We were in the back of the limousine. My Mum was there, Baba was there, my uncle — my mother's brother. I can't remember, I don't know if Dad was there or not . . .

John: I'm sure he would be.

Sue: Mom was upset, and I was ten or eleven years old, and I don't know if I really understood what had happened. I mean, things were going all freaky. I wasn't crying, and Mum kind of just went freaky, and started yelling at me cause I wasn't crying. It was really weird. I mean I understood it then, understood it was because Mom was freaking out about Gramps. I knew it wasn't me so much. Mom was just freaking. And there were lots of really weird things that went on then. It didn't hit me till a while later, much . . .

Dr. F: How much later?

Sue: I started to really get involved with my whole grandfather thing, his stuff, probably about two years later . . . two or three years later. I got very much attached to his memory and what he represented to me. They were like fairy tale grandparents. People started making jokes like skipping a generation and how I should be in sales because he was in sales, and how I like old things and antiques like he did. As the years went by, I felt like I kept coming into these little strings that attached me to him. I never knew him really. He was great, wonderful, and smiled a lot, but I was still too young to know him as a person.

Dr. F: You still carry his memory?

Sue: Oh, yeah. Mom has had to deal with stuff with her father and when some of that information comes out, I really don't want to hear it. I just don't because it kind of smashes up the picture.

Dr. F: Let me ask you this other question now. Do you think that your mother and grandmother ever got over your grandfather's death?

Sue: My Mum did in a way. I don't think completely. She has a lot of resentment and stuff that didn't get cleared up, that she still carries with her. Probably never. I remember she was never the same. We were never the same. Our family was never the same. I mean, Gramps and Baba, it was like parties, and family and food and drink and happiness and everyone having great parties and doing great stuff. And that all petered out. Died with him. I think that whole era of the . . .

Dr. F: A huge loss to the family.

Sue: I think so. I mean more than any of us ever really realized. I think really a part of our childhood went with him. The Christmasses, and the parties, and everything that was going on. My uncle with his nightclub. They were always there and there was always people there. I think a lot of that died, and we became separated from other members of our family. I think, I'm not sure, and we also started to separate from each other. You know, I think while Gramps was there he held it together. There was my Uncle Bob and all his friends, and the nightclubs, and the parties and just all that stuff.

Dr. F: Did you also lose your uncle after that? Did he become less involved with the family?

Sue has made several powerful statements about the effect of the grandfather's death on the family. The therapist opens up this whole area by asking what was different when the grandfather died. Formulating the question to ask what was different, rather than whether something was different, is important. The therapist wants to ask questions that really allow the family member to think about and talk about change over time rather than respond with a yes or no answer. Whenever there is a major event in a family's life, everybody is affected by it. It is a good approach for the therapist to ask how the event affected the family members rather than whether it affected them. The family member can then reevaluate the impact of the change rather than focus on the goodness or badness of the change.

As the interview continues, the therapist asks Sue about the impact of the grandfather's death on some of the extended family members. Sue's uncle had played an important role in the family and had been a bit of a role model for her. We learn that when Sue lost her grandfather, she also lost her uncle. After his father's death the uncle's behavior toward Sue changed. Sue had interpreted the uncle's change in behavior as a rejection of her. In subsequent interviews, it becomes apparent that the uncle was significantly affected by the loss of his father and acted out this loss by distancing from his sister and, consequently, from Sue. Sue responds to the question about losing her Uncle Bob.

Sue: Uncle Bob, yes. It was pretty close to that when I realized that Bob wasn't real to me. Bob was a guy who walked across the U.S. Bob was the nightclub. Bob was nightpeople. He lived a couple of blocks away from us at one point with about twenty-nine people, his girlfriends and stuff like that. But Bob's not real. He's not someone I can touch. He's not a part of things and I remember realizing that very young.
Dr. F: At what age?
Sue: It was at some family gathering and I went up to give him a hug, and he was talking to someone, and he pushed me away. And I kind of went, "What are you doing to me?" And he acted like, "I'm busy. I'm busy. I'm busy." That kind of made me feel yes, OK, fine. I was mad.
Dr. F: It wasn't the same.
Sue: He wasn't . . .
Dr. F: Was that after your grandpa died, this incident?
Sue: I remember seeing it happen, but I don't remember when it was. I don't think my grandfather was around.
Dr. F: John, you were away during a bit of this period that Sue's talking about. You didn't experience it quite the same way, the change in the family after your grandfather died?

The therapist has shifted to John to give him an opportunity to talk about the impact of the loss of the grandfather. It is important that each child has a chance to be heard. John talks with much sadness about his grandfather and how difficult the loss was for him. John is able to explain his sadness without needing to distance from it. Although he defines himself as an emotional distancer, in reality, he is able to talk about his sadness as well as any member of the family. The parents are intrigued with what John has to say. They had never made the connection between the son's distancing and his sadness about the loss of his grandfather and the changes in the family. When John returned to the family after a two year absence, there was intense conflict between his sister and his parents. He sided with his parents, blaming Sue for the tension and conflict. He had not understood that Sue's behavior was a reaction to the family loss and sadness. As Sue and John listen to each other's stories, they become more connected with each other. A subtle but profound shift occurs in the family as they hear each other's stories. The interview continues with John talking about the loss of his grandfather:

John: I remember when my grandpa died. It hit me rather hard. I remember after his funeral when this thing was going on in the limousine, I turned around and said goodbye to him. I knew right away what had happened. I wouldn't see him again. I sort of caught the idea that the family was a little bit further apart now because there weren't the parties that we had. The first Christmas that we had together after Gramps died was really weird. I think since then I haven't been a Christmas person. The past couple of years I prefer to work Christmas Day, just to miss everything. I'm lucky if I can even get gifts for people. That goes for any time of year.

Dr. F: But then you date that to that Christmas?

John: I think so because I remember before he died I would be the first one up. I would be waking everyone else up, I would come in at 5:30, 6:00 in the morning, jump on these guys' bed, "Come on get up." The next Christmas I seem to remember, I slept, and I slept, and I slept. And it wasn't a big thing for me to get up. I would have rather slept, and it's still the same.

Dr F: What was different about Christmas after Grampa died?

John: He was a big part of Christmas. He was there. He was always cracking jokes, making people laugh, being Santa Claus . . .

Sue: Huge gifts under blankets, is what I remember. He never bought anybody like a gold chain, or socks. He bought like a dresser, or a bed, and shoved it in a corner near the Christmas tree and threw a blanket over it.

John: Try to hide it that way. But we started to get gifts that were Gramps! And I got some chests that Gramps got from his father.

Mrs. R: This was from my mother to you, not from us. Let's get that straight.

Sue: Baba had given us a lot of stuff.

Dr. F: Of Grandpa's?

John: And I think that really hit hard too. Don't get me wrong, I really liked it. I loved the chest, but it sort of really hit . . .

Dr. F: The loss?

John: Yeah. When we started receiving his stuff. But it really changed me personally about the way I felt towards people, about the way I felt towards that time of year, birthdays. It really just put a damper on everything, and it still holds.

Sue: That's true.

Dr. F: It never was quite the same again.

John: No.

Dr. F: The memory of Grandpa. How have you talked about that with your mother?

John: I keep my stuff inside. I always have.

Dr. F: Not with your sister?

John: I don't talk about it with anybody. My girlfriend tries to get stuff out of me. It's difficult.

The therapist has taken the son through a series of losses and changes. He now shifts the focus to how the family as a group dealt with each other around these major losses. The therapist describes the losses as representing family sadness and encourages the family members to see how their shared sadness has the potential to connect them to each other. Sue responds to the question about talking to the mother about events following the grandfather's death:

Dr. F: (To Sue) How have you talked with your mother about what happened when your grandfather died?

Sue: Very rarely. Once in a while, Mum will say something, and I, the great communicator, trying all the time to communicate . . . I don't know. Mum relayed bits and pieces of information, but it wasn't like we sat down and talked it out.

Dr. F: I was thinking more of the sadness, whether you talked a bit about the sadness. Your grandpa's loss is very sad. I was just wondering how the family connected on that.

John: I remember hearing about it. I can really picture Mum was crying. She was sitting at the table. She told me to sit down, and she told me I wasn't old enough to go see him in the hospital. They wouldn't let me in. I was upset about that because I wanted to see him. And it was such a shock because I remember hearing that he was getting better, and then suddenly, bang, he was gone. As Bob said, he checked out. I remember that too. And so, I remember crying for quite a while that night, and I remember going to sleep. I kept on waking up thinking I would see a picture of his face in the dark. I know for a while the whole family was sad. I know I was sad. I know Mum was, Dad was too, and Sue was. The dog was I know. The dog really missed him. But I think it really hit hard, when I knew he was gone.

Dr. F: How did your relationship with your Grandma change when he died?

John: Not really. I know me and Gramps were closer than I was with Baba. Maybe it improved a bit, but I had to go away soon after that for two years. I guess maybe after a while when I came back from school, I was a little closer to Grandma, to Baba.

Dr. F: Did it help, John, to be away after your Grandpa died? You went away for two years. Would it have been harder to stay, to deal with that loss?

John: I don't think it would have been harder. I think it would have been different. I would have been able to see what was happening with Sue. I would have seen more of what happened to the family life instead of reading about it in letters. All the news. I think as a result I grew a little apart from the family when I went away because it was that time when Sue was being a ruffian . . .

Sue: I was a what?

John: Ruffian.

Sue: A ruffian.

John: Just raising hell with the rest of the family. I felt distant.

Dr. F: I was wondering how much being away made you an outsider, or made you feel like an outsider.

John: I think it sort of helped that, not that that's good. Since it was that time in my life too, thirteen, fourteen, that young age, my life was changing in myself, and being away from my parents I didn't grow any closer to them.

Dr. F: My guess is that the distance between the two of you developed during that period of time.

John: I'm sure it did. She definitely changed while I was away.

Dr. F: And you weren't involved. You came back to the change.

Sue: You came back to the war . . .

John: I came back to the change. I came back from one, and then I came back into World War III. And I had no idea. They never told me what was going on. So when I came home, it was a big shock. I think we were close when we were younger.

Sue: Sort of.

John: Feed the ducks with grandma, and stuff like that.
Sue: You can just see the family rallying around us to be close, and then they gave up completely.
John: I don't think we've always been like wide apart. I haven't always been the best brother to her, which we all know. There were some tough issues. Later on, I tried to change that.
Dr F: It was hard to change that once it got set in motion?
John: I think it just went too far. If I tried to change it. It would not change the way she felt cause in her memory I would have been the way I was before. So the damage was done.

The therapist is now working on connections. He is trying to reframe the history and challenge the old story. He focuses on the brother/sister relationship and tries to help Sue and John understand that they lost their way around the death of their grandfather and the general anxiety in the family. It is not necessary for Sue and John to publicly address their confusion about some of this history. What is important is that they think about and begin to reevaluate these historical events. To this point, the interview has progressed nicely to covering an important part of the family's history. However, the mother has not yet had an opportunity to express how these events affected her. The therapist is aware that the children's stories are likely stirring up considerable anxiety and sadness in her. The stories are basically about her losses, as well as her children's. Before the therapist has an opportunity to address the mother the foster mother jumps in to say that she has some rather "pressing business." It is important for the therapist to be supportive to the foster mother.

When therapy begins to have an impact, the identified problem child commonly acts out some of his or her anxieties in the family and other settings. The therapist will listen closely to what the foster mother says to assess whether Sue's reactions to the changes in the family are being acted out in her relationship with Joan.

Joan: I have some rather pressing business. I hate to impose it, but I'm not feeling comfortable having Sue at my place right now. I would appreciate some kind of guidance because I want to talk to Brian and Jean and Sue about it. My feeling is that Sue is choosing to make decisions that she's pretty sure are going to be bad for her, and I don't really want to be part of that. I don't want to be involved in her going through that whole number again. I'm not really game for that.
Dr. F: Like what?
Joan: Well, it's simplistic to say the nightclub life, but it is sort of self-destructive behavior where she turns night into day and just has no regu-

larity in her life at all. Stays up very late, sleeps through the day. People phone her in the middle of the night. She makes meals for herself in the middle of the night, is quite inconsiderate of all the people around her in the house, and states that this is very bad for her. She knows it's going to be devastating. The young man she is interested in I have never met, but she has said terrible things about him. She says he is a dreadful young man.

Mr. R: Again.

Joan: He treats her very, very badly, but she is absolutely entranced apparently. She no longer speaks to me or other people in the household. The way she's been talking today is the first time I've seen her like that for a couple of weeks. Except for a few moments here and there, I don't feel I've had any real communication with her at all.

Dr. F: You miss this part of her.

Joan: Yes, very much.

Sue: OK, about these things, I know them up here and I don't know them back here.

Joan: I understand that . . .

Sue: I intellectualize all these wonderful problems, and it's laid out for me. I know it's bad. I know I shouldn't do it. Back here I think maybe it's not going to be the same. I'm not saying all of me is saying this is a ridiculous thing and I'm going to do it anyway. You know it's not that. Half of me is saying I can't do this, I won't do this. Why am I doing this? I'm going to go ahead and do it anyways. OK, I'm doing all that.

Joan: You express that really clearly in your poetry, and so I see both sides. But the fact is fairly clear to me that you are going to go ahead and do it. And I just wanted you to know that I'm not game to be part of that if you have to go ahead and do it.

Sue: I hear that, but I felt from the past two weeks that I can't get to you.

Joan: I can understand your feeling that way because I don't feel comfortable relating to you at all when your voice rises. You start explaining about things and saying things at cross purposes, "I can't stand him. I want to marry him." And so I find it very difficult to relate. Because I don't feel, this is a dreadful thing to say and I'm going to say it because it popped into my mind, I don't feel as though Sue's at home. I don't feel I'm talking to Sue when you're in that mode. It's not somebody that I know how to relate to at all. But I've made little stabs at it, and I have . . .

Sue: I know it's there. It's just a line. There's rationally and irrationally, and it's split right down the middle. Sometimes I feel like it's just straight out luck which one you are going to get today type of thing. I use the rational Sue to control the irrational Sue when things are supposed to be nice. When things are nice, and people keep telling me things are nice, so they must be nice. And when I want to be irrational and say, "Screw this old business. OK, I don't want it. This is not me." I don't let it. I would sooner go downstairs but I feel like this incredible need to communicate with you. I have to and I have to start being normal again and I have to talk and I have to do all those things that I'm supposed to do, and I can't do it. This part, the other half of me is saying, you know, it's a big fight right now. I'm trying to be rational, and I'm not. I'm trying very hard to be rational, but it's not working. You're seeing what's there all the time, but just isn't allowed a lot. And now I'm feeling like everything is going to hell in a handbasket. So this is what there is, take it or leave it. Lots of things are going through my mind. It's also a fight with my pride. I mean I know you probably see that more than you see all the stuff I'm talking about right now, but there's a lot of stuff. I'm not just saying, "I know it's wrong and I'm going to do it anyways." There's like five other parts to that little story. And it's a big deal to me. And I'm getting scared and I'm saying maybe all this nice stuff will lead nowhere, and I'm losing it again. I'm also losing hope. I'm losing belief in that system, that nice system of doing things. I'm losing. It's just an easy place for me to go. And I am capable of turning it around and being a nice person again, but a lot of it . . .

Joan: Why are you talking about a nice person because I don't want you to think that Sue. We've had five months together, and some of it you've been too charming for words, which I find difficult to deal with. And some of it you've been naughty and unhappy. And some of it you've been straightforward, person-to-person. That's what I find the easiest to relate to. But it hasn't been as though you've been five months of person-to-person and suddenly you've gone bonkers.

Sue: No, I know. But that was like a really big chunk of time for me to do anything, to normalize at all. I don't even know how long it lasted, a month or two. That's a big chunk of time for me to be doing some kind of, or at least look like I'm doing a balance, you know. All I can say is there is still all this here.

Joan: I knew that. That was clear, in fact even in that period. You've got your ups and downs.

Sue: I mean half the picture was nice, and half the picture was still a bloody mess. And I still feel like, if I can't get a whole picture, I'm not getting the whole picture anywhere. I'm not getting it here, and I'm not getting it here. I can live. OK, I put labels on this. I can get nice life here, and I can get nasty life here, and I'm not getting either. And I really don't see how they fit together. Tom was talking to me yesterday about finding the balance in the middle somewhere. I don't believe, as rational as I can be, that it's there. I feel like it's a choice, one or the other. I just don't feel like the pieces of my life are ever going to fit together and I am going to get a whole life. I have to choose half a life.

Dr. F: You've decided you have to choose?

Sue: That's what I have to . . .

Dr. F: That's what you feel?

Sue: That's what I feel like I have to do. I feel like that's what's being offered to me. Sue, you can have half a life on the nice side, or you can have half a life on the nasty side. You can't have both. I feel like I'll have a whole life over here and it will be prettier and nicer, but I can't. There is a whole other half that's going to either die, or I don't know. That's just the way I feel.

The foster mother has voiced her anxiety about Sue's behavior. The therapist has to maintain a delicate balance in responding to Joan's concern. He must be supportive without reinforcing the identified problem role of the child. As families change the child's behavior is no longer reinforced in the same way. The child may respond with increased disruptive behavior. The therapist must anticipate this change and be able to reframe the child's disruptive behavior as a sign of improvement. Without this reframing, the family will reintroduce its old ways of responding, try another therapy, or stop therapy altogether. The "R" family therapist must hear what the foster mother is saying but reframe it in a way that encourages the process to continue. The therapist must help the family understand that as the family improves some of the problems may look worse. With this understanding comes a different reaction to the problems.

Dr. F: We're going to have to stop in a minute. Sue, I think's it's the whole family here, not just your own struggle. You are making some sort of peace or some sort of different type of connection with your family. I don't think it's separate from your puzzle, having to choose between those extremes. I don't think any of us can really get that balance until we've made peace with our own history. Our own family. I think that's very important and the reason for the sessions, the reason I'm dealing with the whole family. I think that's true for every member here, not just you. I think it is for John. I think it is also true for your parents. There isn't an urgency of it having to happen at a certain time because it's a struggle, an ongoing one. Over one's life span, we do it better. I don't think we ever do it totally. And probably, if most people were honest, they would say that their struggle is not so different from yours.

But I get a sense of urgency coming from you Joan. You think something has to change now?

The therapist has made a general statement about the importance of working together as a family to make peace with the individual and group concerns. At this point in the process, a general statement is appropriate. The therapist did not want to leave the family focused on the foster mother's anxiety, which would reinforce the parent's reactivity to Sue. As was evident, Sue bought into the foster mother's anxiety and took it on herself. The therapist's statements refocused the attention to the family as a whole and the importance of each member understanding his or her own part in the family puzzle.

Joan: Well, I'm not comfortable with the way the situation is now. I don't feel I'm being at all helpful to Sue right now. And I think I feel a little bit used. I've grown to love Sue, and it's much harder to feel supportive of her when she is in this "Oh, to hell with the rest of you guys' mode." I think probably I'm not very tolerant of self-indulgence. I try really hard to see that Sue is a huge mixture of things. Labeling her self-indulgent has not been useful but certain behaviors really strike me that way emotionally. Whether that's the truth or not, I don't know. I don't really see myself as a therapist or that kind of person. I see myself as a teacher. That's my job. It keeps me really busy. And one of the problems is that I've been quite busy at school and I haven't had as much time for Sue as I had in the summer, and I think she misses that. I have, at times, made time for Sue at my own expense, but I'm not willing to do that while Sue is being this way. So.

Dr. F: And it's hard being able to talk with her about it, this way. But you can now.

The therapist ends on a note of hope. He conveys the message to the foster mother and the rest of the family that they can talk about these issues together although it is hard to do so. He avoids reinforcing the foster mother's anxiety yet conveys to her that he understands her struggle.

This session was illustrative of a typical family therapy session in which the children felt it was safe enough to talk about their concerns through the therapist to their parents. Over time, as the family members feel more comfortable and safe with each other, they become more intimate and clearer about their anxieties, fears, and losses.

Initially, when change occurs, other areas become more conflictual and anxiety producing. The therapist must maintain an overview of the system and recognize that when there is change there is loss. When one family member begins to feel more connected with another, a different family member may feel less connected. When the center of the family attention shifts away from the identified problem child, anxiety and concern will increase for that child. In this latter case, the identified problem child will begin to act out as a way of getting the family back into the more familiar behaviors. When the parents are able to sustain their new position in the family, vis-à-vis the identified problem child, without overreacting or underreacting to the child's anxiety, a profound system's shift occurs. The therapist must also be aware that when the parent/child relationship changes the sibling relationships have to change as well. Change in one subsystem in a family affects all the other subsystems. The therapist must be alert to any change in the system, and must recognize that change has both positive and negative effects on the various interdependent relationships within the family.

Chapter Six

Family Therapy with Couples

SECTION ONE:
UNDERSTANDING RELATIONSHIP PROBLEMS
SYSTEMICALLY

Couples seeking therapy often present a wide range of problems. However, the focus of these problems is usually either the relationship between the partners or the other partner in the relationship. It is rare for one member of a couple to define the problem as arising from his or her concerns about himself or herself. The general assumption that most couples make is that their problems would be solved if the relationship improved or if the other partner changed.

There are several common themes underlying most couples' problems. The most familiar themes are as follows: (1) My partner is too different and I cannot connect with him or her, (2) We cannot communicate, and I feel too alone and separate, (3) Our values are too different and we have different goals, (4) I have fallen out of love and I do not feel enough love to sustain the relationship, (5) We fight over problems with our children or he or she is overinvolved with an extended family member, (6) He or she is depressed, chronically ill, or addicted to drugs or alcohol, (7) He or she is having an affair, (8) We are having sexual problems or he or she has lost interest in sex.

Not surprisingly, the couple's expectation is that therapy will resolve these problems. The therapist must have a framework that will guide intervention. This framework should be based on the knowledge that the problems being presented camouflage or mask deeper concerns.

Most people enter relationships with high expectations. They want to be loved, accepted, and appreciated for their uniqueness. Many hope that their partners will make up for the losses that they have experienced in their own families-of-origin. Some carry the romantic notion that finding a loved one will make everything right in the world. These hopes and dreams are brought into a marriage. However, most of these dreams are not made explicit. Rather, one partner feels that the other partner knows and understands him or her and has similar desires and expectations. For many couples, feelings of disappointment, resentment, confusion, and rejection arise soon after the marriage. A lack of understanding as to why a partner behaves in certain ways or fails to meet certain needs can exist. Many partners will want the other to be more available, more sensitive, and more supportive to them but will find instead that the other partner is preoccupied with his or her own needs and may be critical and judgmental. As these hurts and resentments arise the individual will seek ways to protect himself or herself emotionally. It is at this point that the process of distancing oneself from the other partner and emotionally shutting down will commonly begin. It is important for the therapist to understand how this process develops over time for each couple. The therapist should ask each partner how he or she has explained to himself or herself the failure of the other to meet his or her needs.

Fantasy-making in a relationship will commence at the start of that relationship. Over time these fantasies will block any learning about the other partner. Commonly, when someone feels disappointed or hurt by another, he or she will rationalize the others behavior to himself or herself. This rationalization forms the basis for future myth-making about the other partner. The more negative the myths or assumptions that we carry around about our partners in an attempt to explain why they are not more loving, caring, or available, the more distance we will create. We use these stories and rationalizations to provide ourselves with reasons that justify our emotional distancing. The rationalizations that we construct are the same ones that we originally developed to deal with pain and hurt in our families-of-origin. We are not likely to say to ourselves, "I wonder what is happening with me that I need other to be different." Our usual query is, "What is wrong with the other partner that he or she cannot be more loving, caring, sensitive, and available." It is much safer emotionally to project our problem outward, to blame the other partner and then to use that definition of the problem to justify our withdrawal from the other partner.

There are two common types of defensive reactions to feelings of hurt: (1) to attack and criticize, and (2) to withdraw and shut down. Both reactions are used to make it safe for ourselves when we feel that the "self" is being threatened. The reaction we choose when we feel hurt is the one we learned historically. There is a direct connection between how we dealt with emotional loss in the past and how we deal with it in the present. Over time, we come to define these losses as relationship problems. We feel unloved and so we stop loving. We feel our partner is not available and we stop communicating. We feel rejected and uncared for, and we shut down sexually. To make sense of these various dynamics, the therapist must be able to conceptualize the presented problem as the reactive playing out of the need to protect oneself through emotionally distancing oneself from the partner.

The therapist should be aware that an individual who feels unloved and uncared for by a partner usually deals with the fear of being alone in the world in one of the following ways: (1) by moving up a generation and becoming more involved with an extended family member, such as a parent or a needy sibling, (2) by moving down a generation and becoming overinvolved in his or her children's lives, (3) by turning inward and becoming preoccupied with his or her own emotional and physical functioning, or (4) by moving out of the relationship and seeking someone else to meet his or her needs.

SECTION TWO:
THE FUNCTIONAL NATURE
OF RELATIONSHIP PROBLEMS

Before one can help a couple deal with a problem, it is essential to understand the functional nature of this problem. What purpose does their problem serve for this couple? When did this problem first occur in the life of the couple? Was there a similar problem in the extended family of either partner? How did the couple develop their particular understanding of this problem? Have they previously sought help from other professionals and/or family and friends? Are their perceptions of this problem different from the perceptions of other family members, friends, professionals? Is there general agreement between the partners about the nature of the problem? Where does the couple place the problem in terms of the various subsystems in the family? Is it a parent/child problem, a problem with one member in the family? Is it a husband/wife problem, a problem between siblings? Is one of the extended family members actively involved in the playing out of the problem? However the couple defines their problem, the therapist must develop hypotheses about how it helps the couple to remain connected and involved with one another, even in a negative way.

It follows that the partners' attempts to resolve a problem will flow from their definition of it. If their attempts are successful, then obviously they will not seek therapy. We see couples who are stuck, who have been unable to solve their problems on their own. Their definitions of a problem and attempted solutions do not work. They cannot come up with alternative strategies and approaches for resolving their problem based on their current definition of it. The first step to approaching problems differently is to redefine the concerns of the couple. The therapist must try to understand what a problem represents symbolically. How has the couple learned to deal with their problem in a particular way? Which partner has the most invested in maintaining this problem? What would be the loss for other family members if they did not focus on this problem in a particular way? It is helpful to understand the couple's problem as a metaphor for their historical losses. When the therapist conceptualizes their problems in metaphorical terms he or she begins to reframe it for the couple and to understand how it makes it safe for the couple to function at a certain level.

A basic principle of relationship problems is that the couple's behaviors are reciprocal in nature. Each responds to the behavior of the other. Change in one partner will bring about a response in the other. Change is usually experienced as a loss, and one partner will try to right the imbalance by behaving in a way that will cause the other to return to more predictable behavior. It is very difficult for couples to learn to behave differently with each other.

People in relationships function at about the same level emotionally, and as a result, tend to act out each other's unfinished business. When one person in the relationship begins to change his or her part in the reciprocity and does not respond in a way that maintains a safe emotional distance, the other partner will become increasingly uncomfortable. This partner will show his or her discomfort by becoming more critical, negative, and distant. If the other partner is able to sustain positive involvement in the face of this critical and distant behavior, and can resist using the partner's increased criticism to justify going back to the old behavior, then there will be a profound shift in the connection between the two people. This process may be referred to as "change without cooperation." Change that is sustained without support, validation, and/or cooperation is discussed in more detail in the section on Therapy with Couples.

The basic premise of this chapter is that the functional nature of relationship problems permits partners to maintain a comfortable distance by projecting their problems onto each other. When a therapist begins to tinker with the stories each partner carries around about the other, the anxiety level increases. The couple will respond by bringing in more stories to reinforce their views. The therapist must remain neutral, yet involved, and must resist buying into the content issues. The therapist deals with the couple by asking the partners how holding onto these old conflicts makes it safe for them in the relationship. As either partner becomes more positive and less reactive in the relationship, a relationship shift will occur and the need to hold onto an issue to maintain safety and distance will fade.

SECTION THREE:
THE ROLE OF FAMILY-OF-ORIGIN ISSUES
IN RELATIONSHIP PROBLEMS

In order to be truly intimate in relationships, one has to have made peace with one's family-of-origin losses. How well we have dealt with our initial attachment and separation issues will have a tremendous influence on how well we are able to connect with our partners' "differences." If we continue to have considerable difficulty in this area, we will want our partners to be like us emotionally in order to make us comfortable.

We tend to choose partners whose unfinished business complements ours. For example, if we need someone to take care of us, then we will find someone who feels good about being a caretaker. Of course, no matter how complementary the needs, no one's needs can be met all the time. When someone feels his or her needs are not being met he or she experiences a sense of loss or betrayal. One protects against the sadness of these feelings by shutting down, and then problems in the relationship occur. Adults shut down by using the same defense mechanisms they used as a child, although their responses may appear more sophisticated and refined. Getting angry, withdrawing, projecting, punishing, etc., are devices that we carry into adulthood to make it safe for ourselves when we feel threatened and alone in the world.

In order for us to be different in our adult relationships we have to rethink the emotional stories that we carry around about ourselves and our family. These stories can be part of the problem that we play out in our adult relationships. One of the most profound aspects of the therapeutic process is the gentle challenging of these emotional stories. No one emerges from his or her family experiences with a perfectly accurate emotional memory. Although we may be accurate regarding certain facts and events, the emotional meaning that we give to those facts and events is somewhat distorted. Family members invariably remember the same event differently. We construct our memories so that we feel comfortable around issues of loss and sadness. As we become stronger, our need to hold onto our memories in the same old way lessens. We are more open to others' memories of events and will gradually let go of our need to hold onto old hurts and resentments. This openness allows us to become more curious but less angry, more detached but less distant from our partner, and consequently more intimate with him or her.

A main goal of the therapeutic process is to encourage the adults in the family to make peace with their family histories and rewrite their emotional stories. The therapist's task is to help the adults look at each other and their children separately from their own emotional issues so that they can allow these important people to enter their lives in a different way. The therapist begins the job of redefining the problem in the first interview. From the beginning he or she identifies the themes from the past that each adult has brought to the present family situation. The major goals of the first session with a couple are:

1. To develop a positive relationship with both partners.
2. To understand the problems in an historical developmental context.
3. To begin to reframe the problems from relationship to self concerns.
4. To help each partner begin to identify the family-of-origin themes that are being played out in their definitions of the problem and their attempts to deal with the problem.
5. To construct a genogram that helps the couple and the therapist identify the key family members involved in the problem and the family members who may be involved in therapy to move beyond the problem.

To accomplish these goals, it is important that the therapist see the partners together from the beginning. If therapy is begun with one partner only, there is the potential to create a dysfunctional triangle with the therapist, and one partner will be on the inside talking about the missing partner on the outside.

SECTION FOUR:
BEGINNING FAMILY THERAPY WITH COUPLES:
CASE ILLUSTRATION AND COMMENTARY

What follows is an interview of a first session with a couple. This was a consultation done at a family service agency. It illustrates the process of beginning with a couple using a multigenerational model of family therapy. Many of the major principles of the model are highlighted in this interview. The therapist takes the couple through the beginning, middle, and ending phases of the first interview.

The goals follow a natural sequence. In the beginning phase of the interview, the therapist allows each partner to define the problems. After the problems are defined the therapist begins to reframe them by making use of the genogram to expand on the definition of the problems. Prior to concluding the interview, the therapist makes some connection between the past and the present and helps the couple begin to see how they can work on self-issues.

In the interview that follows, the therapist begins, as always, by asking each partner how he or she understands being in the session. There can be numerous fantasies or confusion about how a session is going to unfold. Ordinarily, the therapist has spoken to one partner in the couple prior to the first interview. The explanation that that partner gives to the other about the process can be quite convoluted. It is prudent for the therapist to ensure that there is clarity about what will happen in the session. When therapists fail to take this precaution, they may be surprised to find that midway through the session someone is totally confused and misinformed about its purpose. The session can be used to greatest advantage when both partners are clear about its purpose. The interview begins:

Dr. F: What is your understanding about what is going to happen today?
Sandy: Basically, we were told that a very good counselor had come to town, that we would like you. You were going to talk to us a little bit about our background and a little bit about why we were going to counseling and stuff like that.
Dr. F: What did you think about that?
Sandy: Sounds fine to us.
Dr. F: Is there anything about that that you are concerned about? You have any reservations about talking to a stranger?
Sandy: Sounds good to me. I've been spilling my guts to strangers for quite a while now.
Dr. F: Jack, how about you? What was your understanding?
Jack: Same as for Sandy. I was probably a little bit apprehensive. I mean, this is going to be a little bit of a new experience. I was wondering how they were going to set it up. If they were going to have thirty people sitting around us, so we make eye contact with people or what.
Dr. F: Do you think it's better this way?
Sandy: A bit, . . .
Jack: Well, maybe a little bit. Maybe a little bit more nervous . . .

The therapist has established that both Sandy and Jack were informed about the purpose of the interview. This couple has been referred for a consultation by a therapist who has been seeing them regularly. Because it was a consultation, the therapist asks the couple what they have been working on in therapy. In this way, the therapist gains a sense of how each partner identifies the problem and understands their efforts to work on it. The questions are similar to those that are asked in an initial interview with a couple who are just starting therapy. In that situation, the therapist asks how each partner understands the problem and inquires about their attempts to deal with it. It is important that the therapist understands where each partner in the relationship places the problem. If the therapist begins by defining the problem for the couple based on the information from one partner or a referring agent, he or she will get caught in the trap of reinforcing a dysfunctional pattern. He or she may also be seen to be siding with one partner and, thereby, alienate the other. The therapist must avoid defining the problem. His or her role is to ask each partner to define the problem and to create an environment that allows each of them to hear the other's point of view. It is not unusual to discover that the partners identify relationship and family concerns quite differently. The interview continues:

Dr. F: Maybe I can get a sense from each of you what you have been working on.
Jack: I was thinking about that today. Like a brief history or . . .
Dr. F: As you understand it.
Jack: We are here for marriage counseling or analysis. Things weren't going that great. We knew something had to change. Neither one of us were that happy. At least, I wasn't that happy. And I know that Sandy hadn't been happy for a while. I was trying to do things to make her happy and some of the things I had a hard time dealing with. Like I like to be on time and early. Sometimes with Sandy, it's a joke with the family, she's late. To try and make myself be a little bit slower and not on time is a hard thing for me to deal with, and I don't know if I want to change that. But I had never been to analysis before so I didn't really know what to expect. I was just hoping that we might get some insight about each other, learn some better skills to communicate with. I really didn't know what to expect. I was wondering maybe this will fix it, and it will be like it used to be. We will be reintroduced to stuff, and it will fix it.

And then, again, after going for a while, we might not fix it and decide that maybe, heh, some people aren't meant to live together or some people aren't meant to be married and that might be a product of it. So it's not like, OK, I'll take the pill now, and here's the cure, you're fixed. It might be you take the pill, and you're still allergic to it. But I'm hoping that . . .
Sandy: So then you go into this thinking that we might not come out of it together?
Jack: No, I didn't go in thinking that, but I did think, what if for some

reason we hit a button that we weren't supposed to or there's just stuff that she wants to give up and I don't want to give up. So how could we live with each other then?

Jack defines the problem as difficulties in the relationship and raises the possibility that they might discover that they are not suited to each other. Sandy is surprised to hear that Jack has considered this possibility. It is already evident that there is some doubt about the eventual outcome of the process. This example illustrates how important it is to allow each person to define the problem and to hear other's thoughts on the problem and its resolution. The therapist asks about the current therapy:

Dr. F: How long have you been seeing Jan? [current therapist]
Sandy: Five, six months.
Jack:: It's about three or four, but problems were beginning maybe two years ago. Sandy used to say that I'm . . .
Sandy: What?
Jack: Inattentive or not supportive. I really had a hard time dealing with what she meant about being supportive — if she meant being supportive by always giving her a hug or being supportive by when I need you I'll call you, but don't bug me in between those times. So I'm going like, "What do you mean by supporting you. I think I'm supporting you," and then she'd tell me, "No, you're not supporting me." And I couldn't like, get like, "Well I need you to hug me, once every five hours," or something. It was like, "I want you to support me, but I can't really define how I want you to support me."
Dr. F: How long have you been married, Jack?
Jack: Four years.
Dr. F: And you are how old?
Jack: Twenty-eight.
Dr. F: And Sandy?
Sandy: Twenty-four.
Dr. F: So Sandy, maybe you can tell me what you see yourself working on this far.
Sandy: Well, there have been some problems ever since we got married, but I never thought that they were too great to overcome or something that was going to split us up. It's like normal. Everybody has problems. And then things started to get kind of bad about a year and a half ago. Things that were wrong with the relationship, a sort of attention thing. It was a feeling that Jack was not involved. That was going on for the first four years we were together.
Dr. F: Four years before you were married?

Sandy: We were together for three and a half years before we were married and that was going on up until about a year and a half ago. Then things started to go a little bit more. I stopped pushing it. I didn't feel like he was ever taking me that seriously, you know the problems weren't that big of a deal. Then the death of a friend of mine sort of threw me into a . . .

Jack: Not just a friend, "the" friend.

Sandy: She was like a sister to me. The closest person in my life, except Jack. And it made all those problems suddenly seem monstrous.

Sandy has indicated their problems became far greater when her friend died. It is not unusual for problems to increase when some significant loss or change occurs in one's family. Such losses shake up the balance in the relationship. Often relationship problems emerge when there has been significant change in one's extended family, among good friends, in the work situation, etc. At this point in the interview, the therapist is still encouraging each partner to state his or her perceptions of the changes in their relationship and their individual understandings of what these changes mean. The therapist asks Sandy more about the death of her friend. He will not begin to reframe the problem until somewhat later in the interview.

Dr. F: What changed for you when your friend died?

Sandy: It was sort of weird for a while. I was dealing with a lot of other things. Then about six months after Sally's death, I moved in with my brother.

Dr. F: Was this an older or younger brother?

Sandy: Younger brother. Last fall for a couple of months. Then Jack took it seriously. I moved back in with Jack around Christmas time, a little before Christmas. I never really moved out. I mean, I would spend the night there. I would come back over to the house to . . .

Jack: She hadn't taken any of her clothes.

Dr. F: So it was actually two months that you stayed with your brother.

Sandy: Yeah, about that.

Dr. F: How old was Sally?

Sandy: Same age as me.

Dr. F: And she died of?

Sandy: In a car accident.

Dr. F: Anyone else?

Sandy: No. Her fiance was injured.

Dr F: And you've known her for?

Sandy: Fifth grade.

Dr. F: Fifth grade. What year did that happen?
Sandy: Last year.
Dr. F: Do you remember the exact date?
Sandy: March 1st.
Dr. F: And she was one of your closest friends?
Sandy: Yes. She was the closest person to me.
Dr. F: Like a sister.
Sandy: She was a lot closer to me than my sister ever was, or probably ever will be.

Sandy's comment that her friend was closer to her than her sister provides a natural opening for the therapist to begin asking questions about Sandy's own family. This line of questioning leads to a reframing of the problem. It is important for the couple to understand the toll the loss of Sandy's friend has taken on the wife, the husband, and their relationship. When Sandy begins to talk about her family and the losses she has experienced within her family, it becomes apparent that Sally was a family replacement. Sandy indicates that she occupied a special place in her family. She was the confidante of her mother and, at times, tried to overfunction for her father as a way of dealing with her discomfort about having this special relationship with her mother. The interview continues with the therapist asking about Sandy's family:

Dr. F: How large is your family?
Sandy: I have one brother and one sister.
Dr. F: Who is the first-born?
Sandy: I am.
Jack: I'm the first-born in mine.
Dr. F: You are both the oldest in your families?
Jack: Yes. We both know we manipulate each other at times because we're used to getting our ways.
Dr. F: Your sister is how old?
Sandy: She's two years younger than I am.
Dr. F: And your brother.
Sandy: Nineteen.
Dr. F: Is your sister married?
Sandy: Yes, she is, and she's pregnant. She got married. She eloped with a guy that she hadn't even known for a year, six months after I got married.
Jack: Was it that fast?
Sandy: Uh huh. She wanted to get married.
Dr. F: So the exact date of your marriage is?

Sandy: March 15, 1984.
Dr. F: And your sister's?
Sandy: August 16, 1984.
Jack: I didn't realize they had been married that long.

The therapist is now taking a genogram of the wife's family by asking some very specific questions about family size and sibling position, and is beginning to obtain a structural, functional, and developmental overview of Sandy's family. With most couples, there is considerable confusion and lack of information about each other's history. As the therapist takes a careful genogram of each partner in the relationship, the partners usually learn more about each other. Another dynamic that occurs is that couples who are conflictual about their current reality can become allies around their common history and will offer help to each other in remembering important dates, names, and experiences that they have shared together. Providing information for the genogram can be a positive experience for a couple. Each partner observes the other reviewing the important experiences in his or her life. The process decreases reactivity and gives form, structure, and safety to the session. It is important that the therapist who is taking the genogram allows enough time for each partner to provide an overview of the major aspects of his or her family history. The genogram is a fluid instrument that evolves and changes over time. In the beginning, it provides a general outline of the major developmental events in the family's life. In ongoing sessions, it will convey in more depth the impact of these events on the individual and his or her functioning in the relationship. The interview continues with its focus on Sandy's family:

Dr. F: And your brother, is he living alone?
Sandy: No, he lives at home. He's living with my father.
Jack: He was living, Sandy's folks recently divorced, well, four years ago.
Sandy: It was more like six years ago.
Dr. F: What was the date of that?
Sandy: My parent's divorce? I was a senior in high school. When did you move in with my dad? That's when they divorced. That was in 1982.
Jack: Dates have no concept for me.
Sandy: I graduated from high school in 1982. They've been divorced for close to six years.
Dr. F: When we finish today, you'll have all these dates exactly in your mind.
Jack: Yeah.

Dr. F: So they divorced in '82. Were they separated before they divorced?
Sandy: Only as long as it took to get the divorce.
Jack: They didn't spend that much time together though.
Sandy: My mum decided she wanted a divorce in 1980. In fact, she had decided years before that that there were major problems and my dad never took it seriously. It came to a point where she wanted out, and by that time, he decided maybe she is serious. And then she asked for a divorce.

It is interesting to note that Sandy described her mother as having problems that her father did not take seriously. This is similar to Sandy's concern that Jack was not taking her seriously. It is not unusual for the problems and concerns one experiences in one's own family-of-origin to be played out in one's family-of-procreation. The behaviors of our partners that stir us up are usually connected with the behaviors that we observed or were affected by in our original families. It is striking that Sandy uses almost exactly the same phraseology to describe the problems in her parents' relationship and those in her own relationship. It is clear that the need to be taken seriously and to be special are important themes for Sandy. As the interview continues, we learn that when Sandy does not feel that she is being taken seriously or does not feel special, she withdraws and distances. Her withdrawal increases Jack's anxiety, which he deals with by becoming critical and demanding.

Jack's particular way of responding to Sandy's withdrawal stems from his own family-of-origin themes, which become clearer as he describes his family. Sandy's need to feel special was satisfied in part by her best friend Sally. When Sally died, her need increased. Jack's inability to respond to or to understand the changes in Sandy resulted in a greater distance between the couple. These dynamics emerge as the interview unfolds. The interview continues with the discussion of Sandy's parents:

Jack: She'd (Sandy's mother) already met someone . . .
Sandy: He said, "Let's go to marriage counseling assessment."
Jack: She'd already met someone.
Sandy: Yeah, but Dad didn't know that. She had already met someone, but there had been problems for years.
Dr. F: Were you your mother's confidante?

This short interaction revealed that Sandy had a very special relationship with her mother. She knew that her mother was having an affair and that her father was excluded from that knowledge. Many times being the special child means carrying the family secrets. Sandy had a special relationship with her mother, but as becomes evident, it created great distance between her and her father. At a later point in the interview, the therapist asks Sandy what she lost in her relationship with her father by becoming her mother's confidante. The question surprised Sandy, who had never considered this side of the issue. The theme of having a special relationship with one person to the exclusion of another is a powerful one in this couple's history. They use other relationships as a way to distance from each other.

It is significant that Jack introduced the information that the mother was involved in another relationship. One of Jack's concerns about Sandy is that she reaches out to other people to the exclusion of himself. Later in the interview, he speaks quite dramatically on this point. At this stage in the interview, the therapist focuses on how being the confidante in one relationship can produce losses in another relationship. This theme weaves throughout the rest of the interview. The therapist begins the exploration of this theme by asking when Sandy became her mother's confidante. If the relationship had developed at an early age, it would have the potential of depriving Sandy of her childhood or adolescence. We discover that she became her mother's confidante at age thirteen. Sandy's assumption of this emotional overfunctioning made it difficult for her to use her mother as a resource for testing out her own confusions and concerns.

This type of relationship with one's parent can cause the child to be developmentally delayed. The child learns that the only way to get to be special is by putting aside his or her own needs to take care of someone else. He or she may wonder whether someone is there for him or her exclusively. These children rarely know how to ask clearly for what they need. Rather, they learn to use relationships to distance themselves emotionally from their own needs. These children have learned that in order to have their needs met they have to take care of their parents. The therapist's task in these families is to help the parents release the child from that role. Children should be able to act out and experiment with their own confusion, knowing that someone more solid and knowledgeable is there to make it safe for them. The interview continues with Sandy responding to the question about whether she was her mother's confidante:

Sandy: Yes. I was, as a matter of fact.
Dr. F: For how many years?
Sandy: It started when I was about thirteen. I went to Europe with her.
Dr. F: Just you and your mum?

Sandy: Yes. We had a group with us.

Dr. F: It sounds like that trip changed your relationship with your mum. When you came back from that trip, you were closer to her in some ways? And she confided in you.

Sandy: Yes. There was a man on that trip who made her realize just how bad things were between her and my dad. They didn't get involved or anything, but it really started her thinking. She had various relationships, but she kept hoping, kept at my dad, but my dad was always on holidays.

Dr. F: How did it affect you when you saw what was happening to your mum and you became her confidante?

Sandy: Well, at that point, I tried not to take sides, I wasn't that close to my father at that time. I was the only one in the family that would yell at him. You know everyone was scared of him. I thought it was neat that my mum and I were friends and that she felt like she could confide in me, that she did confide in me. She tried to confide in my sister once, and my sister had a cardiac arrest. "You're doing what, with who!" She just couldn't handle the idea of my parents having problems.

Dr. F: How did this becoming your mother's confidante affect your relationship with your dad?

The therapist has asked the last two questions so that Sandy will begin thinking about the trade-off between being special and involved with one parent to the exclusion of another. Their purpose is to stir up thinking. The therapist must not belabor the point, or Sandy will put her energy into defending against the question rather than considering its implications. The interview continues:

Sandy: That's an interesting question. I mean, I guess I knew something that he didn't. I loved my dad, but I could see why my mum was doing what she was doing. It was pretty obvious he was more wrapped up in his work than anything else. Later on, after the divorce, I never held anything against my mum. I could understand fully why she did what she did. But I felt sorry for my dad after he realized it was over and he'd blown it because of not taking it seriously for so many years. I took care of him basically. I was the one that cleaned up after him. And I made sure that all the kids were there for certain things. And I cooked. I made sure he had a home cooked meal every week, and you know, the usual.

Dr. F: How did you become so responsible?

The therapist reframes Sandy's involvement with the family as responsible rather than giving it a negative connotation. The therapist's hypothesis is that Sandy, as the oldest in this family, picked up the family's anxiety and acted it out by becoming overinvolved in her relationships with her mother and father. In some ways, she became her mother's husband and her father's wife. She found a place for her father to live and listened to her mother's most intimate revelations. These roles are a burden. Later in the interview, the therapist asked Sandy whom she turned to when she felt burdened, and Sandy talked more about her friend Sally. We learn that when Sally died, Sandy felt truly alone in the world. Her husband was not able to make her feel safe in the way that she had hoped. Her need in this respect created a fundamental problem within their relationship. At this point in the session, the therapist highlights Sandy's assumption of this responsible role and raises the issue of the toll of assuming this role. The interview continues:

Sandy: So responsible. I don't know. I felt sorry for my dad and I wanted to do something for my dad cause I knew he was hurting.
Jack: It'd be nice sometime to have your dad over for dinner, and we . . .
Sandy: But you were just barely coming into it at the time.
Jack: I was living with him. The reason you moved out is to move in with me.
Dr. F: I'm going to get into that. I heard you say that.
Sandy: Yes. He lived with my dad.
Dr. F: The thing I am so curious about, Sandy, is what you had to give up for yourself by taking care of your dad so well?
Sandy: I don't know if I gave up anything. Maybe I had some minor guilt feelings because I knew what my mother had done. I felt like she had very valid reasons for doing what she did, but I still felt like maybe that had something to do with it. And also I'd never really been close to my dad. He never really showed us kids love cause he was always so busy. Maybe in some ways he needed me. I don't feel like I gave up anything to take care of him.
Dr. F: Did you think he needed you more than you needed him?
Sandy: I don't know. I hadn't thought about it that way. Maybe at that particular moment in time. But I needed him more than he needed me before that, and after that. And now.
Dr. F: How old is your dad?
Sandy: Forty-eight.
Dr. F: How is his health.
Sandy: Just fine.
Dr. F: Has he remarried?
Sandy: Oh yes. He's remarried now.
Dr. F: What year did he remarry?

Sandy: Two years ago.
Jack: He doesn't come over for dinner any more.
Dr. F: Does he have any children?
Sandy: No. They're trying.
Dr. F: How old is his wife?
Sandy: Nine years older than me. So thirty-three.
Dr. F: And what do you call her?
Sandy: Beth. Not Mum.
Jack: I don't think she'd feel easy with that either.
Sandy: There is the same age split between me and her as between Jack and his little brother.
Dr. F: And your mum is how old?
Sandy: Forty-six.
Dr. F: And her health?
Sandy: Fine.
Dr. F: And she's remarried?
Sandy: Yes.
Dr. F: What year did she remarry?
Jack: Last year.
Sandy: She had a real problem with that. The guy that she had fallen in love with and one of the reasons why she ended up leaving my dad for sure, he only got his divorce last year. He was married the entire time.
Jack: But was not living with the woman.
Sandy: He was separated, but he couldn't get a divorce. And four days after the divorce came through, they married. I mean, the ink wasn't even really dry.
Dr. F: So they've been together as a couple for how long?
Sandy: Since about two months after we met. They've been together for six years.
Dr. F: Now what do you call him?
Sandy: Pete.
Dr. F: Not dad?
Sandy: No. Just Pete.
Dr. F: Have you ever had any pregnancies yourself?
Sandy: No I've never been pregnant. I've never had a child.
Jack: We have two cats.
Sandy: I have two cats.
Dr. F: Now with your sister having a baby, and you being the oldest, what does that stir up?
Sandy: I think she's an idiot.
Dr. F: What does it get you thinking about?

Sandy: Actually, at the very beginning, when she was talking about being pregnant, it was so important for her to have a baby before me. I knew that, and I'm not really ready to have kids. No way!

Jack: It's funny though. I don't feel Sandy is as competitive as her sister. Her sister tries to be so ahead of her.

Sandy: She's extremely competitive with me. She always has been. I was the first-born. I was the first one to do anything, and to get anything. It really has affected her. When we are together, the normal sister relationship is pretty limited. Mostly, she's reminding me about something that she thinks is better than me, or better than Jack and I. She says anything and everything to remind me that she's pregnant and I'm not. It's really funny. I mean, I don't care, whatever turns her on. I wish that our relationship was a lot better. But you know if that's what she wants to do, that's what she wants to do. She's extremely stubborn, and I know I won't be able to change her mind.

Dr. F: What sort of work do you do?

Sandy: I'm a full-time student, full, full-time. Architecture. I'm at school a whole lot.

Dr. F: So school is important to you.

Sandy: Very.

Dr. F: And your vision for yourself when you think about where this is going to lead.

Sandy: I'll be an architect. Yeah, I use school a little bit as an escape too. You know something that you were talking about.

Dr. F: But you have a vision besides that? A vision for yourself?

Sandy: I don't know about that.

The therapist has taken Sandy through the major structural, functional, and developmental changes in her family. He has also asked about other aspects of her life, such as work, schooling, pregnancies, and so on. It is important to remember that Sandy is a young adult. She is still in the process of moving away from her family-of-origin and establishing her own identity and her own family. It is not appropriate to encourage twenty-year olds to go back and rework certain issues with their extended families. Developmentally, it is a bit premature. Chronologically, the young adult must leave his or her family, establish himself or herself in a career and his or her own family, and achieve a sense of accomplishment in the world. It is then appropriate to rethink one's emotional position in one's family-of-origin. This couple is very much in the beginning stages of their relationship and neither has yet fully separated from his or her own family. There are numerous unresolved issues with their respective families-of-origin. As the couple becomes more solid in their own lives they will become more able to rethink their earlier family issues. At this point in the therapy, it is important that the therapist help both Sandy and Jack to establish their own vision for themselves and to begin to understand the differences that they bring into the relationship. One of the goals of therapy will be to help them to understand what they do to make it safe for themselves when they get anxious. As they come to understand each other's family-of-origin issues, they will be less likely to reinforce these issues by responding with critical, rejecting, and distancing behavior.

In a very brief time, Sandy has provided the therapist with an overview of some of the major losses and shifts that have occurred in her family. Jack has been given the opportunity to begin to rethink some of the themes that Sandy has brought into the marriage. The therapist will now follow the same procedure with Jack. It is crucial that the families of both members of the couple are given equal time and importance. When the therapist accomplishes this in the first session, the major issues that are being acted out in the relationship problems are considerably clearer. The interview continues with the therapist shifting his attention to Jack:

Dr. F: Well, Jack, how large is your family?

Jack: The same.

Dr. F: Two siblings. Who is the closest in age to you?

Jack: Well, actually, I've got one full sibling. My mum was divorced when I was about eight. About two years later, or about a year and a half later, she remarried. I was about eight when they got divorced and I remember the gentleman. They got married. And then when I was ten my mum had my brother, Joe.

Dr. F: Who is eighteen?

Jack: Correct. And my sister is a year and a half younger than me. She's twenty-six.

Dr. F: So your parents got divorced in '68. And remarried?

Jack: Probably '69. And then she stayed married for about seven years again. The seven year itch. Got divorced. I think Joe was about seven then. And then later on remarried to Frank, who is my stepfather now.

Dr. F: That happened when?

Jack: '76.

Dr. F: And you say you love him?

Jack: Yeah, he's very strong. He's like the dad I never had. I mean, he was my best man at my wedding.

Dr. F: Tell me what is special about him.

Jack: Probably he's a lot of things that my real father isn't, and I wish he was. You know we've gotten into this in the counseling. My real father, his patience level, he doesn't really have any. I mean, he can't go out and work on a car with you because if something breaks off he just gets so frustrated he can't handle it and he might just walk away. Frank is the type of guy who will, if it breaks while he's doing it, be able to modify it so that it still works well, and keep on going. He showed me a lot of these things, and he's just an all round good guy. There's a lot of things you could say. If I said, "Hey, Frank, I need your help," and he said he was going to be there in thirty minutes, he'd be there in thirty minutes, unless he got in a car wreck. If I need some help working on the yard or something, he'll say, "What time do you want me to come over, Jack?" And he'll come over.

Dr. F: Was he married before?

Jack: Yes.

Dr. F: Did he have children from that marriage?

Jack: Yes, but it was kind of bitter. He was kind of rowdy in his younger days. He worked like three jobs to support his wife, and then his wife cheated on him. There are probably a combination of things. And she moved with the kids to Seattle, so he didn't really see the kids that often. It was really a bitter divorce where she, from what I understand, would tell the kids how rotten their father was. Where with my mum and dad, now, Father's Day, I have all the fathers over at my place for a barbecue.

Sandy: Oh, Father's Day.

Jack: Well Sandy's dad, not her stepfather, because nobody really gets along with Pete.

Dr. F: We have one, two, three, four, five fathers here so far.

Jack: OK. Joe's father has died. He died of leukemia.

Dr. F: What year was that?

Sandy: 1986.

Jack: Nobody really cared for Tom that much either. I didn't like Tom. I mean, I tolerated Tom. But it was more he wanted to be my big brother, and I wasn't into having a big brother at all. I liked Frank because he is more than willing to show you how to do things or let you do it, just to where you are going to mess it up, then he comes in and says, "Hey, you know, you might want to try this or try that." And usually it works out.

Dr. F: And your mum is how old?

Jack: She was eighteen when she had me.

Sandy: Forty-eight, forty-seven. She says she's forty-two, but she's not.

Jack: She's about forty-six, forty-seven.

Dr. F: And her health?

Jack: No worries at all. I mean, she, the diet thing, women say they are going to be on diets. Well, like my mum is probably twenty, twenty-five pounds overweight. No, I wouldn't go fifty. I mean, I'd like to see her exercise a little bit more, but that's about it. Well, she's big-boned.

Sandy: She's a big woman.

Jack: She's as big as me. I mean, she's six feet tall, but she's big-boned too.

Dr. F: And your natural father, your biological father. How old is he?

Jack: Fifty, or forty-nine. He's a grandfather, and he's highly depressed.

Dr. F: He's a grandfather to?

Jack: My sister just had a child. I am an uncle. A girl. I am an uncle. I think it's great. She's a beautiful kid.

Sandy: She's gorgeous.

Dr. F: That's the first new addition to the family.

Sandy: The first in that generation.

Dr. F: Now has your dad remarried?

Jack: Yes. My dad kind of lost it after my mum and him got divorced. I mean, he got into drugs, and motorcycles, and everything.

Dr. F: He's in Oregon, did you say?

Jack: Now he is. He lived in the Bay Area until about eight years ago, and then he moved to Oregon.

Dr. F: And in his new marriage are there any children?

Jack: Three kids.

Dr. F: He has three new kids from that marriage.

Jack: Correct.

Sandy: But they are not his biological children.

Dr. F: Oh, I see. She had children from another marriage.

Jack: Right. And her husband's dead.

Sandy: Her husband was shot.

Dr. F: Her husband was killed?

Jack: He was killed, and the kids were both about eight years old. There is a boy and two girls. The boy and one of the girls were eight at that time, and the baby was probably about a year or two years old.

Dr. F: You don't know his wife?

Jack: Yeah. Mary, she's not I mean . . .

Dr. F: How old is Mary.

Sandy: Thirty-six. She's not that old.

Jack: Yeah, she's not that much older than I am over Joe.

Jack has described a family background with several divorces and re-marriages. He has emphasized the importance of his mother's marriage to Frank, her third husband. Frank is Jack's "role model" and the type of father that he always wanted. When Jack talks about the qualities he appreciates in Frank, he describes what he needs in his own life to make him feel loved, safe, and appreciated. When the therapist encourages Jack to talk more about Frank and his relationship with him, he gives Jack's wife an opportunity to learn what her husband needs in a relationship. The important technique of encouraging a partner in a relationship to describe an experience that he or she has had that has made him or her feel safe, cared for, and understood permits the other partner to learn about his or her needs in a safe, nondefensive way. The listening partner is able to sit back and hear the other partner's story without having to defend his or her behavior. In this atmosphere general learning about each other is more likely to occur.

In addition to discussing the importance of Frank in Jack's life, the therapist has asked Jack about the importance of fathers in general. It is clear that Jack has worked to try to bring all these father figures together. His inviting all the fathers to a Father's Day barbecue is an important symbolic attempt to make family safe and available to him. The therapist has reviewed the role of all of Jack's fathers in his life, including the death of a stepfather, his disappointment in his biological father, and his sense of acceptance by his third stepfather. This review is important as it defines who has been there and who has not been available to Jack in the family. This theme has significant symbolic meaning for the couple. The therapist has also asked Jack about other relationships within his family. He is looking for other important people who may be available to Jack. In ongoing therapy with this couple, the therapist may wish to expand the therapeutic constellation and invite other significant family members to build on connections and to expand on Jack's family stories. Involvement of other family members is a valuable technique when working with couples.

As the interview continues, the therapist moves away from Jack's family to focusing on Jack's present situation. He wants to give Jack an opportunity to describe how he is managing to function in the world as an adult. Sandy learns something new about why Jack left school. It is not unusual for partners to learn about each other as they listen to each other's stories. Often partners do not explain to each other how they have made major life decisions. In this vacuum, partners make assumptions about each other's reasons for various behaviors. Partners then operate on the basis of these assumptions as if they were fact.

When the therapist asks one partner about how he or she has made certain major life decisions, an opportunity has been provided for the other partner to learn about an important part of his or her life. When Jack is asked about his adult life, he is also given the opportunity to offset some of the stories that he has told about what has not worked in his family. Telling the therapist about his accomplishments will help Jack to feel more solid. Often a person in therapy is more able to look at the issues that have made him feel sad or vulnerable after he has discussed the areas that have made him feel solid and positive. The session continues with Jack:

Dr. F: Jack, what kind of work do you do?

Jack: Repair technician. Computer support technician.

Dr. F: Have you done that throughout the relationship?

Jack: I've worked for the same company since we've been married, but I started in the warehouse and worked into quality assurance. I just kind of moved within the company, but I've been doing the same thing. When we first met, I was going to school for engineering. Maybe that's one of the things that Sandy, you know, ooooh, an engineer.

Dr. F: Why did you stop?

Sandy: Yeah. Why did you stop?

Jack: Man, because college . . . My dad got his GED. My mum went to girls' school. Neither of them ever went to college. And the girlfriend before Sandy, her parents had gone to college, and it was like you don't amount to nothing unless you go to college or have the four year degree. In high school I was an average student, and I worked a lot of the time. I played sports, worked, you know. Grades C, average was fine. "Hey, I'm passing, I'm not failing any courses." Everybody said "Hey, you're doing good." My girlfriend was going to college, so I thought, "Let's go to college. I have an interest towards science. I'll do engineering." After the first year I realized man, this is a grind, and I don't know if I want to be an engineer where they're constantly designing new ideas. I would much rather be using my hands. Not doing physical labor, I would not want to lay concrete cause my back would go out, but I like doing things. I like thinking about things, but I wouldn't want to be an engineer where I design something that's going to work and spend twenty hours on a table just designing and then give it to a technician who is going to build it. I'd rather be the guy that gets the plan, and builds the thing, and makes sure it works all right.

Dr. F: You really thought that one through.

Jack: Yeah. I was freaked out after two years of school. I decided, hey, I could not. It was really traumatic for me because all these people went, gees, am I being a failure. I mean, the easy cop-out after two years of engineering is going into two years of business or change your major. I was getting that from them. Gradually my roommate went on to Washington State and got his engineering degree. And I was kind of like wondering, does this mean I'm a failure? I did think about that for a while, you know, am I being less than I could be? I don't know if I just rationalized it to myself or really thought about it and what it would entail, and I'm really happy doing what I'm doing now.

Dr. F: It's working for you?

Jack: Apparently. They're paying for school, and you know.

Dr. F: Tell me the story of how you came to live with Sandy's father?

Jack: I moved in before I met Sandy. I was about twenty, and I was still living at home, and it kind of developed. I mean, I love my parents and everything, but I respect them in the sense of hey, I'm in their home and it's their rules. And it was just kind of cramped. I mean, I love Frank, and we could do stuff but we still needed that division. So, I knew that Sandy's father was thinking about moving out, and he's not really the type of person to take out a classified and get a roommate. I saw it as a good opportunity for me because I knew Bob and he would never be around that much and . . .

Dr. F: How did you know him though? What was the connection?

Jack: Oh, no. I mean, I didn't know him. I had talked a little bit with him after being with Sandy, and I said, "Hey, Bob, you know, I'm not that happy at home, and I know you're going to be moving out, and I don't know how this . . ."

Dr. F: You were dating Sandy?

Jack: For about three years . . .

Sandy: No. We had been dating for about six months.

Dr. F: You were a couple.

Sandy: Yeah, we were a couple.

Jack: Oh, yeah, we were a couple.

Sandy: My dad knew I had plans. I was going to marry this fellow.

Jack: Sandy didn't move in. I mean, she'd stay, but she didn't move in with us or anything like that. But she was there a lot.

Dr. F: Let me ask you this question, Jack. That's an interesting one to move in with your future father-in-law. How did you talk to Sandy about the wisdom of doing that?

Sandy: Was that my idea to have you live together? I could swear I was the one who brought it up in the first place. I thought it would be great because I didn't want my dad to be alone.

Jack: That and I saw it as a good idea. I don't honestly remember. I knew at the time that I couldn't afford a big rent, and it would work out good for me cause like he'd pay the rent and I'd take care of keeping the house up, just the everyday little things so that when he came home he didn't have to worry about putting the cat out, or cleaning, or doing anything. He could just kind of maintain his little life and, you know, be able to come home and you know, go swimming at the pool . . .

Sandy: Well, yeah Jack, between me and you, I used to help.

Jack: Well, yeah, you'd clean too. I mean you were over there a lot.

Dr. F: I guess what I was wondering about here, when Sandy was saying it was her idea, was whether you felt you were doing it for Sandy or doing it for you. Who were you doing it for?

Jack: I was doing it partially for me because I couldn't afford a lot of rent, and I wanted to save some money. And I knew I could get by with not paying that much but doing things, you know, making sure stuff was taken care of. But then towards the end, before we got married, I couldn't handle living with him anymore. I said, "Sandy, I've got to move out on my own." So I did move out for about four or five months before we got married. I was going nuts because I got to the point where I got tired of him telling me how things were going to be. I just had to get out of there.

Dr. F: You didn't think you were being disloyal to Sandy?

Jack: No, not really. I mean, I felt bad, and we talked about it. I said "Hey, Sandy, don't think it's anything against you, or anything, but I need to get out." And Sandy was a little bit worried for her dad's sake at that point, you know, "What's my dad going to do," and everything. I remember that. Cause he had never really lived alone, and I said, "Hey, you can deal with that or deal with me going crazy."

Dr. F: You are pretty responsible. Both of you. Very responsible. Sandy, let me ask you a question about your saying that you knew that you were going to marry Jack. What was it about this guy, back then, that made you say to yourself that this was the man for you?

Sandy: He was the one.

The therapist has now moved into the middle phase of the session. He begins to ask questions about how the couple met, what they saw in each other, what they needed from each other, and what each of them felt the other could give them that they were not able to give themselves or did not get from their families-of-origin.

The therapist has approached these important issues by asking how it happened that Jack went to live with Sandy's father. This unusual arrangement seems connected with the unfinished business that Sandy has with her father because of being the confidante of her mother. By having Jack take care of her father, she was able to allay some of the guilt that she has because of keeping her mother's secret about her affairs. The therapist moves away from the family history, as history, and begins to tie it in with the current family dynamics. It is important that the couple begin to reframe what each brings into the relationship before they begin to talk about their relationship problems.

After talking about some of the losses and anxieties within their own families-of-origin, the partners begin to think differently about some of the problems that they are having with each other. Sandy's comment that Jack "was the one" gives the therapist a nice opening to focus on what Sandy and Jack need from each other to make them feel that the relationship can work.

The therapist continues by asking Sandy how she made the decision that she was going to marry Jack:

Dr. F: What was it about him?

Sandy: It was a lot of things. I had just got out of a relationship that my parents hated. This one that I had right before Jack, his name was John, and John was my first real love and . . .

Jack: Who introduced you?

Sandy: My mom introduced us, and my mom was in the middle of that relationship all the way through. She cried at the beginning because it was love. And then she cried at the end when I stopped going out with him. And the whole thing was a big mess. I felt like part of the reason why my parents didn't like him was because they didn't think he was going to amount to anything. Like he wasn't good enough for me. And Jack was this nice-looking, clean-cut engineering student that my mom knew. And my mom had learned her lesson, to a certain extent. She didn't want to get involved, but Jack saw my picture and pushed the issue, and so we met.

And Jack was, you know, probably, I mean, he was the best choice up to that point of anybody I'd ever gone out with for husband material and . . .

Jack: Husband material, huh?

Dr. F: Thinking back now, you were how old?

Jack: I thought she was too young to get married.

Sandy: I was like seventeen, eighteen.

Dr. F: You were seventeen, eighteen.

Sandy: I was like seventeen.

Dr. F: What was different about what you needed at seventeen compared to age twenty when you got married and how have your needs changed now that you are twenty-four?

Sandy: That's a huge one. I was seventeen, and what do seventeen-year-old girls . . . I was in high school, rallied, and on all these dance teams and you know . . .

Jack: And with me . . .

Sandy: You know, guys with cars. I mean, the whole thing, and you know. I'm twenty-four, I'm going to be getting out of school in a year . . .

Dr. F: How have you changed? How are you changing?

Sandy: I don't think my needs are the same. I don't think my goals are the same. Well, my goals are similar. But I work at things differently. I think about them in a different way. The death of my friend I feel has also made a big change in this past year.

Dr. F: In your thinking about things?

Sandy: Yeah, I think more about things. I see things differently. I react differently to different things. I mean everything. I don't feel I'm very much like I was at seventeen.

Dr. F: How have you tried to teach Jack about your changes?

Sandy: How have I tried to teach Jack about my changes? I don't know if I have.

Jack: Very good point. I, we've, never thought about that.

Sandy: Good point.

Jack: Good point, doctor.

Sandy: I don't know. He's been with me the entire time. He's seen the changes. A lot of the changes had to do with me trying to be taken seriously about the problems that we had, and finally being taken seriously when I moved in with my brother. That was part of how I let him know about my changes.

Dr. F: Yes.

Jack: Well, I changed a little bit too, I mean . . .

Sandy: You changed a little. You're trying more.

Dr. F: I'm going to get into that. I'm going to ask you some of the same questions, exactly the same questions.

Sandy: Be prepared.

Dr. F: I'm sure curious about what you say to yourself about letting Jack know about the changes and what you say to yourself that convinces you maybe you shouldn't.

Sandy: Shouldn't tell him about these changes?

Dr. F: Yes.

Sandy: I don't think it's a matter that I shouldn't tell him about these changes. I think that it's more I'm a very verbal person and what you might refer to as an extrovert. And whenever things change for me, my opinion is always pretty well known. So in that respect, Jack is always aware of my opinion or of the way I was feeling about things. I mean, I'm not one to hold anything in. So it was not like all these changes were happening inside me and he didn't have a clue what was going on. I mean, it wasn't like that at all. So we would talk about things. We were involved in a group where we did a lot of communicating and writing about our relationship, and a lot of those changes came up then too. So a lot of those changes that I had gone through up to that point were discussed, dialoguing, writing, things like that. The whole thing.

The interview has now clearly progressed to the middle phase. The therapist has begun to ask each partner to become more reflective about his or her own part in the relationship. When the therapist asks Sandy how she teaches Jack about her changes, she becomes more thoughtful about what has occurred to her over the last several years. Jack is also intrigued with the question and indicates that he would like Sandy to teach him more about some of her changes. The important part of this process is that the therapist has introduced doubt in Sandy's and Jack's minds about how much each really understands the other. The therapist's goal at this point is to arouse each partner's curiosity about the other, while at the same time lessening reactivity. Jack and Sandy are no longer defensive and angry toward each other. They are becoming interested in the idea that they don't know each other quite as well as each had thought. The job of the therapist is to continue to emphasize that each has a responsibility to teach the other about his or her themes, anxieties, and needs.

The interview continues along this theme:

Dr. F: You know one of the things that has struck me is that there has been an enormous amount of change in the last six years.
Sandy: Huge.
Dr. F: Huge. It's almost overwhelming, all the things you've had to deal with and try to make some sense out of.
Jack: This might be the third.
Sandy: You are right.
Dr. F: I think it's really quite impressive, with the family changes and losses. People coming in; people going out. One of the things I want to ask you about is lessons learned from your family. What do you think the lessons were in watching your mum and dad deal with relationships? What have you used, and what have you hoped would happen?
Sandy: What lessons have I learned from my mother and father that I pass on to Jack?
Dr. F: Not so much what they said but what you observed, that you carry with you, that influences how you try setting up your own family.
Sandy: Nothing! No, um, I don't know.
Dr. F: Do you think they are positive or negative lessons?
Sandy: Positive or negative lessons. My parents had an argument. Actually, my dad yelled, and my mum cried. So I know a lot about what not to

do when you argue or you fight. My dad didn't spend much time with us kids, so I know how I want, you know as a parent, how to treat a child, to spend time. You just can't compensate with material goods. I guess it's more of a matter of what not to do. They both loved us children to death. That's a good example, learning to love the children and never feel like giving up on one or the other, or anything like that. We took family vacations, had family fun together, about once a year. That was nice. That's something that I'd like to carry on with Jack and I or whatever, family, children, some day.

Dr. F: I was wondering what lesson you learned being the confidante of your mum. I was just curious whether in some way that taught you the lesson that it's safer to talk to someone else rather than to your partner.

Sandy: Yeah, yeah, yeah. I do that too.

Dr. F: And whether that Sally . . .

Sandy: I talked to her all the time.

Jack: And that was frustrating to me because I knew Sandy was talking with Sally.

Sandy: Yeah. I confided in Sally more than I did Jack about a lot of things, unfortunately. And also, Sally was my full means of support. She'd stand behind me no matter what I did, no matter what decision I made.

Dr. F: Like you tried to do for your mum?

Sandy: Right. Sally was there for me always. And Jack, when she died, it was like I wasn't getting the support. Jack had never really done it, but I hadn't really missed it because I was getting it from Sally. So suddenly I wasn't getting it, and all these other problems I had with Jack escalated with the death, plus this support cutting.

Dr. F: When did you become aware of exactly what you are saying right now?

Sandy: I think it was a few months after her death when I started seeing these things. I get more support from Jack now, but I don't get the same amount of support that I got from Sally. I mean, Jack questions my decisions, and questions the way I do what I do and . . .

Jack: Well, I question. I'm just curious about . . .

Sandy: No, you question, Jack. You don't just stand behind me no matter what. You won't just give me that, "Hey, if you think it's good for us, I'm behind you all the way." You won't do that. Sally did that. You do, "Like are you sure that's really what you want. I don't know if that's really . . ." So it's different. I mean, you try, and you're better than you used to be, but you still don't . . .

The therapist is now trying to help this couple see how the changes that have occurred over the last six years have taken their toll. He begins to make connections between their parents' divorces, the death of Sally, and the newness of their marriage and how they see each other and themselves in the relationship. The couple is beginning to talk about their history with a slightly different understanding. They are becoming a bit more curious about what was behind some of their reactions. It is important for Sandy to begin explaining what shifted in her when her best friend died. She recognizes that when Sally was alive she supported her so much that she needed less from Jack. Now that Sally has died she doesn't trust Jack to be there unconditionally for her.

Jack had felt shut out from the relationship between Sally and his wife. It had not occurred to him that the relationship Sandy developed with Sally was, in many respects, similar to the relationship she had with her mother. Sandy and her mother were on the inside with her father on the outside in much the same way that Sandy and Sally were on the inside with Jack on the outside. Although Jack resented this position, he did not understand it. It was a familiar position for Jack, who often felt on the outside during his mother's marriages. It was only when Frank came into his life that he felt that there was somebody there for him. Jack is still trying to achieve this feeling with his wife and has difficulty understanding those behaviors of hers that make him feel that she wants less of him. The feelings of being on the outside serve to increase his anxiety and sense of loneliness. This couple is just beginning to get a sense of how their old themes are being played out in their relationship.

The interview continues:

Dr. F: Sandy, when did you become aware that your relationship with Sally was in some way part of the lesson you learned from your mother?
Sandy: Well, Sally and I had always been really close. Then we started to be best friends about in the fifth grade. Actually, about the same time that my mum started confiding in me.
Dr. F: You confided in Sally?
Sandy: I confided in Sally. I confided a lot in my mum too, but I don't know. I never really made a connection between my mum and my relationship and Sally and my relationship. My mum considered me her best friend there for a while, so I guess there's a connection there. Does that answer your question?
Dr. F: Well, I was just wondering.
Jack: Boy, I mean in my eyes, I'm going, "Ooooh, why can't I get this kind of information when we are just sitting around the TV."

The phrasing of the therapist's question to Sandy assumes that she has made an important connection between her relationship with her mother and her relationship with Sally. The therapist has purposely worded the question in this manner in order to stimulate Sandy's private thoughts about that connection. The wording of the question avoids defensiveness about the connection and encourages Sandy to think about the significance of her relationships with her mother and Sally. The therapist wants Sandy to leave the session thinking about how her involvement with Sally contributed to her sense of distance from her husband in ways that duplicated how her involvement with her mother increased her distance from her father.

Forty-five minutes have elapsed to this point in the interview. The couple has gradually been helped to recognize that they are bringing in some familiar themes and patterns from their families-of-origin to their family-of-procreation. Jack's comment "I'm going, ooooh, why can't I get this kind of information when we're just sitting around the TV," is an indication that there is some new learning occurring. The therapist now wants to give Jack an opportunity to talk about the lessons he had learned in his previous relationships that have influenced his behavior in his relationship with Sandy.

The interview continues with the therapist shifting his attention to Jack:

Dr. F: Well, let me ask you a question then, Jack. The same question I asked Sandy. How old were you then?
Jack: Twenty-one.
Sandy: Twenty-one.
Dr. F: And you'd been involved in one other relationship, you say.
Jack: Oh, man, yeah, I was . . .
Dr. F: That was a significant relationship for you.
Jack: Yes, very significant.
Dr. F: If you were to list significant people, would you list her?
Sandy: Destructive.
Jack: Yeah, very destructive too.
Dr. F: Powerful.
Jack: Yeah, Yeah.
Dr. F: How long did that one last?
Jack: Five years. I graduated from high school, and we started going out then, and . . .
Sandy: Four years.
Jack: OK, four years. But you'd see John a little bit after we met each other, and I'd see Diane a little bit after we met each other. These ties weren't cut. And it was funnier than hell because they got together after we . . .

Sandy: Me and my great ideas. I split up with . . .

Dr. F: Diane and John got together?

Sandy: I set them up.

Dr. F: So Diane was about your age?

Sandy: Yeah.

Dr. F: Tell me when you met Sandy . . .

Jack: I saw her picture.

Dr. F: You saw her picture.

Jack: She looked cute.

Dr. F: And then you met.

Jack: And then I met her.

Dr. F: How long had you known her when you said to yourself this is the woman for me?

Jack: It was longer for me, I mean . . .

Sandy: Was it?

Jack: Yeah. No. I mean, I mean, Diane, I mean . . .

Sandy: I know it. Say it. Go ahead.

Jack: I loved Diane. If I hadn't been so rejected by her, I don't know. You can only be kicked in the face so much, and then there's a point you just have to say, screw it, I'm not going through this anymore. No matter what she says, or what she does, you just cut it off and end it. So it wasn't for a while. I didn't really know Sandy's family. I liked Sandy's exuberance, her openness towards people, that she wasn't always worried about what someone was going to do to her or anything. I don't know if I really came out and just said, "God, she's everything I've wanted." I remember there was a point, like, I mean, I just enjoyed doing everything with her. And I can't remember if there was a point where I said, "Boy, she'd be a good baby maker . . ."

Sandy: Well, what did you tell Joe and Fred after our first date? That's why I was laughing.

Jack: Oh, OK.

Sandy: This was after our first date.

Jack: Yeah. I guess I came home to one of my roommates and said, "Hey, this is a girl I could marry." When I came home from our first date, I said, "Hey, Fred, this is the girl I could marry," cause she was so open and everything.

Dr. F: There is another question I want to ask you. What did you see in her? What attributes, special attributes that you thought you needed for yourself?

Jack: Her lovingness, you know, her ability to give of herself, her cheer . . .

Dr. F: Her cheer?

Jack: Yeah, 'cause I'm kind of like a boisterous person and outgoing, but sometimes, I use that to maybe mask a little bit. I liked her excitedness, saying "Hey, you want to go water skiing, or do you want to go play frisbee, or do you want to go do this?"

Dr. F: Right. Her energy.

Jack: Her energy. You know it was too much effort for my old girlfriend to play frisbee. I mean, she didn't want to run or something. So I mean, I liked that. I was really soured there even after we had been going out for a while and maybe a little bit into our marriage from my other girlfriend in certain aspects. I was really devastated a lot more I think by that relationship than any other relationship. Maybe more than Sandy over John, cause she ultimately cut it off with John. I ultimately cut it off, but it was after her going up and down, saying "Oh, maybe we can get together, maybe we can go out." So, she was kind of the one that cut it off, and I didn't like that reality that she cut it off. That was very hurtful for me.

Dr. F: What do you think you didn't finish off with Diane, make peace with in that relationship, that you've carried over into this relationship?

Jack: I don't know.

Sandy: Good question.

Jack: Good question.

Sandy: Good question, Jack.

Jack: Maybe not ever being able to satisfy her totally. Sometimes I feel either I'm not making enough money, or we're not going out, or we're not doing this. I mean, shit, can't I ever satisfy you. I mean, that was the ultimate thing with Diane. No matter what I did, nobody was ever able to satisfy her, even me. And I finally got tired of trying. And I think sometimes I feel like that with Sandy. That's one thing that really pisses me off when she says "Let's do this or do this." Well, aren't you happy doing this or why can't we do this? I mean, am I not satisfying her?

Dr. F: So this feeling maybe of not being enough?

Jack: Yeah.

The therapist's question about what Jack did not make peace with in his relationship with Diane deals with the theme of playing out past issues in the present. The answer given in the interview is not important. The goal is to stir up both partner's thinking so that when they leave the session they will continue to focus their thinking on their own special relationship puzzle. When Jack talks about his first significant love affair and how it ended, he has the opportunity to tell his wife through the therapist what his sadness and pain is all about. His issues about not being enough and not feeling someone is there for him are clearly evident in his story about his relationship with Diane.

The interview continues:

Dr. F: Let me just jump up a generation. I'm curious about that feeling, considering what happened with Mum and Dad, when you were ten, and then the second marriage with the child, and then the third marriage. Who among all these people made you feel you were enough?

Jack: Frank.

Dr. F: Was he the first one? Before Frank that hadn't happened?

Jack:: Yeah. Really.

Dr. F: Nothing from your mum?

Jack: My mum was my best friend. I mean, my mum would kill for me and do anything for me, but I don't know. I mean, I was a lot of my mum's confidante for a while. And I love my mum, and I'd do anything for her and she'd do anything for me, but I don't, I don't think. I think Frank was finally the one. Hey, if I had to be with someone deserted on a desert island, I'd say Frank. I mean, my mum gives me a lot of security and everything, but she wouldn't be that much fun to be stuck on an island with, if that makes sense. She'd do anything for me.

Dr. F: Not from your own dad?

Jack: No. I can't count on him for anything. I love the man because he's my father. And Sandy says you ought to love him because he's your father and he does love me. But if I said "Hey, Dad, I'm stuck here and I need your help, be here in thirty minutes," it might be thirty minutes, it might be tomorrow. It might be a week from now.

Dr. F: So when that sort of thing happened, what did that stir up in you? What do you say to yourself was happening?

Jack: I'd get frustrated and pissed off, and well, screw you then. I mean, I'll take care of it myself and do it. I do that a lot when Sandy doesn't show up on time or she says she's going to be able to do something and she doesn't do it.

Dr. F: So that familiar feeling.

Jack: Yeah. We talked a little bit about that with Jan, but I don't know if Sandy really realizes the impact that has on me. I mean because I don't really have any respect for my father. I have a lot of respect for Frank. I'd do anything for Frank. You know my father. I love my father but there isn't that bond. I can't say what it's like with my father. He doesn't know how to react. If I say, "Hey, Dad, I'm really hurting you know, I need a hug," he'll say, "Well, hey, you'll get over it." He was never shown any attention when he was a kid. He was raised by a man who he believed was his father until he was seventeen. When he said he wanted to go into the service, the guy says, "Hey, Mike, I'm not your father."

Dr. F: He told you this story?

Jack: Yeah. I can see why my dad is the way he is, but that doesn't mean that I have to love him because of it, or say "Hey, that's OK. We'll forget about everything that's happened. And I love you just as if it never had." And Frank doesn't like my father. He respects my father for who and what he is. But you know Frank.

The therapist has been encouraging Jack to think about the connections between his past and present, as he had with Sandy. Jack's struggle to make peace with the issue of "not being enough" is identified as a major theme for him. Both Jack and Sandy will have to recognize that each brings a fair amount of unfinished business into their relationship. Each carries feelings of inadequacy and is quick to feel alone and abandoned when his or her partner behaves in a way which reinforces this feeling.

The therapist questions Jack about how he makes it safe for himself when he becomes anxious and/or feels somehow lacking. The therapist's question about what gets stirred up in Jack when he feels that someone he cares about is not there for him is an important one. His response is that he feels "frustrated and pissed off" and then says "screw you." He quickly connects these feelings to the feelings Sandy stirs up in him when she ". . . doesn't show up on time, or she says she is going to be able to do something and she doesn't do it." This reaction is a good example of how feelings of loss from one's own family-of-origin are triggered by a spouse's behavior. A partner may feel the spouse is disappointing him without being aware of the fact that the spouse's behavior is triggering old feelings of loss and sadness. Once these feelings are triggered, we tend to react defensively and protectively by withdrawing and/or attacking.

The interview continues:

Dr. F: You heard me ask Sandy about how she's tried to teach you about her changes. You've gone through a lot of changes too. You're not the same person you were when you met.

Jack: I'm not, but I think I'm more . . . I've had changes, but I'm still pretty much the same, as well. I guess Sandy is too, I mean.

Dr. F: You changed careers.

Jack: Yeah.

Dr. F: You have a different vision for yourself.

Jack: But I still feel I feel strong about the things I felt strong about.

Sandy: Do you look at things any differently now?

Jack: I don't know. When I got married, I knew my mum had been married three times, so it was something that I wanted to work. I didn't want to try it three times before I got the right person.

Dr. F: That's a lesson that you learned from your mum, eh?

Jack: Yeah. Maybe we don't get married for infatuation. Maybe, take more time to get to know the person and then have a successful marriage, you know. Don't get married just because you think you've fallen in love with that person.

Dr. F: Maybe your mum's relationships had some interesting lessons for you.

Jack: Yeah.

Dr. F: You would have been ten to seventeen during her second marriage?

Jack: It was seven years maybe that she'd known him, not that they were married.

Sandy: It was close to that though.

Jack: Yeah, because the last time I remember with Tom, I was like fifteen even then. I went and lived with my dad for a year, cause my dad wanted us to see how he lived.

Dr. F: You and your sister, or only you?

Jack: Me only. I went and lived with my father, and experienced his lifestyle, but didn't find it what I wanted at all. So I left.

Dr. F: What age was that?

Jack: Fifteen. Then I came back. In the year while I was gone, my mum had married Frank. And Tom cheated on my mum too. He was just, he was real blah.

Dr. F: Maybe you can tell me, you being the oldest, I would imagine in some ways you were there for your sister.

Jack: Yeah, but I mean . . .

Sandy: Yeah, do you think so?

Jack: Sometimes I tried, but it was weird because something went on between Tom and my sister. And I was having my own identity crisis, really worrying about my father. At that point, you know, ten, eleven, I was seeing my father. And I wanted to get his acceptance. I wanted to go out with Dad and shoot the BB guns and everything. I thought I just wanted to be with Dad. And then when the opportunity came when I was fifteen, my mum didn't want me to, but she thought if she didn't let me go I would resent her for the rest of my life. And we kind of went back and forth. I wanted to go. I didn't want to go. I wanted to go. My dad said "Hey, you're coming down and living with me." So in that year I found out, hell, all these dreams and expectations I had of my father, wanting it to be Dad and son went right out the window. It wasn't anything like that. It was just the opposite. I mean, there was no real camaraderie or any love, you know, hugs. I mean, you know, a father can hug, but there wasn't any of that. And so at that point, I left. For the next couple of years, I kind of dealt with, hey, you know, I love my father, but he's just not the ideal father. And at that time Frank was there, and he's just, like a man's man. I mean, he didn't want to be my father. He didn't say, "Well, now kid I'm your father, and you are going to do it my way." He was really understanding. He used to take me scuba diving and everything. We used to be able to do things that maybe I thought a father and son would do.

Sandy: Did you ever talk to your sister or spend time with her during that time, or anything like that?

Jack: Well you see, Pat . . .

Sandy: Or with your mum or talk to Tom?

Jack: OK. Bouncing back to when I was twelve and thirteen. I was still trying to get my dad's attention, and I was going through a lot of things myself. I was like pushing Patricia away cause I was trying to deal on my own. Then she started developing her own friends and then it's kind of like weird. I don't know if I just kind of blocked some of it out of my memory or what because I didn't like the situation. And now more and more, as I look back to it I can kind of go, "God, you know, that was really awful." We hated Tom. My mum was very unhappy because we moved every year when she was living with Tom. We always had to make new friends and everything.

The therapist has reviewed the major changes in Jack's life by asking him questions about the changes and the lessons he learned from them. Jack's answers help teach his wife about what he has learned from his experiences, what his needs are, and how he protects himself. Jack has raised the issue of possible abuse of his sister by her stepfather. The therapist observes that this is a sensitive area for Jack and is one that should be dealt with in ongoing therapy in order to help Jack mend his relationship with his sister.

The interview continues:

Dr. F: What do each of you need from the other that you didn't receive enough of from your own families?

Jack: Being here all the time for me, I need that.

Sandy: I can't be there for you all the time. I need to have my own life.

Jack: Seems like you're saying that just for your part, right.

Dr. F: What do you hear him saying?

Sandy: I know that I can be there for him when things are a little bit more settled in my own life. But just right now, I have been there for him all the time and been around all the time. I've done all that, but I'm going through a lot . . .

Jack: What about sharing with me. I remember the first time we went down and visited my dad and Ben; you called Sally because something I had done had upset you . . .

Sandy: Yeah. It's a lot better now.

Jack: Right. But, honey, it still sticks in my mind. It's like, I went out in the other room, and she's talking to Sally. Well, why didn't she talk to me about it?

Dr. F: If I asked you that same question, what would you say? What do you need from Jack that somehow is connected with what you didn't get enough of from your own family?

Sandy: I'm learning that I have a need to feel special. I have a need to be really special to someone. And the funny thing is I get that from Jack but yet I'm still not happy.

Dr. F: I'm going to leave you with a thought because our time is up. I really enjoyed talking to the two of you.

Jack: Oh, it was good for me.

Sandy: OK.

Dr. F: I think your struggles are really tough. Those that you shared with me represent some important losses. The job now is for each of you to work on these losses and try to understand how they have influenced your relationship with each other. I think it is important for the two of you together to work on those family-of-origin losses, to begin to have a clear sense of how they influence your perception of what's right, and what's not going right. The therapy should focus on those areas. In some ways you have similar families. It is interesting that you found each other. It's probably not by accident.

Both Jack and Sandy have begun to talk about what they need from each other to make it safe for themselves in the relationship. People often marry because they need something from the other partner to reduce their sense of loss, sadness, and anxiety about their place in the world. When each partner in therapy becomes more aware of his or her themes and less reactive to the other partner's themes, there is a potential for change in and acceptance of the differences in the other partner while still feeling more connected in the relationship. It is important that the first therapy session offer the partners the opportunity to tell their stories without being criticized or blamed for what is going on in the relationship. As the therapist helps the partners to reframe the problem in terms of their historical themes and to rethink how they want to position themselves in the relationship, they begin to develop a sense that things can be different. This process occurred with Jack and Sandy. The couple began by talking about the problems that they were having in the relationship. As the therapist asked questions about their history and the emotional cost that it has entailed, they began to rethink their parts in the relationship. Although they did not feel significantly more connected at the end of the interview, there was a beginning sense of hope that they could see themselves and each other differently. It would be up to the therapist to build on some of the openings that occurred in this session in ongoing therapy.

Chapter Seven

Middle Phase of Family Therapy

SECTION ONE:
DYNAMICS OF MIDDLE PHASE THERAPY

The middle phase of family therapy is proactive. In contrast with the beginning phase which is characterized by family members projecting their self-issues onto other family members and/or relationship problems, this middle phase commences when the therapist shifts the focus away from the other family members and/or the relationship problems onto self-issues. Some family members are able to focus on self-issues after just one or two sessions while others may take up to a year to attain this new focus. However, most families and couples will begin redefining their problems after a few months. After five or six sessions, most partners have gained some understanding of the fact that their reactivity towards their partners has more to do with the issues that they have brought into the relationship than with the problems that they have been attributing to the other partner.

During the middle phase of family therapy, a family member is likely to begin a session by saying that he or she thought a lot more during the week about his or her part in the relationship or that he or she learned something about the self as a result of conflict that occurred during the week. During the sixth session with one of the couples I have treated, the husband listened thoughtfully to his wife's account of some of her struggles with her own family-of-origin. When the husband spoke, he conveyed that he used to listen to his wife with impatience and constantly asked why she was provoking him. In contrast, he now asked himself what was happening within him to cause him to to be triggered off by his wife's behavior. This individual has clearly shifted his reactivity away from his wife to his own issues.

The shift to the middle phase is evident in work with families as well as couples. In the beginning phase of therapy, parents usually focus on the difficulties that they are having with their children. As therapy proceeds, a parent will begin to talk about his or her own issues and how they get played out by focusing on the child's behavior. Parents in the proactive phase will understand that their reactions to a particular child are based on their own issues, such as the child reminding them of their own struggles in their families. They begin to recognize that when the child's behavior reminds them of their own pasts they become anxious and unable to remain detached and curious about the child. This sort of awareness is accompanied by the parents thinking more about their parts in the interaction process with their children and a moving away from blaming their children for upsetting them. This shift in focus is an important one. Once the adults in the family begin to talk about how their own struggles are played out in the present situation, the therapist is able to focus more attention on family-of-origin issues. However, the therapist must be careful not to move too quickly in this direction. If the adults are continuing to project their problems onto other family members, they will simply feel annoyed and misunderstood if the therapist does not seem to be paying attention to their concerns.

As previously mentioned, the job of the therapist is to listen to the complaints of the individual family members but to avoid focusing on those complaints as the source of the family's problems. The therapist will be continually asking family members what it is about certain behaviors that gets them stirred up. As the family members think more about their own parts in the interaction process, the therapist will be able to expand the questioning to issues the family members can work on beyond the immediate family dynamics. This expansion of focus helps the family members to gain some detachment from the family intensity.

In the middle phase of therapy, the therapist serves more as a consultant by assuming a teaching, coaching role. Many families prematurely stop therapy when they move into this middle phase. Anxiety is down, the problems no longer seem so urgent, and the family members are generally feeling more in control and more comfortable. It is up to the therapist to introduce additional agendas for individual family members to work on. It is important that he or she ask the various family members about how they would like other relationships within their family to change. It is time to expand the focus from nuclear family relationships to extended family relationships. This shift permits the therapist to serve as a consultant in important areas, such as helping the parents work through the remaining issues with their aged parents.

When the therapist is no longer being pulled into content issues around nuclear family struggles, he or she is in a good position to ask questions about the unfinished business with extended family members. The efforts should now focus on encouraging the adults to reposition themselves within their extended families. It is important to open up these areas of focus so that the families can sustain their changes. When families terminate therapy at the first sign of improvement, they are rarely able to sustain their gains. As long as family members are supportive of the change, the change will be sustained. However, when another crisis or disruption occurs within the family, the family will usually revert to old ways of responding to these crises. Change has a better chance of being sustained when the adults in the family have begun to work through their unresolved issues with the extended families. This work provides greater depth to the change and a sense of connection with their extended families that can help parents weather additional storms that may occur in their nuclear families. The extended family work can help adults achieve greater depth in their own emotional functioning and is one of the most powerful sources of change. It does not occur to many adults to think about extended family work. However, when the therapist frames this work as an opportunity to gain more understanding about their own issues and also to help them in their nuclear family, they will usually pursue it with enthusiasm.

The role of the therapist changes dramatically once the adults in the nuclear family begin to work on extended family issues. The therapist begins to focus attention on issues revolving around the more important extended family members. The therapist should help the adults plan family visits in which they can gather new information and can experiment with repositioning themselves in their extended family networks.

SECTION TWO:
THE PROCESS OF MIDDLE PHASE THERAPY

Middle phase work focuses primarily on the adults in the family, but it should not involve the entire family. A primary goal of the beginning phase was to shift the focus from the children and/or the relationship to self-issues. When the therapist has accomplished this goal in the beginning phase, then his or her involvement with the adults in the middle phase will focus on the self-issues that are dealt with by the adults in the presence of each other. This process fosters two types of learning; namely, learning about the self and making discoveries about others. It is preferable to see couples together during this phase, although there can be the occasional exception (see Chapter Ten).

The frequency of the sessions will decrease in the middle phase. The family is typically seen on a weekly basis in the beginning therapy pro-

cess; however, at the middle point, therapy sessions are ordinarily sched-
uled every two weeks, or even just once a month. The emphasis in the
middle phase is on encouraging the adults to think about new ways of
relating to extended family members. The important work occurs outside
the session. During the sessions, the adults will be asked questions such
as: What have you been learning about lately? How has your thinking
changed? What have you been experimenting with? What new data have
you discovered? How much new information have you uncovered? These
questions are proactive and emphasize the responsibility of the self in the
learning process.

The major goals of the middle phase of therapy are to help the individual:

1. To construct a new story about the self in the family.
2. To work on connections with extended family members.
3. To spend more time with extended family members as a way of
   learning about the self.
4. To rethink the family history.
5. To minimize regrets about the past.
6. To begin to say goodbye to aged family members.

The therapist's goal is to encourage the adults to make visits back home
as a way to resolve unfinished business, to minimize regrets, and to expand upon the emotional stories that they have constructed over the years.

The difficulties of middle phase work should not be understated. Not all
adults are willing to risk behaving differently with their extended families,
particularly with their parents. Many have such deeply embedded stories
about their families that they lose their objectivity within moments of
returning home. The challenge for a family member is to spend time with
his or her extended family members and to not react in the old ways. The
adults must remember that their families will respond to them as they have
in the past. The only element of difference will stem from how they position themselves vis-à-vis the sameness of their family. Most family members require considerable support for their efforts to behave and to respond
differently within their extended families. It is up to the therapist to prepare family members for the likelihood of their family reacting to them in
predictable ways and to emphasize that their goal is to respond differently
to the same behaviors. Only then will change be set in motion.

One of the therapist's tasks is to coach family members on how to turn a
family visit into a positive learning experience. When there is a high degree of reactivity in the family member's story, it is helpful to involve
extended family members in a therapy session and learn firsthand about

some of the emotional issues that are causing the reactivity in the family members.

The timing of the involvement of extended family members in therapy is critical. The nuclear family adults must be ready to reconstruct their stories. If not, the session with extended family members can be a negative, explosive experience. The therapist should be certain that the adults are motivated and interested in learning something different. When the therapist is satisfied that they are open to this experience, the plans can be made to involve various family members in therapy as a way of expanding on the old family stories. This process will be discussed in more detail later in this chapter.

SECTION THREE: THE MAJOR PRACTICE PRINCIPLES OF THE MIDDLE PHASE OF THERAPY

This section describes the major practice principles that are employed to help family members make peace with their histories and reconnect in a more profound way with their extended families.

1. Going with the Energy

The therapist must understand his or her clients' stories as metaphors for how the clients have constructed reality to make it safe for themselves. Pointing out fallacies within the stories will only increase the clients' anxieties and defensiveness. In fact, any opposition to the stories reinforces them in that it causes the clients to defend their stories more vehemently. Rather than question the accuracy of the stories, the therapist should encourage clients to explain what makes the stories important to them. The therapist's questions will explore what the loss would be for the clients if they were to give up their stories. Understanding the functional nature of the stories and how they allow the clients to maintain safety will offer these individuals the opportunity in a nonthreatening way to reevaluate their stories.

Just as the therapist goes with the clients' energy, the clients must learn to go with the energy when they reposition themselves within their extended families. When they begin to understand how their stories are used to maintain safety, they become more curious about why other family members have had to develop their own stories. Prior to an adult returning home to reposition himself or herself with extended family, he or she must develop some detachment and curiosity about the way the other family members have constructed their own histories. It would be premature for an individual to return to the family-of-origin if what he or she needed was validation for his or her own story. This individual cannot succeed in having this need met. Each member of the family is protective about his or her construction of the past and will invest tremendous energy into maintaining that point of view. When the adult in the nuclear family becomes curious about his or her parents' and other family members' needs to construct the past in their own particular ways, he or she can begin to understand how their histories have shaped some of the unhappiness and sense of distance within the family.

In order for the adult child to have a successful visit with the family-of-origin, he or she must master the principle of going with the energy. If the adult fights against the way the family conducts its business, then the old familiar interaction patterns will continue to exist. In contrast, if the adult child can encourage the very thing that has been resisted in the past and then ask noncritical questions about why family members behave or react in certain ways, he or she will begin to gain a better understanding of how the family operates as a system.

An example of the advantages of going with the energy is illustrated by the efforts of a young couple I saw in therapy. During the course of a session, they were expressing how upset they were because in a few weeks the wife's parents would be coming for a visit. The couple had had severe battles about what had occurred during the parents' previous visits. The wife indicated that upon arrival, the father immediately began to fix things around the house, which infuriated her husband who felt he could do it himself. The mother would rearrange the kitchen and then go out and do the shopping for the young couple. This also upset the husband who saw it as an indication that the parents felt that they were not able to take care of themselves. The wife felt caught in a struggle between her parents' needs to be helpful and her husband's resentment of the parents' intrusion. The couple was adamant that they really wanted this visit to be different and to not be followed by the same old fight after the parents' departure. I suggested to the couple that they should prepare three lists for the parents prior to their arrival. One list would be for the father and would itemize all the things that they needed him to fix in the house. The other two lists would be for the mother; the first indicating what should be rearranged by her, and the second indicating what she should buy when she went shopping. I emphasized the lists should be constructed seriously and presented to the parents in a manner that would solicit their helpfulness. The lists were duly presented. Three days following the parents' arrival, the mother called the daughter into the bedroom for a talk. She then proceeded to tell the daughter that she and the father thought that the couple should realize that they were not going to be around forever and that it was time that they began to take care of themselves. The mother went on to tell the daughter that they could not fulfill the demands on the lists and that it would be better for the daughter and husband if they stopped trying to take care of them that way.

This vignette illustrates that when children cease resisting parental attempts to shape them up, the parents usually lose interest in behaving in that particular way. It is important that the adult child recognize the part that he or she plays in reinforcing the very behaviors that are trying to be changed.

2. Supporting the More Functional Member in the Family

At times one family member may be more prepared than others to work on self-issues. Although the ideal situation is to have the family adults work together on self-issues, sometimes this is not possible. Occasionally, one family member is extremely reluctant and ambivalent about working on the self while a more functional member is prepared to look at self-issues. When this is the situation, it is advisable to focus on the more functional member. If this family member is able to proceed on a self-journey without needing others to cooperate with and to understand his or her efforts, there is potential for the other family members to benefit from these efforts. It is important, however, that the family member work on the self without any expectations that this work will move other family members along emotionally. If the individual requires a certain amount of outcome or support in order to sustain his or her efforts then this work will usually end in failure. Although self-work usually has a positive effect on the family, it is important to realize that there are no guarantees in this area.

It can be a risky business for one family member to work on the self in opposition to other family members. Others may see this work as taking something away from them and making them appear too different. Their increasing anxiety may cause them to attempt to undermine the self-moves and make them difficult to sustain. The anxiety of others, as well as the individual's own anxiety, makes it extremely difficult for an individual to reposition himself or herself within both the nuclear and the extended family. However, the individual who can do some repositioning in the extended family and can sustain those changes in the face of increased anxiety will greatly increase the likelihood that the change can be sustained within his or her nuclear family.

When the therapy is focused on the family members who are the most resistant to change, the family is redefined at its lowest emotional level. The whole system gets bogged down, and there is little room for new learning. It is not unusual for a therapist to become anxious about working with the more functional member because anxiety in the other family members will increase and there will be a shift of focus. Therapists should be aware of their own anxieties and be careful not to collude with the most anxious members in their attempts to maintain the status quo. When the therapy is focused on the more functional members and proceeding well, those individuals will be making new discoveries about their histories and experiencing new connections with their extended families. They will be able to bring this new information into their own families in a calm and detached way without needing other family members to be supportive or understanding of their activities with the extended family. As the nuclear family members realize that the individual who is working on the self will not distance from them and/or overreact to their anxieties, they generally become more calm and more curious about their own histories.

3. Taking a Research Stance to Help Family Members Learn More About the Self and Others

The therapist models proactive behavior for the family. The family members learn about curiosity by observing the therapist's own curiosity. When the therapist takes a research stance with the adults in the family, he or she asks questions, raises doubts, and shows interest. The therapist does not react to the family story, but always wonders how that story got constructed in a particular way. The therapist never puts closure on any story that a family member tells and always wonders who else in the family constructed a story that way. The therapist encourages the adults in the family to contact extended family members and to gain more information about the important stories. Finally, the therapist recognizes the stories that the adults tell are metaphors and symbolic representations of unfinished business.

As the therapist continues over time to model curiosity, the adults in the family become more curious about their own stories. When the adults realize they are not able to answer all the therapist's questions about how various stories got constructed and how they were understood differently by other family members, they become more interested in asking questions themselves of their extended family members. The principle behind taking a research stance is that there is never enough information. As adults in the family become familiar with a wider range of data, they become more appreciative of the complexity of their own family.

4. Introducing New Information to Expand the Definition of the Problem

One of the tasks of the therapist is to provide a framework that permits the adults in the family to understand their experiences differently. When old assumptions and distortions are in place, even new stories are heard as confirmations of the old stories. The adults must understand that they construct their history based on their personal perceptions of reality. Without this understanding, they cannot hear new information differently. In order for change to occur, their cognitive awareness of reality must be expanded upon. The therapy should provide new concepts and new ideas about how the emotional world is developed. New information fed into the old framework will simply become old information. The adults must develop a different set of conceptual tools for understanding information in a new way.

5. Teaching Systems Concepts

This principle is closely connected with the previous principle of introducing new information. In order for the adults in the family to be able to absorb new information, they should have a beginning understanding of how systems operate emotionally. The therapist should be cautious about using too much jargon; however, it can be helpful for him or her to explain to the family how the triangle works and how the overfunctioning of one member puts other family members at a disadvantage. It is also informative and freeing for family members to understand the principle of reciprocity and that there are not "good guys" and "bad guys" in the relationship. Finally, it is important that the family members understand that the stories that they have constructed will tend to lock them into predictable behaviors. These are basic principles of human relationships.

When an individual is no longer in a reactive phase, he or she can use these principles to experiment with being different in his or her primary relationships. The timing of this didactic aspect of therapy is important. The therapist should not adopt a teaching stance at a time when the family is anxious and/or preoccupied with problems. When systems principles are taught during a period of high anxiety, the family members will use the principles to reinforce their own positions and stories. In contrast, when the family is in a period of relative calm, the family members are open-minded and curious about these concepts and can use them to increase their knowledge about the parts that they play in the family struggles.

6. Working on the Self

Working on the self is the single most important aspect of the therapy process. When an individual is prepared to look at his or her part in the family drama, the individual is then ready to take a closer look at his or her areas of reactivity. This work involves encouraging family members to seek out extended family situations and to observe what behaviors stir them up and what reactions these behaviors trigger off inside them. When a family member has some understanding of how systems operate and is able to begin self work, I point out that the process of change follows a fairly predictable pattern that involves a progression through the following stages:

1. The challenge of the first phase involves conscious dissatisfaction with the way the self is behaving in the world. The focus is on the self rather than others.
2. The second phase involves identifying one's emotional triggers and self's knee jerk reactions to these triggers.
3. The third phase involves; first, anger at self for continuing to react in the same old ways and, second, a recognition that the anger keeps the self stuck.
4. In the fourth phase the self moves from anger to amusement about reacting in the old ways. When the self is able to feel more amused and detached about the inability to do things differently, the self has, in fact, gotten a handle on doing things differently. Now the self is ready to behave differently.
5. In the fifth stage, the self becomes so comfortable behaving differently that he or she has trouble remembering the old behavior.

Working on self is the central focus of the middle phase of therapy. The individual is continually asked about his or her own part in any interaction. Whenever the self begins to talk about what others are doing, it is a sign that he or she has lost objectivity and has slid back into the reactive phase. The task of the therapist is to refocus this person's thinking back onto the self. When the self's anxiety rises, he or she will revert to talking about others. When the self feels more comfortable and in control, the individual will more readily look at the role that he or she is playing in the situation. The therapist can help reduce anxiety by reframing what the self sees as failures into valuable learning opportunities. There really are no failures, just opportunities to learn. When the self is able to reframe his or her efforts in this way, anxiety is less and learning occurs from every and all efforts.

7. Repositioning Within the Family-of-Origin

When the individual is working on self-issues, it is time to encourage him or her to visit the extended family. These visits can take place around major family events, such as holidays, or be planned for noneventful times. It is preferable that there be a combination of the two, as visits around family events tend to stir up the family in unique ways. In this phase of therapy, the adult member of the nuclear family is encouraged to put himself or herself in a situation with the extended family that has traditionally been explosive. The adult child's task is to use one of these emotionally explosive experiences as an opportunity to reposition and to be in control of the self while others are reacting in the old ways. If the individual can connect at a deeper level with extended family members rather than distance from them, he or she will find that this new learning will carry over to the family-of-procreation where it will also be easier to deal with emotional reactivity.

The therapist's job is to coach the adult child on family-of-origin visits, with the focus being on learning new ways of responding to the family without using anger and/or distance. Short, frequent visits are preferred, as it is easier to maintain one's objectivity and detachment over a short period of time. Many adults have reported that by the third day of a visit home they have begun to feel very much the child in the family. They are usually able to maintain some degree of amusement and detachment for the first two days.

It is helpful for the therapist to encourage individual family members to be creative about how they want to use the family visits. The therapist may suggest that efforts be focused on particular family members. In that case, the individual family member should try to arrange some time alone with various other family members. An individual cannot reposition himself or herself significantly in a social gathering. These efforts are much more effective in one-on-one meetings.

In coaching people on family-of-origin work, I am very specific about what they need to do to make the visit a different experience for themselves. Their responsibilities include the following: (1) they must be very clear what their agendas are, (2) they should be certain with which family members they want to have different experiences, (3) they must be prepared to spend some individual time with these particular family members, (4) they must be prepared to ask specific questions about the areas in which they want more information, and (5) most importantly, they must be prepared to proceed without receiving outside validation and/or confirmation of their stories. The process of coaching an adult child on the repositioning of the self with the family will be discussed in greater detail in Chapter Nine.

8. Taking an "I" Position

This principle involves letting go of needing others to be different in order for the self to behave in a clearer, calmer, involved, intimate way. By the time an individual reaches the middle phase of therapy, he or she should be able to talk about the self rather than others. As individuals better define their own agendas, issues, values, abilities, etc., they are taking "I" positions. Mastering the "I" position involves letting go of the need to defend the self against others. When others are being critical, negative, or angry, the well-defined self is able to remain objective, calm, involved, and nonreactive. An individual who is overly concerned with others protects himself or herself by responding with aggression or withdrawal when he or she feels hurt or anxious. In contrast, when an individual has assumed the "I" position, he or she is curious rather than defensive and protective about the reactions that he or she gets from others. The therapist models the "I" position for members of the family by responding to their reactivity in a positive way. The therapist remains clear, consistent, and detached, yet involved and curious, in the face of family members' criticism and ambivalence.

9. Involving Extended Family Members to Expand Understanding of Family History

There are times when it is appropriate for the therapist to involve extended family members in therapy. Their involvement provides an opportunity for the therapist to learn more about the complexity of the family by hearing the other family members' stories. It also permits the therapist to ask extended family members questions that the adult child has been unable to ask himself or herself. Equally important is that this process allows the extended family members to share important parts of their history through the therapist without the old reactivity being stirred up. The involvement of extended family members can be a powerful experience for all of the members of the family but it must be done with caution and appropriate structure.

The major purpose for involving extended family members in therapy is to break an impasse. A common impasse is the one that occurs when the adult child persists in telling a story that reinforces his or her need to keep the extended family at a distance. When there is sufficient trust between the adult child and the therapist, the adult child will be willing to invite the extended family members to the therapy sessions in an attempt to discover new information about the family that he or she has been unable to discover on his or her own.

This chapter includes two interviews involving aged parents. The first involves an adult child who was quite reactive to his parents. He had been unable to reposition himself with his parents during a number of visits home. The second interview involves an adult child who had successfully repositioned herself with her extended family and invited her aged parents to the session to "polish off" a few general issues. The therapist positioned himself quite differently in the two interviews. The third interview presents a middle phase interview with a couple. The different therapeutic styles will be discussed in detail in the case commentaries.

SECTION FOUR:
INVOLVEMENT OF THE PARENTS
OF AN ADULT CHILD IN FAMILY THERAPY

When the therapist invites the parents to attend a session with their adult child, the therapist must have a clear idea whether the adult child is in a reactive or a proactive phase. If the child is in a reactive phase then the child will not hear the parents' stories as new information. Rather, the stories will only confirm the child's entrenched view of his or her parents. The therapist must not allow the reactive child to ask the parents questions or react to what they are saying, because the child will probably respond in a way that increases the parents' anxiety and reinforces the old interaction. It is important for the therapist to be in charge of the process and to give the adult child specific instructions about how to behave in the session. Very little should be left to chance when the adult's parents are involved. Many parents are anxious about being invited to a session and believe they are being blamed for their adult child's behavior. Many say that they have done the best job they can and only want their children to be happy. Others say that you cannot blame them for the way that their children have turned out. In any case, they are often confused and bewildered about the purpose of such a session. It is crucial that the therapist make it safe for the parents while at the same time putting the adult child in a position in which the child can learn something new about the parents' stories.

The following vignette illustrates how counterproductive it is to allow an adult child to respond to a parent's story with anxiety and reactivity:

The couple in therapy had been living together for over five years. The woman had had three pregnancies and three abortions. She was now pregnant for the fourth time. When the couple entered therapy, they were in a dilemma about whether to get married. The women told the therapist that she was not prepared to have another abortion. Either they would marry, or she would have this child alone. The man was ambivalent about whether he wanted to marry and to have a family. During the course of therapy, they decided to get married and to have the child together. The man's parents were coming to town for the wedding. Since we had talked about the importance of extended family members, he asked me to see his parents. He was still very much in the reactive phase with his parents, who were both survivors of the Holocaust. He felt that his father was lost in the past, a past that had haunted the entire family. He was not at all curious about his father's stories and, in fact, became quite angry whenever his father referred to anything from the past.

When the parents attended the session, I asked the father a little bit about some of the experiences he had had in his own family and during the war. He began to tell a very moving story about living in a little town in Poland. According to this story, shortly before the Nazis came into the town, the village priest notified the Jewish families that the first-born son in each family would be given a pass to leave prior to the Nazis' arrival. The father was the first-born son in his family but decided that he wanted his brother to leave rather than himself. He asked the priest if his brother could receive the pass and was told it was he or no one. He then left his mother, father, brother, and sister and never saw any of them again.

When the father finished this story, I asked the son if he had any questions for the father about what he had said. The son pointed his finger at his father and asked with anger why he had not gone back to Poland after the war to see if his brother had survived. Clearly, one of the father's fears was that he had not done enough to save his family. The son's attack on the father implied that the father was responsible for not being there to take care of his brother. In some ways, the son's accusations also implied that the father had not done enough to make it safe for him, the son. I erred in allowing the son to raise an issue with the father that made it unsafe for the family to talk about pain and loss. It would have been preferable to focus on other family members and to ask them about what they needed and/or tried to do to make things safe in the family.

This session illustrates how important it is for the therapist to block the reactivity of various family members when their anxiety or old hurts get stirred up. When the therapist allows family members to react to each other's stories, he or she permits the continuance of old family patterns that justify the distance and hurt that already exists.

It is from experiences such as this that I have learned that a therapist must stay in control of the process and keep it safe by being the one to ask the questions. If the therapist can ensure that the adult children will assume an observational position vis-à-vis their parents' stories, there is potential for something new to be learned.

One of the goals of involving aged parents in the therapy is to help family members connect around some of the old family stories. The focus is on helping family members understand the history differently. When the children listen to their parents explain about how some of the major events in their lives unfolded, they become more curious about their parents as people. In eliciting the parents' stories, a therapist should ask about the aged parents' own parents and grandparents. The therapist will want the parents to talk about their experiences as children in their own families and about their memories of their grandparents. It is safer for the therapist to enquire first about the distant past and give the adult children an opportunity to hear how their parents' history unfolded and shaped their lives.

It can be risky to involve aged parents initially around the current family situation and the childhood history of the adult children. When the therapist begins with a focus on the recent past, the parents are more likely to feel blamed for how they raised their children. In contrast, when they are able to tell the therapist about their own lives and what they learned from their parents, they feel more relaxed and understood. When the aged parents have begun to feel more comfortable, it becomes safe for the therapist to ask about the more recent past and the parents' vision about what they wanted for their families. At this time, there is often an increase in sadness among family members as they discover how and why they lost their way with each other. Out of this sadness comes a potential for a greater "connectedness" between family members. At the conclusion of these family-of-origin sessions, the family members generally feel more connected and better understood. The groundwork will have been laid for the family members to feel more at peace with their history and to have a sense of hope for building on that history in a positive way with each other.

It is highly desirable to videotape sessions with aged parents. The intensity of the session can be so great that family members miss a lot of the parents' stories. I have found it very useful to review the videotape with the adult child at a later session so that he or she can sit back and listen to the family story yet again. By reviewing this tape the adult child often hears important elements of the story that were missed during the intensity of the original family-of-origin session. It is also helpful the adult child to review the tape in the privacy of his or her home and then discuss any additional observations with the therapist.

It is a powerful experience for the adult child to listen to his or her parents tell their story to the therapist without having to respond to it. The therapist will have emphasized that the adult child is to simply listen to the story. The adult child's task is not to react to it, to change it or to justify it. Rather, he or she is to try to understand it. Once an adult child assumes this sort of emotional stance towards the parents, he or she has achieved a sense of curiosity, not just about the parents but also about himself or herself, his or her children and his or her spouse. This emotionally curious stance develops slowly over time. The interview that follows took place after a year of planning.

SECTION FIVE:
FAMILY THERAPY
WITH THE ADULT CHILD AND PARENTS:
A CASE EXAMPLE

The following case illustration concerns a client who came to see me shortly after he had separated from his wife and had begun living with another woman. During the first session, he told me that it would be ridiculous to think his parents would ever attend a session with him. This client, who had achieved a high degree of success in his profession, felt his parents did not understand his accomplishments and his way of being in the world. I did not press the point at the first session, but I simply laid the groundwork for raising the issue of involving the parents at a later date. Over the course of a year of therapy, there were numerous changes in this client's life; including such matters as his career, his relationships with his former wife and lover, his connection with his children, and his reconnection with his brother. One day the client telephoned to let me know that his parents were in town for a visit. He inquired whether I was still interested in having a session with them. We set up the session immediately, and I gave the client specific instructions about how the session would be conducted. The client agreed to the following instructions: (1) the session would be videotaped, (2) the client would remain silent throughout the session, and (3) the client would review the tape a week after the session had taken place.

The following transcript is from that session. It illustrates how the themes of the parents get played out in their reactivity towards their adult child.

This session begins with the therapist asking the parents how they understand their attendance at the session. This opening is important in that it allows the therapist to assess the comfort level of the parents and to gain some understanding about their fantasies and agendas for the session. Depending on the parents' responses, the therapist can offer further explanations about the structure of the session and thereby reduce any anxiety based on misunderstandings that they may have about what will be taking place. The session begins:

Dr. F: Maybe I can find out what your son has told you about coming here.

Mr. Myers: Not much. All he did was say that you'd like to meet us and get some background on us and him. That's all we know.

Dr. F: He didn't give you any more details?

Mr. Myers: No. He doesn't even tell us what goes on here.

Dr. F: Did Bob tell you anything about what he was talking about here?

Mrs. Myers: No.

Mr. Myers: Not a thing. Very secretive.

Dr. F: Have you ever been to anything like this before?

Mr. Myers: Oh, once, with Bob.

Dr. F: Both of you?

Mrs. Myers: No.

Dr. F: What was that about?

Mrs. Myers: I was invited out.

Dr. F: You were invited out?

Mr. Myers: Yes. She was dis-invited.

This initial exchange is important in that it informs the therapist that the mother has been left out in the past and alerts him to the importance of making her feel part of the process.

Dr. F: Why don't you tell me about that.

Mr. Myers: Nothing really too much. In fact, I don't even recall too much what took place there.

Dr. F: How many years ago was that?

Mr. Myers: Fifteen years.

Dr. F: Oh. That's a long time ago. You remember being invited out?

Mrs. Myers: Yes.

Mr. Myers: Well, it was in fact lunch. I wasn't eating. It was a different kind of therapy that Bob was going through at that time. You can explain it more than I. (turning to Bob)

Dr. F: How about with your other son? Were you ever involved with anything like this?

Mr. Myers: No.

The therapist has introduced the one member of the family who is not present, that is, the younger brother, Joe. It is important for the therapist to give recognition to the fact that Joe is an important member of the family and has played a part in how the family history has unfolded. The absent member's role must always be recognized. The therapist must be careful not to triangle in or scapegoat the absent member, and yet give weight to his importance in the family.

The interview continues with the therapist giving the parents and the adult son an explanation of the session's purpose. He highlights the importance of family history and moves the parents on to safe ground by asking them about their early memories of family. He begins with the mother to counteract her earlier history of being left out.

Dr. F: Well, one of the things I have been talking with Bob about has been family, some of your family history. And I said to him that the experts in the family history are the two of you. He said that he had the experts visiting so why not take advantage of that. Mrs. Myers, how about telling me a little bit, maybe as a way to tell Bob a little bit, about your beginnings. How far back does your memory go on family?

Mrs. Myers: Almost as old as I am.

Dr. F: Does it go back to your grandparents? Does it go that far back?

Mrs. Myers: No. I didn't know them at all.

Dr. F: Any grandparents at all?

Mrs. Myers: They didn't live here. They didn't live in this country.

Dr. F: So you don't have any memory of your parents' parents. No direct involvement with them?

Mrs. Myers: No. Not at all.

Dr. F: So it goes as far back as your parents. Where were they from? What part of the world?

Mrs. Myers: Eastern Europe.

Dr. F: Where were you born?

Mrs. Myers: I was born in the States.

Dr. F: In the States. Your parents moved to Rhode Island?

Mrs. Myers: Yes. Well, my mother and father married in Rhode Island. But I think I told that to Bob. He recorded it.

Dr. F: He has a lot of that early history of the family. How about your grandchildren? Do you think they know much about that? How it is for parents to have their children so far away?

Mrs. Myers: Well, I don't think we have the best relationship. It's pleasant, and we love each other, but I don't think it's good.

Dr. F: Is it different with your other son?

Mrs. Myers: Yes.

Dr. F: What's different about it?

Mrs. Myers: I don't know why I'm the target this morning.

Mr. Myers: He's talking to you now. He'll talk to me later, I imagine.

Dr. F: I'll make sure you have equal time.

Mrs. Myers: Bob and I have had a damn great, ongoing relationship.

Dr. F: Your other son is in England.

Mrs. Myers: But we seem to see him more often now, and Joe's the late bloomer in family relations.

Dr. F: He's the younger one.

Mrs. Myers: Well, we do see him more often.

Dr. F: Is it that he comes to visit more, or you go to England?

Mrs. Myers: Oh, no. He comes to visit with us.

Dr. F: Have you been to England to see him there?

Mrs. Myers: Been to England to see him? Yes. We did a few years ago. We really aren't that sort.

Dr. F: Would he know as much about family background as Bob?

Mrs. Myers: Absolutely not.

Mr. Myers: He doesn't even know his cousins.

Dr. F: So Bob knows more?

Mrs. Myers: Oh, yes. Bob has a fabulous memory. Joe is not interested. I think he's just becoming interested.

Dr. F: Now that's interesting. So there really is a difference between how much information one son has about family as compared to the other son.

Mrs. Myers: Joe couldn't make family relations. He just couldn't make associations for most of his life. For a long, long time.

Mr. Myers: Don't forget for years they've both been away from Rhode Island. They haven't known family; they haven't seen family.

Mrs. Myers: He wasn't even two years old. He was very little. He would sit in the car. He was born with that, but something happened.

Mr. Myers: He's changed. He doesn't mind visiting with relatives now.

Dr. F: So he seemed more interested later in his life.

Mr. Myers: Oh, yes. Much more.

Mrs. Myers: Oh, yes. I think so.
Mr. Myers: In fact, on one of his last visits, he was somewhere else, and we were going out. My sister happened to be up from Florida. We were out for dinner somewhere. He rushed home and took my other car and came to the restaurant. Before that would have been unheard of.
Dr. F: You mean five years ago.
Mr. Myers: Unheard of. Absolutely. "I don't want to. I don't have time." And I think that from then on he's been more family conscious.
Dr. F: Mrs. Myers, in terms of your own grandparents, was it that your parents didn't talk to you about their parents?

The therapist has learned that the mother is very ambivalent about talking about herself. There is a part of her that wants to connect to her family but a competing part that is angry and vulnerable. She has let the therapist know that he should proceed cautiously with her. The therapist has tried to make the mother comfortable by introducing the absent family members and avoiding putting her on center stage. However, he must be careful not to scapegoat the absent family member. As the therapist listens to the mother, he tries to find an area in which he can connect with her that is both safe for her and yet will move her into a discussion about the family so that she can feel understood by both her husband and her son. By asking the mother about her own grandparents, the therapist is able to involve her in a more comfortable area of discussion while at the same time highlighting an important area of unfinished business between the mother and her own parents, that is, her lack of connection with lost family members. In discussing this area, the mother reveals an ambivalent relationship with her own parents and gives an indication of the degree of unfinished business that she has with her own family-of-origin.

The interview continues with the focus on the mother who has been asked if her parents talked about her grandparents.

Mrs. Myers: My father never did. My mother would talk about her mother. Her mother was blind at an early age. She was blind when she was about thirty-five.
Dr. F: Totally blind?
Mrs. Myers: Well that's what my mother said, and she ran her household. And then when she had a hip fracture she directed other members of the family. Where to find things and how to make them. That's all I know about her.
Dr. F: So she didn't talk much about her mother or her father?
Mrs. Myers: My mother was kind of bitter about what was dealt out to

her. She married a man many years older than she. Bob has this on tape. I don't know if you've heard it.

Dr. F: No.

Mrs. Myers: Well ask him to play it.

Dr. F: Well, what I am wondering about is what you have learned from the family you came out of that you have tried to honor in your own family. What sorts of things did you hope your two sons would honor from your own experiences with family? What did you want to make sure that they did?

The therapist has just begun a major reframe. He has asked the mother to think about which lessons from her own family she has tried to pass on to her children. This line of questioning builds on positives. Rather than encouraging the mother to talk about what did not work in her family, the therapist has asked about her vision for her family. She is given the opportunity to choose an area that she can discuss with comfort. The therapist has made it safe for the mother to talk about areas of sadness that may have blocked her efforts to provide the type of family experiences that she wished for her sons. The theme of honoring one's family is important. When a parent is asked what he or she has taken from his or her own family as a way of honoring that family, he or she is able to discuss areas of disappointment or relative difficulty in a positive framework. The interview continues:

Mrs. Myers: You don't have enough time.

Dr. F: Well, why don't you start to tell me?

Mrs. Myers: No.

Dr. F: Do you know what your wife is referring to?

Mr. Myers: Well, the relationship has not been too good. Superficially it has been very good, but basically there have been ugly kinds of . . . She feels that there has been a lot of . . .

Mrs. Myers: Don't speak for me.

Mr. Myers: I'm not sure. It's been superficial. That's how we feel about it.

Dr. F: So you agree with that, or you have a different feeling?

Mr. Myers: No. We have the same feeling.

Dr. F: The same feeling.

Mr. Myers: Bob can hear this now. It's very seldom that either Bob or Sue (his ex-wife) ever say: "How are you feeling? How are you doing? What are your plans? How's your business? What are you going to do?" It's always "I, I, I," all the way. And there have been some very nasty incidents too. It isn't that we don't love them . . .

Dr. F: But that isn't how you planned it?

Mr. Myers: No, no.

Mrs. Myers: It's not the scenario we saw at this point.

Dr. F: That's what I was curious about. What your scenario was. How you planned it all when you started out.

Mr. Myers: Well, you plan it because they are moving away from home. Change makes planning impossible. There is nothing you can do. You can't direct anything. They don't know whether you are living or dead, unless you speak with them. You develop complete aloneness. It's the two of us against the world, and that's the way it's been. Expect nothing from them. I don't know what they expect from us, but that's how it's been.

Dr. F: For a while now?

Mr. Myers: Its been a distant, close relationship, if you can visualize what I mean.

Dr. F: Yes. I was wondering how different that is from how it was for you with your own family?

The mother has indicated that she is ambivalent about talking about her own family. When the therapist gets close to her pain and sadness, she responds with some distancing maneuver. The therapist avoids taking on the mother's need to distance head on and is able to ease her discomfort by not reacting to her ambivalence. Gradually, the mother's anger and resentment towards her own family and her husband's supportive, somewhat collusive behavior around their sadness begins to emerge.

The family is now moving into the middle phase of the interview. The parents have begun to relax. They are less defensive and accusatory and are more curious and willing to share some of their history. The parents have made several attempts to this point to involve their son in the interaction. The son has honored his commitment to avoid commenting on anything that his parents have said.

As the interview progresses, the parents up their ante and become more and more critical of their son and his children — their grandchildren. Bob is able to remain a silent observer, listening to his parents. As the parents realize Bob is not going to defend, accuse, or react to their comments, they relax and talk more freely about their sadness and anger towards their respective families-of-origin. They now have a platform to share their history. The interview continues with Mr. Myers talking about his family:

Mr. Myers: My parents?

Dr. F: Well, whatever you came out of. Was it different, or does it feel the same?

Mr. Myers: Well, we left home in a different kind of way. I had a very good family life.

Dr. F: If you think about your relationship with your father and your son's relationship with you, what is different and what is the same?
Mr. Myers: Oh, distance is one of them.
Dr. F: Did you stay physically close?
Mr. Myers: Physically, we stayed close until we married. We were still within the area. My mother died at an early age. She was only sixty-three.
Dr. F: She died first?
Mr. Myers: She died first. My father was close to eighty-four when he died.
Dr. F: So how many brothers and sisters?
Mr. Myers: I had two brothers and a sister. My older brother died last year. Unfortunately, we don't miss him one bit. He's no loss to society, or to us.

For the first time in the interview, one parent has been able to talk about his family without the other partner jumping in and adding information. The therapist can now proceed to ask each parent more detailed questions about his or her own family-of-origin. The therapist continues by asking Mr. Myers about the brother who recently died:

Dr. F: Was he the first-born in the family?
Mr. Myers: No, my sister.
Dr. F: Your sister was first-born, and then your brother?
Mr. Myers: Then my brother. Then I, and then a much younger brother. He was younger than I.
Dr. F: What happened to the brother who just died, who you said was no loss?
Mr. Myers: Well, he was married to somebody who kind of ruled the roost. She's been dying ever since 1940 or whatever, 1950 . . .
Dr. F: She's still alive?
Mr. Myers: Oh, yeah, and he's the one that died. It was a strange relationship. One incident with my brother, we were on our way to Japan. I had written three or four letters. I called him before we left. I told him precisely when we were coming back from Japan. We would stay at the Airport Hotel for one extra night, to meet us there. We got to the hotel; he wasn't there. We called, and he said, "Oh, I thought it was next week." He came to the hotel. We walked around the grounds. I took him to lunch. He went home, and that was it. So we said, "Well, forget him.
Dr. F: Was it always that way with him, or did this happen later in your life?
Mr. Myers: No, I think it was after Pittsburgh, wasn't it? In Pittsburgh, we were still friends, weren't we?

Mrs. Myers: Oh, he was smooth. He used to come down from Pittsburgh, and he would always say to my mother-in-law, "If it were earlier, I'd take you to a movie." And she would say, "Nobody is as thoughtful as my Garry."

Mr. Myers: He never took her to the movies though.

Mrs. Myers: He never took her to the movies.

Mr. Myers: I was a good son.

Mrs. Myers: "I'd love to take you out, Mother, but you look so tired, and it's so late." It was a family joke.

Mr. Myers: I was considered the good son. I'd be out driving the truck. I'd get a call, "Come home, Momma's sick." I was always believing Garry. Then she finally went into the hospital, and my sister down in North Carolina came up. "Oh, she can't stay in the hospital. Take her out of the hospital." Then it became my burden. She went back to North Carolina.

Dr. F: So you were the one that was more responsible?

Mr. Myers: I was the one. It was all on my shoulders at that time. I was in the Army. That was during the war.

Mrs. Myers: We both carried the burdens for both families.

Mrs. Myers' last statement is an important one and points to an area of unfinished business for both her and her husband. The therapist forms the hypothesis that their critical stance towards their sons and grandchildren has its origins in their feelings that they were somehow lacking in their families-of-origin. As the interview progresses, it becomes clear that neither Mr. nor Mrs. Myers received the love that they needed. Both of these parents tried desperately to make up for their own parents' losses. They felt that it was their responsibility to make their parents feel good in the world. Both parents reported that they failed in their attempts to make up for their parents' losses. As a result, they felt unloved and uncared for. This dynamic made it difficult for them to be objective about their own children's needs to leave the family and to develop their lives separately from their parents. These parents gave their children two messages, go out and be successful in the world, but stay near us and make us feel loved and special. It is important that the son understand the sense of burden his parents carried in relation to their own parents. He will then be able to understand his parents' criticism of him as having to do more with their own anxiety and sadness about their sense of failure around their own parents' losses than with any real disapproval of him. The interview continues with Dr. F acknowledging Mrs. Myers' statement about their carrying the burdens for their families:

Dr. F: For your own families.

Mr. Myers: Both families, yes. I mean, on the fifteen dollars a week we were both making, we had to give them money.

Dr. F: Did your father ever talk to you about that one before he died? Did he ever let you know that he recognized that effort on your part?

Mr. Myers: I don't think so.

Dr. F: No. Did you sense that he knew what you were trying to do in taking care of the family?

Mr. Myers: He probably did. When we were first married, we had a little car. My father had been in business, but he was stepping down you know, economically, financially, and he got a job as a presser. We would pick my mother up and go out and pick him up afterwards. We were always devoted to the family, Mother and Father, even against our will. We did it all the time. Her mother too.

Dr. F: Very strong family connections, eh?

Mr. Myers: At that time it was, yes.

Dr. F: When you thought about your own children, was this something you wanted to make sure you continued, this very strong sense of family?

The therapist is now carefully pacing the interview. It is important that he builds on the positives that the parents have mentioned. If he moves too quickly into focusing on the parents' pain, loss, and anger he could lose them and/or make them his clients. This is not the objective of the family-of-origin session. The major goal of this session is to encourage the parents to discuss their history and the lessons that they have learned from it in a structure that will foster new learning for their son. If the therapist's conduct of the interview leads to the parents feeling overwhelmed by their sadness and/or puts them into the client role, the therapist will have undermined the objective of this session. The therapist must strike a balance between questions about the lessons they have learned from what worked well in their families and what did not work so well. It is important for the therapist to highlight the positives and to maintain at all times a stance that is respectful towards the parents' efforts.

At this point in the interview, the therapist chooses to focus on the strong sense of family commitment that the parents have conveyed. He asks about how the parents tried to communicate the importance of family connections to their own children. He is reframing a sensitive area. Although the parents felt that their own parents should have been more supportive of their efforts, the therapist focuses on the positive aspects of the parents' efforts to connect with and to care for their families. The interview continues:

Mr. Myers: We would have. We had a sense of family till we moved. We always traveled.

Mrs. Myers: We had a sense of family long after they (the son's family) moved too. We would come here for the girls' birthdays.

Mr. Myers: Yeah, we were here quite often, but we traveled.

Mrs. Myers: That became a negative point.

Mr. Myers: But we traveled a lot when they were younger. We traveled together. We were a good family before.

Dr. F: Did it change after your boys got married? Did that make a difference?

Mr. Myers: I don't really know. It could have.

Mrs. Myers: Did what change?

Dr. F: The sense of closeness.

Mrs. Myers: No. We were very close with Bob and his wife. Very close.

Mr. Myers: And we were close to Joe and his wife too, Gail. They're divorced now but, in fact we're still close to Gail. We correspond with her, his divorced wife.

Mrs. Myers: When our relationship went downhill, I was devastated. I didn't have a clue what happened.

The mother has become more comfortable talking about her own sadness in her family. Her anxiety about moving too close is gone. She now wants to use the therapist as a way of connecting with her son. The therapist must be careful at this point not to let the interview focus on all the losses that have occurred in the family. He must keep the family strengths and the family losses in balance. The therapist responds to the mother by moving up a generation and asking her about what she learned from her own family. The approach allows the mother to talk about her vision of family without focusing primarily on her sadness about family losses. One of the goals of the therapist is to encourage the family members to build on their visions for the family. When a family member talks about how something in the past did not work well for the family, the therapist should reframe it by asking how he or she learned that it could be different. The interview continues with the focus on Mrs. Myers' own family-of-origin:

Dr. F: That's not something you experienced within your own family, anything like that?

Mrs. Myers: No. I was kind of detached from my family. I had growing pains, and they were working class people and were content with their lives. I was too young to appreciate other things at the time, so my sense of family became strongest when I had a family.

Dr. F: When you had your own children?

Mrs. Myers: Yes. And then our house became the place the family came to.

[This brief exchange provides a good example of how to move away from focusing on past losses by giving the mother an opportunity to talk about what she has learned in a positive sense from her family.]

Dr. F: How many brothers and sisters did you have?
Mrs. Myers: I had quite a few.
Dr. F: How large was the family?
Mrs. Myers: Five sisters and one brother.
Dr. F: And you were what age?
Mrs. Myers: The youngest.
Dr. F: The last-born.
Mr. Myers: The little brat.
Mrs. Myers: My parents were rather old when I was born. So I didn't fit into their scheme of things, and there wasn't very much communication at that point.

The therapist now focuses on the major events that occurred in the mother's developmental years. Her spirits lift, and she begins to tell the therapist a bit more of the family chronology. As she discusses the family history, it becomes clear that she has experienced a significant number of losses in her family-of-origin.

Dr. F: How old was your dad when you were born?
Mrs. Myers: He was fifty-three or fifty-four. I'm not sure. Somewhere around there. And my mother was thirty-eight. She was old. She really was.
Dr. F: How old was your father when he died?
Mrs. Myers: He was only about eighty-five, eighty-six.
Dr. F: Did he seem like a young fifty-three?
Mr. Myers: No. He was an old, sweet person.
Mrs. Myers: No, but he was a sweet person. A very kind, wonderful person.
Dr. F: Did your relationships change with your older siblings as you got older, or did you stay the youngest?
Mrs. Myers: They changed because I was a catalyst, if that's the word. I

was the connection really. They talked, but there was a great deal of anger in our family.

Mr. Myers: You're kidding.

Mrs. Myers: They talked with great anger. It got so that for me, as the youngest to be heard, my voice had to rise in crescendo to be heard, because they were very close. When I was born, one was eight, one was ten, one was twelve, fourteen, sixteen, and eighteen. So that . . .

Dr. F: So the closest to you in age would be eight years older?

Mr. Myers: That's not too many.

Dr. F: That's a lot. That's a lot of years.

Mrs. Myers: And then, as they got older, I had more parents than you could shake a stick at, cause everybody had something to say about me. And they didn't know how to handle me. I was very precocious at school, extremely bright. My mother could only think, you've got to work, you've got to learn a trade.

Dr. F: I would guess that your older siblings knew your grandparents?

Mrs. Myers: No.

Dr. F: They didn't know them either?

Mrs. Myers: All of us were born here.

Dr. F: And the age difference between the first born and you was how many years?

Mrs. Myers: Eighteen years, I guess.

Dr. F: Eighteen years.

Mrs. Myers: Well, he left the house first and married a woman that was rather difficult.

Mr. Myers: Demanding.

Mrs. Myers: Very self-centered. Very self-serving.

Dr. F: Was there a falling out between any of the siblings, such as your husband described with his brother?

Mrs. Myers: Oh, periodic. You know, they were angry.

Mr. Myers: But there were no break offs, like they would stop talking to each other.

Dr. F: No cutoffs?

Mr. Myers: I didn't cutoff with my brother. I would write the letters and I would call him, and he would say, "We'll make it but . . ."

Mrs. Myers: I don't remember it really, but if anybody did anything, I was the one to do it. My mother was not well, and their excuse for not doing anything for my mother was that they didn't have a car. My mother lived with one sister. They never spoke during the day to each other.

Dr. F: They lived together, but they didn't talk to each other?

Mrs. Myers: No. And then every Wednesday, when I took my mother out for the day, I knew I belonged in geriatrics then. I would have to listen to, "Nobody ever calls me." It took about half an hour to get her on track, and after that life was fine. I think that's what makes me unique in the work that I do. There isn't anybody who I have found who understands older people like I do. I was born into geriatrics.

We are now getting a sense of the mother's family and some of her sadness about what occurred in her family. Her statement that, "There isn't anybody who I have found who understands older people like I do. I was born into geriatrics" underscores a major area of unfinished business in her life. This statement can be viewed as saying, "I was born to take care of people, but there is no one to take care of me." The therapist reframes the mother's statement by highlighting what she has said about becoming an expert about old people. He asks her what her expertise has taught her about what old people need from their children and others in the world. By asking these questions in this way, the therapist creates an opportunity for the mother to teach her son about what she needs in order to feel safe in her relationship with him. The therapist highlights the positive nature of the mother's involvement with her mother, while at the same time giving her a chance to speak about her own needs without having to defend herself.

As the interview continues, Mrs. Myers' sense of being overwhelmed by her mother's needs emerges:

Dr. F: Almost from the beginning, you became an expert.
Mr. Myers: That's right.
Mrs. Myers: Absolutely, absolutely. It's a sixth sense about it, and everything I do is right.
Dr. F: Well, what is the secret? What is the best way to understand older people? To connect with them?
Mrs. Myers: Well, I always say, "There but for the grace of God go I." I'm sensitive. I'm sensitive to loneliness, and yet lonely for the most part. Lonely, bitter. Some are unusually sweet. I don't know why. I really don't. They do have good family support.
Dr. F: When you have someone who is angry or bitter or lonely, how do you connect with them?
Mrs. Myers: It's not easy, but I'm successful.
Dr. F: Is it just instinct, or . . .?
Mrs. Myers: Absolutely. I find I'm perceptive and intuitive. I find one positive thing and . . .
Dr. F: And you build on that?
Mrs. Myers: Build on that, yes. And every program that I do is the most successful. I had to turn down some people from a particular program because we had no room, simply had no room any more.

Dr. F: So you're working with geriatrics in the hospital?

Mrs. Myers: In a nursing home.

Dr. F: And how long have you been doing that?

Mrs. Myers: Almost eighteen years.

Dr. F: Oh, that's a long time. And before that?

Mrs. Myers: Not much, working for doctors.

Dr. F: When did you decide to specialize in working with old people?

Mrs. Myers: I always wanted to go into geriatrics, and an opportunity arose and I did. I became outstanding, and the lady who was responsible became furious with me, hated me, 'cause she said we could not do what I did.

Dr. F: How much do Joe and Bob know about that part of you?

Mrs. Myers: They never asked.

Dr. F: They don't know about that part of you?

Mrs. Myers: Oh, they may know, but they don't ask.

Dr. F: And if they don't ask, you tend not to talk?

Mrs. Myers: Not any more. I used to.

Dr. F: You used to try. This is a big part of your life, and you feel somehow there is no connection with your boys on this.

Mrs. Myers: Nothing. Charles and I have made a life for ourselves. We're independent and interdependent.

Mr. Myer: We have very few friends now.

Mrs. Myers: We're two facing the world, and that's it.

Mr. Myers: We have no family left.

Mrs. Myers: If we died, they wouldn't even know about it. They wouldn't. Except the call from one week to the other.

Mrs. Myers is beginning to talk more about her need to have someone take care of her. The therapist forms the hypothesis that she devoted herself to her mother in the hopes that her mother would recognize her efforts. When her mother failed to give her the recognition that she deserved, she turned to her son to meet those needs. The son did not feel up to this challenge, and consequently each felt deprived by the other. When the son is able to hear his mother's sadness about her own mother, he can begin to understand her criticism of him differently.

At this point in the interview the therapist begins to ask about the grandchildren. He is interested in seeing whether the mother is able to connect with her grandchildren differently from how she connects with her own children. What he discovers is that she also feels a tremendous loss about her lack of connection with her grandchildren. Her sense of being alone and uncared for in the world is quite profound. Again, if the son is able to understand the extent of his mother's sadness, without feeling defensive and reactive to her neediness, he will be able to find a way to connect with her rather than distance from her to make it emotionally safe for himself.

The interview continues with questions about the grandchildren:

Dr. F: How about your grandchildren?
Mrs. Myers: Oh, we don't hear from them. They're worse.
Mr. Myers: They're worse.
Mrs. Myers: They get angry when we tell them. I work in a situation where kids, some kids, dote on their grandparents.
Mr. Myers: We are never . . .
Mrs. Myers: Our seventieth birthday doesn't mean that much. I got flowers. That was pure guilt. Pure guilt. A collective bouquet of flowers. Didn't mean much to either of us.
Mr. Myers: Not once have Katie or Dana, in their entire lives, called us on their own. Not once.
Mrs. Myers: Or do they send birthday cards.
Mr. Myers: Birthday cards with the family signature.
Mrs. Myers: Their mother thinks that her card is enough to cover it.
Mr. Myers: And I've never heard of a family where grandchildren don't even once call up to see how you feel.
Dr. F: How often do you visit Vancouver?
Mr. Myers: We used to visit a lot. We were here once a year. We were here two years ago on our way to and from the Orient.
Mrs. Myers: If we hadn't gone to Asia, we wouldn't have been here. It's really not high on my list of priorities.
Dr. F: To visit?
Mrs. Myers: I did not want to come here. He wanted to.
Dr. F: How come you wanted to?
Mr. Myers: I don't mind coming here.
Mrs. Myers: He's not as disappointed or angry as I am.
Dr. F: You were going to tell me that you had a vision of how it was going to be.
Mrs. Myers: Even distance wouldn't make it otherwise.
Dr. F: You don't think distance should be a problem?
Mrs. Myers: No, I don't.
Mr. Myers: We know families with distant relatives, and they are contacted much better than us.

Emotions are running high at this part of the interview. The son in the family has had to listen to his mother and father criticize him and his children. If the therapist had not instructed the son prior to the interview to permit his parents to talk without interruption, there would have been an explosion at this point. The son would have defended himself and tried to justify his children's behavior towards their grandparents. Because the therapist had emphasized to the son that he did not have to defend himself or other members of his family, he was able to develop a bit more detachment and become curious about how his parents developed their attitudes towards him and his children. It is extremely helpful when sessions such as these are videotaped so the adult child can watch it later. This material is very difficult to listen to without becoming reactive. Even when the son's attempts to jump in and justify himself have been blocked, his agitation at hearing his parents' criticism of his efforts to be a loving son will distort what he hears them talking about. The critical point is that the son remembers that the parents are not really talking about his children or himself but about their own losses and sadness. This is a clear example of unfinished business.

The degree to which the parents feel that they were not taken care of, loved, and made to feel special in their own families determines the degree of neediness they will bring into their family-of-procreation. Their high expectations for their grandchildren and their own children resulted in their having the same feelings that they experienced in their families-of-origin. Whatever their son or grandchildren did, it was never quite enough to make up for the initial losses. It is important that the son understand this basic principle and move on from there to find areas to connect on with his parents rather than increase the distance between them.

The therapist now moves away from this explosive area and brings back into focus the parents attempts to work on family connections:

Dr. F: I would imagine that there was a message you tried to communicate to your two boys about the importance of family.
Mrs. Myers: We always had family.
Dr. F: What was that message about the importance of family that you tried to get them to think about?
Mr. Myers: We didn't make any special direction on that.
Dr. F: But how come? How come you didn't?
Mr. Myers: It was automatic. The family was the family and that's how it was until they moved away. Perhaps if they stayed in the city we might have had a closer relationship. Most likely we would have. But once they moved . . .
Mrs. Myers: But I don't think that was it.
Mr. Myers: You know distance had a lot to do with it.
Mrs. Myers: It has some to do with it . . .

Mr. Myers: But it also has to do with their personal values.

Mrs. Myers: But we were very close when they first moved out West.

Mr. Myers: Yes. San Francisco too.

Mrs. Myers: Yes.

Dr. F: Do you think it would have been different if you had had a daughter?

Mrs. Myers: No.

Mr. Myers: No. I don't think it makes any difference.

Dr. F: Do you think daughters stay more connected with family?

Mr. Myers: No, I don't believe that.

Dr. F: You've heard that one though?

Mr. Myers: Yes, but I don't know about it.

Mrs. Myers: I've heard it, and I resent it because I think children are children and it has nothing to do with sex. I've seen parents who have miserable situations with daughters. No, I don't believe that at all. I wanted sons. I really did. I thought they were very special. Bob was very special.

Dr. F: What was special about him?

Mrs. Myers: He was so cute, and he was bright and, um, I don't know. He was the first, and I just adored him for years and . . .

Mr. Myers: Bob never minded going anywhere with us. In fact, he was very close.

Mrs. Myers: But we have not been friends for a long time. Friendly for a long, long time.

Dr. F: What would have to change for you to feel that that was happening? What would have to be different?

Mrs. Myers: That's a big question.

Dr. F: What would it look like?

Mrs. Myers: I don't know because so much has . . . We've lived this lifestyle now for such a long time, and I tend to hold grudges. I do. And it hurt so much.

Mr. Myers: Bob has heard this before. We've told him already.

Mrs. Myers: He doesn't like to hear it.

Mr. Myers: No, but we've told him on the phone. Look we have no family. You live there. We live here. We're together. It's not the first time he's heard this. So that he knows.

Mrs. Myers: I mean they lived in Minneapolis. I had a sixty-fifth birthday. It was too much effort to put a candle in a cake to say happy birthday.

Dr. F: If Bob wanted to have a different relationship now, how hard would it be for you to be different with him?

Mrs. Myers: That would be harder on him. Absolutely.

Dr. F: Could you explain that? What do you mean by that?

Mrs. Myers: He would have to prove it and be very sincere about it. I am no longer given to travelogues. He's no different from his uncle. I'm tired of hearing, when I say, "Bob, how are you?" how busy he is, and how much he's got to do. So he's going to have to work very much harder. This is where I'm at, and it's hard for me to change.

Dr. F: So that work . . .

Mrs. Myers: And frankly, I don't want to change. I don't think I did anything that was so terrible.

The therapist is encouraging the mother to talk about her vision for her family. He uses her last comment about not wanting to change as an opening for joining with her. He agrees with her that she has done her best, all things considered. This message is an important one for parents to hear. When they participate in a family-of-origin session, they often feel that they will be blamed for family problems. They should hear from the therapist that he recognizes their efforts. The adult children in the family must assume some responsibility for change. The burden should not rest on the parents.

The interview continues with the therapist supporting the mother:

Dr. F: You shouldn't have to change. Mothers and fathers don't have to change. It's the adult child's work. It's not the parents' work.

Mrs. Myers: He's a big boy now.

Mr. Myers: How long can you blame your parents?

Mrs. Myers: That's right.

Mr. Myers: You become parents . . .

Mrs. Myers: That's right, and they can't go on blaming us forever.

Dr. F: But what would that look like? What would that change look like? What would have to happen for you to say to yourself, "Hey, there is a change here"?

Mrs. Myers: I don't know. I mean that's abstract. I don't know. I would have to see it.

Dr. F: Do you think you would recognize it if there were a change?

Mrs. Myers: I'm very bright.

Dr. F: You think you could.

Mrs. Myers: I'm very sharp and sensitive, and Bob is sensitive. He comes by it easily.

Dr. F: How hard do you think it would be?

Mrs. Myers: For him?

Dr. F: No. For Bob and his mother to have a different relationship. How hard do you think it would be?

Mr. Myers: It won't be easy. Bob would have to work awfully hard at it.

Dr. F: What would he have to do to make that relationship different?

Mr. Myers: What would he have to do?

Dr. F: Yes. If you were Bob, what would you do to make that one different?

Mr. Myers: At this point I really don't know. He's so involved in the work he's doing.

Dr. F: Let's just say he decided he wanted to make it different. What would he have to do? What would have to be different for it to feel different? I'm really puzzled on that one.

Mrs. Myers: That's Bob's problem, not mine.

Mr. Myers: No, I understand what he means. He wants to . . .

Mrs. Myers: Yes, I know. I know.

Mr. Myers: He wants what we would expect from Bob to make it easier.

Mrs. Myers: I understood the question.

Mr. Myers: I know, but I don't know how he would do it.

Mrs. Myers: Bob told his father not long ago, this was really funny to hear, that he was going to take care of us in our old age. We don't need the money. Any caring, if somebody's really interested, he never remembers from one time to the other. If I say I have a very bad cold, I had a infection of the nose for three months; I took tablets. I don't think Bob remembered. Now what shocks me, because I can't even believe this, it's an injustice to Joe, is that he remembers. Bob may not like to hear this, it's true. So I once told him, "Bob you don't even ask me how my cold is because you don't even know I have a cold to begin with."

Dr. F: How much family do you have left?

Mrs. Myers: Well, we are very fortunate. We have a few nephews and nieces. We're surrogate parents to them and good friends, and they are my family.

Dr. F: Do you have any siblings left?

Mr. Myers: None at all.

Mrs. Myers: They have all died.

Mr. Myers: All died, a long time.

Mrs. Myers: It was very interesting. Bob never called me to make a comment when they died, to say I'm sorry. He wrote letters to everybody else, but he has never sent letters to me in seven, ten years, maybe. I don't remember.

Mr. Myers: Frank died after Sarah. And Aunt Miriam, Beth's sister died three years ago.

Mrs. Myers: Two and a half years ago.

Dr. F: That was the last one. Two and a half years ago.

Mrs. Myers: I never got a note.

Mr. Myers: No. In that respect they never showed any interest in any of the family. Except Bob took a very big dislike to my brother in Oregon. I guess it was justifiable.

Dr. F: So you've lost one sibling?

Mr. Myers: Last year.

Dr. F: Even though there was a strain between you and your brother, do you think it changed things in the family when he died?

Mrs. Myers: Not at all.

Mr. Myers: It was as if he never existed. My sister is semireligious, and the brother who died became a Christian. He died as a Christian. He was cremated as a Christian, so she refused to sit Shivas because he was not Jewish. She was hurt more than we were. But I don't think so. Like I say, he never called me. It's like he never existed.

Dr. F: Your mother was the first one who died in your family?

Mr. Myers: In our immediate family? Yes.

Dr. F: How did that change the family?

Mr. Myers: Not especially.

Dr. F: Your father didn't remarry?

Mr. Myers: No. My father was a selfish loner.

Dr. F: Did he became more alone?

Mr. Myers: No. He lived with us for a while and then with my brother, and he lived with my sister mostly. When they moved to the South, he went with them.

Dr. F: He moved around.

Mr. Myers: And he was a surrogate parent to my sister's son. They spent all their time in the movies.

Dr. F: What role did your sister play in the family, as the only girl in the family?

Mr. Myers: Boss lady.

Dr. F: Boss lady. How did she do that?

Mrs. Myers: Well, she's not right, but she tries to assume the rights of a parent.

Dr. F: She's a good parent?

Mrs. Myers: And she does have wonderful children and a super relationship with her children.

Mr. Myers: Her children are very, very close.

Mrs. Myers: I don't know what she's done, but something very good.

Mr. Myers: She lives in California. Her daughter and son live in California. And the other daughter, with whom we're very friendly, lives nearby

to us. So I have one niece, and Beth has one niece, one nephew and another nephew, and that's the whole of it.
Mrs. Myers: I have one nephew and his wife.
Dr. F: So the nephews become important.
Mr. Myers: Very important. They're our family to us. They're our children and our relatives.
Mrs. Myers: In fact, I have to make a phone call if one has a birthday.
Dr. F: Well, when your father died, how old were you?
Mr. Myers: When did Dad die?
Mrs. Myers: Your mother died right after the war, '45. Your father died in '58.
Mr. Myers: '58. I was forty-seven.
Dr. F: You were two years older than Bob is now.
Mr. Myers: Yes.
Dr. F: What changed for you when your dad died?
Mr. Myers: Nothing changed. He didn't live here. He lived in the South.
Dr. F: How about the idea that he was no longer available to you?
Mr. Myers: Not too much changed.
Dr. F: What was left unfinished between you and your dad that you wish you had dealt with?
Mr. Myers: Nothing.
Dr. F: And your sister? Do you think she has the same feeling as you?
Mr. Myers: She was probably even more sensitive about those things than I am, but she lost a housekeeper when he died.
Dr. F: I would imagine you would want to have a relationship with Bob and Joe different from, or maybe in some way similar to, the one you had with your dad. How would you want your relationship with your sons to be different from yours with your dad?

The therapist has encouraged the parents to talk about their own loss of family. They have revealed that they were not involved with their own siblings. Basically they felt cut off from their families-of-origin. The therapist has encouraged the parents to talk about their lack of connection with their own siblings and extended families and has moved from this to a discussion of how they would like their relationships with their sons to be different.

One of the goals of the family-of-origin session is to encourage ongoing connection between family members. The task of the therapist is to help family members to better understand how their past hurts, injuries and/or myths about each other have blocked their potential for reconnecting with each other at a deeper level. The therapist now encourages the family members to consider what has not worked well for them in the past and to use those lessons as a framework for behaving differently in the future.

The interview continues with Mr. Myers responding to questions about his relationships with his sons:

Mr. Myers: At this age?

Dr. F: Yes. At this age.

Mr. Myers: Well, I'd like to be closer to them.

Dr. F: Closer than you were to your dad?

Mr. Myers: Yes. Oh, we were close in a way, but there was not too much communication, because he was quite self-centered.

Dr. F: I think it's an important question. It's one we don't really talk much about. What was that closeness like? The only model we have is the model with our own parents. So what would that closeness between you and Bob look like as compared to what you had with your own dad? How would you know you were closer to your son? What would have to happen?

Mr. Myers: More personal phone calls instead of travelogues.

Dr. F: And how would you know it was more personal? What would have to be talked about to give it that feeling?

Mr. Myers: Things family like to talk about. Father and son. How do you feel? What are you doing? When are you getting out of your business? When are you retiring? When are you going to go bankrupt? That kind of stuff.

Dr. F: Those personal questions.

Mr. Myers: That's all. And those are the things we never hear.

Dr. F: For them to be more curious about what's happening in your life would give it more feeling? And for you to be able to be more curious about what is happening in Bob's life?

Mr. Myers: I think so. We know very little about Bob's personal life.

Dr. F: So it's that sort of thing, a sense of a deeper connection. I imagine from what you're saying that that didn't happen between you and your dad. The two of you didn't talk that much later in his life.

Mr. Myers: No, we didn't communicate too much. He lived, as I say, in the South. He died in the South.

Mrs. Myers: He lived with us.

Mr. Myers: He lived with us, he would . . .

Mrs. Myers: Harold didn't have any closeness. I would get into trouble.

Mr. Myers: He would do his own thing, more or less.

Dr. F: But you were saying that physical distance doesn't have to mean that you feel disconnected.

Mr. Myers: That's right.

Dr. F: So even though your father was in the South, things could have been different if you had felt more connected with him? If he were different with you, would you have been different with him? Here's an interesting question for you. Which one of you could have made a difference?

Mr. Myers: He couldn't change. This wasn't something he was doing voluntarily. It was an involuntary action on his part. He was always the taker not the giver.

Dr. F: You gave up on your dad?

Mr. Myers: No, I just accepted him for what he was.

Dr. F: Do you think you could have made something happen that would have been different between you and your dad if you had worked at it?

Mr. Myers: No. Absolutely not.

Dr. F: Do you think Bob could have?

Mr. Myers: Bob could, yeah.

Dr. F: So what's different with you?

Mr. Myers: Different caliber.

Dr. F: You're different from your dad?

Mr. Myers: I sure hope so.

Dr. F: So you think if Bob put some effort into it, there could be a different relationship; but if you had put some effort into it with your dad, there could not have been?

Mr. Myers: It would not have made any difference.

Mrs. Myers: It's true.

Dr. F: How hard did you try with your dad?

Mr. Myers: I didn't try one way or the other.

Mrs. Myers: I tried.

Dr. F: You tried. When did you stop trying with your dad? At what age do you think you stopped trying?

Mr. Myers: I really don't know, I can't give you an answer.

Mrs. Myers: I tried, but I gave up because it was. . . .

Dr. F: But he was your father-in-law.

Mrs. Myers: Yes. He lived in my house. Harold would read the newspaper and he'd make statements like, "I once saved Charles from falling out the window. He should take care of me for the rest of my life."

Mr. Myers: That's me.

Mrs. Myers: Charles would say, "Listen, doesn't every parent do that?" But I always sensed that he was alone. So if he made a comment I would answer. And then I would get into trouble because he was not the brightest of people and he was very difficult to reach. And then I would suffer for it, but I felt I had to answer. Everybody ought to have an answer. Everybody should get an answer, so I would get into trouble.

Mr. Myers: My father did not . . .

Mrs. Myers: Not so much with him as much as with myself.

Mr. Myers: In our early life, when I was first born up until about 1918, 1919, we had a fairly comfortable economic life. My mother and father would go to the opera. They loved music and the symphony. Then his fortunes went down after the war. He kept getting poorer and poorer and still poorer. And then he became a nothing.

Dr. F: How did that change your mother's relationship with him?

Mr. Myers: I don't know anything about them, that part.

Dr. F: Was he different with you and your brothers and sister as he became more preoccupied with this change?

Mr. Myers: I don't think so.

Mrs. Myers: He was very Germanic, and with that goes Germanic culture. The father is up there, and children have to do what the father says. There never was a closeness. I don't think there ever was.

Mr. Myers: My mother was much more of the doer than my father was. My father was content to sit at home and do nothing. She was the one who liked to be on the go. She couldn't do it too well.

Dr. F: She made things happen more?

Mr. Myers: Yeah.

Dr. F: Let me ask you the same question. I'm really curious about who can make change happen in the family. When your dad died, what changed in the family?

Mrs. Myers: Very little. Very little because my mother had relegated my father to . . .

Mr. Myers: Nothingness.

Mrs. Myers: Nothingness.

Dr. F: The sidelines.

Mrs. Myers: I adored my father. He never was a breadwinner to my mother. And my mother did rule the roost. And the things I hate in myself are the things that my mother had, some of those things. But I didn't get mad at my mother. I find I'm stuck with some of them. But very little. My mother tried to keep the family together but she had a way of creating dissension. Because we were more affluent, she would manage to take from us to give to the others, without our permission of course. It was a little devious and underhanded, and something that I don't look favorably upon. Yet, she made her presence felt for sure.

At this stage of the interview, the therapist has focused primarily on the father and his relationships with his extended family. The therapist has tried to reframe the father's disappointments as lessons that he could use to begin to make some changes in his family-of-procreation. The therapist now shifts the focus to the mother and goes through the same process with her. The son has had an opportunity to listen to both parents and gain some ideas about how he can begin to connect differently with them and with his own children. The interview continues with the focus on Mrs. Myers:

Dr. F: How old were you when your dad died?
Mrs. Myers: Oh, about thirty. And my mother died about seventeen years ago. She was ninety-four.
Dr. F: How old were you then?
Mrs. Myers: Fifty-six.
Dr. F: What did you want to make different with your mother before she died?
Mrs. Myers: Oh, I tried very hard. We did effect some changes. My mother used to say it wasn't stylish to kiss children when you were little, but we would always kiss her upon greeting her. We got her to drink French wine.
Dr. F: Who was the "we," the two of you?
Mr. Myers: We changed her life style completely.
Mrs. Myers: Oh, "we" did.
Dr. F: You really worked on it.
Mrs. Myers: I really did.
Mr. Myers: It wasn't difficult to make her do things the way we wanted her to.
Dr. F: But you had to work on it?
Mrs. Myers: Yes.
Dr. F: She wouldn't have done it?
Mrs. Myers: Oh, no.
Mr. Myers: She would have lived like the other sisters.
Mrs. Myers: They were very much alike, so I had very little to do. But I had this sense of family.
Dr. F: Did you have the holidays at your house?
Mrs. Myers: No.
Dr. F: Passover. Who would do that?
Mrs. Myers: Nobody in my family would invite us. Now there was another story, but that didn't bother us.
Dr. F: But your mother, would she spend Passover with you?

Mrs. Myers: No.

Mr. Myers: No. Alice wasn't kosher.

Mrs. Myers: But we'd make Thanksgiving. There were other occasions, Mother's Day.

Mr. Myers: But we never in all our married life, had one dinner in any of her sisters' homes.

Dr. F: Not one?

Mr. Myers: Not one! We had them over quite frequently. Can you believe that?

Dr. F: It's unusual.

Mrs. Myers: Yeah, it is. It was too much for her.

Dr. F: But you did work on trying to make it different with your mother. I sure get that picture of you.

Mr. Myers: Oh, she was a wonderful daughter. The others were the talkers and she was the doer. Every week she would take her mother out somewhere.

Dr. F: So you know from your experience that if the adult child wants to make something different with parents, it can happen? From your own experience?

Mrs. Myers: Oh, absolutely.

Dr. F: You weren't able to do that with your dad?

Mrs. Myers: It was very interesting. Bob came to Rhode Island with a tape recorder, went to see his uncle, spoke to his father. I really wanted to put no input in that because I was so angry. He sat back as a clinician saying, "Oh, its interesting that you not only took care of your parents but here you worked taking care of your children." I don't think Bob was ever interested in our family. They were not middle class. They were working class people for the most part. Katie (Bob's daughter) came too. She went to a birthday party that Bob created for his father, and she kind of got in a few snide remarks. Her attitude was, "Oh, but look who they are," overlooking the fact that these people are good and kind and can be called on whenever. I mean, she was a snob about it and I resented it. I was quite annoyed. I . . .

Dr. F: What are you most proud of having been able to accomplish with your mother before she died?

The therapist is now guiding the family towards the end of the session. It is important that he end the session on a positive note. He deflects the criticism of the granddaughter. His concluding efforts are directed at a major reframe. He encourages the parents to reflect on their history and the lessons that they have learned from it. He encourages each of them to talk about those parts of their history that they feel most solid about and those areas they still would like to make peace with. He asks about changes that have occurred over the years, how these changes have affected them, and the impact of these changes on their families-of-procreation. He concludes the session by giving both parents an opportunity to explain how much of their own families they still carry with them.

The interview continues:

Mrs. Myers: Oh, I opened a whole new world for her.

Dr. F: That's what you are most proud of?

Mrs. Myers: She never would have experienced that. I would take her out every Wednesday, and sometimes another day. She had gone to museums, which she never, I mean, she was in awe. We would take her to restaurants, and we did, Bob knows that.

Dr. F: That's what you feel you're really happy about.

Mrs. Myers: Yes. That I was exposing her to another life, trying to bring some happiness into her life.

Dr. F: What changed for you when your mother died?

Mrs. Myers: Well, about the following week, I went to work in geriatrics. I told her often, not that I wasn't angry with her, I was a great deal, because I thought that I was a patsy for her often. She used us, but . . .

Dr. F: The following week you went to work though. Your mother died seventeen years ago. When did Bob move away? How long ago?

Mrs. Myers: Oh, long before that.

Dr. F: How many years before your mother died did Bob move here?

Mr. Myers: It was a birthday in the fifties. In the late fifties.

Mrs. Myers: Oh, they were living here when my mother died.

Mr. Myers: They went to Oregon in '62.

Mrs. Myers: When my mother died, they were living here, and Bob didn't come to the funeral.

Dr. F: Joe was still at home?

Mrs. Myers: Oh, no.

Dr. F: He was gone too?

Mrs. Myers: He was away at school.

Dr. F: What did you notice about your wife after her mother died? What changed in your part of the family?

Mr. Myers: There wasn't much change.

Dr. F: You didn't notice much change?

Mr. Myers: No. Because life had to go on, and it did. The only thing is she didn't have any obligation to know that she has to take mother out once a week or whatever. I did miss the phone calls though.

Mrs. Myers: I did that with the sister who died two years ago, who had two children.
Dr. F: The two of you did that together with your mother?
Mrs. Myers: Oh, yes, mostly.
Dr. F: You were devoted to your mother. You were devoted to her in your own way.

The therapist has asked about the impact of the mother's death on Mrs. Myers. He has encouraged both Mr. and Mrs. Myers to be reflective about how her mother's death changed the family. This subject opens up an area of extreme sadness for Mrs. Myers. As the interview continues, the mother reveals that she felt like an unwanted child. She tells of her mother's reminding her that she tried to abort her. This powerful story is at the heart of the mother's unfinished business in her own family. The central theme for the mother is that she never should have been born. The therapist's hypothesis is that she tried to prove to her mother that she deserved to be born yet never felt her mother was happy with her. The father joins with the mother by telling her that she tried her best to love her mother and was the only one who was good to her. It becomes clear to the therapist that the husband tried to make up for what his wife's mother was not able to give her. This touching part of the interview deals with the whole history of loss, rejection, and unfinished business. The therapist allows this history to unfold, as it is important for the son to understand the deep sense of loss and sadness of his mother and the efforts of his father to make up for it. Given the mother's history, it doesn't take much behavior on the part of the son to stir up feelings in the mother that she is not enough. When the son begins to understand this theme, he can be less reactive to his mother's anxiety and sadness, which she expresses by criticizing him for not being "a good son."

The interview continues with Mrs. Myers talking about feeling unwanted:

Mrs. Myers: Well, I was the unwanted child. My mother used to remind me. She once said, "I didn't take enough poison so here you are." And I was a little girl looking for the mother who loved me.
Mr. Myers: And she was the only one who was good to their mother.
Dr. F: How did she recognize that before she died?
Mrs. Myers: I don't know. Did she?
Mr. Myers: She sent us back some money, once.
Dr. F: I mean, do you feel that she communicated to you in some way that she recognized your devotion, your care, your loyalty?
Mrs. Myers: I don't know.

Dr. F: How did she get that across to you?

Mrs. Myers: I think she was pleasant by the end of the day.

Mr. Myers: She bought us presents. She gave us money.

Mrs. Myers: Because she had given everybody else money and when I found out, I was furious.

Dr. F: What did she do to make you feel special?

Mrs. Myers: Nothing.

Mr. Myers: Nothing. She really didn't know how.

Mrs. Myers: Really, nothing. But I was, in essence, the little girl wanting to be loved, trying to ingratiate herself with her mother and . . .

Dr. F: Did any of your sisters tell you that they appreciated what you tried to do with Mum?

Mrs. Myers: Oh, of course not. They were there every . . .

Mr. Myers: They wouldn't tell her but they were very glad that she did it.

Mrs. Myers: Not one ever said . . .

Mr. Myers: It took the burden off all of them.

Mrs. Myers: When I said, "Why don't you take her out for a cup of coffee some time?" "How can we take her out for coffee? We don't have a car." I mean, one walk to the corner.

The therapist now attempts to put a positive connotation on the mother's behavior towards her own mother. He emphasizes that she tried to do her best and that it is important that she recognize her efforts in spite of not hearing from her mother that she was "enough."

The interview continues:

Dr. F: But you feel solid about what you tried to do?

Mrs. Myers: Oh, absolutely. No guilt.

Mr. Myers: Absolutely not.

Dr. F: You made peace with that one.

Mrs. Myers: Absolutely. In every way.

Mr. Myers: It would have been nice to hear.

Dr. F: Did your husband tell you how good you were with your mother?

Mrs. Myers: Oh, all the time. He thanks me. In his own way, he's special.

Mr. Myers: She has nothing to worry about from me.

Mrs. Myers: Oh, he was unusual.

Dr. F: He'd be supportive.

Mr. Myers: Oh, I was very good to her. Much better to her than her own children.

Mrs. Myers: But I was supportive of his parents. We had this thing. My mother never paid me a compliment. When I say not ever, I mean never.

One day she came over, and she said, "I was talking to Mrs. Smith, and there she was boasting about her daughter." And I said, "Did you tell her about me?" because I was one of the precocious little kids who just came waltzing from school. And she said, "No, why should I have told her . . ."

Mr. Myers: It's not nice to boast.

Mrs. Myers: And you know, I think a lot of her friends were not that competitive because my mother was not competitive. Not only wasn't she competitive, but she made it an all time crime to be competitive. To be competitive was terrible. So these things affected me, and I said, "I will never do that to my children." Joe used to say, "Oh, you're so conceited for your children," and that was a complaint because I praised their efforts.

Dr. F: You tried to do it differently from how your mother did it.

Mrs. Myers: Oh, for sure.

Dr. F: But they didn't understand that you tried to give them some of the things that you didn't get from your mother? You tried to make things happen for them differently?

Mrs. Myers: Oh, for sure. Obviously. We talked about this yesterday. I was furious. I'm telling a story. Charles asked if it was Pete, and I said no, it was some kid that I didn't know. They (her grandchildren) giggled, and it infuriated me. It's insensitive. It's rude. The next night they giggled and brought it up, which infuriated me. They've done this over the years, and at this point I don't care. If I don't see them, it doesn't matter. I always say to friends of mine, "I have the greatest grandchildren. They're beautiful. They're terrific. I never see them." So it doesn't matter who they are or what they are. We don't take the pride that we would have. They've given us no reason. Oh, they take from us. They give nothing.

Dr. F: We are going to have to stop.

The interview is now concluding. The therapist tries to reframe the parents' losses as a positive vision. Although he attempts to end the interview on a positive note the mother is quite angry about certain family events and is highly sensitive to perceived slights from her children and grandchildren. This interview does not dispel all the old hurts. However, it does foster a better understanding of some of the parents' reactions. The mother has a need to continue talking about some of her hurts. The therapist permits her to ventilate her hurts without reacting to her. He makes it safe for her to be able to talk about her own neediness without feeling diminished in any way.

The interview continues:

Mrs. Myers: I think Bob should do that. Bob has been a passive father for a long, long time. His wife was furious one day when Charles said, "Why don't the kids send birthday cards?" She got so angry. "Well, I sent one from the family." They're big girls now. They are really big girls. I don't want a thank you note because I gave them a birthday present but there are other times in the year. The only reason they get a check for their birthdays is because I do it. Because I could not cope with it any other way. He doesn't want to send them a check. He's up to not even sending them a birthday card.

Mr. Myers: But I don't know which is right, so we send it.

Mrs. Myers: I can't handle it.

Dr. F: Well, you know I'm happy that you came today, I think what both of you have said is very important. And I think it's very important that Bob finds the opportunity to sit back and listen to what you've said and to think about it. Maybe to hear it in a little different way. So, I think the tape is a treasure in some ways.

Mr. Myers: And I think it's good we came because these are the things we might probably never be able to talk about to Bob that we talked about today.

The therapist has concluded by commenting briefly on the importance of the family-of-origin interview. He defines the son's passive role as a way for him to learn more about the family. The father's closing comments are a good indication that the therapist has accomplished his goals. The therapist has guided the parents through their three generational histories. The son, by adopting the listening role, had the opportunity to listen to his parents' pain, grief, and sadness without becoming anxious, defensive, and reactive. If the therapist had permitted the son to intervene at any time during the interview, it is likely the learning potential would have been significantly decreased.

When the son next saw the therapist, he reported he had been quite touched by his parents' stories. When he listened to the videotape he heard many things he had missed during the session. The only time that he had had difficulty honoring his promise to remain silent was when his parents criticized his children. He was stopped from jumping in and defending his children only by his promise. The son also revealed to the therapist that it had been difficult for him to listen to his parents. However, he discovered that the passive, observant role allowed him to hear things that he had distorted and overreacted to throughout most of his life. He had not been aware of the depth of his parents' sadness and sense of loss about their own families-of-origin. He began to realize that no amount of effort on his part could compensate for this loss and sadness, but that this knowledge should not stop him from connecting with them and staying actively involved with them. He was able to recognize that letting go of his need for his parents to be different actually allowed him to enjoy them without becoming reactive to their criticism and anxiety.

SECTION SIX:
ENDING THE MIDDLE PHASE
WITH PARENTS AND THE ADULT CHILD:
CASE ILLUSTRATION AND COMMENTARY

The next interview illustrates family-of-origin work with an adult child who is in a proactive position. She has worked through many issues with her extended family and no longer needs to distance to feel emotionally safe. Her motivation to involve her aged parents was to consolidate the gains she had made in therapy. The following interview took place at the end of the middle phase of the family therapy. At this point in therapy, the therapist loosens up on the structure of having the parents talk through him to the adult child. He encourages the adult child to ask the parents questions about the family history and, generally, allows for greater interaction between the parents and adult child. Before proceeding with this structure, the therapist should be certain that the adult child is in the proactive phase. If the adult child tries in any way to prove her history and/or be validated by the parents, the interview will not be a positive experience for her or the parents. In contrast, if the adult child has become curious about her parents as people, then she will ask questions that encourage her parents to elaborate on their history in a nondefensive way.

There is less commentary on the following interview. The process is clear. It provides an example of an adult child asking her parents about those aspects of the family history that she is still a little confused about. The therapist begins the session by asking the adult child, Sandra, what she has told her parents about coming to the session. If Sandra were in a reactive phase her response to this question would likely have elicited some type of critical statement about her parents. However, Sandra has progressed to the proactive phase and reveals that she would like to ask her parents about the time she and her three sisters entered a convent. She also wants to ask her parents whether they were disappointed in her when she decided to return home.

The interview begins:

Dr. F: What have you told your folks about coming here?

Sandra: A little bit about what we've been doing. I told them about Paul Senior being here, etc.

Dr F: I thought it was very, very helpful to meet Paul's father. Sandra said, "If Paul's father can come, then I want my parents to come."

Mrs. L: Well, she wouldn't let anyone beat her. That's for sure.

Dr. F: I think maybe a good way to start, Sandra, is for you to ask your folks some questions.

Sandra: Oh, I haven't even thought of where I would start. I suppose the one thing that was talked about the last time we were here with you, and that I thought I would ask about, was when we were all growing up and sort of, one by one, left home. I'm thinking of the four girls and when we entered the convent. I guess, I wonder how you saw that, or what that meant to you, to both of you. I don't know if you were happy about us leaving home. I mean, it was a little strange for four of us to enter the convent.

Mr. L: Yeah. Well, if you ask me, I would say at the moment we were very lonesome and still delighted to think that you were going into the convent. You know, maybe it was something about the order. Apart from that we were lonesome to see you gone. That would be my answer.

Mrs L: I don't know, Pa. They were very young. I'd like to have seen them stay home a little longer, you know, because there wasn't any of them over sixteen or seventeen.

Mr. L: Just thought they should be more mature before they started out.

Mrs. L: But I didn't like to stop them because I didn't think that was the thing to do. They seemed to want to go and . . .

Dr. F: Whose idea was it for them to go?

Mrs. L: The girls.

Dr. F: The girls themselves said they wanted to go?

Mrs. L: Our oldest daughter. From what I thought, maybe she might be thinking about going, but I hadn't never mentioned it to her, and one of the neighbors said, "I hear your daughter is entering the convent." Boy, that's news to me.

Dr. F: Because she hadn't talked to you about it first?

Mrs. L: Hadn't talked to me at all about it. I never mentioned it to her then. I never told her.

Mr. L: There was a lady who was the supervisor at the Bell Telephone. She called up one morning and said, "I want to see Gail this afternoon." Am I right?

Mrs. L: Yes. She put in her application there for the holidays to work for them, and it was so hard to get in . . .

Mr. L: So, I guess Gail was out at the time. And then she came home, and we told her about it, that some Mrs. Smith had contacted her and said they'd like to interview her and that they will have a job for her at the Bell Telephone. And Gail says "I don't think I'll want any job at the Bell Telephone, Mother. I'm think I'm going to enter the convent." And oh, Mother was quite surprised, and of course, I was very surprised too.

Mrs. L: Not really.

Mr. L: Surprised because I knew there was something a little different about that girl. She was so genuine.

Sandra: Special.

Mr. L: She was special.

Mrs. L: We thought she was special.

Dr. F: When the four girls went, did any of the children stay? Were the boys at home?

Mrs. L: No, the boys were still at home.

Mr. L: Two boys.

Dr. F: They were still at home?

Sandra: But they were both married by the time I went away.

Mrs. L: No, they just got married before you went away.

Sandra: That's right. By the time the four of us went away, then everyone was out of the house.

Mrs. L: Yes.

Dr. F: So no adult children.

Mrs. L: No children.

Dr. F: So that was the first time, I guess, for the two of you to be alone in a long, long time?

Mrs. L: Yes, and there wasn't much visiting when they were in the convent. You know, they don't get home very often.

Dr. F: At what age do you think it would have been better for the girls to have left?

Mrs. L: Well, now they wouldn't take them at that age. I would think if they were twenty, or twenty-one, they would have made it in.

Mr. L: I think they should have been twenty, twenty-one, around that age.

Sandra: Were you disappointed when we came home?

Mrs. L: No.

Mr. L: Not at all. We didn't ask any of you girls to go. We're never going to say to stay. You were as welcome as you were the day you went away.

Mrs. L: You knew that too.

Sandra: Well, I just wondered for all of us. I remember my experience, particularly with you, Dad, when I came home. I think you were a little worried because Alice had such a difficult time. I remember you just saying, "Well, OK, what are you going to do? Are you going to university, or are you going to finish your nursing?" You sort of grabbed the bull by the horns.

Dr. F: Were you worried that your parents might be upset? Was that a concern of yours?

Mrs. L: She thought we might be disappointed.

Sandra: For two reasons, I thought they might be disappointed. It made the family very special, particularly in the RC community. I think we all knew that, that four daughters were committed to the religious life. The other thing was that my sister Alice had had a very difficult time when she came out and got quite depressed, and I thought they would worry about that.

Mrs. L: The rest of you would do the same . . .

Sandra: But I remember, when I walked in the door, I remember a sense of my dad saying, let's get on with our lives, sort of thing. And that was a great relief to me.

Dr. F: It was.

Sandra: That often happened with Dad. We were sorta friends.

Mrs. L: He could see it faster than me.

Sandra: And remember, Mum, you and I visiting. We just didn't have enough time talking because we had missed all those years.

Mr. L: Just talking about having four nuns in the family. There was times when you had mixed feelings. You wondered if it was something to be proud of or if it was the opposite, you know. If you felt that it was something that didn't occur very often, there must be something weird in the house.

Sandra has already learned something from her parents. She had not been aware of her parents' ambivalence about their daughters entering the convent. She had assumed it was important for her parents to have their daughters become nuns. She now learns that her parents tried to be supportive of their daughters' wishes. They did not wish to put pressure on their daughters but were a bit sad to have them away from home. It is not unusual for children to misconstrue their parents' expectations of them. Parents and adult children seldom discuss this subject, and there can be considerable confusion around it. Here we discover that the father wanted to remain on the sidelines and to allow his daughters to make their own decisions but was delighted to have them return home. This piece of information is an important one for Sandra who thought her father had wanted more distance from her. When she hears her father talk about wanting to have his daughters nearby, she feels free to ask him some more questions about his role in the family.

Dr. F: Are there any nuns or priests in either of your families?
Mrs. L: No.
Mr. L: Well, not in our immediate family.
Mrs. L: But there was quite a while before. I guess, he would be a great uncle. He was the founder of a brother's college. And then, one of my uncles was out there. And three or four of my cousins. I think there was about six of them altogther. So there was a bit of that.
Dr. F: More distant, not your brothers or sisters?
Mrs. L: Oh, no, no, no. Distant.
Dr. F: More distant. So the thought of having four nuns, or one or more nuns in your own family caused a mixed sort of reaction?
Mrs. L: I just wanted them all to be happy. I didn't want them there if I thought they were bothered or troubled.
Mr. L: Worried or want to get home and thinking that they couldn't come home.
Dr. F: Did you try to communicate that to them in any way?
Mr. L: No, except when I thought that there was someone to come home, and then I came right out with it. "We're not trying to keep you in there. We didn't ask you to go in. You are as welcome home as you were the day you left."
Dr. F: Did you hesitate about saying you'd like them to come home for fear that you were putting pressure on them to come home?
Mr. L: No.
Dr. F: Did you hold back saying that?
Mr. L: No, I don't think so.
Mrs. L: I don't think so.
Sandra: I don't think so.
Mr. L: I wouldn't have made any suggestions, any way or the other. No, either one way or the other. While they were in there, I was very careful not to let them think that we didn't approve.
Dr. F: You did that consciously. You didn't want to put pressure on them.
Mrs. L: It was their own idea.
Dr. F: That's interesting. I understand your family was large, six?
Mr. L: Seven.
Dr. F: Seven children.
Mrs. L: We had eight.

Mr. L: We had eight. Four of each.

Mrs. L: But we had two boys who were stillborn.

Sandra: Two of my brothers died at birth.

Dr. F: Eight pregnancies. Four of each, with Sandra being the last-born. Was there anything different about her coming along at the end of the family?

Mrs. L: No. I would just as soon not have had her.

Sandra: You're going to get it from me, Mum.

Dr. F: You were ready to be through with that?

Mrs. L: I sure was. At that time, I got arthritis in my knee. But she was a darling. And she was a good baby.

Mr. L: Look at all the trouble we have now just with her.

Dr. F: You wouldn't be here.

Mrs. L: I couldn't bring her home when I came home, so my sister-in-law took her for us and kept her for a while because I wasn't able to do anything. I think she would have kept her, but her father said, "No Sir." Sandra was an awful good baby, so we enjoyed her, have all her life.

Sandra: This is Dad's sister, Meg, who only had one child, so that I guess she took me for the first three months. My older sister tells a story that she overheard my Aunt Meg ask Dad if she could keep me and raise me. This is a story I used to ask my older sister to tell me all the time, and Dad said, some comment like, "It's like asking me for my right arm or something." That's a neat story I used to ask my sister to tell me.

Dr. F: Do you have any questions for your dad or your mum about being the youngest in the family? How that affected your relationship with either one of them?

The therapist is encouraging Sandra to open up the areas of confusion that she would like to become clearer about. One of the major issues that Sandra has discussed in therapy is how she felt aligned with her mother and cut off from her father. While still at home, she felt she was a confidante of her mother and saw her father as being on the outside. In therapy she has been working on reconnecting with her father and rediscovering him as an important part of her life. When the confidante of her mother, she heard information about her father that contributed to her feeling alienated from him. As the session continues, it becomes clear that Sandra felt closer to her father when she was younger. The distance increased during her late adolescence when she became a confidante of her mother. The parents were experiencing various difficulties in their relationship at that time. Since Sandra was the last-born she became the ally of her mother. One of Sandra's major goals is to try to understand a bit more about that part of her history and to be able to maintain solid relationships with both parents.

The interview continues with Sandra asking questions about her earlier years:

Sandra: Well, I can remember both feeling some really good things from being the youngest and a lot of things that had a lot of self-interest in it. I remember some special favors because I was the youngest and that sort of thing I liked. I remember Alice and Pat complaining to you that you were babying me. You used to dress me on your knee, and they would say, "Look, she's old enough to dress herself." And you would say, "Well, she's my baby." And you'd let me down the wrong way off. I remember things like that, that I got off on because I was the youngest. I also remember feeling kinda bad when I started to go to school because you talked about losing your baby. And there was some pressure on me around Grade One. I used to feel badly leaving Mum, leaving you at home.
Dr. F: You want to check that out with your mother, maybe?
Sandra: Can you remember that time, Mum?
Mrs. L: Oh yes, and you said to me, well that year Sister Evelyn had entered . . .
Sandra: Well, no, I was about ten or eleven then, 'cause I was in about Grade Six.
Mr. L: That's right, I remember now.
Sandra: But you were at Oscar's because before I went to school, I remember walking down the street to meet you on the way when you used to come home for lunch. And then we'd have lunch, and then you and I would go take a nap together. Remember? I was six. I don't know, I guess it was a way to get me to take a nap if I went with Dad. That's a nice memory.
Mrs. L: Yeah.
Sandra: Yeah.
Dr. F: On that note, how did you try with such a large family to spend time with each one of the kids?

The therapist is now trying to get each parent to differentiate between their children and to identify the special qualities of each child. One of Sandra's issues is whether she was seen as special in the eyes of her father. She felt special to her mother by virtue of being her confidante. This role is a mixed blessing. Being one parent's confidante can mean losing a degree of intimacy with the other parent. It can also involve giving up a piece of oneself to take care of one's parent. Sandra's job is to understand that she does not have to play this role in order to be special.

When adult children can hear their parents differentiate between them and recognize their special features, it frees them from taking on their parents' anxiety as a way of being special.

The interview continues:

Mr. L: I don't think I ever did that as much because I didn't realize that it meant as much as it does now. I realize it would have been better to, but I worked very long hours for one thing. And the kids were always good. You never seemed to have to chastise them. They had work to do. There was so many reasons. I've got all kinds of excuses now, but . . .

Dr. F: Coming out of a large family yourself, you are the oldest in a large family, was this family any different from the family you came from?

The therapist is now encouraging the father to review his own family. He asks about the lessons the father learned from his family that he has tried to apply to his family-of-procreation. The father talks about his role as the first-born son and the special relationship that he enjoyed with his own father. As the father, and then the mother, talk about their own families, it becomes clear to Sandra how hard her parents worked to make their own family both different from and similar to their families-of-origin.

It is interesting to note that both Sandra's mother and father had more positive relationships with their fathers than with their mothers. Sandra's father's way of trying to take care of his family in some ways honored his father's ways. He described his father as being very supportive, but indirect in his love. Sandra's mother described her mother as being critical, demanding, and inflexible. These descriptions are similar to Sandra's descriptions of her parents. Sandra saw her father as being on the sidelines and nonjudgmental; she viewed her mother as critical and central to the running of the family. She had not understood that her father's remaining on the sidelines was not his way of distancing himself or a sign of his lack of caring, but rather, his way of repeating a pattern that he felt worked in his own family with his father. As illustrated in this family, children often develop faulty assumptions about their parents as a result of not having any information about how their parents' experiences in their own families influenced the ways in which they chose to position themselves emotionally with their children.

The interview continues with Mr. L responding to the question about whether this family is different from the family he came from:

Mr. L: Not really. There are always differences, but never anything that is opposite to the way that you were brought up yourself. We were raised on a farm, and of course, we were over two miles from school and I had to walk it most of the time when I started out myself. At least until my sisters grew up, and then we drove all the time. And of course, by that time, I was a little older and more capable about handling the horse and we used to take a horse and buggy or cutter, myself driving into town and stable the horse until night, you see. Feed it at noon. And then when I got home, I had chores to do, you know, unhitch the darn horse and put him in the stable. And change your clothes and get this. So there was that much.

Dr. F: No stopping.

Mr. L: No, there was no such thing. It was all work. And at that time, you know the pioneers in this country, they had to dig in. There wasn't a lot of money. There was no money to be made. Everybody was in the same shape. Poor as church mice, you know. I didn't know the luxuries. At least we got along all right, pretty well. But the times that they had then, people couldn't stand it now. They wouldn't put up with it.

Mrs. L: They wouldn't like to have such a big family either.

Sandra: That's true.

Dr. F: Did you have any time with your dad alone, being the first-born?

Mr. L: Well, yes. I was the oldest born, and we had a lot of time, but it was working.

Dr. F: Working together?

Mr. L: Yes, we worked together an awful lot. Haying, the harvest. And we always got along good. We never had any quarrels. I don't ever remember having a quarrel with my father. We might not agree with each other at the time, but we never quarreled about it.

Sandra: Dad loved his dad. Has always. It's been real obvious any time he talks about his dad that he really loved him.

Mr. L: Yeah, he was a wonderful man.

Dr. F: Are you the closest to him of all the children, do you think? Do you think you spent the most time with him, got to know him the best of your brothers and sisters?

Mr. L: Yes, I knew him well, with the exception of the next in the family, a boy, a brother of mine, Tom. Of course we worked a lot together too, even though he was a couple of years younger. We worked too, you know, when he got up a couple of years. The level that I started in, now we worked together. Dad worked with me. So we teamed up that way. My sister, she was a sister to me, but we didn't have the same chance. She was working in the house. I was way back in the back fifty.

Dr. F: So there was that separation between the boys and the girls, the boys worked outside with your father and the girls took care of other stuff.

Mr. L: That's right.

Dr. F: Now in your family was there a difference between your relationship with your sons and your daughters?

Mr. L: I don't think so. I don't think so. Do you think there was? The only thing there was, the only thing that I can say about it, Lorne, our oldest boy, he was a tinkerer.

Sandra: Hellion was the word you used to use.

Mr. L: He was a good guy you know, but he was mischievous. And he was so busy, into everything.

Sandra: I was saying "hellion" was the word we've used for Lorne. He was . . . lots of energy.

Dr. F: Who was the easiest among the kids?

Mr. L: The easiest? Oh, Tad, the next boy. Well, he was to me. Maybe, mother will think about some of the girls being the easier but he was to me. I always thought Tad was very easy.

Dr. F: What would you say Mum? Which one would have been the easiest for you?

Mrs. L: Well, the oldest. Sister Evelyn was very easy. Alice was hard. I hate to say that. She's the closest one to us now. And she's always there at every beck and call, but she was more like Lorne. But Tad was quiet and easygoing. Sandra was too. So was Pat and Sister Evelyn, certainly.

Sandra: But we were so different when we were kids.

Dr. F: That's right. Each one is different. When you think of Sandra in the family, was she willing to be available for most things? Was she easy too?

Mrs. L: She used to have to get her little talking once in a while. But she got it too.

Mr. L: She was no trouble as far as control was concerned. She might get into a little mischief with the rest of the girls.

Mrs. L: She was always good at school.

Dr. F: What was the most mischief she got into?

Mrs. L: She was always good at school.

Mr. L: I can't think of anything. There was nothing serious or I'd remember it.

Dr. F: Sandra, your dad has said how busy he was and how looking back he would spend more time with each individual child. Did you think your dad wasn't there? Would you like to have been more involved with him?

The therapist is now pressing Sandra to ask her father about her theme of his not being there for her. Previous therapy sessions have indicated this is an important issue for her. She continually doubted whether her father was there for her. In her large family she felt she was somewhat ignored by her father from the age of eleven on. Although she remembers her father being supportive at various points in her life, her alliance with her mother increased her sense of feeling cut off from her father. As she explores this area with her father, she begins to discover that, in fact, he was quite tuned in to her and cared about her in many different ways.

The interview continues:

Sandra: Oh, yeah, I would have liked more time with Dad, but it's true that we were a pretty traditional family, and we saw Mum as the caregiver. If you had hurts or you had bothers, you came to Mum and she was there. Dad was the hard worker, the steady man. He never drank, and he was a good wage-earner. And as I say other than the times when there was a real crisis and I just had that sense of my Dad that he may not be available to me for all my hurts, I wouldn't have bothered him with that. There was some sort of a message that Mum would take care of that. But if there was a crisis, I would think of my Dad.

Mrs. L: Yes, because he handled it better.

Sandra: I would think my mum would get upset at me. I never remember him letting me down for that, never. I mean, I remember it when I came home from the convent. I remember when I broke off my engagement to Ken about three weeks before we were going to be married. Um, I remember when I came home and said that Paul and I were together and that Paul was not an RC. He was a divorced Episcopalian with two sons. Those are about five black marks against him, and Mum and Dad were both wonderful about that. I wouldn't worry so much about Mum because it would be easier to talk to her about that, and I wouldn't always know what Dad was thinking. We were talking out in the lobby when we were waiting for you, about how much quieter my Dad is and he doesn't make his needs known. Like, my Mum really knows what she needs, and we get it for her but Dad is quiet. I remember when I came home to tell him about Paul and asked him to take some time to see if he could accept it because I didn't want to bring Paul home if I thought it was going to be too hard on everyone. My dad said that he had waited a long time to see me involved with someone and he just took the pressure right off and said, "Yes, bring him home." And Mum did the same thing. So always in a crisis.

And yet I am sorry that I didn't spend more time with Dad, and I know since I've moved out West, and probably even more since I've been seeing you, how I've called on so many memories. I mean, I have lots of memories with Mum because I was so constantly with her and I act a lot like my Mum. I've sorta hung on to so many memories of you, Dad. I remember funny little things. When Paul and I are walking down the street, this is pretty old-fashioned, but Paul will always walk on the outside. I think it is more a habit than anything else. And I remember as a little girl you teaching me that. You saying to me, you were coming home from work and I went to meet you, it was before I was in school, I was about five years old, and you saying to me, "You walk on the inside and I'll walk on the outer." And you told me why a man does that, and I don't think that whoever does that that my father doesn't click in my mind. I mean, I wish I had lots more, but I think I have lots of . . .

Dr. F: You think your Dad might have some memories of being with you that you don't have? You care to ask him those sorts of questions?

The therapist is now encouraging Sandra to work on her connection with her father. Sandra's parents are in their late seventies. One of the goals is to help Sandra to begin to feel at peace with her history with her parents. Reminiscing with her father about pleasant events from their past creates an opportunity for Sandra to feel connected with and special to her father and to minimize her regrets.

The interview continues:

Sandra: The last time I was home, I asked him a little bit about a couple of memories that my sister Alice had told me about. My Dad couldn't remember them, and then I got scared and stopped asking because I didn't want to know that he couldn't remember them. Alice says that she remembers when I was a little girl we would sit on the veranda, and I would be on your lap. She was real envious because I was spending so much time with you. This was before I was in school, of course. She used to get real mad at me because I seemed to be absorbing Dad's time. And I barely remember that.

Mr. L: Well, I can remember being on the veranda. Taking her on my knee. Rocking with her, and so on. Maybe just sitting there, but I can't remember anything more than that about the incident.

Dr. F: Would you remember spending more time with Sandra than the other children because she was the youngest?

Mr. L: That's the only reason. Just because she was the baby. I just had a babyish feeling for her, that's all.

Dr. F: That's right. Do you remember any experience that you had with Sandra that stands out in your mind as she was growing up?

Mr. L: I can't think of anything.

Dr. F: Mum, can you remember any one between Sandra and her dad that stands out in your mind?

Mrs. L: I don't think I can. I remember the hours spent where he was working and things like that.

Sandra: That's pretty special. The dog.

Mrs. L: The dog was always after Sandra.

Sandra: I would go and see my Dad.

Mrs. L: It would sit there and wait for her to come home. And her next sister always made such a fuss about the dog, and she never went with her, did she? She used to wait on you all the time. You always knew you were coming home because she'd be out in the front waiting for Sandra to come.

Mr. L: Good old Sally.

Sandra: Do you remember me in your little office Dad, at work?

Mr. L: Oh, sure. I remember the morning that you came over there and you went out the back way, and the dog Sally was sitting at the door outside of my office. Do you remember that? And I chased her three or four times because I knew that Sandra had went out the other door and went home. And by golly I spotted the dog outside the door, so I went out and chased her, and she came right back. She didn't know that Sandra had gone. She thought she was still there, and she was bound she was going to wait on Sandra.

Mrs. L: You had to go back for her.

Sandra: My dad called home and said send Sandra back and get the dog out of here.

Mr. L: That's right. I had to call home and tell Sandra to come and get the dog.

Dr. F: It seems to me that you went there and spent some time with your dad, little bits.

Mrs. L: She used to go over there a lot.

Sandra: Yeah, I hadn't thought of it that way.

Mrs. L: But he was usually pretty busy, I guess. Were you?

Sandra: I never had that feeling, never . . .

Dr. F: That he was too busy?

Sandra: Never, no. If I went over there. Well that's not true. I always had the feeling he was busy. I often had the feeling he was busy, but I never got the feeling that I had made a mistake by coming. Never. He was a shipper for Oscar's Meats. He did that for something like seventeen years. He had this sort of small office where he'd make out his delivery forms or something. He'd always sit me up on this high stool, and he'd leave me in there as long as I wanted to stay. He'd give me paper and pencil.

Mr. L: Sometimes I used to have to go out, you know.

Dr. F: Now, did all the kids do that?

Mrs. L: No, they didn't.

Dr. F: Did they all come and visit Dad?

Mrs. L: No, I was just going to say, you were the only one that went.

Sandra: I think the others were all in school.

Mr. L: I don't know why that was.

Sandra: I don't know. I think you're right. It was being close to Dad, being close to you.

Mr. L: It must have been.

Mrs. L: You just liked to go.

Dr. F: Mum, did you encourage Sandra to spend more time with Dad? Did you think that was a good idea?

Mrs. L: No, I don't think I did. I don't think I said anything.

Sandra: I don't remember you discouraging me to go over there.

Mrs. L: The only thing I would think he might be busy, you know.

Sandra: I remember you asking him if I bothered him. "Was she bothering you today? Did she bother you when she came over." I think you were just checking with him, and he said, "No," because I remember listening for his answer.

Mr. L: She never bothered me, but sometimes I had to work like hell after she left.

Dr. F: To make up for it?

Mrs. L: You know. Pat never went over there because she couldn't stand the meat. You never even looked at the meat.

Sandra: No.

Dr. F: How old were you when this was going on?

Sandra: I would say about four or five.

Mrs. L: Not any older than that.

Sandra: I was old enough to open the door, but I remember Dad used to have to come to the door because it was too heavy for me.

Mr. L: She must have been a little older than that because usually she would go to school after that.

Sandra: I think I would have been. I'd forgotten that though, how often I would go over there.

Dr. F: How about as you were growing up, your teen years and later? Did you feel comfortable spending time alone with your Dad? Did that change?

Sandra: Yes. It became sort of less comfortable, I think, as I grew up. Dad was real protective of his daughters. He watched very closely who we went out with and who we spent time with. I mean, you didn't sit in a parked car in front of the house very long or you'd hear about it, either from Dad directly or through Mum.

Dr. F: Would it be more through Mum than Dad?

The therapist now moves the interview into a new direction to focus on some of the differences in the roles played by the mother and the father and Sandra's confusion over who played which role. He also encourages Sandra to begin to ask the parents about areas in which they were supportive of each other's involvement with the children.

Sandra: Most times. To this day I'm not sure whether what came from Mum was from Mum or Dad.

Dr. F: Well, find out.

Mrs. L: I think we kinda worked together.

Sandra: You may have, but sometimes I remember your saying to me, "Your father said such and such . . ."

Mrs. L: Well, I reckon he did then if I said that.

Sandra: I wasn't sure if he in fact had said that or you thought it might have more clout if you said it came from my father cause my father could get real cross.

Mrs. L: I don't remember any of those incidents. I remember one, a guy he didn't like. I thought he was a nice guy.

Sandra: Not Sam McKay?

Mrs. L: No, I like Sam. You know the fellow who . . .

Sandra: Pete . . .

Mrs. L: Yeah, Pete. He had no time for him. I didn't mind him.

Mr. L: Oh, yes.

Mrs. L: Well you'd just come home from the convent then, and Daddy thought you were quite an innocent girl.

Dr. F: Needed some protecting eh?

Mrs. L: Yeah.

Sandra: I always got that from him.

Dr. F: Suppose you check it out with your father, the way you felt he helped.

Sandra: Well, I always felt you were very uptight about who we dated. Well, I'll just ask you. Were you nervous or were you frightened something was going to happen to us?

Mr. L: No, not really, because I never saw any signs of any of you dating any person that I wouldn't approve of. Just once, once only, Alice dated a guy. Do you remember?

Mrs. L: She spent the night with him.

Mr. L: She dated a guy, and I gave her quite a tongue thrashing, and that settled it, without one blow . . .

Sandra: What were you worried about Dad?

Mr. L: Well, because he'd got an awful reputation, and he was four or five years older, maybe more than that. That's all I did. I give her quite a talking to that time. She never went out with him again. That was one of the best things that ever happened. I think that guy is still in jail.

Mrs. L: One of those people, you know that don't turn out . . .

Sandra: Don't turn out very well.

Mr. L: That was the only time that I ever had to speak to any of them.

Dr. F: That's slightly different from what you're saying.

Sandra: Uh huh. I felt you were always sort of vigilant about who we were seeing and what time we got in, and I guess, a little nervous that we would be somehow sexually involved or that we would get pregnant.

Mr. L: Maybe, I think that . . .

Mrs. L: I didn't ever think that.

Mr. L: I think that goes through every father's head, you know. From what I knew of them, they were always from respectable parents and good families, and what more can you do than that anyway. There's a limit. But I knew this one guy was a good-for-nothing, you know. I sure didn't mince any words.

Sandra: No.

Dr. F: It sounds like you had a lot of confidence in your daughters' judgment.

Mr. L: Oh, yes, I think I did. But of course I told them to only communicate or talk to or be friendly with people of good, respectable parents.

Dr. F: Did you feel your Dad thought you were pretty responsible, level-headed?

Sandra: I think so. I think he would be shocked if we did anything wrong.

Mr. L: When I started out, you know, my dad asked me after I had been out to a dance who I had danced with and so on. And he said to me, "One of the first things you must learn is to respect the girls." I didn't know what the hell he was talking about. But he kept it up until I finally knew.

Dr. F: Till you figured it out, eh. That was his message. That was his consistent message.

Mr. L: We'd come home, and of course, then the next morning, he would get me up and tell me, "Come on get up and get your clothes on and get down. Get some chores done." It didn't matter who sat down to breakfast first. When we came together and we were at the table, he'd say, "Well, who'd you see last night that you liked better than yourself?"

Sandra: I remember Dad asking us that the day after a party or a dance. And he always had a great laugh cause it reminded him of what his dad said.

Dr. F: He'd always ask you that question?

Mr. L: Yes. He asked it many times, many times. It wasn't very long until he knew who it was that I liked better than myself.
Dr. F: Well, Mum, in your family, the family you grew up in, did it work the same way?

The therapist reinvolves the mother at this point. Although one of the agendas of the session was for Sandra to reconnect with her father and to better understand his involvement in the family, it is also important for the mother to tell her story. The objective of connecting Sandra and her father has been achieved. The therapist now shifts focus and asks the mother questions about her own family, particularly the lessons she learned in her family-of-origin that she tried to apply to her family-of-procreation.

The interview continues:

Mrs. L: Yeah. I had three brothers and one sister.
Dr. F: You were the first-born girl in the family. That put you in a more responsible role. You took care of the younger ones?
Mrs. L: Yes. My parents were very strict too.
Dr. F: Very strict.
Mrs. L: Yes. I remember the first party I went to. I came home, and I talked so much about it my mother said, "Well, you're not going again for a year," and I didn't either.
Sandra: Because you talked too much about it.
Mrs. L: I talked too much about it.
Dr. F: Talked too much, and you showed too much excitement, were too happy about it.
Mrs. L: Oh, yes.
Dr. F: How old were you when you . . .
Mrs. L: I would say about seventeen.
Dr. F: And it was a year before you were allowed to go again?
Mrs. L: I never even asked to go. I just thought, "It's no use. I'm not going to bother." My mother was very strict. My dad would do anything.
Dr. F: Your dad was easy?
Mrs. L: Very easy. If I said to Dad, "Can I go?" I know he would have said, "Yes," but there was no use in getting his side and not my mother's.
Dr. F: Because it still would have been no. If Mum said no, that's no. No matter what Dad would have said.
Mrs. L: Yes.
Dr. F: So she was the one that really made the family . . .
Mrs. L: Made the laws.

Dr. F: Made the laws in the family. So when you met your future husband, how was that handled in your family?

Mrs. L: Oh, very good because we always knew his people. It was sort of like old times, I guess. I don't know.

Dr. F: They approved.

Mrs. L: Oh, yes.

Mr. L: My father dated Mary's mother a few times.

Sandra: I didn't know about that until recently.

Mr. L: When I told my dad he said, "Sure. I know her mother real well. Took her out to a couple of dances myself."

Mrs. L: So that was fine on both sides.

Mr. L: And then, of course, Mother got the surprise when she heard who it was because my mother had no knowledge of the family at all until my dad told Mum about it.

Sandra: It's interesting that both Mum and Dad were both closer to their fathers than their mothers, both very much closer to their fathers. You don't hear anything bad about either grandpas, but you hear lots of little stories about rigidity on the part of the grandmas on both sides.

Dr. F: You see the fathers as somewhat softer.

Mrs. L: Mine was, very much.

Mr. L: Oh, yes. I think my dad was too. But my dad had just a little different way of handling things. He got to you without any trouble at all, where Mother would come out very blunt and give it to you.

Dr. F: It was a softer way. You came to like that approach better?

Mr. L: Oh, yeah. Much better.

Dr. F: Did you try to use that with your own kids? Your dad's approach?

Mr. L: I think I had that. I tried to have an easier way of handling it than being like my mother was. Because I never appreciated the lectures she would give me.

Dr. F: Do you think sometimes your dad was so subtle that you missed the message?

Mr. L: I know one thing. Mother would give it to you so quick and so hard that the first thing you knew you wouldn't tell her. Dad would get all the news. You knew you could tell it to him, and that would be the end of it.

Dr. F: So basically what happened was that Mum would hear almost nothing and Dad was someone you thought you could talk to.

Mrs. L: I think I told my mother a lot.

Dr. F: Even though she reacted, you still did?

Mrs. L: Oh, yes.

Mr. L: I was different that way. I didn't tell Mother anything.

Sandra: Yes, you've told me that. I've heard that before.

Dr. F: I asked your dad whether his father was so subtle that he would miss the message. I get a sense your father has tried to be subtle too. Do you think that has ever happened to you? That you have missed the message?

This last question to Sandra is an important one for her to consider. The therapist reframes the father's subtlety as being his way of honoring his own father. Sandra's response to this question indicates that there were areas about her father that she missed completely. The therapist encourages Sandra to talk about what she has learned about her parents in the session. She has heard several things differently. This response is not unusual for adult children in the proactive phase of therapy who begin to hear their parents' stories with a better appreciation of their parents as people. Once the adult children let go of their need to be validated and have their own history confirmed, their parents' stories enhance rather than diminish their sense of themselves in the world.

The interview concludes with Sandra reviewing what she has heard:

Sandra: Some things that Dad has said today I've missed completely. One is what he thought a couple of visiting days before I actually left the convent. I think there was an indication that I was unhappy, and Dad gave a very subtle message about the fact that if I was unhappy that I should come home. But I wasn't sure of it. I did not hear it the way I know he meant it now. I understand why it was subtle, what the spirit was. Dad could get very upset and there would be open conflict in the family but I would say 90% of the time he was quiet, thoughtful, pensive with his pipe, and solid. Often I wasn't that sure where he was or what he was thinking or how involved he was or whether he was involved. That's unfortunate.

Dr. F: You're hearing it differently now.

Sandra: I'm hearing it very differently.

Dr. F: That's interesting. Would you like to ask one last question before we stop.

Sandra: I don't think I have any particular question. I was just thinking about last night when I was crawling into bed and Paul was real tired. And Mum and Dad had gotten home and they had gotten into bed. And I could hear them kinda chatting before they went to sleep, and Paul said to me, "I can't believe your excitement." I didn't sleep all night, I was so excited about having them. He said, "You are like a little girl again." I just feel real lucky to have them as parents.

Mrs. L: Thanks, darling.
Mr. L: Thank you.

Sandra has ended the interview with a very strong, caring statement about her parents. This is the desired ending for a family-of-origin session when the adult children are in the proactive phase. Their parents' involvement is seen as positive and nourishing, and they are generally touched by their parents' stories. These family-of-origin sessions facilitate a deeper connection between the parents and children and they create an opportunity for adult children to let go of any last pieces of unfinished business, thereby feeling more complete and at peace with their history.

SECTION SEVEN:
FAMILY THERAPY WITH COUPLES – MIDDLE PHASE:
CASE ILLUSTRATION AND COMMENTARY

Once a family has moved into the middle phase of therapy the therapy shifts from the parents and children to work with just the parents. After the parents have stopped focusing on the identified problem child and have redefined their issues, the therapy focuses on the husband's or wife' self-issues. Earlier interviews with this family were presented in Chapters Four and Five of this text. Several significant changes occurred between the earlier interviews and the one which follows. The focus is no longer on the young adult children who have left home. The parents have begun working on their own issues. During the course of therapy, the mothers of each parent have been seen. The parents have also been encouraged to involve other extended family members in therapy sessions. This session illustrates many of the middle phase strategies discussed earlier in this chapter.

In middle phase therapy the focus shifts from the functioning of the nuclear family as a system to the reconceptualizing of the functioning of the couple as a husband/wife unit. The partners are asked to consider what they have learned over the course of therapy about positioning themselves differently in the marriage. The therapy helps the partners understand how anxiety contributes to relationship stuckness. Partners look at how their ideas have changed about the way they function within the family, both nuclear and extended, and in their work environment. During the middle phase, couples gain an understanding of how family systems work and learn to deal with their relationship at a higher level.

In the interview that follows, it is clear that the husband and wife in the "R" family are in the middle phase of family therapy. They are less reactive and more thoughtful and curious about how each functions in the world. This interview is in marked contrast to the earlier interview in which the parents were anxious and reactive and generally feeling overwhelmed by the family problems. Mr. and Mrs. R have a sense of excitement about their future and are hopeful about their ability to make things happen in a positive way in their family. They are far more comfortable talking about sensitive areas, such as the suicide of the husband's father and the death of the wife's father. They both appreciate the importance of involving their mothers and see their families as positive resources in their lives. The children are no longer seen on a regular basis. The primary focus is on the self. As the therapy continues both partners will have an opportunity to experiment with major self-shifts.

In the following interview the therapist helps each partner see the other partner's changes as an opportunity to connect at a higher level rather than as a loss. He raises the issue of how anxiety producing some of these changes can be and helps the couple deal with the anxiety. If the anxiety level is too high, the couple will revert back to an earlier way of functioning. It is important that the therapist raise issues that the couple have not considered in order to help them sustain their self-changes. The therapist is able to accomplish this in the middle phase of therapy when the couple's anxiety has been reduced and they are able to take on additional anxiety without becoming defensive. If these issues are raised too early in therapy, they would add to the couple's already high levels of anxiety and simply lead to more defensive, reactive behavior.

In the following interview the focus is on helping Mr. and Mrs. R recognize what areas they need to work on in order to sustain the significant family changes that have occurred. The therapist begins the interview with a general question about how the couple's thinking about their relationship has changed over time. The husband responds by introducing his concerns about his siblings and their involvement in the therapy. This response is a good indication of rethinking on the part of Mr. R. When the couple first began therapy, they were most hesitant to involve any extended family members. Now that massive changes have occurred throughout the extended family, it is quite natural for them to think about involving other family members as a way of connecting with important people at a deeper level.

The interview begins:

Dr. F: I wanted to see you without your children to find out how each of you have started to understand things differently and how all this has affected your relationship with each other. Do you have other agendas before we get into these two questions?

Mr. R: My brother Joe has expressed an interest in therapy. He and I have had some talks about the family. I have given him the interview tape which his interviews are on. He asked me not to let anyone else listen. I've asked him if he would listen to it, and then give permission for Bill to listen to it. And if he gives that permission, then I'll let my wife listen to it because I don't see there is anything on there that's such a big deal. But he was afraid that he was going to be critical of people and didn't want anyone else to hear the criticism. I'm not sure that I would let my mother listen to it because he was highly critical of her. My brother Bill spoke to me last week asking for my help in helping him as he proposes to look at some issues in his life. He feels there are some unresolved issues in his life. He referred to my telling him that the two, his perception and his younger brother's perception, were entirely different on the family. So when he gets back into town in September, he wants to sit down and talk to me about that and I said, "Fine, be happy to do that."

My mother and I have had some interesting talks about the family, and she said for the first time that I can recall that she felt resentment when her husband killed himself. I never heard her say that before. So I validated that by saying I felt the same way and it's OK to feel like that, to feel resentment that your husband departs in that manner because she saw it as a rejection of her. And I was able to share some things with her about what I felt was lacking in my upbringing, and then to say to her, "You did the best you could." I said to her, "When you look at where you came from and what happened to you, and the fact that you were an orphan by the time you were thirteen and came from a very judgmental family, well, that's how you were made! You did the best you could." So, we've started to talk along those lines which I found very positive.

I have had a couple of sessions with Sue. Sue sees her relationship with me as her big problem. I took Sue out for dinner last night, and we had a very nice talk. And she was talking about what she thought my shortcomings were as a parent, what was missing in me, and how she sensed that I had this tremendous anger in me. She always knew where her mother was coming from, but she never knew where I was coming from, never knew when I was going to explode, and all that. I was being positive saying, "Well, it's great that we are dealing with these things, and I'm sure things are going to get better." And she was getting a bit despondent, and then she said, "I don't know where we are going to end up." So I grabbed her hand and said, "Together and in love." So she burst out laughing. But there was a sense of some bridging going on, some understanding. I mean it's going to take a while.

Dr. F: How did you know to take her hand and say that?

Mr. R: I just thought what would David Freeman want me to do?

Dr. F: How did you know that was the right thing for your daughter?

Mr. R: I don't know, instinct.

Dr. F: I think you've been listening to her very carefully, and it's also natural.

Mr. R: And I knew I should not be defensive, saying, "Yes, but . . . yes, but . . . you did this . . . you did that." So I just listened and tried to be attentive.

In previous sessions Mr. R has tended to overfunction for his daughter and had been generally reactive to her anxiety and behavior. In contrast, he now tells about an event in which he was able to embrace his daughter's sadness rather than distance from her. The therapist has highlighted the fact that the father has managed to react differently. As the interview continues the therapist introduces the concept of anxiety and comments that when anxiety is down one's natural abilities are more in evidence. This comment lays the foundation for helping Mr. R to understand how his anxiety debilitates him. Mr. R's pattern has been to overreact to his daughter's anxiety-producing behavior. The daughter in turn feels diminished and unable to connect with her father. The therapist's goal in this interview is not to focus on the father/daughter relationship but rather to stimulate Mr. R's thinking about his different reactions as a way of better understanding some of the changes that have taken place in his relationship with his wife.

The interview continues:

Dr. F: It's interesting how once the anxiety goes our natural instincts begin to show themselves.

Mr. R: Sue has been saying to her mother, "Well, I don't think I can ever get along with my dad." And Jean has been saying, "Well, I don't know if the two of you are ever going to be able to get along." And I think, "Well, of course we can." So as far as our relationship, I see more progress in my relationships with others. I still have some issues that I've got to deal with myself, personally. And still some issues to deal with with Jean, but things are better than they were two years ago.

Dr. F: We'll come back to that. I'd still like to get your reply to those questions I asked. What did you learn from having your mother here and how has it translated to the relationship?

Mrs. R: Well, first of all with regards to my mum, I was so glad she came. Getting her here was not easy. She was glad she came after she came, but there was . . .

Mr. R: Does he know the story on the back and forth on that?

Mrs. R: Oh, she phoned up three days before. And I wasn't home fortunately. That worked out perfectly because if I'd been home I would have said, "Oh, well. OK." But you relayed the message to me . . .

Mr. R: Well, I was home. I was listening to the answering machine, and someone had called our number about twenty times during the day. No messages.

Mrs. R: Mum never uses the answering machine. She would never use the answering machine. She doesn't approve of them.

Mr. R: So she finally got ahold of me, and she said, "I just can't go. I'm sorry, but I can't go to meet this doctor person." So I said, "Well, my mother felt the same kind of concern. She didn't know what was going to happen. She thought she was going to get criticized. She thought she was going to get clobbered and that it was going to hurt. It turned out not to be that at all. It was just fine. Everything was cool and warm, and I understand why you would be concerned. My mother is a very uptight person, and it was fine with her." She said, "No, no. I'm just not going." So, I tried to reassure her. And then, I started to get annoyed with her and I said, "You're not doing this for yourself, you're doing this for your daughter." So, she just said, "No, I don't care, I'm just not doing it." So I said, "Well, why, what is your concern?"

She says, "I'm just not doing it. That's all. I'm just not going to do it. It's not for me." And she was obviously terribly wrought up. I could just feel it. So we sort of hung up not on good terms, and then she called back early the next morning . . .

Mrs. R: I didn't return her call that night. I was supposed to call back, and I was so mad I didn't . . .

Mr. R: And the first thing next morning, she called and she said, "I thought about what you said, and. . . ."

Mrs. R: So I never had to talk to her about . . .

Mr. R: "I've decided that you don't have to cancel the appointment."

Mrs. R: So he handled it. It was fine. And I stayed right out of it. I was so mad so that was good. So getting her here was a major undertaking was what I started to tell you. So I really enjoyed the whole dialogue, and I felt it was wonderful, as I said before, to have all the pieces come together in one hour. The problem with a normal relationship is that you get such bits and pieces and there is no picture. It's just all over the room and you fill in the blanks yourself with your own imaginings. I think that's what probably happens. There was some information that was corrected. So there was some misinformation that I had. So that was interesting to me too. So I found that very useful, and she was really relieved and happy when it

was finished. I think she now understands. I don't think she understood what we've been doing. She has not understood what we've been doing.
Dr. F: So that made a difference to her understanding?
Mrs. R: Yes. I think it was important for her to understand what our counseling was about, what our therapy was about. She had a vision of it, which was really not very good, not a very pleasant image of what could be happening. Basically she has this image of critical, heavy discussions. I think she had a wrong image. And that family therapy is completely different from many other kinds of therapy. So, that was good.

In terms of our relationship, my feeling about my mum is just to accept her. There have been a lot of problems with me since my dad died because I have wanted her to be more, maybe nurturing isn't the right expression, but more alive, more involved with life. And I've been angry at her around that. But I also recognize that she has choices to make, and I can't make that happen for her. That has been very difficult. There have been nine years of it, for me, with her. I don't think until my dad died I was aware as much. I knew she was a very dependent person, but I wasn't so aware of how dependent she was and how she really lived her life through other people. Now that my father is gone, it's like half of her is gone. Maybe even more than half. So the resentments I've put aside.
Mr. R: Although the changes started to occur even before your dad died?
Mrs. R: Well, yes. There was more. There were some changes before he died. My father was concerned about it and would come and discuss the problem. You know, she's not an alcoholic in the sense of a person who drinks all the time, but she is addictive, and I'm aware of that. In the evenings most people will cut it off after two. She will go for three, maybe. Not four or five, but three. And by three she's had way too much. My sense is that it's a depressant for her. Also, she has a lot of anxiety. She worries. She's very obsessed with her fears. I think the alcohol covers those fears and those worries.
Dr. F: Jean, let me ask you a specific question about your anxiety about your mother which I guess increased before your dad died, with your dad talking to you about his concern . . .
Mrs. R: Yes. He would see her every day. I would only see her at dinners and so on . . .

This portion of the interview demonstrates that when couples are working together, they reinforce each other's attempts to be different in their extended families. Mrs. R was ambivalent about bringing in her mother to a session, and it was important that Mr. R was supportive of her efforts to involve her mother. If Mr. R had not been supportive, Mrs. R could have used her mother's anxiety as an excuse to avoid following through on her attempts to involve her. Ideally each spouse will be supportive of his or her partner's efforts to reposition himself or herself in family. When there is even a mild negative reaction on the part of one, the other will often use it to justify remaining stuck. In contrast, when both spouses are making similar efforts, there is a greater likelihood that neither will reinforce the negative side of the other's ambivalence.

At this point in the interview, the therapist focuses on Mrs. R's relationship with her mother. Mrs. R carries a high degree of anxiety about her mother. The therapist will gradually shift the focus from the way Mrs. R positions herself vis-à-vis her mother to the way she positions herself in the husband/wife relationship. His hypothesis is that the way Mrs. R deals with her anxiety about her mother is carried over into her relationship with her husband. Her anxiety leads to caretaking, which in turn contributes to her feeling stuck and frustrated in her relationships. As the interview proceeds, the therapist tries to help Mrs. R see the connection between the way that she deals with the anxiety stirred up by her mother and by her husband.

The interview continues with Mrs. R talking about her caretaker role:

Dr. F: How do you think your anxiety about your mother, and then your whole loss around your dad's death, affected your marriage?
Mrs. R: Well, it obviously had to because it would divide my time to a certain degree. You know, I have this problem with being all over the room. I have my clients. I have my children. I have my husband. I have my family and because I'm the caregiver, or whatever I am in this dysfunctional family, my way of coping with life was to be responsible for everything. I guess that was a rule in my family that was taught to me when I was very young. It was expected that I would do that. And I guess I resented that underneath. I didn't know I resented that. I thought I liked that.
Dr. F: When did you begin to rethink that?
Mrs. R: Well, probably through the therapeutic process.
Dr. F: Not before?
Mrs. R: Well vaguely, but it wasn't as focused.
Dr. F: A vague feeling about it?
Mrs. R: Yes. I remember having high blood pressure in 1975 when I was working for the government. At that stage, it was just bizarre. I was really feeling exhausted. I was managing two small children and a very big job with the government. Then there was my concern about my parents, and I was involved with my friends. I tended to be a caregiver to my friends as

well. In other words, I would listen through all their divorces and their separations and everything else. And I just thought that was what I did. I mean, I never really questioned until my health broke and I was warned that I was going to have to find a way to slow down. I couldn't do it all. I thought I could do it all.

Dr. F: So that was the beginning of the notion. In the last year or so you've become even more focused . . .

Mrs. R: More focused. More aware really of my inability to say no. My inability to get away or flee from a problem. So there was a lack of assertiveness in me in valuing me as a person. That's still a hard concept for me, that I have a right to have vacations and holidays and time when I'm not a caretaker. I think I've been shifting those gears and feeling less guilty. I'm sure there is still a thread of guilt involved when I'm not a superwoman. You know, that concept.

Mrs. R has begun to see how her caretaker role has contributed to her being stuck in her extended family. The therapist has tried to help Mrs. R understand how she was encouraged to assume the role of caretaker because of her father's anxiety about her mother. She vaguely understands that she was in a triangle with her mother and her father. Mrs. R is encouraged to think more about how she acted out the family anxiety for her parents and how this influenced her own role in her nuclear family. Mrs. R is quick to recognize the downside of being a caretaker. The therapy must proceed with caution here. It is important that Mrs. R understand that there are significant losses involved in giving up the caretaker role that can result in increased anxiety. The therapy is directed towards helping Mrs. R become aware of the losses for her, in both her extended and nuclear families, and to consider how prepared she is to deal with these losses.

The interview continues with a discussion of the potential loss involved in giving up the caretaker role:

Dr. F: What are you worried about happening? What would the losses be in your relationship with Brian, if you continue to pursue this new position?

Mrs. R: It's really dangerous. I suppose as a person who is seen in a certain light, one expects that the person married you for the same qualities. I mean, you are going to be attracted to somebody like that because they have those qualities. When they start to take that off, and say, "Hey, I don't want to do that," there is going to be conflict. The person doesn't want the change because the roles are rigid, and you know . . .

Dr. F: You're violating the unspoken contract . . .

Mrs. R: The unspoken contract. Yes. So for me when I say, "Brian I want to work part time. I don't want to work full time because I get so involved that for me to work full time and be as heavily committed as I am with family, children and so on, I'm looking like my father who died at 64 of a heart attack, a stroke." Do I want to be like him? And I tend to be like him. So, these are the issues that I'm grappling with, and I'm getting ready. I'm still getting ready. I haven't actually got to the stage where I've taken the plunge, but I know I'm getting ready to do that.

Dr. F: A certain degree of anxiety though in doing it differently.

Mrs. R: Yes.

At this stage in the interview the therapist is emphasizing the down side of change. Whenever there is change, there are losses. At times therapists are so eager for their clients to behave differently that they actually collude with them to deny that there are some functional reasons for maintaining the status quo. It is critically important to highlight the losses that accompany change. When family members are able to look at their need to hold on to a particular behavior they begin to see it in a different light and approach change for more solid reasons.

The interview continues with the focus on the implications of change:

Dr. F: How do you think the anxiety gets expressed? The ambivalence about keeping things the same or doing things differently?

Mrs. R: I've already described what the anxiety is when I change. So, the anxiety if I stay the same, I guess the key here is how much do I really want to live. What it really comes down to, and this has always been a little vague for me, what I tend to do is just put it out of my mind that I could die, or I could be sick, or I could be crazy, or whatever. I don't think I'll be crazy. I think I would die first rather than be crazy. I mean, I have two choices. Or have an accident or do something, because I know that's what stress does to me. I mean, I teach stress management, which is even more horrendous. I'm laughing at myself as I say that. It's good for other people but it isn't good for me. You do what I say, but don't follow what I do. No, I recognize the risk, and I guess what I'm still working on is really internalizing the fear of that so that that corrects me.

Mrs. R is beginning to understand that behaving differently will bring about anxiety of a different nature. This new anxiety stems from change without cooperation. Once a family member behaves differently, other family members react to the change with surprise, and some degree of concern, and behave in ways that put pressure on the individual to return to his or her familiar way of being in the family. Unless an individual can withstand the pressure from other family members, he or she will quickly give up the change.

The concept of change without cooperation is an important one in the middle phase of family therapy. It is during this phase that the individual family member learns that the negative reaction of other family members to his or her change does not necessarily mean that the change is bad for or hurtful to the family. The negative reaction is understood as the other family members' way of dealing with the anxiety that is stirred up by new and unfamiliar behaviors in the family. This creates anxiety of a different nature.

The interview continues:

Dr. F: I think you've heard me say that if change is going to occur it has to occur without cooperation. So if you really have a sense of how you need to be different, then you have to let go of Brian supporting that. How do you go against your nature and your history and maintain new behavior without cooperation?

Mrs. R: It's going to take a lot of work.

Dr. F: Have you been thinking at all about that?

Mrs. R: How do you do that? Yeah!

Dr. F: Because you know how to reduce your anxiety by being a caretaker.

Mrs. R: Yes. That's the way I did it.

Dr. F: Now you have to go against your nature and history and increase your anxiety to be different rather than reduce your anxiety. Because there's no guarantee of cooperation. Inviting your mother here made you anxious because it made her anxious. But you were able to sustain the request, rather than say. "Oh, well it's not necessary, Mum." That's new.

Mrs. R: Yes. I hung in there.

Dr. F: So besides bringing her in here to hear her story, you also did something different in your relationship by getting her here. Because it wasn't to get her better, it . . .

Mrs. R: It was to help me.

Dr. F: That's right. The same principle applies to the marriage. You're doing these things differently for yourself. Not because it's good for Brian, but because it's good for you.

Mrs. R: And I'm starting to change with Sue. Like, she'll phone me and say, "I want to go out for dinner with you tonight." And I'll say, "Well, I'm sorry, Sue. I just took my shoes off, and I'm really tired, and I've got my dinner started and its not convenient." And she'll say, "Well, I'm broke. I've got to leave the place I'm living in." And I'll say, "Well, I'm sorry. Tonight is not a good idea." That's hard for me.

The therapist has emphasized that Mrs. R has been able to make some changes within her extended family and to sustain them in the face of increased anxiety. The focus is now shifted away from the extended family to the relationship between Mr. and Mrs. R, particularly the implications to the marriage if Mrs. R gives up her caretaking role.

Dr. F: Let me ask you another question about you and Brian. How do you think your caretaking role has affected the marriage?
Mrs. R: Well, I guess I must have had resentment because people who are caretakers aren't always just so perfect and wonderful, doing it cheerfully. A cheerful giver is the nicest giver there is. So there's probably a part of me, at least underneath, that hurt Brian because of times when I was taking my frustration out on him, that anger of the role. It would have to deflect, and you would have examples I'm sure. So that it would affect the marriage because I would be living with these expectations that I couldn't live up to, or was hoping to live up to, or trying to live up to, and then being resentful of the people who were making demands on me.
Dr. F: And that resentment would show itself in what sorts of ways?
Mrs. R: Short temper. Critical.
Mr. R: And perhaps projecting onto me, by saying to me, "Well, you want me to work full time, and you expect me to do this. And you'd be disappointed if I do that, therefore I can't."
Mrs. R: Well, I suppose. But, I don't really believe you. You know, there's still a part of me that's saying, "No, no, no . . ."
Dr. F: That's the next stage.
Mrs. R: But I have to believe you. That you really mean that.
Dr. F: Well, I'll turn to Brian in a second, but I'm really intrigued with this dilemma for you. The loss for you in doing it differently. What would you lose?
Mrs. R: OK, I get a lot of respect. A lot of positive comments. There's a lot of nice things that come your way when you're a caregiver. You've got a lot of people very supportive of that. I've just got it everywhere.
Dr. F: Being the good guy.
Mrs. R: Yes. It's nice. Really nice. So I wouldn't be that person anymore. I'd have to settle for not having that. So that would be a loss.
Dr. F: What other losses would there be? The gains are obvious but what would the losses be?
Mrs. R: I guess it would be to do with control. I don't know. Something around that. I'm just working on that. That was a way I controlled my life.

That was a way to be important, to be special, to be unique, and to manage — function. So I would have to find new ways of managing. A different management style.

Dr. F: A different way of finding meaning?

Mrs. R: Yes. Authority. All those things.

Dr. F: So being special and having purpose are also involved in doing it that way.

Mr. R: Are we talking about losing your employment or losing your role as caregiver?

Mrs. R: Caregiver. Employment might be part of that, or half of my employment might be part of that.

Mr. R: But you've always held out volunteer work as an option.

Mrs. R: Yes, because it's manageable.

Mr. R: Which is an outlet for caregiving.

The interview has reached a point where it is timely to introduce the idea that Mr. and Mrs. R's ways of dealing with anxiety have to do not just with themselves but also with how they take care of each other. The therapist hypothesizes that when they sense anxiety in each other they behave in ways that cause a reaction to their behavior, thereby, shifting the partner's focus away from his or her own areas of discomfort.

The interview continues:

Dr. F: I'm going to push you a little bit on this one. I think that part of your taking on a caretaking role is a way of reducing anxiety.

Mrs. R: Yes. I know that. I agree with that.

Dr. F: You know that.

Mrs. R: Yes. Some people drink too much. I care too much.

Dr. F: OK. Here's my question.

Mrs. R: This is my addiction. That's my addiction.

Dr. F: That's a good way of looking at it.

Mrs. R: I think it's my way.

Dr. F: OK. So that's one way. Your way of reducing anxiety. You no longer want to do it that way. What do you do with your anxieties?

Mrs. R: What do you do in place of it?

Dr. F: How do you deal with your anxieties? That's the big question.

Mrs. R: That's a really important question. That's the most important question. Well, it comes back to trust and self-esteem and stress management. I have to think about it for a minute. Well, if your expectations of yourself are lowered, then that should reduce the anxieties and that should lead to more self-acceptance. I mean, it's a spiritual/emotional question. It's really complicated. I think you know it's a state of being. It's a more philosophical approach to life. It's letting it happen. Knowing you can't control it all and not taking responsibility for it. So what do you do with the anxieties? Well, when you stop taking responsibility, then hopefully, that should lessen the anxiety, your perception of it.

Dr. F: What do you begin to be able to think about then? The anxiety allows you to focus on other things. You don't need to do that as much anymore . . .

Mrs. R: So you develop other parts of yourself.

Dr. F: What does it free up in you to think about? I'll leave you with this question for the next time I see you. I do think that anxiety blocks us from our sadness, from what to do with our sadness, and there's a lot of sadness.

Mrs. R: So I have to feel it, and in order to deal, to cope, I have to feel it. That's the grief, recovery process.

Dr. F: Jean, let me ask you one last question about your father's death. Is there any unfinished business around that part of the history? When we throw away all the other stuff that makes it safe, we're left with making peace with that part of ourselves we had the distance from. When you take care of your mum, you don't have to think about your mum's sadness, you're taking care of her. You don't need to take care of her as much any more. She can then talk to you about that other part of herself. Some people aren't prepared for that shift. They don't want to get into the sadness so they replace one anxiety for another anxiety.

Mrs. R: I think I did escape. Caregiving allowed me not to have to really feel how dysfunctional, how unhappy, the whole situation really was.

Dr. F: Do you think you are better prepared now to stay with that feeling rather than be scattered with all those needs out there? That just keep you exhausted and unfinished?

Mrs. R: Yes. It's really important.

Dr. F: Caretakers have a way of distracting themselves with everybody's needs. They don't think about themselves.

Mrs. R: That's what I've been trying to say. I think I need more time. In order for me to deal with these issues, I need to give myself more time. There just isn't enough time. I am busy. I drop at eleven o'clock.

Dr. F: The day you make that happen for yourself is going to be really interesting. No one is going to help you with that.

Mrs. R: I know. Everyone is going to be upset with me. I know that's why . . .

Dr. F: That's right, and that's lovely that you understand it this way. You're changing the unwritten contract, but you'll come out of it in a very different way.

Mr. R: Who would be upset with you other than me?
Mrs. R: Oh no, no, no. Other than you. At least you admit it. I'm glad to hear you be honest.

The interview has been focusing on Mrs. R's anxiety about change. The therapist proposes to shift the focus now to Mr. R. Mr. R's comment, "Who would be upset with you other than me?" indicates he has some discomfort arising from the interview's emphasis on the need for change in the relationship. The therapist must be sensitive to how Mr. R has heard the discussion up to this point. The therapist's hypothesis is that Mrs. R's relinquishment of her caretaking role will be experienced as a loss for Mr. R and that he will make efforts to get her to resume her old role. Because Mrs. R is so ambivalent about changing her role in the family, she will be very sensitive to any shift in Mr. R's behavior towards her and may use it to justify not sustaining her change. In this way, the couple would collude to avoid change. Mr. R is encouraged to discuss what the losses would be for him if Mrs. R behaved differently. Making these concerns explicit provides some insurance against the couple conspiring to maintain the status quo.

The interview continues:

Dr. F: Let's talk about that. Let me ask you the same question that I asked Jean. How have some of these changes snowballed into your rethinking your marriage?
Mr. R: It's hard to say. There have been so many changes in the last two years that it's difficult to say what is cause and effect. In the last two years, we've been through a lot with our children, resulting in us becoming empty nesters. And then I went through a turmoil in my work life, as well as the therapy. So it's hard to sort out. I feel more relaxed now and less tense and less guilty, and I've had more emotional energy for Jean. But I am aware that I'm still blocked. There are still some things in me that come not from my father's suicide, because I was twenty years old when that happened and I think my personality was reasonably well formed. I think the problems have to do with abandonment at an earlier age, at a very young age. And I'm still wrestling with that. And I won't really be a free man until I can deal with those issues. And I have a problem with women who are close to me. With my mother, my wife and my daughter. So I'm probably blaming my mother, probably blaming her for my father as well. So things are better, but I've still got a lot of work to do with myself. And as I said to Sue last night, "My main relationship problem is with myself, and if I can deal with that one, then other relationships will work out or improve."

Dr. F: Brian, when I first met you, almost exactly two years ago, this wasn't your theory. Can you explain to me the process you went through to develop this new theory of what you need to work on for yourself?

Mr. R: I'm not sure of the question.

Dr. F: Well, your theory has to do with abandonment and these three important women. How did you develop this theory?

Mr. R: How did I?

Dr. F: Yes. How did you come to that? Two years ago you would have said to your daughter something about shaping her up. You would have talked about yourself. You wouldn't have talked to her about what she needed to do for herself.

Mr. R: Yes. I have been aware for at least ten years that I had some personal issues to deal with, and that's why I went into the various counseling and therapies and other things. In the last two years, I've become more clear about what those issues are. It was becoming aware of abandonment and the importance of that and how important it has been in my life. It's also been a struggle for me to come to terms with guilt, being a guilt-ridden person, and I've become more aware of that. And the therapy, and the discussions that Jean and I've had, and the things that we're doing now. We're doing John Bradshaw, sort of listening to him, reading his book and that all helps me understand. But what's hard for me is to deal with the feeling side of that. I can understand it intellectually. I can feel it intellectually, but that doesn't get to where the hurt is. That part where the hurt is is still quite well defended in me.

Dr. F: When that gets stirred up, how does it change you?

Mr. R: Well, I'm not sure it has been stirred up. I've become more aware that it's there and what it is, but I have a feeling that I still haven't done a lot to break through, or to break out.

Mr. R's theme of feeling abandoned by important people in his life reemerges in this session. An important issue for Mr. R will be how to experience change in Mrs. R without feeling alone and abandoned in the world.

The interview continues:

Dr. F: Let me be more precise in my question. If Jean rethinks how she wants to be in the world, how much of that will cause you to feel abandoned by her?

Mr. R: Um, I'll adjust.

Dr. F: No, that's not my question. How much of that will cause you to feel abandoned?

Mr. R: Well, I can only go on past experience. Well, not only, but let me talk about past experience because Jean has been in and out, and up and down. And then she's done this, and then she's done that. And then she's stopped working, and then she's gone to school. And then all the moving we've done. I have trouble with the transitions, and whenever Jean starts talking about it's being time to move, I just say, "No. I don't care. I just want to stay here. Leave me alone." And then things keep working away. And then, finally I'll say, "Well, we'll move. What the heck." So I would move, and then I'll settle down again. And the same with when she works or stops working, or changes jobs. I have difficulty with the transition, the possibility of change. But then after it's over, I say, "Well, that's fine. That wasn't so bad." So, if Jean wants to work part time, or work no time, I will be able to adjust to that. And after it's been done, I'll feel OK about it. I had not thought of that in terms of abandonment. That's an interesting way to look at it.

Dr. F: If you found yourself starting to feel abandoned, how do you think you would make it safe for yourself?

Mr. R: Possibly by recognizing that after the change has been made that the roof, the sky didn't fall. Sort of looking around and saying, "Well, you know, it's OK."

Dr. F: But before you get to that point, what happens? How do you let Jean know that you are struggling with this one? How do you teach her about that part of yourself?

Mr. R: Well, she says to me in so many words, "Is the reason you're objecting because you're afraid I'm going to abandon you." I mean, you don't put it in those terms, but that . . .

Mrs. R: Pretty close to that.

Mr. R: But essentially, that's what you are saying. So I guess I say, "Logically I know that, but the feeling is still there."

The therapist, by describing Mrs. R's changes as "stirring up (Mr. R's) old feelings of being abandoned and alone," lays the groundwork for Mrs. R to understand Mr. R's reactions differently from how she has in the past. The more Mr. R talks about these feelings, the less likely he is to act them out in a way that encourages Mrs. R to take care of him and to keep the relationship stuck. The therapist is fairly direct about reframing Mr. R's reactions with the intention of helping Mrs. R see Mr. R's behavior as stemming from anxiety, fear, and vulnerability rather than not caring. This is an important message for Mrs. R who is sensitive to feelings of anxiety in those around her and will likely give up attempted changes in her behavior if she feels these changes are causing discomfort in others. The interview continues:

Dr. F: I think Jean is very sensitive to anxiety. When she picks up your anxiety, she acts it out for you, and then you react to her. It gets sort of confused, who is doing what for whom.

Mr. R: Which is better, which is safer than me reacting to myself.

Dr. F: That's what I'm trying to get at. That's the idea. That's exactly what I was wondering about.

Mr. R: So I feel anxious. She picks up the anxiety and expresses it. Then I'm able to react to my anxiety, which is kind of outside of myself and therefore safer.

Dr. F: And keeps things the same, and there's no headway in that one for you. That's what I mean by change without cooperation. She stops doing that for her own reasons, not as a way of making it better for you, as she gets clearer about how she wants it to be for herself. There's a gain, and there's a loss.

Mr. R: Well, sometimes I get annoyed at her being anxious. She'll say, "Well, I'm not sure that I want to do that because you're not in favor of it . . ."

Mrs. R: Typically me.

Mr. R: And then, I say, "Jean, if you want to do it, do it."

Dr. F: When have you become aware, Brian, that her taking on your anxiety has been a way of her taking care of you?

Mr. R: How long have I been aware of that?

Dr. F: Yes.

Mr. R: Oh, gosh. It's been two or three minutes now.

Dr. F: Well, then let me ask you another question. If she stops doing that, what becomes different for you? What's the loss for you? The gain is obvious. What's the loss?

Mr. R: That maybe I'll fear that she doesn't love me, that she isn't there for me. It's another significant person in my life that has abandoned me.

Mrs. R: Oh, dear, yes.

Dr. F: You would see it as something being taken away from you emotionally? Those feelings would get stirred up?

Mr. R: If she didn't get anxious in response to my anxiety?

Dr. F: Exactly. That's the question. Let's put her on the sidelines. Go on.

Mr. R: I don't know how to respond. I mean, there is a logical side of me that says I wouldn't have to put up with her anxiety because that's a hassle . . .

Dr. F: That's a gain.

Mr. R: But at the feeling side, at the feeling level, I really don't know.

Dr. F: That hasn't really happened for any significant period of time yet.

Mr. R: What hasn't happened?

Dr. F: Jean hasn't stopped taking on your anxiety.

Mr. R: I don't understand. She has stopped doing this, or is going to stop doing this, or might stop doing it.

Dr. F: Well, I was just wondering if you had ever experienced that with Jean. Has she gotten on the sidelines around your anxiety?

Mr. R: It depends whether it is anxiety related to a decision that she has to make or is thinking of making. It's quite different when it's anxiety relative to something that I am doing or might have to do. It works differently.

Mrs. R: I have an example.

Dr. F: Yes.

Mrs. R: One of them would be that I'm not cooking as much. I cooked for years and years, and now we have a microwave, and it's really easy. You just have to put it in and there you go, and we're both in and out and rushing around. So Brian will announce, "Well, you realize that I've cooked three nights," and I say, "Oh, really," and I don't react. Whereas, I think a few years ago, I would have felt very upset with myself. I would have felt that I was a bad wife. So in that case I'm not reacting to your anxiety.

Dr. F: That's about you being different, that sort of thing.

Mrs. R: So that caregiving is less now than it was, and that's a big risk. I mean, that's scary for me to do that.

Mr. R: Well, there's an anxiety about what you might do, and there's anxiety about what I might do. And Jean doesn't respond very well to my anxieties about myself and about my life, but she does pick up on my anxieties about her.

Mrs. R: I don't get anxious about your life? Ooooh . . .

Mr. R: In the same way. If I'm having trouble, or don't know what I'm going to be doing, or I'm in difficulty at work . . .

Mrs. R: Oh, I don't think that's true. When you were going through that period of unemployment, I found it very difficult. I'm always picking up on the anxieties. And what you're saying is that you may not have felt that I cared enough, but I did. I was . . . My sense is you're saying something else.

Mr. R: But I think you responded in terms of how it was going to affect you.

Mrs. R: Oh, I was concerned about how it would affect you as well, not just me.

Mr. R: Anyway, the important thing here is what happens if you stop reflecting my anxieties. Then I would have to deal with them myself, rather than counting on you to do that, feeling for both of us.

Dr. F: And not feel abandoned.
Mr. R: And not feel abandoned.

This segment of the interview illustrates in greater depth the delicate maneuvering that goes on between Mr. and Mrs. R. Each takes care of the other in an unusual way. The therapist hopes to convey to the couple that they can better meet each other's needs when they are not overreacting to each other. It is also important that they understand that their private thoughts, even in the absence of any overt reaction to the other's anxiety, can impede their ability to understand their own concerns, worries, and vulnerabilities. For example, when Mr. R's thinking shifts to his theme of abandonment, he views his anxiety as being caused by someone else's behavior towards him rather than by what is being stirred up inside him emotionally.

The interview continues:

Dr. F: Once you've shifted into feeling abandoned, then you feel differently about your anxieties.
Mr. R: So the thing is not about feeling anxious, it's about what you think when you feel anxious.
Dr. F: What story you tell yourself the anxiety is about.
Mr. R: Yes.
Dr. F: And if you give other responsibility for that, then you're not really allowing yourself to understand what it is about. That's what I was saying about when you shift the focus. What you're left with sometimes is more uncomfortable feelings. The nice thing about shifting it to blame, "other isn't there for me," "other is abandoning me," is we don't have to think about whatever the loss, or the sadness, or the vulnerability is about. You can shift it to a safer place. If we feel hurt about other not being there for us rather than what we're struggling with inside of ourselves, it makes us safe. It keeps us stuck. The reason I'm saying this to you is because this is the part of the work that is the most difficult. It takes a long time just to get to this point but it doesn't make it better. At this point, really, what one is left with is one's own sense of sadness, one's struggles, one's vulnerability, one's confusion, one's uncertainty, one's master plan. Other is there is some ways and willing to take on our anxiety by reacting because they see the struggle. They see the vulnerability, and they get anxious about that. Couples take care of each other in a convoluted way by playing out each other's anxiety. I think a real intimate relationship is one in which neither person needs to act out the other's anxiety or needs other to be OK to feel good in a relationship.

You have to understand where self stops and other begins. Anxiety is really where we lose it. Not being familiar, comfortable, safe. Those I think are the major losses in letting go of the old dance. What replaces them are sadness, sometimes vulnerability, and confusion. How long you can stay with those three things before someone jumps in and takes over will determine how solid you feel. A lot of people get the most twitchy at the point when the comfort, safety, and familiar are replaced with sadness, vulnerability, and confusion. That's why a lot of people don't change. You have to be able, if you love someone, to have confidence that they will come out of this clearer. But as soon as you jump in and take it on, it bogs down the process. I think you are smack at that crossroads.

Mrs. R: I think I've gone a little over the crossroad. My son says that I've changed in my interaction with Sue, not a 100%, but much, much better. And I'm doing some things for myself. I'm still not clear about that line. I'm not saying I've got it all figured out but . . .

Dr. F: But it will change too . . .

Mrs. R: But I'm doing more for myself then I did two years ago. Oh, yeah, definitely.

Dr. F: And it will change because your mother is getting older . . .

Mrs. R: Oh, and I'm doing less for my mum than I did two years ago. That confused her, and it's created some problems. I mean, she is handling it better than I imagined she would, but when she gets really mad at me she'll bring it up, "Well, I never see you." So there may be that kind of thing going on between us.

Dr. F: And it changes with your siblings?

Mrs. R: Yes.

Dr. F: You know there is real change when every major relationship feels different.

Mrs. R: So there is a crossroads. I don't think we're there. I think we've gone a little past that.

Dr. F: Yes. I would say so. It's a funny thing about change. When all the important relationships no longer feel comfortable, you know you changed something fundamental. It's an odd one.

Mrs. R: Yes. I find myself failing the most with John. It's hard for me to tolerate all the confusion and the problems, and I know I could smooth them out.

Dr. F: And not do that.

Mrs. R: And not do that because he's really a challenge.

Mr. R: So then you say to me, "I don't want to get in and change his life," but you do it.

Mrs. R: But you go do it.

Dr. F: And you have to say to yourself, anxiety! It's not a matter of caring or not caring.

Mrs. R: But it's also that I want to do some things for him. It's very hard to find that balance . . .

Dr. F: Well, watch for this now because we have a principle. The principle is, whenever we do something for other out of anxiety, it's not what other needs, it's what we need to get comfortable. Our timing is always off when we respond out of anxiety. It might be the right thing, but the wrong timing, because it's our anxiety that dictates it.

Mr. R: So whenever we try to help someone out of anxiety we're working on our needs not theirs.

Dr. F: Exactly! If you can get a handle on that and slow yourself down, then you'll be clearer.

There is a didactic component to the latter part of this interview. The couple is taught about anxiety and relationship principles with the intention of helping them understand how complicated and delicate change actually is. The common dynamic of reacting to other to maintain emotional safety is explained. The couple is also helped to understand that the shift away from a preoccupation with the other to thoughts about the self can actually increase one's sense of feeling alone, vulnerable, and confused. Unless individuals understand this reaction they will look for behavior that allows them to distance from their uncomfortable feelings about themselves. The individual attempting to change must be alert to this process. The major objective of middle phase work is to help each partner define himself or herself through an understanding of this process.

Chapter Eight

Family Therapy with Siblings

SECTION ONE:
WHY WORK WITH ADULT SIBLINGS?

The sibling unit is one of the most important subsystems within the family. Sibling relationships are usually the most longlasting relationships in a person's life. Siblings share a common history although in some respects they usually experience the same family quite differently. Factors such as sibling position, gender, and the developmental stage of the family at the time of the sibling's birth all affect the sibling's development.

It is crucial that a therapist take into consideration sibling relationships when working with a family. The way parents deal with their children's sibling relationships and the way the siblings deal with them are significant barometers of the family's functioning. Parents' attitudes towards their children's relationships with each other are determined in part by the messages that they received from their own parents in this area. A multigenerational approach provides a perspective on how the parents' experiences with their own siblings influence their approach to their own children's sibling relationships.

To gain a fuller understanding of the family system, the therapist should inquire about the relationships the adults in the family have with their siblings. How connected the adults are with their siblings and the extent to which they rely on their siblings as resources are both indicators of their sense of family. Children learn about the importance of siblings by observing their parents' connections and involvement with their own siblings.

One of the goals of the middle phase of family therapy is to encourage adults to reposition themselves with their siblings. At the beginning of therapy when adults are telling their stories about their families-of-origin, the therapist should ask whether their siblings carry similar stories. When the adults begin to consider the different ways in which their siblings experienced the family, they begin to have some doubts about their family stories. They become more curious about their experiences within the family and begin to wonder about how their siblings constructed the family history. Once this curiosity develops, the timing is right for the therapist to encourage the adults to seek out their siblings and to ask them more questions about their family.

Siblings offer each other a unique opportunity to work on unfinished family business. They are usually the most important link to the parents and have their own memories of the parents' roles in the family history. Sibling relationships also provide an opportunity for an individual to begin to reposition himself or herself by relating to his or her siblings in other than his or her traditional role with them. For example, an adult who was the first-born of the family is probably accustomed to assuming a senior role in relation to younger siblings. It is unusual for a first-born child to ask a younger sibling for help. It is a major change for a first-born to reposition himself or herself with these siblings. When a first-born asks younger siblings how they perceived the family unfolding over time, a realignment of relationships occurs in the family. In similar ways, the youngest child can reposition himself or herself in family. Many youngest feel a need to rebel or resist the efforts of the oldest who try to take care of them or shape them up. The younger siblings can effectively reposition themselves by encouraging their older siblings to provide their opinions and more information about the family. In this way, the younger sibling takes on some responsibility for maintaining the relationship. When both younger and older siblings seek information from each other about family, a more balanced sibling relationship is set in motion.

Working on sibling relationships is a middle phase strategy. An element of research is introduced into the therapy. The emphasis is on becoming more knowledgeable about the extended family and understanding how the family history shapes the way one positions oneself in the nuclear family.

SECTION TWO:
GOALS OF WORK WITH SIBLINGS

In working with adult siblings, one of the primary objectives is to tackle issues that have increased the distance between them. The emphasis is on connections. When siblings are given the opportunity, in a safe, neutral environment to tell their stories, they begin to learn about each other's sadness, loss, confusion, and ambivalence about family. As they discuss how their history has affected them and how they have constructed their memories of family members, they begin to reframe parts of their history.

Work with the younger siblings differs in several important aspects from work with the older siblings. Younger siblings may be vying for their parents' attention or acting as combatants in playing out their parents' unfinished business. When the therapist involves these younger siblings, his or her primary goal is to soften the animosity and/or anger that is acted out between the siblings. When parents are not able to give balance to their relationships with each child and/or act out their own issues by becoming inappropriately involved with their children, the children will act out the parents' issues with each other. Left to their natural inclinations, siblings are supportive and caring towards each other. Their rivalry is a sign that they are taking on parental issues and acting them out for their parents. As parents become more able to deal with their own issues without involving their children, the children's relationships with each other become more balanced and less conflictual. When working with the younger siblings, the therapist will also want to help them to understand that they need each other and that not all of their issues stem from their sibling relationship. This work is preventative in nature, encouraging more positive feelings and a sense of security between siblings.

When siblings are first seen together as adults, the idea that their sibling problems are a reflection of how their parents dealt with family issues is new to them. They are further intrigued by the idea of their parents playing out their own parents' historical themes. Once they begin to look at their history in a new light, they become more curious about their brothers and sisters. It is at this point that the involvement of the siblings in a session is especially productive.

A major reason for involving adult siblings in therapy is to reframe past issues. The siblings are helped to understand that they all had to find ways to make it emotionally safe for themselves when the family was under high anxiety. They are tremendous resources for each other. Most siblings are convinced that their stories about family are pretty much the same as their siblings'. Once they become able to appreciate that their siblings' stories are different, there is potential for a new type of connection to develop. As these connections develop between siblings, they become more important to each other and play a more vital, central role in the lives of each other's families. When siblings are connected with each other, other relationships are strengthened as well. Uncles, aunts, cousins, and other extended family members all become more important to each other. The general outcome of adult sibling work is an expanded family boundary within which the generations are more actively involved with each other.

SECTION THREE:
PROBLEM AREAS IN WORK WITH SIBLINGS

It is common for siblings to reduce tension in their relationships by focusing on their parents as "the bad guys." Siblings will try to use the therapy sessions to talk about their parents in negative ways. The therapist's task is to prevent the siblings from triangling in the parents and to help them to focus instead on their own experiences in family and how they tried to stay connected with each other. There are several important questions to ask siblings, such as: (1) what happened when the first sibling left home, (2) what changed when a sibling became ill, (3) how did sibling relationships change when another child was born, etc. These types of questions help the siblings remain focused on their relationships and how important family events affected them and their involvement in the family. The therapist must take an active role in focusing the discussion or the siblings will be likely to scapegoat their parents, another sibling, and/or an extended family member.

A client of mine, Paul, told a story that illustrates how significant family events have far-reaching effects on sibling relationships. Paul, at the age of thirteen, persuaded his parents, apparently against their wishes, to allow him to attend a Catholic boarding school. He was the oldest of four children, three boys and one girl. Paul indicated that he never really returned home after leaving for this school. From the age of thirteen on, he effectively was out of the family. When I asked him how his leaving affected his siblings, he replied that it was probably, ". . . just fine with them because they had each other." He felt his current relationships with his siblings were strained, particularly his relationship with his brother closest in age to him. He saw no connection between his departure from the family at age thirteen and the current problems in his relationships with his siblings. We arranged a session with all the siblings. I began the session by asking the second oldest to describe what changed for him when his brother went away to school. The younger brother told a story of feeling deserted and abandoned by his brother. His brother had been a role model for him, and he had counted on his brother to pave the way for him with friends, in school, and at home. When his brother left, he felt alone in the family and in the community. He went on to say that he had always resented the fact that Paul had left without preparing him in any way. This news came as a revelation to Paul who had not been aware of how important he was to his brother and how his brother had carried this loss all through the years. After Paul had the opportunity to hear this story, the two brothers began to mend their relationship and understand each other a bit differently.

Another potential problem that can arise in sibling sessions is the confirmation by siblings of each other's stories about the family history. This occurs most often when the siblings triangle in a particular family member. It is important that the therapist understand this dynamic as the siblings' attempt to reduce family and sibling anxiety. The therapist should ask each sibling precise questions about how a particular story affected him or her. As the siblings provide more details about how a major family event influenced their thinking and feeling about family, the differences in their accounts emerge and new knowledge is introduced into the sibling relationships. In contrast, if the therapist allows the siblings to confirm each other's stories, the session will provide just another opportunity to play out the ongoing distance existing in the family.

Another difficult aspect of work with siblings is the reactivating of old issues. Many family members try to bury their old hurts. The therapist's questions about family history stir up some of this pain. Siblings may want to avoid looking at certain parts of their history that they feel unfinished about or for which they feel guilty and responsible. The therapist must be very gentle and supportive when opening up certain areas of the family's life. The therapist must respect the siblings' pain and provide a safe environment for them to talk about what they have learned from their history. In this atmosphere, the therapist will be able to reframe some of the old issues in a positive way.

A fourth problem area in sibling work is that of focusing too much on content. The therapist should guard against the siblings simply using the session to tell family stories. Storytelling can be useful; however, too much storytelling can serve to reduce anxiety and maintain distance. The importance of the content is what it reveals about the process. It is up to the therapist to keep the focus on the process by asking questions about what a particular content issue meant for the self, how a content issue shaped one's life, and what the self learned from a particular content issue about how he or she strives for safety in the face of anxiety. The therapist uses content issues symbolically to help siblings connect at a deeper level.

The therapist who works with siblings must also be on guard against the keeping of family secrets. Siblings may wish to tell a family secret and swear the therapist to secrecy. These secrets tend to be about a parent's affair and/or some other major historical event that one sibling knows about to the exclusion of everyone else. It is important that the therapist not get drawn into the trap of keeping secrets. He or she should make it clear to the siblings that there should be no secrets and that any important family events should be shared and understood by all the family members. The therapist should help the siblings to understand that secrets serve to exclude family members, thereby increasing distance and adding to the general dysfunctioning of the family.

SECTION FOUR:
HOW TO MAKE A SESSION SAFE FOR SIBLINGS

A therapist must have a clear strategy for making a session with adult siblings safe for them. The siblings should be invited by the sibling client, not the therapist. It is prudent for the therapist to commence the session by asking the newcomers how they understand being there and what they would like to get out of the session for themselves. In this way, the therapist begins to communicate to the siblings that he or she will be respectful of their wishes and will try to make the session an experience that they will own in their own right. After these introductory inquiries, I usually proceed by telling the siblings that I would like to hear how each of them understands how the family developed over the years. These stories give an indication of the degree of each sibling's unfinished business. The individual siblings will each tell his or her own story involving old hurts, resentments, anger, and other unresolved issues. The task of the therapist is to begin to reframe these stories in a positive way. In doing so he or she will help the siblings understand how their stories, if left intact, will maintain the distance between them. He or she creates an environment in which it is safe for them to let go of some of their old stories and to become more curious about how other family members have constructed their similar histories. It is important that the therapist end the session on a positive note, emphasizing how the family members can become more connected as they work together as adults to honor their family history.

SECTION FIVE:
INTERVIEW WITH ADULT SIBLINGS:
CASE ILLUSTRATION AND COMMENTARY

The following interview involves two brothers, Bob and Joe. Bob was the adult child in the interview contained in Chapter Seven, Section Five. There were various references made to Joe in that interview. The six major goals of family therapy with siblings are illustrated in the following session. They are: (1) building on connections, (2) reframing past issues, (3) developing siblings as resources, (4) beginning to write a new story,

(5) dealing with distance, and (6) expanding family boundaries. As the reader may recall, the session with Bob and his parents had been taped, and Bob had watched the tape following the session. Prior to my seeing them together, I encouraged Bob to have Joe view the tape as well.

Joe's having reviewed the tape was tremendously helpful. It gave him a sense of the therapeutic approach and helped stimulate new thinking about the family. In the interview that follows, it was important for the therapist to avoid the pitfall of focusing on the parents' story and concentrate instead on how their story affected the way in which each brother dealt with important family issues.

In my work with Bob, I had given him an open invitation to invite his brother to a session. He did so spontaneously without notifying me ahead of time. Accordingly, I began the session by trying to get a sense from Bob about how he happened to arrange the session at this particular time. After I had obtained a brief explanation from Bob about why he invited Joe to this session, I shifted the attention to Joe.

The interview began as follows:

Dr. F: What brings you and your brother here today?

Bob: Well, it occurred to me this morning, and I didn't know what Joe's schedule was. He came back last night, and he's got a bunch of errands. I thought, "Why not? Invite him into the session like I did with Mum and Dad."

Dr. F: Good.

Bob: I showed him the tape, and he said that was interesting. And you did something we have not been able to do. I think what you did was you asked questions. I think that was it.

Dr. F: I just let them tell their story.

Bob: Exactly. And I don't think anybody has ever done that.

Dr. F: (Turning to Joe) Since you listened to the tape, I'd like to hear your reaction to it.

Joe: That was very interesting. I mean, it was stuff I had sort of figured out before. I mean, I was not very surprised. There was certain stuff I didn't know about my mother and so on, but it didn't come as a shock.

Dr. F: Yes.

Joe: I discovered things about my grandfather, I suppose, that I didn't really know because I don't really remember him that well, my father's father. But it's easy to see how things get passed down. I have a thirteen-year-old boy as well who just showed up yesterday from Europe. He's in Rhode Island. So, I mean, you try to break the chain along the way, but it's not always that easy.

Dr. F: If there were a theme from that tape that you would like to do differently, what theme would that be?

Joe: Listen to what your kid has to say whether it bores the shit out of you or not. You know, sit there with open ears. Ask him what he's doing, what's he up to, and listen. You know, if you have to fake it, you fake it, but at least you're there. Spend as much time as you can. Devote yourself to him when you can. I mean, I'm divorced, and he lives with his mother, so it's a little bit different. Or maybe it just magnifies it. I would say that was about it.

Joe's comments have given some indication of his unfinished business with his parents. The therapist must be cautious not to triangle in the parents by permitting the two brothers to scapegoat them. By asking about the brothers' reactions to the videotape, the therapist shifted the focus from the parents to what the brothers have learned about themselves, their family, and their relationships with each other.

The interview continues:

Dr. F: I am curious about how your mother's and father's relationship affected how the two of you developed your own relationship as brothers.

Joe: Well, I don't know. Since 1962, when he left, that's the last time basically that we lived together, except for the three years that I was here. There was a time I hadn't seen him in seven years. So you know, I didn't know him. You know we each developed some way, and I went my own way. I suppose when I was a kid I used to idolize him.

Dr. F: Did you feel he deserted you?

Joe: No, not at all. Not that I feel like it.

Dr. F: I have a theory. I think I have mentioned this theory to Bob. I'll mention it to you. Can I do that?

Joe: Yeah. Sure. Go ahead.

Dr. F: The theory that I've developed listening to your mother's and father's story is that they experienced a lot of losses in their own families-of-origin and they both felt for different reasons that no matter how hard they tried to be there for their parents, they couldn't be there enough. It was a very powerful story that your mother told about her mother. Even on her deathbed, her mother still got her mixed up with another sibling. And your dad also kind of took on this burden with his dad. But they had you two, and I think in their hopes and their dreams they hoped that you two would make them feel loved enough. And you needed to get away from that. That's my theory.

The therapist has offered an hypothesis about how the parents' stories have influenced the brothers' relationships with each other and their roles in the family. He is attempting to gently challenge the brothers' stories that they have constructed about themselves in the family. The hypothesis reframes the parents' behavior towards their children. The therapist suggests that the parents attempted to take care of their sons as a way of making up, through their sons, for the losses they experienced in their own families. The therapist implies caring, not blame. The reframe encourages the brothers to think about their parents in a slightly different way. The emphasis on the parents' experiences with their own parents fosters a more curious, less judgmental attitude towards the parents. The therapist, in introducing the hypothesis, hoped to introduce some doubt and uncertainty in the brothers about the stories that each had constructed about his parents.

The interview continues along these lines:

Joe: The first half I agree with. Probably that's true, but they never sort of paid their dues as far as I'm concerned to justify it. Right. To this day my mother has never, and my father has never, asked me really what I do. So they never listened. They still never listen. I was talking to Bob about this. I'd go on a trip. They'd ask you a question, sort of like in an oral exam, you know, "What'd you do?" "I went to the Chicago's fair." "Oh, yeah. We were there." This launches up a whole diatribe about where they've been. So, I became sensitive to this maybe ten years ago, and I'd say, "Well, this is the way they are."

Dr. F: What did you see happening? What explanation did you give yourself?

Joe: For their behavior? It's to show their insecurities. Kind of show that we've been there. We know it. We know just as much as you do and we're cool. OK. Fine. But it's very competitive, you know, and I'm not a very competitive sort of person. I'd rather switch then fight. OK. You want to be that way. But then, I turn off. So my mother would say they never asked us what I did. Well shit, you know, you never asked me. How do you expect me to generate interest in what you're doing if you never did it for me. So, I can't remember if this fits your theory or not.

Dr. F: They weren't there for you. It's very hard for them to let go of their own agenda, switch over to hear yours.

Joe: Sure. So they can't really expect that we'd reciprocate when they never put out.

Dr. F: So you would have to find some way to make it safe for yourself, protect yourself, when that would happen. What would you do?

The therapist is now encouraging Joe to think about how he has used distance in his relationships. He is opening up the subject of how Joe deals with anxiety and loss. The therapist is aware from previous contacts with

Bob that he tends to define the distance in his relationships with Joe as a sign of lack of caring or lack of need rather than a sign of vulnerability and a need for safety.

The interview continues with Joe's response:

Joe: Oh, you mean me. Why I left. Well, I had this need to leave. I went to City College for two years, and I had this need to get out, to transfer out. Part of it was because I lived at home. I was only eighteen at the time, and I wanted to leave. Part of it I guess, maybe subconsciously now in retrospect, probably what you say has some truth in it. Let me out of here. But also I had this need to see how the other half of the world lives. So I had this kind of wanderlust, which I guess I still have. I get a chance to travel quite a bit. I also wanted to get out of Rhode Island. You know, it was probably the best thing in my life that I ever did. I have to thank my parents for putting out, for paying the bills, letting me go. Some parents would say, "Sorry, we don't have the money." So yeah, probably part of it was escape. Even to this day it's hard for me to be at home. I say, "You're going to bite the silver bullet. You're going to have to put up with their shit, that they don't listen to you and all that stuff, and they don't care, and what they do doesn't really interest you." What my father does sort of interests me because it's technical. I like that kind of stuff. But listening to my mother talk about the old age home, part of it I fear myself, old age, you know, nobody likes to hear that. But the thing itself doesn't interest me. It's like someone who works in social work or something. You know it's interesting for five minutes, but personally, it doesn't interest me. So it's hard for me. When they came down for my son's bar mitzvah, I went almost off the wall. Especially my mother. She can't tolerate anything. She's a very difficult sort of person. She has to have it her way and I'm much more easygoing. So fortunately my girlfriend is much more tough. She's a stewardess and has the skin of an elephant, because you have to if you are a stewardess for very long. She took them around, which was very nice. You know, it took the heat off of me. If I'm with them for more than a few hours at a time, I go off the deep end.

Joe's response gives a clear indication of how he uses distance as a way to be safe in the world. His last comment about going off the deep end is a strong indication of unfinished business. Joe's comments have given Bob an opportunity to rethink Joe's behavior in the family. The therapist now wishes to focus on the brothers' relationships with each other and asks Joe a direct question about how the family patterns affected his relationship with Bob:

Dr. F: How about with Bob then? If you weren't able to connect with your mom and dad back then, and Bob was three and a half years your senior, were you able to connect with him?

Joe: Well, he wasn't around. In '58 he went off to school for a couple of years. Then he came back when I was finishing my senior year in high school, I guess, and then he was here in my freshman year, something like that. After I finished my freshman year, he left again. So it was only, in any kind of mature life, it was only two years there of overlap. I don't even remember those years too well, and he was doing other stuff.

Dr. F: It's not something I gather you've talked with Bob about, how he's tried to make peace with your mom and dad.

Joe: I guess, sort of, we have. We've talked about it to some extent.

Dr. F: Later in life or?

Joe: Oh, no. Just now.

Dr. F: Just now, but not before?

Joe: No. Because we were never really in the same venue at the same time.

Throughout the interview the therapist has tried to reframe the old stories and encourage the brothers to think about their history differently so that they can connect on it rather than feel cut off and defensive about it. The therapist proceeds by asking Joe one last question about how the theory he has constructed about the family affects the way he relates to his brother and uses distance to stay safe.

Dr. F: Well, what's your hypothesis about the distance now, the fact that the two of you don't try to spend more time together?

Joe: What? Me and Bob?

Dr. F: Yes.

Joe: Well, we're at other ends of the world for one. It's sort of by luck, and my being at the right place at the right time, that I could actually get here, because of my work. If it weren't that, and maybe the occasional trip to Rhode Island when we just happen to overlap, you know, physically it's hard to see him. I'm not a millionaire. If I could, I'd probably be over here more often. That's the nuts and bolts of it.

Dr. F: Do you think the reserve comes from you or from Bob?

The therapist now uses the word "reserve" rather than distance to describe the brothers' relationship with each other. In using the word reserve, he is encouraging Joe to rethink his behavior towards his brother and consider why he needs to maintain that behavior in the present.

Joe responds:

Joe: Reserve? In terms of what?

Dr. F: Between the two of you.

Joe: Him.

Dr. F: More Bob.

Joe: Yeah. He's more reserved than I am. It's manifested also in the kind of work he does. It's a much more conservative and reserved kind of job. I mean, I haven't worn a suit to look respectable in twenty years. Because I don't have to. I mean, I can teach in shorts and so on. So I'm much more informal. The job I do is much more informal, among more crazy people. So there is very little formality and reserve and so on. So I'd say I'm less reserved than him. But maybe he looks at it differently. I don't know.

Dr. F: Well, what do you think about this theory? You had to find a way to make it safe for you around your parents, and you did that by finding some ways to distance.

Bob: You know, I think you're probably right. I did have a job in Rhode Island when I graduated, and then I decided I wasn't really that keen on doing that. I would rather try the West Coast, and you know, I ended up coming here. There's nothing that I can think about that would refute the hypothesis.

Dr. F: Well, how do you think it affected your relationship with Joe? What was the spin-off?

The therapist has again asked a specific question to ensure that the focus will be on the sibling relationship rather than on the parents.

Bob responds:

Bob: I don't know. I never looked at it that way. I guess, if one directs the number, we both acted the same way. Probably we're very close to being as far away as you could be on the globe.

Joe: Pretty much, with Rhode Island in the center.

Dr. F: This is accidental, more job-related?

Joe: Yeah, I think so.

Bob: Joe would like to be closer. If he could get a job here, I think he would jump at it. My guess is if he had choices in North America, this would be one of the places he would . . .

Joe: This would be the top of the list.

Bob: We are ten or eleven hours time distance and close to nine thousand miles away from each other. You know, I think that's a result of the hypothesis. You know it's certainly plausible. If you had like Mum, Pop, Joe and me, and we were going to set up distances I can certainly see setting up distance from them, but I can't see setting up distance from him. I could see it as a consequence, more than desire or intended.

Dr. F: You don't think it is conscious, not an overt attempt to keep distance.
Bob: I don't think so.
Dr. F: No.
Joe: I myself wouldn't want to live in Rhode Island for anything. Even if you gave me ten million dollars of your salary.
Bob: Well, ten million of my salary, but short of that, I wouldn't live there. I just couldn't deal with it anymore. I've spent too much time outside of the city. And to get them to move out of Rhode Island is impossible.
Dr. F: Well, let me ask you another question. I'll ask you this one, Bob. How do you and Joe use each other as resources? You both have gone through divorces, major upheavals in your life. How have the two of you connected on that?

Here the therapist is choosing to focus on the positive nature of the relationship between Bob and Joe. Rather than focus on what has not worked in the past, he is directing attention to what can work in the future. The ultimate goal of this sibling session is for the brothers to feel more connected with each other and more hopeful about their relationship in the future.
Both brothers respond to the question:

Bob: I think we talked once about that . . .
Joe: Yeah, a year ago.
Bob: I think it was maybe more in the context of Pam than anything else.
Joe: Well, it was the last day when I was here a year ago. You got a subpoena, so I was asking you all about the stuff because I got it all over several years before that.
Bob: Pam was studying for exams, and she wasn't in. Joe and I made a Seder for the kids. So in the middle of the Seder, this subpoena server comes and says this divorce petition has been filed with the courts. Sue said she had this terrible feeling, but we knew it was coming. We split the cost of the subpoena server.
Joe: Oh, really.
Bob: Well, I did that. I mean, I agreed with Sue that whatever the legal costs are we split them fifty-fifty. She said she had this terrible feeling that it was going to show up at a time like that, when the girls were together. So I guess we talked a little bit then.
Joe: Not much. It's so different. Such a different kind of divorce set up. You know. It felt really comfortable. Maybe these days there's more cam-

araderie getting divorced than not. Since so many people do it. But there's not really much to it.

Bob: You know I'm still close with Sue by choice. I mean, we really care for each other.

Joe: Yeah, I think if an eraser would come down on my ex-wife and make soap eraser dust out of her, I'd be real happy.

Dr. F: You're still angry?

Joe: Yeah, I'm fed up. You know, with her pettiness, and I'm sure she thinks I've got my own problems. And it's totally different today. I mean, age differences and so on. So it's not really the same.

Dr. F: So if you could change one thing, one aspect of your relationship with your brother, what would that be?

The interview is now shifting into the middle phase. Each of the brothers has talked a bit about how the family history has influenced the distance between them. The therapist now begins to take a more proactive stance and encourages the brothers to begin to talk about how they would like the relationship to be different. He encourages each to consider how much responsibility he is prepared to take for making it different. The therapist emphasizes the point that each brother must be prepared to work on the relationship without needing help or cooperation from the other. It is common for family members to take the position that change is not possible because of other's refusal to cooperate. Anticipating this response, the therapist encourages each brother to talk individually about what he would like to occur in the relationship rather than approach change as something they need to work on together.

Joe responds to the question about what he would like to change in the relationship:

Joe: I'd like to be closer.

Dr. F: Closer in what sort of way?

Bob: Oh, physically. I mean, if we were closer physically, then we could work on other things. Joe not being here very often, it's very hard.

Dr. F: What would being closer look like? If Joe were here, let's just say for the sake of discussion, what would that closeness look like?

Bob: Well, I mean, we had a really nice night last week or two, I don't know . . .

Joe: A couple of weeks ago.

Bob: A couple of weeks ago. We just stayed around, and one night Dana came over. Then the next night, we were just by ourselves and we barbecued something. Then we watched some tapes together. We had a chance to talk. It was just really pleasant. So it would be like that. It would be more opportunity to talk, just come over for dinner. When you have the time, it's not like each minute you've got to worry about. We could go out to baseball games. We could go watch movies, and we could do stuff together without feeling like there is so little time. And that's the trap I had to get out of with the kids when I was in Europe. I had to get myself out of thinking, "Gosh. It's so great having them. I better maximize each minute." I said "Schmuck. If you really want to kill this trip, that's got to be the optimal way to do it." So I backed off, and you know, we had a great time. We would just be doing the kind of things brothers do together. And Joe likes to do much more outdoor stuff than I like. I like doing more urban stuff, but he would be around. I'm sure he could drag me off to go for a hike in the bay. And I'm sure I could take him, and we would do urban things. It would be a nice time. It would just be nice having him around, having a friendlier, closer bond.

Dr. F: Do you think about that loss, not having that? Is that something that occurs to you every now and then?

Bob: When it occurs to me is when Joe shows up and a lot of times he gives me no notice. I remember two years ago when Joe was here, I was really angry at him because I have a crazy schedule. I had no idea he was coming. Then he comes and says, "OK, I'm free for lunch." I wasn't free for lunch. And then he got all pissed off because I wasn't free for lunch because he was here. Give me a day's notice and I'll rearrange the lunch.

Joe: Well, I couldn't plan it. I just couldn't. It depends on airlines. What could I do?

Bob: Well, when you do plan it you still don't know your schedule.

Joe: I did this time. I told you exactly.

Bob: You told me exactly that you may be leaving to go to the site on Sunday, Monday, or Tuesday.

Joe: Well, I couldn't get through to him. It's not my fault. That's the nature of the game. You know, it's not like business guys who are sitting in their offices. I mean, it's not the same kind of thing. Our hours are a little different and the realm of people I work with is much more fluid. It's not so much like the business world where, well, I got this dinner here, I got this lunch here. I have an appointment book. When people call me up, I try to do it, but still it's not the same sort of world. I mean, I try as much as I can but more often it depends on them.

Joe's comments provide a good example of how one sibling can use the behavior of another to justify the distance. These responses are predictable. Siblings, like couples and parents and children, will say they can't change without cooperation. As mentioned before, the therapist must introduce the notion that for change to occur the self must be able to behave differently, even in the absence of cooperation from other.

The interview continues with the therapist asking Joe how he would like the relationship to be different:

Dr. F: Well, how would you answer that question, assuming you were physically closer? What would you want to have different?

Joe: With him?

Dr. F: Yes.

Joe: Drag him outside. He lives in probably one of the most beautiful cities in the world, and one of the most beautiful environments in the world, and he looks at the buildings all the time. This is like a personal life view, you know. I like the buildings because I think it's a nice place. But I, in the last two weeks, have been working in the interior, and yesterday, I was down in the islands, and for me, it felt like I was tripping around, like twenty years ago, because it's a beautiful place. And here he lives here and he does not appreciate it. Or maybe he appreciates it, but maybe everybody who lives in a place gets jaded after a while. But to pull him outside, to show him what a great area, to have him slow down a little bit, and not be so intense at what he's doing. To loosen him up a little bit. Loosen some of the joints. He used to, when we would go to summer camp, he used to love being outside, and then something happened to him.

Dr. F: How long ago was that?

Joe: Twenty or twenty-five years ago.

Bob: I think we stopped in 1958 or something like that.

Dr. F: How about the other question I asked Bob about the loss? Do you think about not having your brother available to you?

Joe: Well, yeah, to some extent. Especially when I was in England. I was working with a colleague of mine. He's really close to his parents. Close to his mother, his father, and he's got a brother he's real buddies with. He plays Kung Fu and this and that, and they're real close. I said, "Gee, it would be nice if I had a relationship like that." Of course, they live five miles away and so it would be nice to have that. And also they share similar interests. It's much more overlapping, what they do and like compared to what Bob and I do and like. But I said it's like a goal to strive for. It would be nice, but I don't pine away all the time.

Dr. F: Your parents are in Rhode Island and your brother is here and your son, where does he live?

Joe: He's not so far away, but it's not so easy. He's at the age where it's hard to see him. His friends are more interesting than his old man, whose out-to-lunch already.

Dr. F: So do you feel disconnected from family?

Joe is beginning to talk about how he would like things to be different for himself with his family. When the therapist asks Joe whether he feels disconnected from his family, he gives Joe an opportunity to tell his brother, by way of his answer to the therapist, that he really wants to have more connection and that family is important to him. Commonly family members distance as a way of making it safe for themselves. Unfortunately other family members view the distancing as an indication that the family member doesn't wish to be involved and reciprocates with more distancing. The therapist reframes the distancing as a sign of caring and vulnerability, not a sign of lack of interest. Once the family members interpret the distancing behavior differently they are unlikely to use it to justify further distance.

The interview continues with Joe's response:

Joe: Yeah. Sure, I feel all alone. I mean, London is really kind of a lonely place. Other than everything else there, I wish I were back on this continent, or somewhere else. For whatever reasons. Family is one, but just life style is another. I would much rather be back here.

Dr. F: But if you were here and your son stayed there, what would that be like?

Joe: It's a conflict. Pretty tough. But he's getting to the age now where . . . Like he came yesterday all by himself.

Dr. F: Came on a plane?

Joe: Yeah. Got on a plane. He used to be an unaccompanied minor and all this stuff. And this morning when I spoke to him it was like, "No sweat, you know. Got my bag off. Went through the customs and that's it. Everything is fine." In London kids are much more independent and grow up much faster than they do here anyway. I think being a kid of a broken family, he's much more sensitive and street smart to maintaining his own whatever. So to answer your question, if it boils down to having to live here and regretting it rather than to suffer there because he's there, I'd rather be here. I mean, it's a selfish decision, but I've got no choice.

Dr. F: So you've thought about that.

Joe: Oh, yeah, all the time. Sure.

Dr. F: For your boy and his sense of family, what does he carry in terms of your definition of family?

By asking Joe how he communicates his definition of family to his son, the therapist is sending the message that Joe's work on family is important to the next generation as well as the sibling relationship. He encourages Joe to talk about how he would like his son to think and to feel about family as a way to emphasize the point that this work has implications for all levels; in effect, between siblings, between parent and child, and between other adults in the family. As the interview continues, the therapist focuses on the siblings' development of a sense of family, both for themselves and for the next generation.

Joe responds to the question about his son's sense of family:

Joe: Probably minimal, I would say because his mother's family die like flies. They have this sort of black, scorpion cloud over the whole family. His mother had a sister who died of a brain tumor and then a brother, who, because his family was devoted to the sister while she was dying, committed suicide. And then ten years ago her mother died of cancer, at the age of fifty-three. So it's like catastrophe. And when we got married in London, on the night of the wedding, the only relatives of her father who were still alive in London got killed in a car crash.

Dr. F: On their way to the wedding?

Joe: Yeah. So it's like a death cloud over the family. And I don't have a family there. I mean, his only family relationship from his father comes from me and my girlfriend, who he gets along with pretty well and his grandparents, my parents, which is obtuse to say the least. I mean, when I told my mother, I'll get back to the answer, but when I came here three weeks ago, my mother said, "Well, when is Justin coming? I hope it's on a Tuesday." I said, "Jesus Christ," I said to myself not to her, "I mean, this is your only grandson. He's thirteen. He's the only one and you can't take a day off from work to do something with him." This is not the first time she acted that way. This is a couple of years ago as well, and all of a sudden it clicked in. Well, if she's that way to her grandson, it's not a new behavior pattern. It must have been that way to me as well. Like I don't have time for you for some reason. So I think it really makes sense. How much did she really put out? Can't you go take off from work? She's seventy-two years old, so she'll miss fifty bucks. And when he's there, she never relates to him because she's sleeping till ten o'clock. It's some kind of a crazy problem she has. She never puts herself out to do anything for him. And here's a kid who comes seven thousand miles away to do something, and she doesn't have the time. Or she can't be bothered or what am I going to do with him. I mean, what to do with him, just sit around and talk to him. But she's probably so afraid of herself that she can't really relate to him. So now what is the answer to the question? I'm getting back to it, just all these diversions.

Dr. F: His sense of family?

Joe: Ah, yeah. So he has that from my parents. I don't know how much . . .

Dr. F: How about his grandfather? What about with your dad? What is different about his connection with your dad?

Joe: A little bit, but you know, I think now my father is changing a little bit. He's more willing to play cards and do stuff with him. But its not like most grandparents. They are doting. Their kids will come, and they'll drop everything they can just to be with their kid and play with him. Do something. Go to the movies. Take him out bowling. Just do something with their grandchild. I see it all over London and everything like that, and with them, it's intellectualized. "What are we going to do?" So, OK, I realize it. Once you realize it, then can you maybe deal with it and treat it.

Dr. F: So that's a loss for you, I gather.

Joe: Well, they could do it. They connect. They love him, and he's really nuts about them and stuff, but it's real limited. You know, it's not really this kind of unzip my heart and emotion, because they are probably all afraid of getting put off and rejected and all that stuff. So yeah. It's a loss. It's too bad.

Dr. F: And with his uncle?

Joe: Oh, with Bob. I don't know. I mean, they see each other so little. I mean, he knows who Bob is and so on but I don't know what kind of attachment there is. It's like blood is thicker than water, but I don't know how much more because he's kind of an abstract figure. Bob was there in '84, and he didn't see him, and '85.

Bob: I saw him for a couple of days then.

Joe: Yeah. Right. But more than that, Justin knows that he exists, but . . .

Dr. F: So very little sense of family for your boy.

Joe: Yeah, pretty much. It's tough on him really, but what can I do? I can't manufacture a family overnight just to make him feel that way. So for me, it's important when he comes here that I can do stuff with him.

Dr. F: It's important that he connect with his cousins and with his uncle?

Joe: Here? Well, I think it would be nice, but I think there's no connection. I mean, the connection between him and his cousins is next to zero. There is no connection.

Dr. F: Not much with Dana?

Joe: Zero. They are two different mind sets.

Dr. F: They are not so far apart are they in age?

Joe: Well, he's thirteen, and she's nineteen.

Dr. F: Six years.

Joe: And it's just a different mentality. He's sort of very English in certain ways, and she's very North American, and there is probably nothing in common.

Dr. F: How about Katie?

Joe: Katie, I don't know. Maybe. She used to read stories to him. I remember, when he was here in 1980, Katie read to him. Stories, comics or whatever.

Bob: They've only met two or three times.

Joe: They don't really know each other that well.

Bob: Maybe what you should do is have him come next summer. We'll send him to this camp over on the island and get him out of London.

Joe: That's not up to me. It's up to his old lady. But if I come here on sabbatical next year, I want to bring him totally. Maybe now I could do it, but it's hard at that age. He doesn't want to leave his buddies just to get uprooted to come with his father to some place that he sort of vaguely knows. He doesn't want to leave all his pals. I could work on it, but I get zero support from his mother. If his mother would say, "You know, Justin, it's going to be tough, but I think it would be good for you to spend the year abroad with your father," but she would never do it. Never. That's part of the problem. So part of his lack of family identity I think relates to geopolitics and to his mother, I think as well. She's got sort of a heart like ice.

Dr. F: Bob, when you listen to Joe talk about his son and all this, what do you find yourself thinking?

The therapist has decided to give Bob an opportunity to comment on his nephew's history of loss. The theme of loss runs through the generations in this family. Bob's comments have the potential to foster a connection between the brothers. The therapist considers Bob to be in the proactive phase of therapy and expects that he will be touched by his brother's story and will be able to use it to connect with him. In contrast, if he were still in the reactive phase and feeling angry at his brother, he would be likely to criticize his brother's story, thereby increasing the distance between them. It is therefore crucial that the therapist be quite sure what phase his client is in. The goal is greater connection. If there is significant reactivity, it is too risky to ask one family member to comment on the story of another. However, if solid repositioning has occurred and members are no longer blaming each other for the distance between them, then there is potential for them to connect around each other's sadness.

Bob responds without reactivity:

Bob: Well, it makes me sad. Justin is a very sweet kid. He really is. That's why I thought it would be nice to send him over here and let him stay with me. I'll send him to camp for a couple of weeks and we could do stuff together. You know, like get him out of London.

Dr. F: He's never stayed with you before?

Bob: No. Only in 1980. He was six.

Joe: Five. When you took him out to the sushi bar, I remember. He liked it too.

Bob: We went to a baseball game in 1985. We did do some stuff at the Chicago Pizza, I remember. He's really sweet, and I have the money, and I realize that I'm his uncle and the kids are his cousins. And you know those are close family words. It would really be nice to have some kind of relationship with him. I saw him in London in '84. I was there for three weeks and I spent a fair amount of time with him. We did some swimming and we toured the wax museum together. So we did do stuff together. But there's got to be more for him.

Dr. F: So he doesn't have any, if I follow this story, uncles, aunts, and cousins on his mother's side?

Joe: Yeah. He has cousins. They would be second cousins. It's his mother's cousins.

Dr. F: No first cousins though?

Bob: Now he's an only child.

Dr. F: He's truly an only child.

Joe: Yeah, he's really by himself. It's like school of hard knocks. In lots of ways, I really worry. You know, drugs and all that. I mean, he's thirteen and all that stuff.

Dr. F: Has being in London become like family? Is it that sort of feeling for him?

Joe: Well, I think he's more tied to his buddies at school than he is to anything else.

Dr. F: They've become even more important with the lack of family?

Joe: Yeah, sure. And his father's not around that much, you know. Always going someplace around the world. Here and there and the other place. That's part of my job to get out of there whenever I can, which I do.

Dr. F: Does getting out of London feel like getting out of Rhode Island?

Joe: No. It's not because of feeling. It's just I don't like being there.

Dr. F: So Rhode Island was getting away from family?

Joe: I guess subconsciously it was getting away from family. Now that I look at it more, I realize that that's partially true, but I don't think it was all that. This kind of yearning to see, you know, I had friends who went away to college. You see on TV, football games, and things like that.

Maybe the yearning to see a football game and be with crowds of people that are not just the same kids I went to high school with. So I think that was part of it. I'd say half, if not more.

Dr. F: And it's different now. Your wanting to move away from London has a different basis to it?

Joe: Oh, yeah, totally. It's more like nuts and bolts of the daily life and colleagues and things like that, which I could do without. The job that I do there basically is kind of interesting, but I'd like to do that kind of stuff somewhere else in the world. Being raised in North America, I'd prefer that to being over there.

Dr. F: You're going to do a sabbatical over here next year?

Joe: I hope. I'm taking a sabbatical one way or the other. I'm going to see if I can arrange to do it here. I tried to do that for this year, but the money fell through. I couldn't get enough money out. I'm going to try to teach here or something. Even if that falls through, at least, I'll have more money for my sabbatical pay. So I'll try and stay here anyway.

Bob used the opportunity to comment on his brother's story to build on family resources. He expressed his sadness about his nephew's losses and spoke about wanting to have a relationship with him. During the interview Bob has also talked about the importance of the brothers' spending more time together and becoming more involved in each other's lives. The sibling session has successfully fostered a general increase in connection between the two brothers. Also of importance is that other family members have been discussed in a positive way, stimulating new thinking about family.

The interview continues:

Dr. F: Well, you know if you were here for a year, it would be interesting to see how your relationship would evolve. I guess it would be the first time in your adult life that you would be close to each other.

Bob: He was here for four months in '85.

Joe: But I was away a bit, and he went off to lots of different places . . .

Dr. F: I am wondering if that's what you would repeat in the year. A similar pattern even though you lived close together.

Bob: Well, in the three weeks we certainly did because I think we had dinner together three times maybe.

Dr. F: So it's almost like not having each other nearby.

Joe: Well, to some extent yes. That's right. Because you get so much in the groove of living a certain life style of well, I've got to go here, or I've got to go to there and give a lecture here and see the people, you know.

Dr. F: I think it's a myth to think that one has to live close by to have a connection. I think it helps, but it's not the amount of time one spends that makes one feel connected. It's how much you connect part of yourself with other. And I still have the theory about your family that it's safer to keep a certain degree of distance. I think you learned that at a very young age, without even realizing it. And I think a lot of times when we need emotional distance, we orchestrate our lives to fit that need. And then we say it's because we have this life style that we live like this. We think it's our life style that is responsible. That's the myth that we carry about ourselves. I don't think it's the life style. I think it's the need, and we use our life style to support our way of keeping it emotionally safe. When you think about the next generation, your son and your daughters, to what degree will you be able to help them break that pattern?

The therapist now attempts to build on connections for the future. Throughout the session he has encouraged the brothers to rethink the lesson that they learned in their family about maintaining distance to feel safe. He emphasizes the point by asking about the brothers' potential for passing on different ways of relating to the next generation.

Joe responds to the question as follows:

Joe: I agree. You're probably right. But for my son and his kids, it's too late, dead. There's no hope instilling any feeling of family between them because of probably just the way they are. If you do not grow up with somebody like cousins, how do you know? What kind of a relationship can you have? You don't feel anything I suppose.

Dr. F: If you had this concept back then, do you think you would have done it a little bit differently?

Joe: Our children do you mean?

Dr. F: Yes, and making sure there were more connections going in all these different ways.

Joe: I don't know. That's a good question. I'm not sure. It's harder. I mean, really, if I were living on this continent, it probably would have been easier to get together and sort of instill something. But when you know the two circles never touch, and when they do touch half of them have grown up already, you know, past a certain age, I imagine it sort of becomes more academic than emotional when you realize that you have a cousin somewhere. I mean, you know you have a cousin, but so what. It could be Joe Blow on the street.

Dr. F: I was just sitting here wondering how your kids would react to hearing the two of you, watching this tape. What sense they'd get listening to their fathers and their uncles talk about this family puzzle, and how they'd apply it to themselves. Well, I think that someday it would be valuable to them just to listen to it. It would be fascinating. But what do you think about that question? The need to distance and somehow develop a life style that supports that?

Bob: No, I think you're right. It's been going on in my head, when you asked Joe at the beginning about being reserved, and to hear his perspective, because I think he's much more reserved than I am. I mean, he has an image of me being very conservative because of the meetings I have. And I have a reasonably structured kind of existence just because of all the demands on it, so I've got to slot them in. But I consider myself on emotional things to be much less reserved and much more keen than Joe expresses. Maybe not anymore keen than he is in fact, but much more keen than he expresses. And so, when I look back, obviously his perception when he was here before was that I was too busy to do anything with him. My perception was, yes, I was very busy, but there wasn't anything in my business that I would not have rearranged to make time for us to spend together. So I was hurt because I knew we only had three days together in four months. And when I said, "Let's get together," Joe would have something else to do. My perception was it was never a question of my time, because no matter how busy it was, I was able to rearrange. His perception is a very different one.

Joe: Yes, the opposite. Because I was just going to say, exactly a direct quote. There were times I would call to say, "Let's do something." You would say, "No, I've got this meeting," or "I'm going over to Hong Kong," or something like that. I'd say, "We've got to get together and smoke some cigars and drink some booze," and I'd wait for the time for you to call me up and say, "OK. Let's do it," and it never happened.

Bob: I do remember one night we did that together, and you spent the whole night ironing.

Joe: Well, maybe I had to iron, I don't know. But that's part of, I mean, but that's OK. I don't think there's anything wrong with that, if you are with somebody you like. What difference if he stands on his head, or eats . . .

Bob: Because I sensed that you were busying yourself with these other things and that you were there, but not there, a bit like Pop.

Joe: But so what?

Bob: Like Pop was there, but he wasn't there. I mean, physically. It's what you talk about that counts.

Dr. F: The meaning that each of you gives to the other's behavior has not been talked about. Yet you see the meaning as reality. It's not the other person's reality, but you make it your reality.

Here the therapist has directly challenged the story each brother has constructed about himself and his brother. His goal is to help each brother understand how his thinking that his reality is the other's reality serves to keep them stuck and distant in their relationship.

Bob: I told you I have this grammatical construction I named after you, the positive semi-indefinite. I'd say, "Hey, Joe, let's do something," and he'd say, "Oh, that's great, but . . ." And then I remember a number of times when you'd call Pam and me up, the next morning and say, "Hey, I was going to go out with you guys." Well, along came seven-thirty, and we were going to go to a movie, and we went, and you were waiting for something else to jell. And the next morning you'd say, "I was going to go out with you."
Joe: I don't remember that.
Bob: You would keep your options open to the point where there were no options because they would disappear. After a while I would say, "Gee, you know I do have all these other things," and I would clear everything else up to do something with you, but then you would say, "Well, I've got to keep the options open," and then, pretty soon, my option to keep an option open closed.
Joe: I guess I just don't remember.
Bob: I guess this is one thing I can get across. No matter how busy I am, if you called to say, "I'd really like to do something," I will clear it up. I mean that but I've got to have notice to rearrange things. With a couple of days notice, I can make time. I would like to.
Dr. F: On that note, before we end, I have a question I want to ask each of you that may puzzle you. Why do you want to spend more time with each other? Wouldn't it be better to leave it the way it is?

This last question is a paradoxical one. Rather than trying to convince the brothers they should be better connected with each other, the therapist plays the devil's advocate role. He puts the brothers in the position of having to convince the therapist, and, in turn, themselves, that better connections are preferable to distance. The therapist does not wish to assume the convincing role. He moves out of the role of trying to make something happen and focuses instead on helping the brothers to understand why they need their relationship to be a certain way, what they would lose by changing it, and how each needs to go about being different in the relationship for his own reasons and not as a way of taking care of other and/ or pleasing the therapist.

Bob responses to this paradoxical question:

Bob: Well, I mean, I like him. It's not dependent on being my brother. I like him. So that's one. And secondly, it's just a lot of things. I like having a brother. I mean, the stuff with Mum and Pop has been eating at me for a long time. I like being able to share that experience with two different perspectives. It's really important to me to be able to say, "Hey, look. I grew up and this is the way it looked to me. Am I totally out to lunch? I mean, how was it for you?" Being able to have that. Because we did. We've been away for a long time. But we did have twenty years together, and we've had twenty years subsequently. Even more, you're forty-four.

Joe: Three.

Bob: So I mean, just being able to share these experiences and kind of test things, you know, would really be special. So I miss not having that opportunity.

Dr. F: Can you answer that question, Joe? Why would you want to spend more time with him?

Joe: Well, I like him. He's an interesting guy to talk to. Even though we don't have that much in common, and he's also my brother. As I say, blood's thicker than water, so.

Dr. F: What do you think the risk is?

Joe: What do you mean, the risk?

Dr. F: That's the question I thought would puzzle you.

Joe: Yeah it does because, it's not, the risk . . .

Dr. F: I don't know if you can answer the question, but think about it. What do you think the risk is of getting closer?

This last question touches upon a difficult area. When the brothers realize there is some risk and/or loss in becoming closer they are better able to understand the parts that they play in maintaining the relationship as it is. It is important that they understand that they will lose something by giving up the old stories that preserve the safe distance. By drawing closer to each other, they will have to be different in some way. First, must understand what they need in the relationship to feel comfortable. They they must let go of needing other to be different in order to feel safe. The difficult question is how they make it safe for themselves regardless of whether other is different. This fundamental question must be addressed before one prepares to risk being different in the relationship.

The interview continues:

Joe: Oh, I have some ideas.

Dr. F: Do you want to keep them to yourself?

Joe: I don't care. It's up to you. I could think about it more if you want, I mean . . .

Dr. F: That's up to you. Bob, what do you think the risk is?

Bob: I think it's just the risk you always have in getting close. You get close, and then you get hurt and disappointed. So it's kind of a standard, government-issue risk. That's one I'm getting more happy to take.

Dr. F: That's a dilemma for the two of you. When I met your parents, I learned that they had difficulty giving to you emotionally what they did not get from their parents. You learned how to make it safe emotionally by distancing.

Joe: Yeah. Sure. I see it in my own kid.

The therapist has reframed the parents' behavior towards the brothers as arising from their losses with their own parents rather than from any lack in their sons. This reframe makes it easier for the brothers to think about their own reasons for distancing. When they no longer justify their distancing as a reaction to critical parents, they have to come up with some other reason for their behavior. Once a family member gains a three generational perspective it becomes difficult for him or her to maintain distance in the same old way.

The interview continues:

Dr. F: That's the risk. To be there for each other you have to change the pattern.

Bob: Well, yeah. You had to go and build that wall, because without it you'd just sit there as a little kid. You'd eat your heart out. You know, why aren't they ever there on my terms. Why don't they ever ask you what you need. So pretty soon you reach two conclusions. Either you're not deserving, which is not a nice one. I lived with that for long enough. Or you reach the conclusion you are not going to get it anyway so you better go take a little concrete and cement over that hurting place. And those are the two choices.

Joe: It sounds right, but I don't know how much is conscious or operationally conscious. Somehow now as I get older, maybe more brain cells die off, I try to realize it and say, "Well, that's the way it is." I strive with my own kid to avoid some of the things, but it's hard if you have no model to be a father. It's very hard to know how to behave with your own son. So you had only daughters. Maybe it was a little different or easier, and you were married when the kids grew up. When I broke up with my wife, he was five, and it's like trying to be father and you try doing these

search routines in your head to find out what kind of implantation, or what do you call that with birds?
Bob: Just instinctive behavior.
Joe: No. Imprinting. There's no imprinting for being a father so it's hard to relate to in certain ways.
Dr. F: Bob, you told me a very interesting story about how you had trouble with that one with your daughters. I don't know if you ever told him that story or not. About playing and your saying to them not to get discouraged.

The therapist has encouraged Bob to repeat a story from a previous session that highlighted the principle of working on the self without needing other to be different. The story involved Bob identifying a pattern that he had learned from his family-of-origin that he was acting out with his children. He encouraged his children to continue certain behaviors even though he was having trouble being different with them. In fact, by explicitly encouraging and accepting these behaviors he was being different with them. Bob proceeds to tell the story.

Bob: Yeah, years ago I felt really bad I could never play with the kids. They were always asking me to play with them, and it would always get me angry. And then I realized one day, well, I'm angry because I always wanted Pop to play with me. And he didn't. So when the kids asked me to play, it just stirred up a lot of hurt. So one day I turned to the kids when I realized this, and I said, "Look. I want you guys to understand if I don't play with you, it has nothing to do with you. So you should never, ever in your life feel guilty because a kid's job is to go and ask their parents to play. So you're doing the right thing. If I can't do it, then it's my sadness but it's not, you should never, ever feel guilty about it." And I think saying that, having it clear, made it possible for me subsequently to play with the kids. And be able to look forward to playing with the kids, and I realize with a boy it is going to be different, because I think there are some special things with fathers and sons. There are a lot of things which aren't different, and this one isn't different. The other thing with the role model, I think, yeah, that's very different. There are some things I want to leave the kids in terms of values, but it's not about being a mother and a woman. In that they really need a woman role model. That's a very different burden.
Dr. F: Before we finish, I just want to leave you one thought about going beyond the reserve. I think, this is again just pure conjecture, I think that you've learned to get discouraged very quickly. If you try to make some-

thing happen with Mom and Dad, and they call themselves into center stage rather than asking you about yourself and that can get very discouraging. It's a very easy one to give up on and just find some other way to get satisfied, go out of the family on that. When I listen to the two of you talking, the examples that you give, you're very quick to get discouraged if the other person doesn't follow through. You make the offer, and if there isn't a taker, then you go about your business. If you listen to the tape, I think you will hear that, and I think that is reminiscent of a family experience. So you wouldn't go the extra mile because there has been no evidence that if you hang in there for the extra mile there is going to be a different result.

Bob: We were just going to get hurt more.

Dr. F: The two of you play that out in a very nice way, each of you wanting more, accepting less. To break through that wall might affect how well you'll do up a generation and down a generation. It might help if you could do it across the generation. It might.

Joe: Yeah, I don't agree totally, but that's OK.

Dr. F: Something to think about. But it's an interesting pattern.

Bob: Well, you know, I invoke your model increasingly. I always ask, if worse comes to worse, I just ask how it is.

Dr. F: How was it for you to be here today?

Joe: Oh, it was interesting. I thought it was very interesting.

Dr. F: I sure enjoyed meeting you.

Joe: Oh, yeah. It was nice to see the man. All I saw was your knees.

Bob: I was really happy it just worked out this way because I really wanted to talk to Joe about this.

Dr. F: Yes. I told Bob there's an open invitation. If you're ever in town, he should drag you in here.

Bob: It didn't occur to me till this morning. I realized that Joe is here and we could do it.

Dr. F: It really helps to hear each side of the story.

Bob: And it's hard. I mean, these things are so important that it's really scary to talk without somebody who can kind of help get the question out the way you really meant it, without getting hurt and defensive. I appreciated the opportunity.

Dr. F: So that's what we'll have on tape. I think it would be really interesting to hear how your kids would reflect on family and how they experience how you two, their fathers, describe family. They might have their own version of what some of that feels like. Different from what you think it is.

The therapist has concluded by attempting to tie the hour together. He highlighted the positive parts of the brothers' stories and he has ended on a note of optimism. He encouraged the brothers to look at the tape of their session together with the hopes that they will hear the caring and connection that exists between the two of them. He has repeated the theme that distancing is a sign of caring and wanting things to be better rather than a lack of caring or criticism. He suggested to the brothers that their work on being connected may be the legacy that they pass on to their children.

Chapter Nine

Family Therapy with Individuals

SECTION ONE:
WHAT IS FAMILY THERAPY WITH INDIVIDUALS?

Few family therapists consider it appropriate to work solely with individuals. The popular view in the field of family therapy is that in order for families to change the whole family must be involved in the treatment; however, I have discovered that it is occasionally appropriate to work with individuals. There are times when an individual is strong enough and/or solid enough emotionally to work on repositioning himself or herself in the context of the family. This repositioning produces a powerful, positive ripple effect. When the individual takes a new position, the family has to respond to it. However, few individuals can sustain the change in the face of the family anxiety that is triggered by the change. Typically the individual gives up his or her new position and either distances from the family and/or resumes the old predictable behavior patterns. It is difficult for an individual to maintain work on the self in the context of the family when the family responds to those self-moves in negative, critical, or rejecting ways. Therapy can help the individual sustain the change by allowing him or her to understand the family's reaction to the change differently.

It is important to be able to assess when it is appropriate to work with individuals in the context of family change. The approach is significantly different from individual therapy. In family therapy with individuals, the individual must seek out his or her family and actively reposition the self vis-à-vis other family members. There are many individuals who are separated from their families by thousands of miles. However, an individual family member may be willing to experiment with repositioning himself or herself in the family through letters, telephone calls, and regular visits. This situation is the most common one in which it is appropriate to work with an individual to effect family change. The individual must be creative in his or her attempts to behave differently in the family context.

The first phase of family work with individuals involves helping the individual rethink his or her story about the family history. He or she must become both more curious about the family and less reactive to the family's behavior. Therapy begins by helping the individual to develop a different framework for understanding family behavior. He or she is helped to understand the old family stories as metaphors for loss, sadness, and unfinished business. In this work the individual will have to let go of the need to be validated, supported, and understood. If he or she continues to be reactive to the family, any attempts to discover new information will fail. The therapist's job is to raise questions about the individual's old stories and to foster curiosity about his or her parents and their stories about their families. The idea that the individual's story is connected with the grandparents' stories is a powerful one. When an individual begins to wonder about the parents' and grandparents' stories, he or she is usually ready to make a trip home to fill in some of the blanks in the family history.

In the therapy sessions, the individual is continually encouraged to tell the therapist the stories that he or she carries around about the family history. The therapist gently questions the stories and raises new questions for the individual to consider. The therapist must avoid joining in the story or criticizing the story since either stance would reinforce it and hinder movement by the individual into a position of curiosity about the family history.

A useful tool for helping the individual understand his or her history is a multigenerational genogram. With the genogram in place, the blank areas of the family history are more readily apparent. The therapist will continue to inquire about the history by raising areas the individual has not considered. The therapist expands the definition of family beyond parents and siblings to include grandparents, aunts, uncles, cousins, in-laws, second cousins, great aunts and uncles, etc. The expanded definition of family increases the resources in the family that the individual can approach to obtain more information about family.

In the therapy sessions, the individual is encouraged to discuss the family rather than focus on the dilemmas and issues that he or she is experiencing in his or her daily life. When a shift from family to a relationship problem or work problem occurs, the therapist should refocus the attention back onto the family by asking questions about the family history and how the current dilemmas may be connected with unfinished family business. The therapist keeps the focus on the family history and on the framing of questions for the individual to raise with various family members. Over time the therapist identifies the most reactive relationships, the major themes, the safe relationships, and the most likely resources in the family for expanding on the family story. As the sessions proceed the therapist develops hypotheses about which family members can help the individual to develop a different sense of the family history.

SECTION TWO:
THE PROBLEM AREAS
IN FAMILY THERAPY WITH INDIVIDUALS

The therapist doing family work with individuals must be vigilant about the development of triangles. The individual is, after all, coming in to discuss his or her family. It is easy for the therapist to be triangled in around family issues. The client may describe the family as horrible, rejecting, angry, etc. The therapist may collude with the story by encouraging the individual to ventilate his or her feelings about the family. This process is basically dysfunctional. It reinforces the individual's story and keeps him or her stuck. For change to occur, the therapist should maintain detachment towards the individual's stories about the family. The therapist should not judge the family, take sides on the family issues, or feel overly sympathetic or reactive to the issues that the individual raises. The therapist should maintain a sense of curiosity and a healthy element of doubt. It is not the job of the therapist to validate the accuracy of the story but to encourage the individual to obtain more information from various family members about the story. The therapist's curious, nonjudgmental stance will often have a powerful influence on the individual. Most people that the individual has known will have colluded with his or her definition of the story. When the therapist raises doubt about the certainty of the story, the individual's anxiety increases. The therapist must gauge the level of anxiety that the questions elicit. A moderate level of anxiety will propel the individual into wanting to discover more information about the family and to connect with family members in a more positive way. However, when anxiety is too great, the individual will feel overwhelmed at the prospect of letting go of the story, or uncovering some unwanted information within the family. The individual's other tendency will then be to avoid getting more information and the old story will be reinforced. There is always the possibility of considerable sadness and loss in one's family. When an individual repositions himself or herself with his or her parents, sadness and loss become more evident. The therapist must proceed with caution and explore with the individual what the loss will be for the individual in letting go of the old stories and learning more about his or her parents' losses.

The interview that is presented later in this chapter is with a woman whose parents had experienced tremendous losses. For a long time, this woman felt vulnerable and needy. She was overwhelmed by her parents' losses and needed a lot of distance from them. Only as she became more solid and felt more in control of her own emotions was she able to hear her parents' story. Timing is crucial. The therapist must assess when individuals are ready to learn about their parents' losses and sadness without becoming overwhelmed or feeling engulfed by their parents' neediness.

The individual in family therapy may find the work is lonely. There is little support from the family for the changes that the individual is trying to maintain in the presence of the family's sameness. If the individual requires validation and support from the family for the attempts at change, then his or her efforts will fail. The therapist must understand and accept the principle that the family stays the same. The only thing that changes is his or her reaction to its sameness.

The individual's ability to let go of outcome and approval is influenced by developmental factors. Young adults in their twenties and early thirties have difficulties with this principle. The repositioning of the self in one's family-of-origin is less threatening and developmentally more appropriate for adults in their late thirties or older. Before an individual can let go of outcome and approval, he or she has to have attained some sense of accomplishment and validation in the world. Until this validation has been achieved, it is risky for him or her to go back and reposition the self. At the first sign that one's parents are critical or rejecting, most young adults will become reactive and defensive. It is the therapist's job to prepare the adult child for the possible negative reactions of the family members. It is helpful for the therapist to review a number of possible scenarios with the individuals. It is also helpful for the therapist to help the individual build in some safety valves for dealing with the family intensity. Timing is particularly important. Short visits that allow some time on one's own away from the family intensity are preferred. Long visits with no time to oneself often leave the individual feeling trapped in the family home. These visits, which don't allow the individual to leave the emotional field, are usually doomed to failure. Visits should be well planned and structure must be built in. The individual must be prepared for old emotional issues to pop up, and he or she should have thought about new ways of responding to them.

Another difficulty in this approach is that the individual's reports of his or her work with the family may be biased and distorted. What the individual chooses to reveal to the therapist is not necessarily an accurate reflection of what is going on in the family. The individual's tendency to distort the family experience increases as his or her anxiety increases. The therapist must remain consistently neutral and curious about the individual's reporting of the family experience. If the individual describes the visit as successful, the therapist should ask questions about what has been learned from the success versus what would have been learned if it had not been successful. If the individual reports the family visit was a failure, the therapist should ask various questions about what he or she learned from the failure and how this learning would have been different if he or she had not viewed the experience as a failure. The job of the therapist is to avoid buying into the reporting of the individual. The therapist must continually introduce new questions to stimulate the individual to rethink the experience.

When doing family therapy with an individual as opposed to the whole family, there is a greater tendency for the individual to develop an intense relationship with the therapist. It is not desirable for the family therapist to play a central role in the individual's life. In this type of therapy, the individual should view the therapist as a coach or consultant. In the beginning phase of family therapy with an individual, the therapist will typically see him or her on a weekly basis. The focus of these sessions will be on helping the individual develop a different framework for understanding the family. Once this framework has been developed, the therapist will begin to decrease the frequency of the sessions and assume more of a consultant role. The therapist should not be seen as the key player in the individual's work on family. It is important that the individual assume ownership of the change. The family therapist's job is not to own the change but to help the individual develop more solid, less reactive connections with various family members.

Finally, it is important that the therapist choose to work with individuals for the right reasons, not because of the therapist's anxiety about seeing couples and families. It is appropriate to do family therapy with individuals when there is no family geographically accessible and the individual is not actively involved in a significant relationship. Even in these latter situations opportunities may arise for involving other family members. Often family members will come to visit the individual. When this occurs, they should be invited to a session or sessions to talk about the family story. The structure of the sessions will depend on whether the individual is still reactive towards the family or has moved to becoming more proactive.

An example of an interview with visiting parents of an adult child working individually on family issues has been provided in Chapter Seven.

SECTION THREE:
MAJOR GOALS OF THE MIDDLE PHASE
OF FAMILY THERAPY WITH INDIVIDUALS

The individual is in the middle phase of family therapy when he or she has replaced reactivity with curiosity about the family as an historical unit. He or she no longer needs to defend the self from family and is ready to make efforts to reposition the self in the family. The major goals of this phase are: (1) repositioning of the self in family, (2) becoming more proactive towards the family's sameness, (3) expanding the family story, (4) reconnecting with various family members, and (5) minimizing "cutoffness."

1. Repositioning of the Self in Family

An individual has succesfully repositioned himself or herself in family when he or she is able to stay connected with family members without reacting to their behavior in the same old way. When family members are critical, negative, or withdrawn, this individual avoids reacting to those behaviors in a way that reinforces the distance. Instead, he or she asks better questions and remains involved in a way that reduces the family members' anxiety and defensiveness and frees them to talk about themselves in new ways. A major repositioning occurs when a family member reacts to an individual in old, negative ways and the individual is able to respond in a positive, caring manner. The individual is able to see the caring behind the criticism, the sadness in the anger, and the anxiety in the distancing behavior. When the individual is able to reframe the family members' behaviors as being the ways that they make it safe for themselves when they feel anxious and vulnerable, he or she has made a major shift emotionally. This individual will be able to connect more intimately with family members even when the family members need to react to feel safe and protected.

2. Becoming More Proactive

Becoming more proactive is connected with repositioning oneself. Whenever an individual feels the need to defend the self, to justify his or her behavior, or to protect the self emotionally by blaming or criticizing others, he or she is in a reactive position. Many individuals believe that they can only feel safe in relationships if others behave in ways that will not make them feel anxious or hurt. These individuals put the responsibility for their feelings of satisfaction in their relationships on others. The proactive individual is able to respond in a caring, positive way even towards someone who is being negative and critical. This individual maintains an element of detached curiosity when other family members respond in peculiar and defensive ways. It is easy for an individual to be different when the family cooperates and makes it safe. It is much more difficult to be different when the family members respond with high anxiety. Becoming proactive involves immersing oneself in the family intensity and learning that even in the middle of this family intensity one can have safety inside himself or herself. The proactive individual is able to stay emotionally involved, yet sufficiently detached, to try to understand why others react as they do. He or she does not try to prove or validate himself or herself or seek approval. The proactive individual is able to define his or her sense of self, values, and position without needing understanding or agreement from others. When others react negatively to his or her position, the proactive individual responds with curiosity rather than defensiveness.

3. Expanding the Story

Expanding the story requires the individual to seek out various family members and ask them about their history. Ideally the individual will be able to spend time alone with his or her parents to discover each parent's story. He or she will ask about such areas as how the parents have dealt with their own parents' and grandparents' deaths, what the family legacy has been throughout the generations, what memories each parent carries about his or her own family history, and what the parents hope the next generation will remember about them. While expanding the story, the individual begins to work on minimizing the regrets that he or she has about family relationships and to obtain some feeling of peace about the part that he or she has played in these relationships.

4. Reconnecting with Various Family Members

This reconnection flows from the individual's work on expanding the story. As the individual expands on the family story and understands each parent's sense of history, family loss, and connection, he or she becomes more connected with various family members. As individuals reach their thirties and older, it becomes particularly important for them to begin to make peace with their aged family members. Work on these relationships will minimize the regrets that exist when a family member dies. Work on reconnecting with various family members will also honor the family and give one memories to carry throughout life. Getting to know the parents better and understanding how they said goodbye to their parents will help one to understand how to say goodbye to and to remember one's own parents.

5. Minimizing "Cutoffness"

In any family one may be cut off from various family members. There may be fights between siblings, a child may feel rejected by a parent, or a horrible incident may have occurred that has left permanent rifts between various family members. Frequently children buy into their parents' stories about how they were cut off from their families and consequently found themselves cut off as well. When an individual repositions the self with the family, he or she begins to mend the separation that has occurred over time. The individual who is better able to connect with lost family members feels in charge of his or her life. The individual does not allow the behavior of others to dictate his or her involvement and may choose not to remain involved with certain people after establishing contact with them. However, by now the individual should have learned that the ability to involve himself or herself with them still exists. This knowledge, although somewhat freeing, may also produce a certain degree of sadness. Sometimes one must recognize that although one is prepared to be involved with another, the other may not be able to reciprocate. This recognition allows us to mourn the loss of that relationship without needing to feel angry or hurt to make it safe for ourselves.

SECTION FOUR:
FAMILY THERAPY WITH AN INDIVIDUAL:
INTERVIEW AND CASE COMMENTARY

The following interview was conducted with a young professional woman who had no family in the area. Ms. S had moved across the country to distance from her family's losses. In previous sessions, Ms. S had talked about feeling engulfed by her parents' neediness. She felt that she needed at least 4,000 miles distance between herself and her family to be free. On the other hand, she felt that she had deserted and betrayed her family by moving so far away from them. On her visits home, she felt overwhelmed by the family intensity. Yet, whenever she left, she felt guilty and responsible for her parents being alone in the world. She found it took her two months to "recover" from each visit home. She was unhappy being near her family and unhappy being away from her family. Ms. S's life was generally unsatisfying to her. She was unable to sustain any permanent relationships with the opposite sex. Although a highly qualified professional, her achievement in her work was marginal. She felt conflicted about settling into her career and a home of her own, seeing these behaviors as a betrayal of her parents. When I first began seeing Ms. S, she was in her thirties. She was the first-born of two children, a son and daughter. Her brother was three years younger. Her parents were survivors of the Holocaust. She described her parents' pain over their war experiences as being so great that they had never been able to tell her the story of what had happened to them. Ms. S felt she carried the burden of her parents' losses on her shoulders. She felt alternately angry and sad towards her parents because of this burden. Ms. S had been in various previous therapies that she had not found helpful. At times she felt suicidal.

In the course of my work with this woman, I encouraged her to have frequent, short visits with her parents. The goal of each visit was for her to reposition slightly with each parent. During the initial stage of family therapy with Ms. S, I asked her to tell me the family story and began to gently raise some doubts about the story. As Ms. S moved into the middle phase of therapy, she became increasingly comfortable about visiting her parents and asking about their history and their war experiences. Initially, Ms. S had described her mother as being unable to talk about her war experiences. The session that follows is the interview that took place after Ms. S raised the whole area of war time experiences with her mother. Ms. S discovered in that discussion that her mother maintained her silence about her story as a way of taking care of Ms. S. This time, as Ms. S's mother began to tell her the story of what had happened to her own mother (Ms. S's grandmother) during the war, Ms. S began to cry. As soon as she became tearful, her mother stopped telling the story and said she couldn't go on. Ms. S responded by saying to her mother, "My tears are not about not being able to handle the story, and I wish you would go on and finish it." At this point her mother said that she had always wanted to tell Ms. S the whole story and willingly continued on to finish the story. It was a revelation to Ms. S that her mother's silence over the years stemmed from her wish to protect her. When her mother finally finished her story, each felt more connected with the other. At the conclusion of the visit, Ms. S felt less conflicted about leaving her mother.

The following interview illustrates how the home visit can be utilized to encourage the individual to rethink the family story and to involve the self differently with family. The process is an ongoing one. The therapist encourages the individual to learn from each visit how to make the next visit different and more meaningful.

The interview commences:

Dr. F: What have you been working on since I last saw you?
Ms. S: About three weeks ago, I was having doubts about whether it was going to be possible, financially, to go back home. But after checking with the bank, I realized I could, and I went ahead and went home. And I'm fine, but I went through this emotional turmoil. It's just incredible when I go back home all the things that go on. A lot of the things that we've talked about, of course, are highlighted because of my awareness of them. And there is just so much material I could just go on and on and on. And I got a couple of tapes. I got some very, very good taping done with my mom. I got a little bit done with my Dad. He was difficult. He really is a difficult character, and you'll be able to tell from the tape.
Dr. F: Let's slow down a bit and start with your decision to go.

The therapist slows Ms. S down a bit to take her methodically through her visit. He wishes to discover what she learned about herself, each parent, and possibly other family members during the visit.

Ms. S: Even though I had already been there a couple of months ago, I wanted to get as much as possible done before we broke for the summer. You know that was important to me to progress with the taping a little bit about a lot of things we've talked about. I wanted to be there to sense the situation, and you know, it's just a good time. I remember missing it very much at holiday time last year, at the Passover holiday. My father, having been raised in such a religious, orthodox home does a very, very traditional affair. He used to have a very beautiful singing voice before his hearing deteriorated so much, and he and his brother used to carry it. I don't know. I seem to have a sentimental appreciation of it. It really moves me, the whole thing and the rest of the people are sort of just bearing with it.

Also you know, it created a lot of conflict about my relationship to my Jewish culture, heritage, identity, and what it means to me. And it always does because I find that somehow it moves me so much. It is so important to me, and I have a very strong background and identity with that culture. And yet I have little day-to-day expression of it and exposure, and so that always somehow calls up a lot of conflict for me too. So that was why I decided to go when I realized that I could afford it. I wanted to, and I think it was a very positive experience.

There were some moments of tension, but maybe because it was short and because I did try and structure it a bit more, it didn't get carried away. And I was able to have more of a sense of humor about it with my parents.

I think that I wasn't completely successful. I did in a few instances, which I will tell you about in time, manage to stay involved without getting defensive and without reacting in my old ways, but there were times when I did so. It wasn't completely successful in that regard. I was only there basically for three and a half days, and it was a renewal of the four most intense relationships that I have in my life, with my brother, my mother, my father and with a very, very good friend that I've had for thirteen years, a female friend. It really stirs up a lot of feeling in me. When I'm there, I always can see myself as going back and living there for those reasons. It felt more like home than here.

Ms. S has started to describe how she worked on repositioning herself with her parents. She has indicated that she was, at times, able to avoid getting defensive and reactive. It is important that the therapist help Ms. S analyze how she managed to respond differently to her parents' behavior. Helping Ms. S assume an observational stance towards her interaction with her family will give her the opportunity to learn even more from her visit.

The interview continues:

Dr. F: When did you first start entertaining that idea?
Ms. S: I always entertained it a little bit, but this time, it seemed to me a very positive idea. I always think about it because of the tremendous messages that I get from them that they would like to have me nearby. And, in part, guilt. In part, I realize how positive it is that we are so connected in many ways, how rich the relationship is in spite of its negative qualities and the doubts that it arouses in myself. You know, how positive it is that we are so involved with each other and are very, very honest and open with each other. And there is less, in contrast to other families and people that I know, less underground. I mean, it's hard to cope with, but there is an awful lot aboveground. It's all sitting right there and that can be very difficult, but on the other hand, it's good. You know, my brother's fiancee said to me that the only time she sees my father really alive is when I'm home. My mother said that too. She said there is nobody else that makes him happier, that he's happy when he can talk to me, that he relates to me so well.

And I know that that is true. I know we've concentrated mostly on the relationship between my mom and I and I've tried to say that there is a great deal between my father and I, but my brother is definitely the apple of her eye and I'm my father's counterpart. I know they may not be around too much longer. If it doesn't interfere with my life or doesn't drag me down, who am I to deny them that? I can't help but feel guilty. I also feel that if I can enrich their lives, and I'm not sure that they can't enrich mine, I'm not sure that I need to be away from them. Then I feel like, maybe, I should be back there, all other things being equal. Those are some of my thoughts, sorry.

The latter part of Ms. S's response is important. It reflects her ongoing reactivity, feelings of guilt, and sense of responsibility. It is interesting to note that her brother's fiancee has reinforced her role as the emotional caretaker in the family. The future sister-in-law's comments about how important she is to her father make it more difficult for Ms. S to consider repositioning herself in the family. It is quite common for other family members to reinforce an individual's way of being in the family.

The interview continues with Ms. S discussing her ambivalence about her involvement with her family:

Dr. F: What did your future sister-in-law's comments about your father coming alive stir up in you?
Ms. S: A sense of responsibility to him. It's nice to be cared for. Even here I have some very close friends who I know care about me a great deal. I guess there is a different quality to it. Nobody that thinks himself the center of the earth, but that's not something I think to be treated lightly. I'm caught between the North American ideal of a person becoming independent and leaving the family goals and having their own, and the European values of still being very involved with the family and maintaining an intimate interaction, I guess, which seems to be the pattern.

The therapist has singled out the future sister-in-law's remarks because it is important that Ms. S be able to reframe these and similar remarks. Ms. S will need to hear these comments differently before she can let go of her old emotional story, that is, that she is the one who keeps her parents safe in the world.

The interview continues:

Dr. F: I imagine one of the things you worked on during your visit was staying involved while at the same time not losing a sense of yourself.
Ms. S: Yes.
Dr. F: How close did you get to that? If you take it day by day, . . .
Ms. S: Forty-eight hours.
Dr. F: You managed forty-eight hours? It was the third day that was a little bit difficult?
Ms. S: Yeah, not even the third day, the forty-ninth hour.
Dr. F: OK. Was the first day easier?

Ms. S: The first day, though I did go away. The first night was the first Seder night. Then the second day, I went shopping with my sister-in-law-to-be and my brother and came home for dinner, and then we all had dinner together. The third day, I did a little taping with my mom in the morning, and then spent the afternoon and lunch with my friend and then came home for dinner. So that was, you know, forty-eight hours. And then, it was just me and my parents, and that was the first time that it was just me and my parents. That was the most intense situation, and that's when it, my self-composure and my resolve to stay involved, was a little bit . . . What happened, the issue was that my father deems himself to be a great expert in all things, and he's like that. I accept that. He's argumentative and develops these fantastic, and actually very clever, theories to explain all sorts of things which have nothing to do with reality but are very clever.

And he was expounding on one of these and also was telling me how I should choose an accountant. I have an accountant who was his accountant, and I realize this is an issue which sort of focuses on my being away from there for him. He is now working for that accountant as a bookkeeper. He went to a retraining course and is working for that accountant and admires him a great deal. You know, I'd heard about twenty times since my visit began how wonderful the accountant was, but I've expressed the desire and the interest to get an accountant here because I need advice from time to time. It's very inconvenient to have somebody so far away and to communicate only by long distance phone calls or by letters. And so, I had already resolved that it was too late in this year to send my return, but that for next year, if I were to stay here, I would get an accountant. I had already decided that within myself, but it is very difficult to communicate with my dad and to let him know. I had tried to say that to him, but he didn't get the message. He was going on about this is what I should do, this is what I must do. You know he's so forceful that it is very difficult for me not to be reactive. It's almost the only way to get through. To be understated or to speak in a natural tone or not to speak over-emphatically is basically not to speak at all to him. So that's why so often there is confrontation. He invites it, and he also has a great deal of difficulty listening. So he was telling me, going on and on about what I should do, and I said "ENOUGH," and then his response to that is to sulk. He says "OK," and then he clams up.

That evening I wanted to get some taping done with him. My mother and I had had a very, very emotional session in the morning. In spite of her crying and breaking down and my breaking down, I insisted we continue rather than backing off as I had done previously. We just kept through it, and so we did get to some very, very emotionally charged issues, and I think she found it good in the long run to stay with it. My father, I know how to deal with him, I think it is probably the reason that he enjoys my company. And, I think, in a way he knows how to deal with me in that we are both people who will, if pushed, push back, and react to that. We need to be, perhaps it's a fault, tiptoed around sometimes when we are feeling sensitive. And so my father retreated. We were getting dinner ready. He retreated into the living room to read the paper or to watch television. And then I said to him, "I'd like to do some taping with you." He said, "No. No. I'm not in the mood." I left it alone knowing that I would go back to it later. I know that if I had said to him, "Oh, why not? Let's do it tonight. This is the only time," he would just become entrenched in his stand. And that's the kind of thing my mother would do. She would say, "Yes. You must do it right now!" And she doesn't know when to back off. That is the way she has always dealt with me too, and that's why there is so much tension between us, because she will sort of charge ahead. If I'm on ground where she's really too shaky, I won't. You know it's less easy for me to cooperate or relate. She's not sensitive to that kind of feeling. Not that it is her fault. That's the way she does it.

So then, I just said that to my dad, and then we called him for dinner and we had a pleasant enough time. But any time the three of us are alone together, the subject always comes around to why don't I get married, why don't I go do this, why don't I move back there, what am I doing, what kind of a life am I leading, etc? It's always like that. It just goes on and on, and so that was another thing. I just withdraw. I just sort of say nothing. There is nothing. I don't know how to. I can't say anything because they don't listen. Anything I say is taken as an argument, so they will start screaming and yelling.

In the work with Ms. S, the therapist has encouraged her to think about balance between being involved with and being separate from her parents. Ms. S has been working on being close to each parent, while separating herself emotionally from their reactions. She has been able to do something quite different with her mother. In the past, she would have backed away from her mother's tears, and the mother would have stopped talking about her story as a way of making it safe for her daughter. Each would have been confused about what the other was reacting to. The therapist now shifts his attention to Ms. S's relationship with her father, which in some ways is a much more difficult one for her to handle. If the therapist had concentrated too much on the enthusiasm of the breakthrough with the mother, he would have lost an important opportunity to use that break-through as a basis for Ms. S to think differently about how to be involved with her father. The therapist's role is to stay neutral and detached without becoming overly excited about a particular breakthrough in the family. The change in one relationship can be used as a springboard for encouraging a family member to begin to experiment with other relationships, preferably the more emotionally difficult ones.

The interview continues:

Dr. F: You are saying, "they." Are you talking about both of your parents?

Ms. S: Both of them, yes.

Dr. F: Not Dad?

Ms. S: They are in cahoots at that point.

Dr. F: So you take them on together at the dinner table?

Ms. S: So I just withdrew. I couldn't help it . . .

Dr. F: When you have them separately, are the dynamics the same?

Ms. S: Sometimes, yes.

Dr. F: Is it easier?

Ms. S: Yeah, oh, yeah. It's a bit easier because they egg each other on. It builds to a crescendo, and neither of them will listen. One person will be talking and trying to make a point, and the other person will start telling you a tangentially related story about the people three doors down's daughter's cousin who did this and this and this. Then the other person is going on in their own track and it sort of goes back and forth. You know, my brother's way of dealing with it has always been to say, "I agree with you." He says it in good humor. He says, "I agree with you," and he won't argue with them. And neither will I anymore. Both of us shut them out in our own way.

It is important to remember to differentiate between the mother and the father. Many adult children refer to their parents jointly. It is difficult to know how the adult child's relationship with each parent differs from the other when the therapist allows him or her to refer to the parents as a unit rather than as separate individuals.

Dr. F: Did you have a chance at all during this short visit, to change the social setting for engaging your mom and dad separately?

Ms. S: It's difficult. I have done that with my mother. My father, because of his hearing problem, couldn't go to a restaurant. He enjoys going out for coffee or tea, but again with the three days it was difficult. Not this time. This time, it was all within our home but I did insist that my mother be separate, that my mother be away when I was talking to my father. What happens is my mother will follow me into a room. I think I've said this to you before. I'll go into a room to change, and she will sort of tag along behind me and follow me into the room and close the door, and now she's got me cornered. Or I'll go into the bathroom, and she'll follow me into the bathroom and close the door behind us. She's got me cornered and she can tell me what she wants to tell me.

Dr. F: What do you do with her?

Ms. S: I don't try to corner her. I don't need to. She doesn't withdraw I guess. She withdraws in her own way. When she has had enough of listening, she'll talk. She'll shut it out and talk. She has her own way of withdrawing. What she hears is what she wants to hear.

Dr. F: How do you think your father would react if you had him alone? Let's say you took him for a drive. Does he like to go for drives?

Ms. S: Yes, he does.

Dr. F: OK. Let's say you take him for a drive. If you talk loud enough in the car, can he hear you?

Ms. S: No. It's better face to face contact. What often happens is he'll get me into the car for a drive so he can talk to me. This is what they both want to do. They want to hear. He sort of made a joke. He said, when I finally got him to talk about things to me, "Well, now can I interview you?" I said, "Well, I'd like to get some facts from you." As far as I am concerned, he has all the facts, but he always wants to provoke. He wants to get me to express my opinion, to tell him what I think, even though I've told him many times, so that he can argue with it. Because I no longer express my opinion, he's always saying to me, "Isn't that right? Isn't that so? What do you really think? What are the real reasons you're on the West Coast?" I'll tell him what I think are the real reasons, and he'll argue with them. And I'll say, "Those are the reasons I'm there," but he'll argue how they are not valid.

Dr. F: You answer when he asks you a question?

Ms. S: I just sort of smile now cause he knows what the answer is and there is nothing new to add. He obviously feels he's being kept in the dark. He said to me, "Now do I get to interview you? I'd just like a few facts."

Dr. F: And what did you say when he said that?

Ms. S: I said, "Dad, you have all the facts." And then he says, "Not enough facts."

Dr. F: That's interesting. And this happened where?

Ms. S: This is up in my bedroom when I was taping him.

Dr. F: When you were taping him?

Ms. S: Yeah, in between.

Dr. F: Now, when you had your dad alone, it was a bit easier to engage him than when you had the two of them together at dinner?

Ms. S: A bit. Only because they interrupt. My mother cannot stay out of the conversation. He finds it very frustrating, and I find it very frustrating. But when I was taping him, I wasn't engaging him. Like I would say to him, "Dad, I want you to tell me about this," and he would say, "Fine. I want to tell you about this." There was no way I could direct him. It was him directing. He was the one that had to be. I was not really engaging him. He was just talking.

Dr. F: So, he likes to be a parent.

Ms. S: Oh, yeah. And he wants to tell me what he wants to tell me when he wants to tell me. And if I say to him, "Can we talk about this for a while?" He says, "No. No. No. I have to talk about this right now." So I said, "Fine." I figured we could get back to it. But he cannot feel too passive, too directed. He has to feel that he is in control.

Dr. F: What does this stir up in you, when he does that sort of thing?

At this point in the interview, the focus is on encouraging Ms. S to begin to reposition herself with her father. The therapist helps Ms. S re-think her relationship with her father, becoming both more curious about him and less reactive to him. He encourages her to think about arranging a physical setting that will be more cordial to change. When an adult child is working on repositioning with a parent, it is helpful if he or she meets with the parent away from the family emotional field. A neutral setting in which the adult child can ask questions without interference from other family members is best.

The interview continues with the focus on Ms. S's reaction to her father's behavior:

Ms. S: Well, it didn't bother me too much, really. I was feeling exasperated with him, but I understand him and that does not upset me too much. Except, you know, that quality can be very, very upsetting if you are trying . . . Our family was never able to do anything cooperative because of that quality. He was never able to consider other people in the scenario. He was never able to consider other people's desires or needs in the family. He would say, "Now we are going here, and this is what we are going to do." It was just him. He was very autocratic. He could not receive. He could not cooperate or be flexible. If I got him aside and in a very normal, slow tone of voice explained to him what our considerations were and why we had to accommodate certain things, then he would listen. He would say, "OK." It wasn't that he was innately uncooperative, but it was difficult for him to receive messages and understand why. You know, it is just so much effort to communicate with him. That was the basic problem. And also the basic problem with him feeling that he needed to be the leader and organizer, and that everything was going to be chaos if he didn't do that, which was true. It made it very difficult.

Dr. F: As a child, how did you understand what was happening?

Ms. S: It's difficult to remember. I was afraid of his anger. I was very afraid of his anger. He was never physically abusive, but there was this glowering anger within him always that I sensed, and I was terrified of that. It was always just upsetting. It was upsetting to go anyplace with him. We never did things as a family because there was so much turmoil before. There would be so much screaming and yelling. So much anxiety about simply going out to relatives, for instance, or going on any outing. Now that I think of it I know it must have raised tremendous anxiety in him. Any sort of venture into the outside world would raise a tremendous anxiety in him. There would be screaming and yelling, and it was just so unpleasant that that's why I remember mostly just unpleasantness about it. There was never lightheartedness or nice feelings about it. And how I perceived it as a child was just anger and unpleasantness. I don't remember . . .

Dr. F: How did you understand these feelings?

Ms. S: I think I always perceived it as anger and despair at everything, at the world. I think I always did. I don't think I ever thought it was directly related to me, although it could be aimed at me if I sort of called attention to myself in some way.

Dr. F: How much responsibility did you take on for making your father less angry?

The therapist is now attempting to help Ms. S work on the self. He is focusing on helping her differentiate her reactions from her father's reactions. The last question about how much responsibility Ms. S took on for making her father less angry is really a question about how emotionally fused Ms. S is with her father. This question is asked not for an immediate answer, but to stimulate Ms. S's thinking about where she stops and her father begins emotionally.

The interview continues:

Ms. S: I think I always felt I wanted to make it more pleasant. I think I always felt like, if only I could organize or coordinate it enough ahead of time, then we could avoid these huge confrontations. If only I could, that perhaps, it would . . . I think I did feel that it was my fault in some way. Perhaps if I had done something, I could have avoided it. That reminds me of a trip we made to New York for a wedding as a family. This was something we hardly ever did, and there was such tremendous anxiety and build-up for it. I did not expect a wonderful trip to New York. I knew that it was going to be very difficult, and so I sort of girded my loins. I geared myself up for that kind of thing. I thought I'm just going to do the best that I can and try to keep my temper under control and try to not let him get to me. And my father just developed a tremendous anxiety about the whole family, because you know, we've just never been able to successfully have a pleasant time altogether. To be in the same car for twelve hours was going to be very difficult. This was perhaps when I was twenty-three and my brother was I guess, eighteen, or something like that, and I knew this was going to be a major trial. And that's what I accepted, but my father just couldn't believe that we were actually going to do something like that. He always does this as the time gets nearer to do anything like this, he'll say, "No, we're not going to go." He'll look for any reason to not go, or say, "No. We're not going. We can't go."

And we went, and I was the peacemaker the whole way. That's not my role normally, but I sort of took it upon myself this time. Normally I'm the one that creates as much bad feeling as anyone else by reacting to them. And we went, and it was horrible weather, and the car broke down. Our family, our home, was the kind of home where if a glass of milk was turned over it was a major disaster. It could ruin the week kind of thing. So the car breaking down, this was, you know, the trip was not meant to be. This was bad luck, and we're going back. And I said, "No. Even if we can't take our car with us we should rent a car and continue on." And I just somehow kept sanity, and I was the one that was always placating my father. The other thing about driving, going on a trip like that is that because you can't communicate with him, he makes all kinds of wrong turns, and he also can't be shown to be in the wrong. He just really goes off the deep end if you show him to be in the wrong. Rant, and rave, and really bring down the wrath of God if he is shown in anyway to have made a small mistake. A very difficult person.

So he made all sorts of wrong turns. My mother was going, "Oh, my God." My mother's also sort of learned to grin and bear it. My brother was going bananas in the back seat, and I would just say to him, "There's the sign," and show him the map, and say to him, "This is where we have to go, we have to turn around." I just kept calm the whole way and when we got to New York, it turned out he had brought the wrong suit. He didn't have the right tie, and I took him to help pick out a tie. All the way he's saying, "I just won't go to the wedding. I don't have the right clothes. I just won't go." And I took him out and bought him the proper tie, and I took it upon myself. I felt responsible the whole time to try to avert so much of this unpleasantness. But that was the first time that I actually did that. I always think that I ought to or I could have done something or that I should have done something. That was the first time that I actually did that and I think I've done it since. Sort of try to somehow make it better for him by showing him the way, by providing, by buying him the right things, by I don't know. They seem so cut off from reality, from the rest of the world. They are in their own little world. They are both convinced that the world works in this peculiar way, what I see as peculiar. They may be in the right, I don't know. I may be peculiar. They sort of go along in this cocoon, not really receiving many messages from the outside and interpreting things to corroborate their view of things.

Dr. F: Let's get back to your sense of responsibility. As you remember it, until this trip, when you were twenty-three, you hadn't actually taken on these responsibilities.

Ms. S: No, I don't think so.

Dr. F: But at that time you started to do something differently. Keeping things OK for your father was a way of taking care of the family.

Ms. S: Right. That's true.

The therapist has just offered a hypothesis for Ms. S to consider about her relationship with the father. He begins to raise questions about what Ms. S gains and loses in taking on this caretaking role. In some ways Ms. S carries more anxiety about her father than about her mother. The story of the car ride illustrates how powerful her father is in the family and how much of his anxiety Ms. S assumes. As the interview continues, the therapist tries to help Ms. S understand that she need not continue playing the caretaker role. Attention is focused on how she can use future visits to begin to reposition herself with her father. It is important that Ms. S not be left with a sense of success about her efforts with her mother and a sense of failure about her struggles with her father. Prior to concluding the interview, it will be helpful for her to have some ideas about how she can work on her relationship with her father.

The interview continues:

Dr. F: Is it possible for you to stay involved with him when he is stirred up without feeling the need to do anything and still feel good?

Ms. S: Again, that's rather tough. I think that would be very, very tough, but if I ever get to that point, that would be very far from where I am now.

Dr. F: I think that in order to make a return home really successful you would have to be up for this challenge.

Ms. S: Yes, it's very different. I'm very aware of that.
Dr. F: Very interesting. I was just wondering whether you could see yourself asking your father about the comment that he seems to come alive when you're around.

The therapist is continuing to encourage Ms. S to develop some new ideas about how to approach her father. At the same time, he begins to challenge the myth that she is responsible for her father's well-being. He encourages her to ask her father about this perception, which may be mainly a fantasy of other family members. In this way, he introduces some doubt into the old family story.

Ms. S: Yes, I could say that to him. I received that message from my sister-in-law-to-be, my brother, and my mother. They all said, "He just glows when you're around."
Dr. F: What is the double message there?
Ms. S: Oh, yes. It's a very manipulative message.
Dr. F: I imagine that with the strong feelings of responsibility that get stirred up in you, that would be a tough message to handle.
Ms. S: They were all giving me messages that they would like to have me back. You know, either consciously or unconsciously trying to invoke my sense of responsibility by their need of me. All except my girlfriend, but her boyfriend came to me and asked in an indirect way, "Shouldn't you really be here." So I got that message too although I know she was very careful about intimating or insinuating because she knows and understands what I go through and why.
Dr. F: How does this compare to previous messages to come home?
Ms. S: They are always at it, but somehow it was the clearest message this time. And the one from my girlfriend, we've talked about it before, about it's being too bad we're in different cities now because, actually, as the years have gone by, we've become closer and closer. We've known each other since high school, and we've shared a great deal. The relationship just gets better and better, and she has always kind of said to me, "Well, you seem very happy there." We'll actively try not to suggest that she would be happier or that she would like to have me back here. Even so, it was the most sort of united front of the four people who I am most intensely involved with in my life, and they are all there. And here I am, so I don't know. No, I've always gotten those messages clearly, and my last visit, my brother even more strongly suggested that. I don't quite understand why he says that. I moved out when he was fourteen, and prior to that, our relationship was on big sister, little brother terms. Of course, he's grown up an awful lot since then. On the visits home when I was

living there, there was a bit of alienation. He was rebelling against me because I was really his only authority figure. Then, as he grew older, that changed. It's become more and more of an equal relationship, and it's become closer and more and more affectionate. We've never really lived together when it was mutually supportive. I'm always surprised at him expressing a desire to have me in the same city.

I know that he doesn't talk very much about personal things whereas I find it a lot easier. He's not very forthcoming. I know he won't discuss family with his friends, nor even up to any great extent with his fiancee. There's a lot of things I feel she's not aware of that I freely talk about because he won't say. He tends to feel that it's none of anybody's business, and he tends to be very protective about the family. I always used to cause him so much distress because that's what I would talk about with my friends. Sometimes that's what I would share with my friends so he's the opposite of me. I know that he will talk about it with me, so perhaps he needs that outlet. But what I'm trying to say is that I'm still confused as to why he's giving me these messages that he wants me to come back. Whether it's kind of my mother trying to get him to influence me, which could be my mother talking to him because I know she's often dropped hints to me to try to influence him, knowing how much we respect each other, or whether it's really from his own feelings of wanting to have me close by.

Dr. F: How have you tried to talk to him about it?

Ms. S: He's a little bit cagey. I've said to him, "Why is it so important to you to have me in the same city?" He said, "Well anybody that knows you wants to have you close by," or something like that. Or he says, "I don't want you. I think it would be really sad if you settled down someplace far away from me and had children and I didn't know them," and all those things I think are true, but I'm not sure how emotionally true, you know what I mean. He'll say those things or he'll say, "I can talk to you. There's many times I would like to call you up and ask your advice and I'd like to be able to help you." Right now I'm having all kinds of problems with my (business) partner, and he said, "I'd like to help you with any legal problems you have. We have a lot of resources in this family. It would be nice to pool them." So those are the kind of answers he gives me.

Dr. F: The statement about your father coming alive when you're around is a statement about their lack of influence in him as much as a statement about your influence on him. I think that's an important opening for you with your brother. What sense of responsibility and involvement does he see himself having with your father? Your mother too. It's also a statement about where she is with her husband and where she perceives you. I think it would be interesting to get back to this with your brother.

Ms. S: There's so much I haven't told you yet, and one of the things is she really wants to separate, and I know that things are very, very bad. My mom is very, very depressed. My father, they don't get along at all. And my father, because of his own lack of self-esteem right now in his work, is really dumping on her so much and making life so difficult for her that she is very, very depressed. It's very, very sad. A lot of the hypotheses that you say I have about my mother, that you're not certain about, a lot of those things I think were corroborated on this visit. So much is expressed directly. She would say, "This is the way it is," and it came from her. You've questioned whether my mother asks my advice because she really feels inadequate or because she gets that message from me or because it's a way of making me feel inadequate. I think that that's sort of what we were talking about. There were so many times that she actually expressed it directly, not in looking to make me feel good, but in saying, "I can't do this one alone. I'm not good at this," and constantly, constantly, constantly asking for reassurance. Someone complimented her on her salad. She says, "Oh, nothing else is good." That's the way she is. It's so exasperating. Constantly she'll say, "Oh, the meat was too dry." "No, the meat was fine, Mom." "No, no, no, it was too dry." "Really, was it OK?" "Yeah, really it was delicious." "Oh no, no, no." She'll constantly ask for reassurance, not believing. She's a funny lady. She's a wonderful lady, and there's a side of her that is impossible. She's extremely . . .

Dr. F: Think of this one when you think of your parents. I had this thought while you were talking about your dad at the beginning. It's about his need to be in control. Let's use the word "survivors" because both of them have managed to survive under very difficult circumstances. Two people like that married. Can you have two survivors in a relationship? Is that possible? Think about that with your parents. Look back to the beginning when they both survived (the Holocaust), and then when they met and how they had to struggle. These are hypotheses which I hope you are going to get more and more into with them as you do this work. How do they accommodate each other's very strong sense of having to be in control to survive? That was the bottom line during those times. How do you manage a relationship when you both need to be in control to survive?

The therapist has just attempted to reframe Ms. S parents' controlling behaviors as their way of trying to survive. If Ms. S does not expand her understanding of her father's need to control, then she will continue to distance from him as a way of maintaining control of herself. However, if she understands his behavior as his way to survive and reduce his anxiety, then she can become more curious about him and less reactive. We are dealing with parents who are both survivors. We can hypothesize that there is a degree of high anxiety in their relationship and in the family. One way to reduce anxiety is to become dogmatic and to try to control the behavior of others. Ms. S has traditionally responded to her father on the basis of her belief that he needed control. The therapist is interested in seeing how her response to him would be different if she saw his behavior as related to his need for survival.

The interview continues on this theme:

Ms. S: That's a very interesting point and wait 'til you hear my father's tape. And actually, I was very interested because I don't think I've got it on tape, but at one of the dinnertime conversations, my father said to me, and he came up with this completely spontaneously, he said, "What you have to remember is that you're the daughter of two survivors." He just came up with this on his own. Again, as I say, he's a very, very intelligent man and will do a lot of interpretive and theoretical thinking, talk about things all the time. He said, "Somebody that was weaker than either your mother or myself would not have got through what we went through." And he said, "We had to be really strong. Not only physically, but mentally." At this point my mother went, "I guess I don't know," and he said, "That's why you are so strong physically and mentally because you've got all the genetic components." And my mother of course thinks that emotionally I've got a great deal. It's funny, you know, because she asks me, "I don't know what it is. Sometimes I'm just working and tears will pour down my face. What is that?" She has no insight. I say, "Are you thinking about something sad at those times?" And she says, "No. Nobody's bothering me. Nothing sad has happened," and I know she's miserable. She doesn't understand that she's depressed. I'll say, "Mom, I think you're feeling really sad about a lot of things in your life," and then she will break down crying. I don't do that anymore. I used to cry. I'm not tearful. I'm not easily brought to tears anymore. And yet, she sees me as emotional and very unstable because I have said to her, "I'm depressed," or "I was depressed," meaning feeling low, and she sees that as a mental illness in quotes. Because in her day nobody talked about being depressed. She says, "I lived with 100 girls and nobody was ever depressed." She says, "Why is that? What is wrong with people now?" And yet, she's so much sadder than I am. But anyway that's a digression because she again made this sort of face, and she said, "Emotionally, you're not strong, are you?" That's what I mean. There's no balls made about what she really thinks.

Dr. F: There's another notion I've had about your mother and about strength. Your father's comments about survivors being strong are very interesting. Your mother, as you present her and as I hear her on the tape and what you've said just now, made me think that her way of surviving was to give up some self. That was really her way of showing some strength.

This last statement by the therapist is another major reframe. The idea that the mother takes care of the family by giving up a piece of herself is a new one for Ms. S. Rather than the mother being seen as weak, this reframe defines her as a strong person who takes care of the family by positioning herself as submissive to her husband and unable to deal with his anger or anxiety.

Ms. S: That's what I was going to say although when I think of my mom I see an image of a very, very determined, very stoic, very strong woman in many ways. The way she dealt with my father when the two personalities married is she tried to give in. She gave in, and gave in to his stronger will and ideas. Thinking this was a way to make him happy, this was what she had to do. And I think that as time went by, she did that less and less. I mean, many years, maybe fifteen years or so when I think about it. But if he wanted to do something she was very unhappy about she would do it anyway because this might make him happy. She tried to accommodate herself to him. When I think about it, she has a very strong personality.

Dr. F: She might be the stronger of the two in some ways.

Mrs. S: Yes, as a matter of fact. I was telling my friend about what you and I talk about, and she said to me there does seem to be more involvement with my mother. And she said, "I think you see your father as being able to take care of himself," and I said, "I see him as much more fragile, much more fragile in many ways." Because my mother can make her way. She can adjust. My father, just the least little thing will set him off. I see him as much scarier. He's a much scarier person. There's something else I was going to say. I don't know if we have time.

Dr. F: We'll save the rest of the tapes for next time because I'm really interested in hearing them.

Ms. S: Oh, yeah, there's just so much that was happening.

Dr. F: This work is to help you define where you stop and your parents as separate entities begin.

This last statement by the therapist is a clear statement of the objective of family therapy with individuals. Ms. S, by assuming the overfunctioning, caretaking role, has prevented herself from learning just how adequate and resourceful her parents are. Until she has this knowledge, she will remain anxious and guilty about their behaviors. Redefining their behaviors as their way to survive and manage in the world can help reduce Ms. S's reactivity and anxiety about letting her parents down.

The interview begins to wind down:

Ms. S: It's going to be a tremendous relief if I ever get there because I know I do lose so much of my sense of self. That's why there is so much emotional turmoil and confusion. I literally am quite depressed when I come back. I can function, but I question my whole way of life, and I question who I am, and I don't really know.

Dr. F: As you begin to respond differently to Mom and Dad, my hunch is Mom and Dad and brother will begin to respond differently to you, and each other. When that happens it is going to seem like a bit more turmoil.

Ms. S: I wonder if it's very difficult to do long distance because it's occasional. I guess its easier for me because there is respite, but it slows down everything. Although I suppose my phone conversations with my mom . . .

Dr. F: It would be a bit more difficult if you were there.

Ms. S: The detachment. I don't know what the time is because I don't have a watch, but this is what I was going to say. This is what I remembered about my brother. I think for the first time I'm not there to cushion him from my parents, and I know that he spent last summer with them and saw the pathology in all its glory. I think that perhaps it might have been one of the first times that he actually experienced it, and I think actually was frightened. I think he wants to share the responsibility. I think he started to feel responsible and usually I carry that role and he just came and went. And he actually started to feel the pressure, and he actually expressed this when I came to visit. And I'm totally detached, and I don't know. I mean, I know, but it's a vague idea. I don't have to live with it. And he said to me, "What are we going to do?" He was sort of desperate. "What are we going to do about them? We've got to do something." This really floored me. I mean, from my brother, "We've got to do something." First of all, the idea that we had to do something, that anything could be done, and secondly, that he felt that he had to do something and that I had to do something for them or with them. And I know that part of him wanting me to be there is that I'm family and he wants family, but he doesn't want to be involved with them so much. He wants detachment from them so badly that he's going out of town to work, and he's worried. There is tremendous friction between my mom and his fiancee, which is all erupting now. There's a whole other story there, and he's definitely going to go with his woman. He's not going on the side of my mom.

Dr. F: So it would be easier for him if you were there.

Ms. S: Yeah, it would be. So I think that may be a part of why he wants me there. Plus, they are all desperate to get me married. Here I sort of go along, and it makes me wonder maybe my approach is too lack-a-daisical. I mean, I just sort of see people and they all sort of feel that I'm going to miss the boat, and maybe they are right. He wants me to be there so that if he has any friends or associates that he thinks that I might like, he can introduce me and they all feel that I need help.

Dr. F: I think that in some ways it is probably better for your brother not to have you there with family. You know there are two ways of being involved. There is being involved by being there and being involved by not being there and maintaining this detachment business. A lot of people get confused about that. They think that physical closeness in itself means emotional involvement.

Ms. S has begun to take on the reframe. She understands a bit more about the way her parents have coped in the world. Her comment that it would be a tremendous relief for her to have a sense of herself separate from her parents is an indication to the therapist that he hasn't moved too quickly. Clearly, Ms. S is beginning to rethink her role in the family. The issue of the role her brother plays in the family dynamics has been introduced. As the brother becomes more involved and Ms. S less involved, the family members will reposition themselves vis-à-vis each other. In the past Ms. S has been a caretaker to her brother as well as her parents. Her moving to the sidelines of the family intensity has allowed her brother to play a more central role in the family.

The interview concludes:

Ms. S: Not necessarily, but they are related in some ways.

Dr. F: They can be. Hopefully one achieves a balance with family between being involved and detached simultaneously.

Ms. S: I'm trying. I'm working on getting my mom to come in July, so it might be that she will be able to come in.

Dr. F: That would be interesting.

Ms. S: It would be. I don't know if you will be around but it would be nice to have a session then.
Dr. F: Good idea. Let's discuss it at a later interview.

The foregoing interview provides an example of family therapy with an individual. The family is one in which there's a lot of tension and anxiety. The daughter has dealt with this by assuming the overfunctioning role of caretaker. The fact that the parents are survivors of the Holocaust adds to the family intensity. The dynamics dramatically illustrate how adult children take on their parents' unfinished business and act it out for them. Untangling this complicated, emotional web requires a very methodical, cautious, well-planned strategy. The therapy has involved encouraging the adult child to return home to reposition herself with family members. She has been helped to recapture a sense of family without needing to maintain distance to make it safe.

Chapter Ten

Endings

SECTION ONE:
THE TERMINATION PROCESS

There are various signs that it is time to terminate family therapy. While it is true that working on the self never ends, the formal family therapy process should have some closure. A major indicator of the readiness of a family to stop formal therapy sessions is the ability of the family members to deal with anxiety and tension without resorting to the old reactive behaviors. During the course of therapy, the therapist will be evaluating the degree of change within individuals and in their relationships with other family members. As the family therapy progresses family members will consistently be able to talk about difficult situations in new ways. A marked decrease in blaming, focusing on other, and general defensive behavior will be evident. Individual members will display an increased sense of responsibility and desire to work on their own issues separately from the issues of others. The general tone of the sessions will become more relaxed and family members will show more curiosity about themselves and how others operate in the world. The therapist will find that questions that formerly evoked reactive responses will now stimulate thinking about the meaning of the questions. The therapist will see a general repositioning of family members within both the nuclear and extended family. When the family is ready to terminate, it will have been crisis free for a period of time; however, individual family members will have maintained their interest in and motivation to work on self-issues.

When the therapist thinks the formal family therapy is coming to a close, it is timely for him or her to suggest that the family attend a session to evaluate the treatment process. Although the family members may have made significant gains and learned to respond to problems in different ways, they will not necessarily have integrated these changes sufficiently to handle stress in a more creative fashion. The formal evaluation session is an important part of the overall process, both for the therapist and the family. It provides the family members with an opportunity to evaluate what they have learned about themselves and the family. It offers the therapist an opportunity to learn from the family about the impact of the therapy. At this point, the family members are the experts on what has worked for them. This feedback is an important source of data for the therapist who is continuously modifying his or her theory and model. The therapist must avoid structuring the session so as to validate the therapy with the family. The formal evaluation session should allow the family members to be critically analytical about their overall experience in the therapy. The therapist should be determining what did not work with the family and what the family members would like to have experienced differently in the therapy. When the therapist encourages family members to evaluate their experience in a critical way, he or she can learn a great deal about his or her sense of timing. The therapist's questions will cover such areas as: (1) how family members experienced various suggestions made by the therapist, (2) the introduction of new family members into the therapeutic process, (3) the redefinition of certain problems, and (4) the general timing and pacing of the therapy. The family's evaluation of the therapist's judgment in these areas permits the therapist to assess the appropriateness of the model with that particular family. In this manner, each family provides new data for the therapist. The therapist is able to expand the model and generally develop more depth in his or her understanding about what families need. It is helpful for the therapist to position himself or herself in a learning role with the family members prior to terminating with the family. If the family members compliment the therapist on how well the therapy has gone, he or she should not accept the compliment at face value. Rather, family members should be asked to explain what made sense to them about various interventions, how the experience would have been different without those interventions, and what else the family would like to have experienced other than those interventions. These questions are all important in flushing out the range of experiences that family members have had in the family therapy process.

A helpful exercise in the terminating session is for the therapist to raise possible future scenarios and to ask how the family members would use their new learning to deal with these scenarios differently. The scenarios will involve issues that family members have traditionally had difficulty with. The therapist should listen carefully to how the family members respond to these scenarios. If they are defensive, confused, or generally reactive, it is possible that this termination is premature. On the other hand, if the family members understand that they will not be problem free and will need to continue working on finding more creative ways to respond to ongoing problems, then it is likely that the timing for ending the formal therapy is appropriate.

Prior to terminating, the family members should understand that the family can always return for a consultation. It is unrealistic to assume that the family will not get bogged down again. However, a consultation session may be all it takes to get the family back on the right track. The therapist should emphasize that returning for a consultation is not a sign of failure but rather another opportunity to learn more about how the family system works. This reframe is an important one. If the therapist fails to introduce the possibility of a future consultation, the family members may simply get discouraged if they find themselves returning to their earlier reactive behavior and know that they cannot seek help. If they have been forewarned that family members may get bogged down in periods of high anxiety, they are more likely to seek additional help.

Quite frequently families will return after six to twelve months for a consultation session and be able to deal with certain issues in more depth following the session. Numerous events, such as the death of a parent, a divorce of a sibling or a physical problem in a child can trigger increased tension and anxiety in the family. When family members seek consultation around such crises, the crises become opportunities for more learning about the self and the family.

SECTION TWO: WHAT DOES THE TERMINATION SESSION LOOK LIKE?

There is a formal structure for the ending session, which should be planned. In the session preceding the termination session, the therapist should ask the family members to review the therapy process and come to the last session prepared to evaluate it. The therapist should structure the formal termination session to give the family members the opportunity to share their overall experiences in the therapy process. Family members should be asked to evaluate their success in handling old problems as well as their effectiveness in coping with existing concerns.

As mentioned previously, the therapist should leave the door open for the family members to return if they encounter difficulties. The therapist should define his or her role as that of a consultant. When the family views the therapist as a consultant, they will redefine their reaching out to him or her in the future. When family members view the therapist in this light, they will be able to work through dilemmas in the follow-up sessions more quickly. In contrast, when the family interprets its needs for future therapy as a sign of failure, their reentry into therapy is more difficult. It is important at termination to convey to the family that the need for an occasional consultation is not an indication of failure.

The interview that follows provides an example of a termination session. It follows the general format that I have discussed. First, each member is encouraged to discuss the highs and lows of his or her experience. This discussion helps the therapist assess which experiences were especially useful and which were unhelpful or disappointing. It is illuminating to have family members go into some detail in describing their highs and lows and to see how other family members have related to the same events. Second, the family is assessed for the changes that have occurred in each of the subsystems within the family. Of particular interest is how each individual's functioning within the family has changed over time and how the husband/wife, parent/child, siblings, and total family unit have been affected by the therapy process. Third, the family is evaluated for its effectiveness in dealing with current concerns. Fourth, the possibility of future consultation is discussed with the family members.

SECTION THREE:
TERMINATION SESSION AND CASE COMMENTARY

The following interview provides an illustration of a termination session with a couple who had been in therapy for one and a half years. The couple had been married for several years prior to seeking therapy. It was the second marriage for the husband, who was in his fifties. He had two teen-age sons, who lived with their mother in another city. It was the first marriage for the wife, who was in her early forties. The wife was the youngest of eight children. The husband was the oldest of two children. His younger sister was fifteen years his junior. The husband's mother had died a number of years previously. His father was still alive. The wife's parents were still alive.

The couple sought therapy after the wife discovered her husband was having an affair. She felt devastated and she wanted to end the marriage. The husband was contrite and desperate to save the marriage. They began therapy by wanting to use the process to analyze their marriage and decide whether or not it could be saved. The husband presented himself as the transgressor and the wife as the injured victim. At the conclusion of the first interview, I suggested to the couple that they could use this affair as an opportunity to learn more about themselves and the potential of the relationship, or they could use it to justify distancing and ending the relationship. I also suggested to them that if they continued in therapy it might be appropriate to involve their parents at some point. They reacted strongly to the idea of involving their parents and were confused about how the affair could bring them closer. Nonetheless, they decided to continue in therapy. As the therapy proceeded, they became more motivated to look at self-issues and family-of-origin themes. Over the course of the therapy, the husband's father and sister and the wife's parents were seen. (The interview with the wife's parents is reported in Chapter Seven.)

Numerous changes occurred over the course of therapy with this couple. The wife had traditionally viewed her husband as the perfect male. The husband had felt that he had to perform in a certain way to make it safe for his wife. These rigid roles were dropped. The husband became more involved in a positive way with his sons, his sister, and his father; the wife became significantly more involved with her extended family, particularly with her father from whom she had generally felt cut off. As these partners respositioned themselves in their extended families, they became more intimate and less reactive to each other. They had each been therapists and in the beginning found it awkward to look at self-issues rather than focus on their relationship problems. However, as they rethought their own parts in the relationship struggle, they became more comfortable with and less anxious about the other's differences.

The following interview is the formal termination interview with this couple. The therapist begins the session by stating that the purpose of the hour is to evaluate the therapy process. The wife (Sandra) responds by briefly reviewing significant changes that have occurred within herself and the relationship. She comments that ". . . the whole concept of separating and work with the self has been so important to me that it has spilled over into a lot of other relationships, and that has been an interesting process to watch."

This statement is an important indication of the depth of change that has occurred. If change occurs within the self, it should affect not just the marriage but other relationships as well. Sandra has experienced differences in many important parts of her life. Her experiences indicate that something basic, rather than a merely cosmetic change, has occurred. Sandra goes on to discuss how she has been able to reframe certain experiences in her life, which has allowed her to learn from some failures rather than to feel discouraged and inadequate. She concludes her brief evaluation by raising her ambivalence about whether they are ready to terminate therapy. This ambivalence is not unusual and the therapist must be careful not to use the ambivalence as a reason to continue therapy. However, it is important to address the ambivalence. The therapist reminds the couple that the change that has occurred has been as a result of the work that they have done outside of the therapy session.

The session begins:

Dr. F: Let's start out with how each of you would evaluate the process of therapy.

Paul: We were talking today because we knew that we would be spending time evaluating the whole experience, taking the various roles you have had with us, the changes that have happened, and the areas we still need to work on. Sometimes you have been a catalyst to get us to look at things we would not have otherwise done. Sometimes you had to slow us down and say, "If you ever reach that point it would be nice, but don't put too much pressure on yourselves." And I guess, more than anything, there is a safety in knowing that every X number of days or weeks, we are going to have a chance to let you look at, test out, get some feedback, give each other and ourselves feedback in a safe situation. It has been an extremely important process for us.

Sandra: We were both expressing some anxiety, particularly this morning, that our life has been in a whirl. Since we last saw you we decided to go to Europe, so we haven't talked a whole lot about this discussion. But several times, Paul, particularly, said we should probably set aside some time and talk about our last session with you. So this morning, over coffee, we talked a bit about it and realized that both of us were having some anxiety about it being our last session, and we wanted to talk to you about the possibility of having some sort of follow-up session in the Fall. I think that is valid because I have always been really hard on some of the clients who have hung on or been dependent, etc. But when I think of our situation, I see the steps as small, but the overall change as quite mind boggling in terms of my thinking of this relationship and in terms of thinking of who I am. It may sound trite, but they are questions that I don't think I ever wrestled with before our experience with you . . . before we were in crisis. I have found the sessions really helpful. There were times I came to the sessions with a bit of an agenda and never got to it, and that was just good to know that you kept me on track. I always left the session feeling like, even though I didn't get to my agenda, it really wasn't an agenda. You helped me get under that and see what was really going on. And that was helpful.

The other interesting thing that happened to me during all of this was that while we really worked hard at our relationship and our interaction with each other, the whole concept of separating and work with the self has been so important to me that it has spilled over into a lot of other relationships, and that has been an interesting process to watch. I have a really good friend in the city and have had some real struggles with her last year. I didn't have the same expectations of a relationship and of myself in a relationship, and she has had a real hard time because she is dealing with different parts of me and her. It has been difficult. I have seen it in my work situation too. More than the changes I have seen, I recognized the pitfalls. That happens every day. I don't think a day goes by when I don't feel myself slipping into a pattern that I don't particularly like. You have always been really reassuring about it not really mattering what happens as long as you look at it and try to figure out why. You talk about that little part of your mind that you keep up here as opposed to the heart level.

That has been helpful because before I would be so self-critical and so unhappy with myself. I really disliked myself so much I wouldn't give myself too much encouragement to change. But now it seems OK to fall into those pitfalls. I don't need to fault myself quite as much. I am more able to move on. That was one of the spinoffs that I wasn't expecting. And of course, had to happen if the relationship was going to improve. We were both doing a lot of work with self.

There have been instances just during the past weeks that the amount we have changed has just been so dramatic in my head. Because things have changed so much. I am not talking about the pain now but the joy to change, if you like. We really feel we are right dab in the middle of the process and the thought of terminating this is frightening.

Before addressing the issue of ambivalence, the therapist shifts Sandra's focus to evaluating the impact of involving her parents in the therapy process. The therapist is curious about what gets stirred up in Sandra (and others) when it is suggested early in the therapy process that it may be necessary to involve extended family members. He is also curious about how Sandra's initial reaction changed over time. Sandra's answer confirms the therapist's hypothesis that she wanted distance between herself and her extended family. Over the course of therapy, she reconsidered the appropriateness of this stance and became more interested about involving her parents. Sandra points out that her husband's involvement of his sister and father was a major influence on her decision to invite her parents. This dynamic is another example of why it helps to have both people in the relationship working on the self. When one partner makes a self-move and/or repositions the self in the extended family, it usually spurs the other partner to consider a similar move.

The interview continues with the therapist raising the issue of involving extended family members:

Dr. F: Before we get into that, let me ask you about the beginning, and looking back, what sense you make out of it. Remember when I suggested involving your family and, Paul, you had your reservations about it, and, Sandra, I think you had a few yourself. Could you comment on that and the effect it has had on you over the last six months?

Sandra: The effect that I think that it had on me is that . . . first of all, I don't think I did a great job reconnecting with my family. I was highly anxious. I wasn't terribly satisfied. I avoided certain areas. I taped Mum and Dad. The tapes are very factual, very little process involved. It was partly them, but it sure was mostly me. While I am not very happy about the way I did it, I think in my head and in my every day life, I have probably been more connected with them than I ever have been before. Something I don't even think I shared with Paul was that when my friend C. and I run into trouble. It so often reminds me of the trouble I have with my sister T., who I have mentioned occasionally. There are really areas of pain there. We have both shut down. We decided we would be doing a great thing if we said we would respect each other's space and if you are ever in trouble call me. And that is what our relationship consists of. But that is not really true because I carry all sorts of feelings about T. and I worry about the sorts of feelings she has toward me. There is a big chunk of sadness around that relationship and that comes out in my relationship with C. and in my relationship with Paul. Some of the stuff that goes on between T. and I, I can see where we both got it, in our relationship with our parents. It's a mess. So I guess when you talk about family-of-origin, I don't feel very successful in concretely reconnecting with them. But in my head I have connected with them in such a way that brings to light almost everyday, particularly with Paul, and that has been a helpful process. The more I catch hold of it, the more I feel able to change it, or be aware of it, and say, "Hey, that is like my mum . . ." That has been helpful.

Dr. F: What was your reaction to my pointing out the importance of family?

Sandra: I sure hated it when you first started talking about it. My reservations were that, first of all, I didn't understand what you were doing because my orientation in dealing with people in trouble was so different. Paul is a reality therapist . . . you heard his dad on tape. I thought it was lovely that little poke about him being a reality therapist. And to go back to family-of-origin went against both of our grains. And I thought, "Oh, no." We asked around a lot before we approached you because I thought both of us needed someone who would not let us get away with any bull-shit. Both of us in our own way are still therapists and have fooled a lot of people, mostly ourselves. And I was real disappointed when I realized the approach that I perceived you taking. When you assured me, and I think this was the second session, that you weren't talking about reinvolvement with the family, that was the turning point. I thought if I had some control, if he is asking me to love my father, I am in trouble. So when I realized you were asking me to understand more of the reality, not just my perceptions, by just hearing someone else's perception, and in fact, that I could change some of those awful feelings, that was the turning point. That was reassuring, not because it took some fear away, but because I saw some real validity in it. The other big turning point that I remember is when I realized Paul was getting into it. And we talked one time about my fear of going ahead, and Paul not, but he got into it even more than I did. Took some real risks and got excited about it.

The therapist now pushes Sandra a little bit. He points out that at the beginning of therapy Sandra saw herself as being more connected with her family than Paul was with his; however, as it turned out, Paul was more willing to involve his extended family. He asks Sandra to reflect on this dynamic. Sandra's response indicates that Paul's willingness to involve his extended family forced her to rethink the myth that she carried about her own connection and comfort with her family.

Dr. F: Was that a surprise to you? Because when you both started you were the one who seemed a bit more connected and open about family.
Sandra: As it went on it changed a bit, and also it changed a bit in my perception of how connected we were. I think he is as connected as I am. I made a lot of noise so it seemed that I was more connected.
Dr. F: How did it change your sense of Paul when you observed him reconnecting in a different way with his family?

This last question is to assess whether the changes that have occurred in the relationship are perceived as gains or losses. Sandra could view Paul's connection with his extended family as being at the expense of his involvement with her. Or, as was the case, his movement towards his extended family could encourage her to rethink her position with her own family and propel her to reconnect in a different way.
Sandra responds:

Sandra: Some interesting things have happened, actually, now that you have asked that question. One was his letter to his dad when he decided not to go home. I wondered whether or not that was a cop-out. There were lots of reasons why he couldn't go that were valid but I felt his relief that he wasn't going home. But immediately after that he wrote a letter to his dad, and it was one that had been given a lot of thought, he asked me if I wanted to read it before I sent it. And I remember thinking that he is really very serious about this. But more than that, I think what helped change my perception of Paul and his involvement, or lack of involvement, was when we listened to his dad's tape together and I saw how really important his dad's words were . . .

He jumped up and played over the words again many times. He was sad. He was fighting tears. He cried. Just so often throughout this whole process, I have made assumptions about Paul that aren't true. One of the biggest assumptions that I made was a lack of strength and the depth of his involvement with people. He would be quite glib and talk and write people off easily. I don't believe it anymore. He doesn't tell me as much any more really. That has been really helpful because what it has done for me (I am not real good at it yet) has made it easier for me to say what I want and not have to worry that Paul will crumble. He may get depressed. He may withdraw a little bit. But he will cope. I don't have to worry about that as much.

Dr. F: What has that done for you?

The therapist persists with Sandra to assess if Paul's work on his own family has influenced her rethinking her position with her family. She initially answers the question by talking about how encouraged she was about her husband's work on his family. It would be a mistake for the therapist to leave the focus on how one partner sees the other partner's work without reflecting on how that work has influenced his or her own change or lack of change. It is interesting that Paul's work has been freeing for Sandra. She has been able to let go of her preoccupation with his behavior and focus on her own relationships and how she would like them to be different. Her comments illustrate how she has been able to begin to separate herself out from her husband's behavior. In the beginning stages of therapy, Sandra had been preoccupied with her husband's reactions. She worried about his disapproval and his lack of involvement with other people in the world. As she began to separate herself from her husband emotionally, she became able to experiment with how she wanted to be in other relationships without being preoccupied with Paul's approval or reaction to these changes.

Sandra responds to the question about the impact of Paul's work on her:

Sandra: It frees me to deal with the feeling of not being needed as much. That is still something I grapple with, things that make me feel real needed. That is right at the forefront. It also releases me. It gives me a freedom that I haven't known before in the relationship. I can do what I want to do. I still worry about his reaction, but not as much. And where there is a reaction, I can give it more time. Actually, we need less time now. And I stick to what I want. It happened over the weekend, going out when I didn't want to go out. Ordinarily I would say, "OK. We will go out." He reacted when I didn't want to go out. I just said I really didn't want to and that was fine.

I got a letter from a friend who Paul doesn't waste much love on, truly, and she and some other friends of mine are going to be in Reno and wanted me to go along, right after we get back from Europe, just for a weekend. And I really want to go. Paul was working late last night and got home late and I told him about it. When I told him about it, his reaction was that he wasn't surprised I wanted to go. Ordinarily I would sit on that letter. I would think that we couldn't afford it. It is over a long weekend, etc., etc. I would have myself in a tizzy before I would even present it. And then I might not present it—I might just write back and say it is out of the question. And then over that weekend I would be depressed and couldn't say why. And I would have resented it.

When I read him the letter last night, I said that I would really like to go, knowing that when we got back from Europe we wouldn't have much money. And he said that he wasn't surprised that I would like to go . . . some friends of mine from back East would be there. So I said I hadn't made up my mind if I wanted to go, but I said that I would look into it. It seemed OK with him. Then, I was glad he said them, he said that he had some feelings because it is a long weekend and he will be off. If he hadn't said it . . . he said it in a way that wasn't accusing me, but it was just what he was feeling. But there was no pressuring me. That was a major thing. It could have been a major issue. But it just wasn't because I thought, I have a right to state what I want. Paul has a right to react, but that doesn't have to make me change what I want. And that is a new process. In my life, not just with Paul. A year ago I would have been walking around with a three-day depression, and he would wonder where the hell I was coming from.
Dr. F: I would like to ask you a question about the beginning. I remember you starting in the first session with this image of the relationship and how disappointed you were that because of the "incident" this image was shattered. Do you have any thoughts on that?

The therapist is now asking Sandra to reflect back on the affair. It is important to talk about the affair in the context of the changes that have occurred in each of them and in the relationship. The therapist also wishes to assess the degree of reactivity that currently exists around this powerful incident in the couple's history. The therapist could not be certain that termination was appropriate at this time without asking about the affair and Sandra's and Paul's rethinking about its meaning for themselves, their relationship, and their future. If Sandra and Paul are still stuck emotionally, they will use the affair to define the relationship on the basis of the old hurt, blame, and anger. If there has been significant change, they will talk about the affair in terms of what each has learned about the self rather than their anger and hurt towards the other.

Sandra responds:

Sandra: I used the word "magical" a lot. And that was a good word to use because that was exactly what it was. It was magical and quite unreal. I had an image of Paul that he had to meet and couldn't possibly meet, and everytime he didn't, he got shit. The one statement, I think I told you this before, that was really helpful to me was that when I see something in Paul that I am criticizing, I am really making a statement about me and not Paul. That was the magical part. That was the part that turned me around. To me the amount of freedom I am feeling right now, I mean, I know you know that I am only in the beginning and I am working from a real tight spot still, but to me the relationship is magical. I am just stretching myself in all kinds of areas. I am stretching myself in feeling strong, deciding who I am and what I want, and saying that, sometimes with a lot of assurance and great pride. And I feel myself exploring outside the relationship that I didn't do before because of fear. And I think I was so trapped into the image I had of Paul, and the one that I wanted him to have of me, that I was immobilizing myself. So that when something happened like the "incident," that was outside the image . . . I mean, I don't think I came to you with any real sincerity. I came to you thinking that it is going to blow, and at least, I can say that I am seeing someone for help. I don't think I came to you really believing that this could be worked through. I believed we were really finished. At some level that is true.

Dr. F: When you heard me say at the beginning that an issue or an "incident" could bring people closer or farther apart, how did that hit you?

This last question is another attempt to learn from the family. As mentioned previously, the therapist had stated in the first session that the affair could be used as an opportunity to connect at a deeper level or to distance. He wants to learn more about the power of these types of statements on people in the early part of therapy. This statement is based on the assumption that the couple will be able to hear the reframe and use it. However, the therapist wishes to check it out later on in therapy to determine if his assumption is valid. The therapist learns that, in fact, the couple found this statement quite useful. It permitted Sandra to become clearer about her own agenda, which at the beginning of therapy was to end the relationship. When the therapist reframed the affair as an opportunity, she had to take responsibility for her own need to distance in the relationship.

Sandra responds to the question about the impact of this statement:

Sandra: That was really powerful. I still have it written in the back of my book. I went back to my office and wrote it in the book. And we had another meeting in two weeks. And I struggled with that statement for two weeks. The reason I struggled with it is because, as I said it over in my mind, it did two things. It made me somewhat equally responsible for the "incident." I sure didn't like that because then I had to stop blaming. And yet a big thing it did, once I accepted the fact that I was in this situation too, equally . . . that was the word, I could give lip service to the fact that I "probably fed into it," that is such a nice, safe statement, but when I was saying to myself, "I am as responsible as Paul is. We are in this together," then I let my anger go. That was a huge movement for me. Probably the first time something had happened that made me angry at Paul, and I had to accept equal responsibility and give up the anger. Then I got into the process. That was probably the biggest turning point. Lots of turning points. That was the big one.

Dr. F: Well, Paul, how about some of the same questions for you? Going back to the suggestion that the family-of-origin might be an area to take a look at.

The therapist is now shifting the focus from Sandra to Paul. It is important that he ask both members of the couple the same questions and give them both an opportunity to evaluate the therapy process.

Paul responds to the question about his reaction to looking at his family-of-origin:

Paul: Well, I was really resistant. I really did not want to be here. And in some ways, I haven't, and in some ways, I really have. I have in the sense that I have a deeper sense and a lot of interest in knowing more about where I come from and what my patterns are. That was really important to me. I got a sense of some stuff that I never had, once I heard, and I had to hear it several times, that reconnecting did not mean that I had to like everyone. And like I still do funny things. Like getting ready for this trip for Europe, I made a list of my family I needed to write, and I didn't put my sister on the list. Sandra had to point it out. I kind of laughed and said, "There I go again." But it was not a gamey thing, which it would have been in the past. I don't think I will ever particularly like her, but I am more connected with her in ways, and I have a much deeper understanding of why we are so different. It has done a lot for me with Sandra in that I think I see her as a piece of a system and have a much greater understanding about where she is coming from. And I don't see it as her. The other night she was saying something to me, and I said, "You are even looking like my sister right now." So it kind of enriched me in terms of . . . as I see her working at her place in her family and the whole thing around families. It has been an interesting process.

As I said, I will probably be out in the fall and I am looking forward to having some chance to talk, and I don't know how that is going to go. I have taken so much pressure off myself, that if there is any big change in me, I am not sure I comprehend what happened to me in the past. And I don't really give a shit. I just know that I am so much more at ease living in one skin and living in this relationship than I ever dreamed possible, although I always thought I should be able to be different. I never could quite tolerate me. Now I am just enjoying it. I don't need to have answers, and I don't need to have everything tied up. I always had everything in point form. Sandra used to tease me in the first months because whenever I would say anything I would say good point, one, two, three. And she would say it in reverse the next time, and I would say, three, two, one. Everything in a lock step form. And somehow, life has become more comfortable and less regimented.

Sandra: Could I just mention this, because you may want to know this. When Paul got his leave, in our typical fashion, we decided, "Let's go to Europe," and in two days we had a 30-day tour booked in Europe. And never worried about the money. So we are leaving next week. Our summer is usually filled with family, from May to September. It is usually a very stressful time for us. This is in response to how I see Paul's connectedness with his family. We decided, after quite a bit of discussion, that we were going to safeguard Paul's leave. And both of us felt strongly about it, and I probably came down first and said there is no way . . . we waited for this for so long. You are 51. You have never had a break from work. The family will hear that he is off work and that is it. And sure enough, Paul's dad phoned and said he would like to come out the last week in July and a couple in August. We weren't ready for this because we hadn't had all of this discussion yet. But we said we would get in touch because we are still making plans for summer holidays, etc.

Paul came home from work and had produced this letter that he had written to "Dear family." And this was going to his dad, the two boys, his sister (who had gotten on the list), his ex-wife, because he wanted her to understand what was happening, and his aunt and uncle. It was a letter that kind of shocked me, pleased me, confused me. It shared with them some of the struggle he had over the past few years at work, and this is the big, strong Paul who everyone turns to in trouble, and no one knows what the hell goes on inside of him. He talked about how bone weary he was of worrying about fundraising and the finances. He thought of quitting and then talked to several people and then decided he was in no position to make this kind of decision, but a break would give him a chance to get some distance in order to sort out his options. How then we decided to go to Europe. He talked about how guilty he felt telling his family he was going to Europe. Spending money on himself and not the boys. And this is something he really wanted to do. It will bust us financially, and therefore, a lot of goodies that are usually available for the boys in the summer will not be available. They may sound like small things, but coming from Paul, I know the strength that it has taken to say that. And that we are safeguarding the summer. Therefore, neither he nor I were having family members out this summer, and that he hoped everyone would understand and love him through the process.

And he had that letter done before I had any letters done to my family, and you know "I am the organized one." And then he enclosed an individual letter to each of the people so that it was personal. So to me that is a good answer in terms of the question of how he reconnected with his family. He has become a person, and I am sure they are having a hard time with it. I am also sure they are quite enjoying it.

Dr. F: So you wouldn't have seen yourself doing that a couple of years ago? It wouldn't even have been within your thinking? Never tell them you were having a tough time?

Paul: Never acknowledge that I was having any personal problems, talk work with them, or pressures or strains. Like the first letter to my dad that Sandra and I were in therapy. It really shocked Sandra. Surprised her because I had just not let them know anything about me or what was happening to me. My oldest son phoned two or three nights after the letter. "Hi, Dad. Hear you are taking some time off. Got your letter." Like no big deal. "Maybe I can come out in September. Is that OK?" etc., . . . Somehow the boys have been much more behind my veneer, more accepting, and understanding than any of the rest of the family. Much more open.

Dr. F: Let's go back to the very beginning, something that I found very interesting, your thinking that maybe this wasn't going to make any difference anyway, but that Sandra could at least pat herself on the back for trying. How about for you?

The therapist is now reintroducing the subject of the affair. It is important that the therapist ask Paul how he heard the therapist's comment that the affair could be used as an opportunity to connect or distance. Sandra has been given a chance to talk about the impact of the statement on her, and the therapist now wants to give Paul the same chance. The impact of an important intervention should be checked out with both partners.

Paul responds:

Paul: I think I was more committed to it than Sandra was. I found you. I am the one who actually did the phone calling. And Sandra, I think, did her enquiries because I was. But I think they turned their back on me . . . a couple of my buddies. Again I don't share any problems, so the only way to do this was to phone and say, "I need a therapist. If you were going to go who would you see?" And one of them, who has since separated, said he wished he had gone to see you instead of someone else.

I came. I don't know whether I said it. I certainly thought it was a real opportunity. You used all kinds of words that bothered me. But I had thought that we could use this either as something that will make our relationship something we always believed it could be, or it can kill us. One or the other. Thinking about it, when we finally got ourselves back together again, living back together again, and decided to come and see you, I had some hope that it could work. I wanted it to. The "incident" still crops up, and stuff around it still does, and it can still put a dark cloud on it. I get angry at myself and heavy . . . Sandra still does, not often. And maybe always will. I don't know.

Dr. F: When you heard Sandra talk about the magic and the expectations that are usually attached to that, what impact did that have on you?

Paul: You mean the magic we talked about we used to think was there?

Dr. F: Yes.

Paul: I don't know how to answer. We had ourselves locked into a theory of relationships that I really believe made us really resistant to any alternate proposals. And very scared of any alternate proposals. Either make it work or there was nothing, no alternative. It was very scary and still is at times. I feel those flights of panic at times. I know now they are flights of panic and they don't last.

Over the past while, Sandra said there was a new kind of magic in the relationship that has to do with a kind of freedom, somehow, to be more involved in ways and be able to give each other a kind of support. A kind of cheering section. It's OK to be stupid or unknowing about some sharing. Sandra has opened up some vulnerabilities in areas where she felt vulnerable to me in the past while, and sometimes, I am sort of dazzled. I am trying to catch my breath and catch up. The way she has made herself vulnerable in quite little ways. So incredibly vulnerable in terms of where it is going. At times I feel I am so privileged. But not obligated. I know I have a hell of a distance to go in dealing with this feeling of obligation, but I have made some incredible strides in terms of being obligated to have the answers.

I still do it in a funny way. Sandra is not really interested in history. It's the small thing or the huge thing. All her life has denied any interest in history. And now, she is reading a history book, and sharing it with me, and enjoying it tremendously. And I am the historian in the family and she will ask me what I know about that. It is an exciting process we are going through in terms of a sharing. Somehow for me the whole thing about history is a symbolic type of togetherness, where Sandra can reveal her lack of knowledge and an incredible interest in wanting to learn this whole field, for a whole variety of reasons . . . her family, her mother, hearing stories from her as a kid. They can't understand why she turned off of history . . .

But there is an uneasiness sometimes. Pain still. Some hard times.

Dr. F: One of the things I remember you reacting to, besides the hesitancy to get involved with family, is the concept of separateness. Maybe this is part of the magic of "we are one in the world" rather than separate. I remember you having some uneasiness. You reminded me just now when you said you did not want to entertain in the beginning the different ways of looking at the magic. How did you become more comfortable with that?

The therapist is now probing Paul's thinking about where the self stops and the other begins. There is usually some ambivalence about working on self-issues. The tendency of many couples is towards fusion. Commonly, the therapist's suggestion that one should not define himself or herself by other's behavior is greeted with a certain degree of unease. The therapist, in asking Paul how he worked on the principle of separateness when he entered therapy, is also interested in discovering how people work on changing their thinking.

Paul responds:

Paul: I don't think I know how it happened. I know it isn't always there. Sometimes I am very nervous about it. I just know that somewhere along the line I am getting excited about it, but I don't think I can point a finger and say what it is. The last session, when you raised the issue, was an important one. It is also Sandra's break from me. If I am going to be off doing my thing, she is going to have some time left. It scared me. I thought it was OK for me to be doing this because it left me in control.

I still feel those waves of fright, but somehow now I know they will pass and that I have to hang in there with myself and give myself some time . . . give Sandra some time. I am not always able to do this.

Dr. F: When you are not able to do it and when you weren't able to do it in the past, what did you do with that feeling?

Paul: I would withdraw. Get sullen. Try to make Sandra feel guilty.

Dr. F: What were you trying to do?

Paul: I think it is a way of punishing her for making me feel uncomfortable. I think the end result is that I pulled her back in. When it happens now, I don't want to pull her back in. I don't like the feeling of pain and discomfort. I am not good at figuring out how to get out of it. When it gets to that point, that I withdraw, I am still feeling trapped by some need. I obviously have some areas that I haven't unlocked. Maybe it is because I haven't figured out . . . I have been excited about the sense of freedom of being more independent and trying on a few things of my own in some of my plans for the summer without really looking where that began to happen or what is involved in that. Maybe that is what I hope will happen over the summer, to try that out . . .

Dr. F: When Sandra raised this issue about Reno, what got stirred up in you?

Paul: Well, I really dislike this person, this old friend of hers. She is a classical 100% pain-in-the-ass, from my point of view. A good friend of Sandra's. I have gradually, over the years, come to get less angry and diffuse myself. So when the letter came yesterday, I was not surprised because Sandra had told me that they talked about it in Toronto. And at the time, I thought it was a good idea. They really have a good time together. They are an old bunch of friends who do crazy, silly things together. Laugh and laugh. So that I could well understand why she would like to do that. I would really like to support her doing that. The other thing that goes off is that it is a long weekend, one of the few times over my break that I have a claim on her time, and all of a sudden . . . I suspect that over the summer that I am going to cherish Sandra's time off, because I am going to have a lot of time. And I have to keep reminding myself that she is a working lady. So I have to learn to respect that piece of her. So suddenly, to have the possibility of a long weekend taken away from me, I got a little tight on it.

Dr. F: It is interesting hearing you talk about that, because in an indirect way you answered the question. And it makes me think how difficult it is when you look at a piece of behavior. It looks the same, but the reason for that behavior is different. I asked you how comfortable you have become with your separateness. That was a struggle for you. A struggle for both of you. Now that is a part of that magic. In the first session, I heard that you had been one together. When you had the affair, you broke away from that. You did something that threw that into question. And the struggle was to get back to it, in whatever way possible, to that magic. But you said when you came in that it could never happen again.

Now all this time you have gone on working on the things you have been talking about. And Paul, your discomfort with the implications of separateness, you have come a long way on that. So now when Sandra presents this proposal to spend a few days away from you with friends, your reaction to that, as I hear you, has to do with a lot of other things besides the discomfort of separateness. All these issues you just raised, your free time, you have a lot, she has little free time. So you make a demand for her not to go. Is that demand heard as an old demand or something different from that? Did you experience the old Paul or the new Sandra? Because the behavior is the same. It is still a demand, "I prefer you not to go." But is it because of the old issue, "You are breaking away, and I am losing control," or the new thing, "I have a lot of free time now and the few days that we have free are precious." I find that the most difficult thing in working with families and couples is that the history is so strong that even when there is change, the behavior is understood in terms of the old issues. The behavior is the same, but the reason for that behavior is fundamentally different. But do we feel it, see it, as fundamentally different? Do you follow me?

The therapist is now taking a more didactic approach, teaching some systems principles to the couple. He raises questions about how each of them is able to differentiate between the old stories that they have constructed about each other and the new learning about themselves and their relationship that has taken place.

Sandra responds first:

Sandra: Oh, do I ever.
Paul: There were times in the past when I felt, when we had some strains in the last week or so, I felt floods of the old anger and the old frustrations, and I think, my reaction has been an automatic one, that this is the old Sandra. I have even said that to myself, "There she goes again. There it is again."
Sandra: It is like back to the family-of-origin. It goes back further than that. But what you said . . . bells are going off in my head. Last night,

when Paul came in, we started chatting, and I said I got lots of mail today, and so I showed him one, two, and three. And the third letter was the "one" and as I read it, I saw his reaction. And in my head, what was going on was "Oh, oh. I knew this would happen." And then two seconds later I said, "Oh, shit. It isn't happening." And then "Oh, yes. It is happening." I couldn't figure out if it was the old Paul or if he was being perfectly reasonable. And I was just fascinated. One thing that was sure was that I didn't feel that I had to compromise what I perceived might be the old Sandra. Now I realize that it probably wasn't, and that was why I didn't compromise.

Paul: I didn't vent all this feeling last night because I thought that if she decided to go, I would probably prefer her to stay, but there are other things that I could do anyway. Schedule a trip around that. In my head, I had assumed that somehow whatever I would do I would be in the city or available when Sandra had a long weekend. That would be what I would put into my summer plot. So it was an open option to me.

Dr. F: It perplexed you a bit.

Paul: Uh, hum.

Dr. F: But you (Sandra) said something interesting, "If it had been the old Paul, it would have been different." You don't know for sure but that is your hunch. You picked up something inside of him that made it easier for you to maintain . . . It would have been interesting if the old Paul showed himself to see if you would have maintained that stance. Because if you have to have the other person be different before self can be different, you wait a long time. As you heard, when he answered your question about Reno, the reasons were of a different nature than the old need to have you.

The therapist has now reiterated the important principle that if change is to be sustained, it has to be sustained without cooperation. Therapy has been directed at helping the couple understand that if they want to be different in the relationship, they have to be different for their own reasons, not to please other or to make the relationship better. Only when one can change without cooperation will one be able to sustain change.

The interview continues:

Sandra: How could I possibly choose to be with someone else when I could be with him . . . You are right in terms of the old reactions with each other. It has happened. We are smack dab in the middle of this process . . . where I heard his reaction as an old reaction and compromised and was unhappy with myself. On Sunday when I didn't want to go out, I felt his whole reaction, but I felt that is OK. I still don't want to go out. I will still be mad at myself if I do go out. So, he will get over it. But going through a struggle with it, feeling he is under so much stress, I can talk myself into compromising very quickly. But I didn't, and he was fine, and we had a nice evening. We wouldn't have if I had compromised.

Dr. F: So you are getting clearer, it sounds, about the need to have one person be different rather than having to have both be different.

Sandra: Yes.

Dr. F: Even if you feel that pull to somehow have something that tells you to resist. And that can work for either one of you.

Paul: One of the things that you have said is that only one of you can be doing it, and most of the time that is the best you can hope for. That has been an important statement. And something I have been saying to myself is that sometimes I am not clear whether it is the old or new me, or the old or new Sandra . . . but I have to live with that. Sometimes when I get out of it, some kind of strain, I get an unhappy feeling that it is the old me that is paramount. And I am trying not to let the anxiety get added to this. To get that anxiety added to it, then, who knows, I feel that I will get crippled by the process. Sometimes now when I withdraw, it is because I really don't know what the hell is going on with me. I just know I am feeling miserable at the time. And so if I back off a bit, I can get a chance to sort it out. Whether I feel miserable for lousy reasons, selfish reasons, or I am miserable because Sandra is being a bitch. That is a strong word but she has done something that is not fair given the situation. Once that becomes clear, then it becomes so easy to resolve. Some situations are so easy to clarify and resolve. We don't get ourselves caught in the wondering of whether it is the old or new self.

Dr. F: So even a withdrawal has a different meaning?

Sandra: It just means space, not a punishment.

Dr. F: But how do you know that? Or do you need to know that?

Sandra: Sometimes I don't know.

Paul: Sometimes I don't know. My style is to withdraw, so I will probably go and stand on the balcony sometimes . . . I don't know if I am out there because I want to leave and never come back, or sometimes I am just out there because my head needs a time to sort out and think out and clarify sometimes . . .

Sandra: Sometimes I have heard you say to me, "Is it an old pattern I'm going by?" I was always amazed, Paul comes out of unhappiness much more quickly than I, and he is almost always willing to talk about him and what is happening to him more quickly than I am. I am much more likely to blame.

Paul: That is the old you.

Sandra: Right.

Dr. F: Well, I guess the underlying principle is that if you need the other person to be different for self to be different then you are really vulnerable.

Sandra: The other turning point for me was your explanation of the paradox of the closer you are, the less intimate you can be. The universal paradox. It hit the nail on the head for me when I was able to put into words this morning our major task being establishing a healthy balance between separateness and togetherness.

Dr. F: The universal struggle is that. I think the best time to work on those things is now. Most people would say the best time is when you are in crisis but I think this is the best time. The potential is far greater because you are not bogged down. The issues really cloud working on self. For a lot of people, as soon as they get those issues resolved, that is the end of the work. You can get into a comfortable balance. After that, like now, it is time to take a look at the fundamental issues.

I would like the two of you to remember that if you need to come back to see me as a consultant, I would be open to that. I think you have gone quite a ways in the process, and each of you has been able to do some very important work, both in your extended families and in your relationship with each other. If you find yourself getting bogged down in the future, it might be helpful to come back to see me once in a while just to get some new questions asked as a way of getting unstuck. I would like to leave the door open for that possibility.

Paul and Sandra: Sounds like a good idea to us.

In this termination interview the therapist guided the couple through a fairly comprehensive evaluation of the treatment process. He concluded the interview with an emphasis on the need to develop balance between the self, the other, and the relationship. He highlighted the principle that intimacy is the ability to allow each other to be different while at the same time feel connected. This positive message should help sustain them in their ongoing efforts. The therapist left the door open for future consultions which are framed as a natural part of the process.

Chapter Eleven

Special Therapeutic Issues

SECTION ONE:
INTRODUCTION

There are a number of situations that arise during the course of therapy and present unique dilemmas for the therapist. Well-founded principles of practice will, at times, have to be modified by the therapist when he is faced with certain situations. Although the general principles of a model are usually effective, there are always exceptions to the rule. Whenever exceptions are numerous, they will give rise to a new rule or principle. While, at other times, they merely require an adaptation of practice. This chapter will examine common therapeutic dilemmas that require the therapist to modify a principle of practice. It is important to remember that even when the approach is changed, the modification of the principle should remain consistent with the basic values, goals, and theoretical premises that govern the model.

This chapter discusses the common issues or dilemmas that confront the therapist and provides some suggestions on how to deal with them therapeutically. As always, the approach to these issues attempts to achieve balance between the goal of increasing family members' sense of connection and sense of self.

SECTION TWO:
SPECIAL ISSUES AND DILEMMAS

1. Secret-Keeping

Secret-keeping is probably one of the most negative processes that can occur in a family system. It is not the secret itself that is important but the process in which the family engages to maintain the secret. Secrets divide family members. Secret-keeping is based on collusion and exclusion. Although excluded family members are often, in fact, aware of the secret, they feel unable to address the issues the secret represents symbolically. Secret-keeping is a dysfunctional family process that makes certain family members feel special and connected while excluding other family members who are seen as being vulnerable, responsible, and/or outside important family matters.

Family members who keep secrets will usually attempt to involve the therapist in the secret-keeping process. It is critical that the therapist avoid becoming a party to secrets. At times, it is necessary for the therapist to state clearly to the family in the beginning phase of therapy that he or she will not be a party to information that is kept from other family members. The therapist should make it clear to the family that his job is to be even-handed with all family members. The therapist must be able to ask any questions that he or she thinks are appropriate. The family needs to understand that the therapist who participates in secret-keeping restricts his or her freedom to ask those questions that help family members to understand their dilemma differently.

Occasionally, a family member will telephone a therapist and proceed to tell him something in confidence. Before this process can be halted, the therapist may already find himself in the middle of a secret. When this happens, it is best handled by the therapist telling the family member that the secret cannot be kept. The therapist should advise the family member that it will be necessary at future family sessions to talk about secret-keeping in general and the secret itself. It is helpful for the therapist to tell the family member that the secret should be revealed at a time when it can be experienced by the other family members as new learning rather than a negative message. Often when the therapist takes this position, the individual who is carrying the secret will have revealed it to the family prior to the next session. Refusing to keep a secret constitutes a powerful intervention. When the therapist participates in keeping a secret, he or she can contribute to the maintenance of a dysfunctional generational pattern, as the following example illustrates:

I was asked to provide a consultation to a therapist who had been seeing a young couple for several months. I requested that the therapist give me just a brief overview of her work with the couple prior to my interview with them. During the course of the interview both the husband and the wife indicated that each had had a parent who had been involved in extramarital relationships. When the wife was just thirteen, her mother had confided in her about an affair she was having and had sworn her to secrecy. The wife had felt guilty about possessing this knowledge and not being able to talk to her father about it. It was obvious during the consultation session that the secret-keeping and the guilt associated with it were issues for the wife. In discussing the couple with the referring therapist I learned that soon after the wife got married she had developed her own extra-marital relationship. When the couple first started in therapy, they were seen together and the wife did not tell the therapist about her liaison. The wife asked to see a therapist individually and revealed her secret to the individual therapist. She swore this therapist to secrecy. This therapist then told the couple's therapist about the secret and swore her to secrecy. Then both therapists knew about the wife's affair. The only one who was excluded was the husband. The therapeutic situation now duplicated the emotional system the wife had come from, and the therapists had inadvertently reinforced the pattern.

In a family systems model, it is not so important what the therapist understands. What is important is how the family members understand themselves and each other. The therapist acts as a force for allowing new information to be exchanged between family members. When therapists become involved in dysfunctional triangles, in effect, secret-keeping, they actively work against the open exchange of information.

2. Management of the Absent Member and Introduction of New Individuals

There are times when it is impossible for all family members to be involved in the family therapy process. Most commonly, physical distance prevents some members from being involved. It is important that the therapist be respectful of the absent member and avoid scapegoating, triangling, or focusing on this member. The therapist should make it clear to the family that the absent member should not be discussed in a negative way. If the individual participates in the therapy, the concerns the family members have about him or her can be addressed at that time. The therapist who permits family members to focus on an absent member reduces the potential for that member to be involved. When family members talk about an absent member, they do so to distance and maintain the dysfunctional triangle. If the absent member is involved, the anxiety of the other members increases. They are fearful of the absent member's reaction to hearing what has been said about him or her and also miss the "safety" of being able to focus on his or her behavior. The presence of the new member will shift the focus to the others in the family. There can be an unspoken collusion between the absent member and the other family members to keep the absent member away as a way of maintaining a safe distance between family members. The therapist must be alert to this possibility and must ensure that the member's absence does not serve a dysfunctional role in the family therapy process. It is helpful for the therapist to point out that the absent member's point of view is important, although unknown and that in the future it might be desirable to involve that person in the therapy to gain a more balanced picture. In giving this message, the therapist is showing respect for the absent member and maintaining him or her in a more balanced position in relation to the other family members.

As discussed in previous chapters, as therapy continues the therapist may wish to involve additional family members in the process. The therapist must be very clear about the reasons for doing so. The new person will enter the process as the outsider. He or she will have been told stories about the family therapy process and may have received messages about the reasons for his or her involvement that are quite different from what the therapist had in mind. The way the person is involved in the process will determine how constructive the person's involvement will be.

When the therapist introduces a new member to the process, he or she must do so in a natural and sensitive way. The newcomer will have numerous fantasies and concerns about what the experience will be like. He or she may feel ill at ease and guarded. Often a new member will be hesitant to say anything for fear of upsetting what has already happened. Because of these natural concerns, when there is a new member present, I always begin the session by introducing him or her to all present and then asking about what his or her understanding is about what has been going on, who has told him or her about the sessions, what his or her expectations are, and what sorts of goals he or she may have for the session. When the new member is given an opportunity to articulate his or her thoughts and feelings about the process at the beginning, the new member's role, as well as the roles of the therapist and the other family members, can be clarified. This clarity facilitates the new member being quickly engaged in the work at hand. It is important for the new member to be able to identify what he or she needs to have happen in order to feel that the time is well spent. Unless the new member feels the benefits of attending the session, then he or she will tend to remain ambivalent about the process. If there is a high degree of ambivalence, then the negative aspects of other family members will be highlighted as away of distancing from them and keeping the anxiety about getting too close under control.

3. Sharing Information with Outside Agencies

At times, a therapist is asked to provide information about a family to other professionals or agencies. The therapist must do so with a great deal of care. He or she should attempt to facilitate a positive perception of the family. Regrettably, a great deal of information that is shared between agencies emphasizes the more negative, dysfunctional aspects of the family. Various professionals who are involved with the family judge the family on the basis of their personal views of what family should be like. The family therapist must be careful not to feed into this process. My practice is to provide a genogram to other professionals who request information. I resist providing subjective impressions about family members and avoid explaining how families function. I provide the structural outline of the family and explain to other professionals that my job is to help the family members with their connections. Unfortunately, many professionals express frustration over my not providing more information. However, in my opinion it is more useful for professionals to form their own impressions about the families they see. My role, as I see it, is to encourage them to become more curious about the families that they are inquiring about, rather than rely on my impressions. In my practice, I avoid using information from others or from written records as guides to my work with a family. I attempt to remain neutral and detached from other professionals' work with the family. I find the more information that I have about families prior to seeing them, the harder it is for me to ask fresh, crisp, provocative questions. My guiding principle is that the best informant about the family is the family itself.

4. Therapy with Families in Which a Member Is Placed Outside the Home

Family therapists are occasionally asked to work with a family in which a member has been placed in a setting outside the home such as a hospital, residential treatment center, foster home, etc. This situation presents a dilemma for the family therapist. It is difficult to engage the entire family when one of its members has already been removed from the family home. The treatment is further complicated by the fact that the professionals who are involved with the absent member have vested interests in how the therapy should proceed. This latter difficulty presents one of the most difficult hurdles. For example, it is common for the inpatient staff in hospital settings to overidentify with the plight of the hospitalized patient and to feel overtly or covertly antagonistic toward the family. During case conferences or on rounds on hospital wards, one often hears staff comment that the patient would do much better in a different home. The triangulation that occurs between the professionals and the other family members can present a serious constraint to commencing family therapy. One way to limit these hazards is to use the time the absent member is outside the home to prepare the rest of the family for family therapy upon the absent member's return. The formal therapy should not be commenced when one member is placed in a setting that reinforces his or her identification as the problem in a family. As long as the absent member is in such a setting, it is difficult for the other family members to recognize that a redefinition or rethinking of the family's concerns is necessary. Their thinking has been reinforced by the professional community, and they are firm in their belief that their focus on just one of their members is legitimate. With these families, the absent member is at a marked disadvantage. Until he or she is on an equal or near equal footing with the rest of the family members, the family therapy process can have only limited success.

One of the most common outside placements the therapist encounters is the foster home. Placement of a family member in foster care raises several therapeutic issues. Over the last several years, I have tried bringing foster families and natural families together with quite encouraging results. Quite often the natural parents are antagonistic towards the foster parents and view them as competitors. In turn, the foster parents, who have been informed about the failures of the natural parents, fail to appreciate how the parents can provide a positive environment for their child. As a rule, there is considerable misunderstanding between the foster family and the natural family. The welfare agency may play into this estrangement by feeding very selective information to each family, thereby increasing their mutual distrust and the distance between them. As a result, the foster child is usually the main communicator of information between the two families. How and what the foster child communicates are influenced by his or her own struggles. Ordinarily, these communications result in further antagonism between the two families. The family therapist can bring the foster family and natural family together to their mutual benefit. The two sets of parents have similar goals. They can be supportive of each other and, in fact, learn from each other. However, this rarely occurs without some assistance. The therapist must assume an active role in helping the two family systems recognize that a mutual respect and understanding is helpful to the child and themselves. (An example of an interview that involved the natural parents and the foster mother was previously reported in Chapter Four.)

5. Concurrent Therapies

Concurrent therapies present special dilemmas for the family therapist. In exceptional circumstances other therapies may be required. There may be a need for a specific type of service that the family therapist cannot provide. When other therapies are indicated, it is important for the therapist to be aware of their influence on the functioning of the family. Chapter Three discussed the difficulties that can arise when more than one therapist is involved with the family. The greatest risk is that family members will use other therapies to maintain their stuckness or reactively reduce their anxiety. Therapists can become part of this dysfunctional triangle. When there is more than one therapist, there should be a clear understanding between them about their respective roles. Except in rare circumstances, I will not see a family if some members are involved in other therapies. My experience has been that concurrent therapies usually undermine each other. I make my position clear to the family members and suggest to them that they discuss my concerns with their other therapist(s). The family therapist who takes the position that multiple therapies are undesirable should be careful not to suggest that one therapy is better than another. The family therapist should make it clear that the concern is about how effective he or she can be when family members are engaged with other therapists. He or she may wish to point out to the family members that the basis of family therapy is that they have one setting where they can talk about self, relationship, and family issues together in order to learn about themselves and each other. When one or more of their members sees someone else, it has the potential to undermine the connections flowing from this process. The therapist should define this position, but make it clear that the family members have to make their own decision about where they want to put their emotional energy in working on their concerns.

It is important to remember that when change occurs in a relationship or family, there is increased anxiety in the short run. Unless the family or relationship can handle the increased anxiety, family members will resort to old ways of dealing with anxiety, in other words: triangling in other people, including other therapists, around their story. The therapist should be observant about how various family members involve themselves with other people in the community to reduce their anxiety. If the therapist is not able to control this dynamic, the chances are that the family will move slowly or not at all in experimenting with ways to change their interactional patterns.

6. Affairs

When one member of a couple entering therapy is involved in an affair, it is difficult to make progress. In many ways, the affair serves as a device for the members of the couple to maintain distance and stay stuck emotionally. When either party uses another relationship as a way to deal with difficulties in his or her primary relationship, it is difficult for that individual to begin to learn about his or her own emotional reactivity. Commonly, when one partner is unhappy in a relationship, he or she will move out of the relationship and into another for comfort. He or she becomes safe but has not learned anything new about the self. When the other partner discovers the affair, his or her reactivity and anger around the affair keep him or her stuck as well. The couple begins to fight about the affair, but neither has learned anything new about what has been happening for the self in the relationship.

In order for the therapist to be effective when one of the partners is involved in an affair, the therapist should bring it to the forefront. Some of the therapeutic dilemmas previously discussed in this chapter are present when there is an affair. There is usually secret-keeping. Certain people have information others do not, etc. The other participant in the affair is the ghost in the therapy session. Even when the couple is not discussing the affair, their thoughts are on it. When the therapist encourages the couple to become more connected with each other, one or the other will introduce the affair as a way to maintain the old, comfortable distance. An effective way to deal with affairs is to talk openly about them. At times, it it helpful to invite the other member of the affair to a therapy session. Once the therapist makes this suggestion, he or she becomes unhooked from treating the other participant in the affair as the ghost haunting the therapy process. Quite often the couple's relationship begins to change once this invitation has been made. There are times when a member of a couple has not mentioned to his or her lover that he or she is involved in family therapy with his or her spouse. When the therapist insists that this other party be invited to a session, the dysfunctional triangle that exists when two people know something to the exclusion of the third begins to dissolve.

When the party involved in the affair attends a session, the principles previously discussed for introducing new individuals come into play. The new member is made part of the process, and his or her agendas are addressed.

In dealing with affairs the most important principle to remember is that the therapist must not collude with one partner to keep the affair a secret. The task of the therapist is to make the affair public, to address the issues directly, and to make it clear to the couple that so long as the affair continues the chance of therapy being effective is minimal. The therapist should suggest to the couple that they will have to make a decision about where to put their energies. The therapist should help them understand that staying stuck on the anger, hurt, and guilt around the affair will serve to maintain comfortable distance. In contrast, if they are prepared to work on self-issues and look at what the affair represents in terms of the issues that they brought into the marriage, the affair can be the basis for making progress in the therapy.

7. Crises and Emergencies

During the course of therapy, it sometimes happens that a family member will call the therapist in a state of crisis. The person may ask to be seen alone. The therapist's response to these crises is important. The therapist should avoid working out any individual arrangement with the caller. The family member who calls when there is an emergency is typically the more anxious, reactive member at that particular time. The therapist who relies on the information provided by the caller to deal with the crisis may find that he or she has unwittingly joined with this anxious member in an approach which undermines the other family members. When the therapist takes the approach that the family members should meet together to discuss how they wish to deal with the issue at hand, the more anxious family member generally calms down. In contrast, if the therapist becomes anxious about the crisis, then he or she is more likely to collude with the anxious family member and overfunction for the family.

It is usually my practice to wait half an hour or so to return calls about crises, as I have found that in this short period of time the crisis often abates somewhat. When I do speak with the caller, I always ask about what he or she has learned over the course of family therapy that can help him or her to deal with the issue. I try to stimulate thinking about the issue after the initial ventilating of the problem. I conclude by stressing the entire family should be seen to address the problem.

Quite often, by the time the family attends the next session, the crisis has passed and there has been some new learning. The therapy can now proceed on course. The therapist should always keep in mind that crises can be used as opportunities for family members to learn more about each other and the ways in which they deal with anxiety. If the therapist gets drawn into the anxiety around the crisis and overfunctions for the family, then he or she contributes to the family members' being stuck and relying on their old, familiar ways to reduce anxiety.

8. The Use of Time and Frequency of Contact

It is up to the therapist to ensure that the therapy time is used purposefully. There is a beginning, middle, and ending to each session. The family members make the best use of time when there is a clear understanding about how long the session will last. Family members will occasionally introduce a new issue at the end of a session in order to extend its length. The therapist should respond by recognizing the importance of the issue and pointing out that it should be raised in the next session. When the therapist remains in control of the time, family members will use it to their best advantage. The predictable structure of the session also provides some sense of safety to the family members. On those occasions when a therapy session is not going well, the therapist will not improve matters by extending its length. In fact, increasing its length will likely make the session seem even more out-of-control.

The frequency of therapy sessions will vary depending on the phase of therapy. If the family members are in the reactive phase, more frequent sessions are indicated. After they have moved into a more proactive phase and are involved in working on the self, longer periods between sessions are desirable. When beginning with a family, it is important to meet regularly, usually on a weekly basis. If too many weeks elapse between the first and second sessions, the second session feels too much like starting over or the family may drop out before the second session is held. The anxiety level of the family members just starting therapy is high. After the first session, they usually feel relieved they got through the hour and may even feel a little better. However, the old issues usually resurface not long after the session. If too much time elapses prior to the next session, the initial enthusiasm and motivation will be replaced by feelings of discouragement and even defeat.

After four to six weeks of regular weekly sessions, the family members generally have a sense of how useful the therapy will be. The time is then opportune for the therapist to negotiate with them about the frequency of contact. As mentioned previously, if family members are still in the reactive phase, it is best to see them weekly or, occasionally, biweekly, until they begin to redefine the problem. Once their focus shifts away from the other and relationship issues to self-issues, the therapist assumes more of a consultant role and the frequency of the sessions can be decreased to once every two to four weeks. The task of the therapist is to gradually and purposely remove himself or herself from a central role in the life of the family. As individuals assume more responsibility for the self, their need to use the therapist as a safety valve in their relationships lessens. The therapist must be sensitive to this shift and change his or her involvement from that of therapist/expert to consultant/coach as appropriate.

9. Co-therapy

It is difficult to develop effective co-therapy teams. It takes a great deal of time and practice, and there are no short cuts. I have found that it is helpful to work together, first, as individual therapists with one therapist in any given session observing, but taking no part in the actual process. When both therapists reach the point where they can anticipate the other's questions, chances are good that they will be able to work together.

There is general support for the idea that heterosexual co-therapy teams provide useful models for dealing with differences between men/women, husbands/wives, fathers/mothers. Although I do not disagree with this premise, it is not particularly relevant to my approach. My model of therapy involves encouraging people to return to their families-of-origin to rediscover how their families conducted the business of life. I try to foster a curious, research stance in my clients that will help them discover their own models based on how their families developed over time.

There are several dynamics that can undermine the co-therapy process. The most common are competition between therapists, lack of a similar framework and the unfinished business that gets acted out in the co-therapy relationship. The co-therapists must take responsibility to see that these factors do not interfere with the services they provide. It is productive for co-therapists to spend some time before each session discussing their agendas and setting up guidelines about how to proceed during the session. At the conclusion of the session, it is recommended that they review the progress of the session as well as how they worked together. It is a useful learning format for therapists to take turns conducting the sessions for the first six months of their working together. This process is less chaotic than the one in which the co-therapist asks questions or makes statements to the family at unpredictable times. By taking turns each therapist is able to observe how the other works in a way that is not possible when both are actively involved in the session. Spending an hour just observing how a family is involved in a therapy session also provides a great deal of learning about the family.

The issue of whether co-therapy teams should consist of opposite or same sex therapists has not been fully researched. My belief is that the sex of the co-therapist is less important than his or her ability to use the other in a proactive, spontaneous way. If there is no competition between therapists and both are comfortable observing as well as acting, then there is potential for a great deal of learning on the part of both the family and the therapists. Notwithstanding the potential benefits of co-therapy, I think it is necessary when training to be a family therapist to work with families on one's own. The family therapist should be able to use himself or herself without the support of another person in the session. The involvement of a co-therapist in the therapeutic process should come from strength and confidence in one's work, and not from fear and anxiety about what might occur during a session.

10. Contraindications for Family Therapy

There are times when family therapy is contraindicated. Family therapy with psychotic individuals, severe character disorders, severely addicted individuals, or those individuals with thinking impairments that make them unable to understand what is going on around them, is ill-advised. When an individual behaves in such a disturbed manner that his or her presence prevents the rest of the family from thinking about themselves or other family members, then his or her involvement is detrimental to the family therapy process. People with severe character disorders are well defended and are usually unwilling to look at or to take responsibility for their part in the process. Their presence also undermines the work of other family members. The job of the therapist is to reduce the anxiety of family members to a level where they can begin to think more effectively about themselves and other members of the family. The therapist cannot accomplish this when there is a psychotic family member or a family member under the influence of drugs or alcohol attending the session.

Family therapy is appropriate in most family situations. The basic principle underlying a multigenerational approach is that it is the framework that is utilized, not who is seen, that defines the process. One can do family-of-origin work with individuals, couples, or entire families. It is not the constellation one involves but the goals, objectives, and questions posed that facilitate the process of change within the self. When one family member creates undue anxiety, then the therapist has to find other ways to proceed so that family members who are more functional can work on their self-issues without being preoccupied with the least functional or more disturbed members of the family. When possible, the family therapist should try to offer a structure that reduces the anxiety of the most disturbed member so that the effect of his or her disturbance is less powerful. However, if the more anxious member continually dominates the session with his or her behavior, then it is appropriate to see the more functional members of the family without the more anxious member, and begin to coach the more functional members to make self-moves without the cooperation of the more reactive family member. This process is based on the principle that when one or more family members works on self-issues in a positive way without using other family members to define themselves or justify their reactivity, then there is a positive ripple effect throughout the family.

It is naive to think that family therapy can change everybody. Certain individuals are so disturbed or so stuck in their situation that they are not prepared or able to work on self-issues. The job of the family therapist is to discover which members of the family have the greatest potential for change and to work with them in a way that fosters the possibility of change in others flowing from the change in them. The family therapist should not define the family in terms of its least functional members. The family therapist's major objective is to free family members up from each other's issues so that the most positive creative parts of themselves can be expressed. In essence, the family therapist's task is to help family members become more masterful about their sense of self in the world and to help them to have the ability to be positive and proactive in all the relationships that are important to them.

Bibliography

Ackerman, Nathan (1966), *Treating the Troubled Family*, New York: Basic Books.

Anderson, Carol and Susan Stewart (1983), *Mastering Resistance*, New York: Guilford Press.

Allport, Gordon (1968), "The Open System in Personality Theory," in *Modern Systems Research for the Behavioral Scientist*, Walter Buckley (ed.), Chicago: Aldine Publishing Company.

Aries, Philippe (1962), *Centuries of Childhood: A Social History of Family Life*, New York: Alfred A. Knopf.

Auerswald, Edgar (1968), "Interdisciplinary Versus Ecological Approach," *Family Process*, Vol. 7, No. 2.

Bandler, Richard S. and John Grinder (1975), *The Structure of Magic*, Vols. I & II, Palo Alto, CA: Science and Behavior Books.

Bank, Stephen P. and Michael O. Kahn (1982), *Sibling Bond*, New York: Basic Books.

Beatman, F.L. (1967), "Intergenerational Aspects of Family Therapy," in *Expanding Theory and Practice in Family Therapy*, N.W. Ackerman (ed.), New York: FSAA.

Bell, John Elderkin (1975), *Family Therapy*, New York: Jason Aronson.

Bennis, Warren G., Kenneth Benne, Robert Chin, and Kenneth Corey (1985), *The Planning of Change*, 4th ed., New York: Holt, Rinehart and Winston.

Bergmann, Martin and Milton E. Jucovy (1982), *Generations of the Holocaust*, New York: Basic Books.

Bermann, Eric (1973), *Scapegoat: The Impact of Death-Fear on an American Family*, Ann Arbor: University of Michigan Press.

Bertalanffy, Ludwig von (1968), "General System Theory," in *General System Theory: Foundations, Development, Applications*, New York: George Braziller.

Bertalanffy, Ludwig von (1981), "Theoretical Models in Biology and Psychology," Chapter 10, "Toward a Generalized Theoretical Model for Psychology," in *A Systems View of Man*, Paul A. LaViolette (ed.), Boulder, CO: Westview Presses.

Bloch, Donald A. (ed.) (1973), *Techniques of Family Psychotherapy: A Primer*, New York: Grune and Stratton.

Blom, Djuwe Joe (1986), *Inside the Milan Interview*, London, Ontario: Somerset Press.

Boszormenyi-Nagy, Ivan and Geraldine Spark (1973), *Invisible Loyalties: Reciprocity in Intergenerational Family Therapy*, New York: Harper and Row.

Bowen, Murray (1960), "A Family Concept of Schizophrenia", in *The Etiology of Schizophrenia*, Part VI, D.D. Jackson (ed.), New York: Basic Books.

Bowen, Murray (1966), "The Use of Family Theory in Clinical Practice," *Comprehensive Psychiatry*, Vol. 7, No. 5.

Bowen, Murray (1978), *Family Therapy in Clinical Practice*, New York: Jason Aronson.

Bowlby, J. (1969), *Attachment and Loss, Vol. I: Attachment*, New York: Basic Books.

Bowlby, J. (1973), *Attachment and Loss, Vol. II: Separation, Anxiety and Anger*, New York: Basic Books.

Bowlby, J. (1980), *Attachment and Loss, Vol. III: Loss: Sadness and Depression*, New York: Basic Books.

Braverman, Shirley (1981), "Family of Origin: The View from the Parents' Side", *Family Process*, Vol. 20, No. 4.

Broderick, Carlfred (1971), *A Decade of Family Research and Action*, Minneapolis, MN: National Council on Family Relations.

Brody, E.M. and G. Spark (1966), "Institutionalization of the Aged: A Family Crisis," *Family Process*, Vol. 5, No. 1.

Buckley, Walter (1968), *Modern Systems Research for the Behavioral Scientist*, Chicago: Aldine Publishing Company.

Buckley, Walter (1967), *Sociology and Modern Systems Theory*, Englewood Cliffs, NJ: Prentice-Hall.

Bugental, James (1987), *The Art of the Psychotherapist*, New York: Norton Press.

Carter, Betty and M. McGoldrick (1988), *The Changing Family Life Cycle: A Framework for Family Therapy*, 2nd ed. New York: Gardner Press.

Chess, Stella and Alexander Thomas (1986), *Temperament in Clinical Practice*, New York: The Guilford Press.

Colon, Fernando (1973), "In Search of One's Past: An Identity Trip," *Family Process*, Vol. 12, No. 4.

Danica, Elly (1988), *Don't: A Woman's Word*, Charlottetown, P.E.I.: Gynergy Books.

David S. Freeman 383

Epstein, N.B. (1973), "Family Therapy—State of the Art," *Canadian Psychiatric Association Journal*, Vol. 18, No. 3.

Erickson, Eric (1964), *Childhood and Society*, 2nd ed. New York: W.W. Norton Press.

Erickson, Eric, Joan M. Erickson, and Helen Q. Kivnick (1986), *Vital Involvement in Old Age*, New York: Norton Press.

Farber, A. and J. Ranz (1972), "How to Succeed in Family Therapy: Set Reachable Goals—Give Workable Tasks," in *Progress in Group and Family Therapy*, C. Sager and H.S. Kaplan (eds.), New York: Brunner-Mazel.

Feldman, Francis and Francis Scherz (1967), *Family Social Welfare: Helping Troubled Families*, New York: Atherton Press.

Ferber, Andrew, Marilyn Mendolsohn, and Augustus Napier (eds.) (1972), *The Book of Family Therapy*, New York: Science House.

Bloom-Feshbach, Jonathan and Sally Bloom-Feshbach (1987), *The Psychology of Separation and Loss*, San Francisco: Jossey-Bass.

Fine, S. (1974), "Troubled Families: Parameters for Diagnosis and Strategies for Change," *Comprehensive Psychiatry*, Vol. 15.

Framo, James (ed.) (1972), *Family Interaction: A Dialogue Between Family Researchers and Family Therapists*, New York: Springer Pub. Corp.

Framo, James (1982), *Explorations in Marital and Family Therapy*, New York: Springer.

Freeman, David S. (1976), "A Systems Approach to Family Therapy," *Family Therapy*, Vol. 3.

Freeman, David S. (ed.) (1980), *Perspectives on Family Therapy*, Toronto: Butterworth and Co.

Freeman, David S. (1976), "Phases of Family Treatment," *The Family Coordinator*, Vol.25, No. 3.

Freeman, David S. (1977), "The Family Systems Practice Model: Underlying Assumptions," *Family Therapy*, Vol. IV, No. 1.

Freeman, David S. (1974), "The Potential Contribution to General Systems Theory of Social Work Knowledge and Practice," in *Unifying Behavioural Theory and Social Work Practice*, D. Finlay, E. Stolar and D. Freeman (eds.), Ottawa: Canadian Association of Schools of Social Work.

Freeman, David S. (1981), *Techniques of Family Therapy*, New York: Jason Aronson.

Freeman, David S. (1985), "The Involvement of Children in Family Therapy," *Canadian Social Work Review*.

Freeman, David S. and Barry Trute (eds.) (1981), *Treating Families with Special Needs*, Ottawa: Canadian Association of Social Workers.

Freeman, David S. and Barry Trute (eds.) (1973), *Canadian Journal of Community Mental Health*, Special Issues on Family Mental Health Practice, Vol. 2, No. 2 September.

Friedman, Alfred (1965), *Psychotherapy for the Whole Family*, New York: Springer Publishing Corporation.

Friedman, Edwin H. (1971), "The Birthday Party: An Experiment in Obtaining Change in One's Own Extended Family," *Family Process*, Vol. 10, No. 3.

Friedman, Edwin H. (1985), *Generation to Generation*, New York: Guilford Press.

Gerard, R.W. (1968), "Units and Concepts of Biology" in *Modern Systems Research for the Behavioral Scientist*, Walter Buckley (ed.), Chicago: Aldine Publishing Co.

Giles-Sims, Jean (1983), *Wife Battering: A Systems Theory Approach*, New York: Guilford Press.

Glick, Ira and David R. Kessler (1974), *Marital and Family Therapy*, New York: Grune and Stratton.

Graham, Lee Combrinck (1985), "A Developmental Model for Family Systems," *Family Process*, Vol. 24, No. 2.

Gray, William, Fredrick Duhl, and Nicholas Rizzo (eds.) (1969), *General Systems Theory and Psychiatry*, Boston: Little, Brown.

Grinker, Roy (ed.) (1956), *Toward a Unified Theory of Human Behavior: An Introduction to General Systems Theory*, New York: Basic Books.

Group for the Advancement of Psychiatry (1970), *Treatment of Families in Conflict: The Clinical Study of Family Process*, New York: Science Books.

Group for the Advancement of Psychiatry (1970), *The Case History Method in the Study of Family Process*, New York: Vol. VII, No. 76.

Group for the Advancement of Psychiatry (1970), *The Field of Family Therapy*, New York: The Group.

Guerin, Philip (ed.) (1976), *Family Therapy: Theory and Practice*, New York: Gardner Press Inc.

Hader, M. (1965), "The Importance of Grandparents in Family Life," *Family Process*, Vol. 4, No. 2.

Haley, Alex (1976), *Roots*, Garden City, New York: Doubleday and Co. Inc.

Haley, Jay (1971), *Changing Families: A Family Therapy Reader*, New York: Grune and Stratton.

Haley, Jay (1980), *Leaving Home: The Therapy of Disturbed Young People*, New York: McGraw-Hill.

Haley, Jay (1969), *The Power Tactics of Jesus Christ and Other Essays*, New York: Grossman Publishers.

Haley, Jay (1976), *Problem Solving Therapy: New Strategies for Effective Family Therapy*, San Francisco: Jossey-Bass.

Haley, Jay (1973), "Strategic Therapy when a Child is Presented as the Problem," *American Academy of Child Psychiatry Journal*, Vol. 12.

Haley, Jay (1973), *Uncommon Therapy: The Psychiatric Techniques of Milton H. Erickson, M.D.*, New York: Norton.

Helfer, Ray and Henry Kempe (1974), *The Battered Child*, 2nd ed., Chicago: The University of Chicago Press.

Henry, Jules (1971), *Pathways to Madness*, New York: Random House.

Herman, Judith L. (1981), *Father-Daughter Incest*, Cambridge, MA: Harvard University Press.

Hinde, Robert and Joan S. Hinde (eds.) (1988), *Relationships within Families: Mutual Influences*, Oxford: Clarendon Press.

Hoffman, Lynn and Lorence Long (1969), "A Systems Dilemma," *Family Process*, Vol. 8, No. 2.

Hoffman, Lynn (1981), *Foundations of Family Therapy: A Conceptual Framework for Systems Change*, New York: Basic Books.

Irving, Howard (1972), *The Family Myth: A Study of the Relationships between Married Couples and Their Parents*, Toronto: Copp Clark.

Irving, Howard and Michael Benjamin (1987), *Family Mediation: Theory and Practice of Dispute Resolution*, Toronto: Carswell.

Ishwaran, K. (ed.) (1976), *The Canadian Family*, Toronto: Holt, Rinehart and Winston of Canada Limited.

Isaacs, Marla Beth, B. Montalvo and David Abelsohn (1986), *The Difficult Divorce*, New York: Basic Books.

Jackson, Don and Irvin Yalom (1964), "Family Homeostasis and Patient Change," *Current Psychiatric Therapies*, Vol. 4, Masserman (ed.).

Kantor, David and William Lehr (1975), *Inside the Family*, San Francisco: Jossey-Bass.

Kaslow, Florence (ed.) (1982), *The International Book of Family Therapy*, New York: Brunner-Mazel.

Kerr, Michael and Murray Bowen (1988), *Family Evaluation*, New York: Norton.

Koller, Marvin (1974), *Families: A Multigenerational Approach*, New York: McGraw-Hill Co.

Krell, R. (1972), "Problems of the Single Parent Family Unit," in *Canadian Medical Association Journal*, Vol. 107.

Kubler-Ross, Elisabeth (1975), *Death: The Final Stage of Growth*, Englewood Cliffs, NJ: Prentice-Hall, Inc.

Leichter, Hope (1961), "Kinship, Values and Casework Interviews," in *Casework Papers*, New York: National Conference on Social Welfare.

Lerner, Harriet Goldhor (1985), *The Dance of Anger*, New York: Harper Row.

Lerner, Harriet Goldhor (1989), *The Dance of Intimacy*, New York: Harper Row.

Levinson, Daniel (1978), *The Seasons of a Man's Life*, New York: Alfred A. Knopf.

Lidz, F. (1960), "Schizophrenia, Human Integration and the Role of the Family," *The Etiology of Schizophrenia*, Part VI, D.D. Jackson (ed.), New York: Basic Books.

Litwak, E. (1960), "Occupational Mobility and Extended Family Cohesion," *American Sociological Review*, Vol. 25, No. 1.

Luepnitz, Deborah (1988), *The Family Interpreted: Feminist Theory in Clinical Practice*, New York: Guilford Press.

McFarlane, William (ed.) (1983), *Family Therapy in Schizophrenia*, New York: Guilford Press.

McGoldrick, Monica and Randy Gerson (1985), *Genograms in Family Assessment*, New York: Norton.

Madanes, Cloe (1981), *Strategic Family Therapy*, San Francisco: Jossey-Bass.

Miller, Alice (1984), *For Your Own Good: Hidden Cruelty in Child Rearing and the Roots of Violence*, New York: Farrar Straus, Giroux.

Miller, Alice (1981), *Thou Shall Not Be Aware, Society Betrayal of the Child*, New York: New American Library.

Miller, James (1955), "Toward a General Theory for the Behavioral Sciences," *American Psychologist*, Vol. 10.

Miller, James (1969), "Living Systems: Basic Concepts," in *General Systems Theory and Psychiatry*, William Gray, Frederick J. Duhl, Nicholas Rizzo (eds.), Boston: Little, Brown.

Minuchin, Salvador (1974), *Families and Family Therapy*, Cambridge, MA: Harvard University Press.

Minuchin, Salvador (1967), *Families of the Slums: An Exploration of Their Structure and Treatment*, New York: Basic Books.

Minuchin, Salvador (1981), *Family Therapy Techniques*, Cambridge MA: Harvard University Press.

Minuchin, Salvador (1978), *Psychosomatic Families: Anorexia Nervosa in Context*, Cambridge, MA: Harvard University Press.

Murray, H.A. and C. Kluckhohn (1953), *Personality in Nature, Society and Culture*, New York: Knopf.

Napier, A. and C. Whitaker (1978), *The Family Crucible: The Intensive Experience in Family Therapy*, New York: Jason Aronson.

Neill, John and David Kniskern (eds.) (1982), *From Psyche to System: The Evolving Therapy of Carl Whitaker*, New York: Guilford Press.

Nichols, Michael (1984), *Family Therapy, Concepts and Methods*, New York: Gardner.

O'Neill, Nena and George O'Neill (1973), "Open Marriage: Implications for Human Service Systems," *The Family Coordinator*, Vol. 22, No. 2.

Papp, Peggy, Olga Silverstein, and Elizabeth Carter (1973), "Family Sculpting in Preventive Work with Well Families," *Family Process*, Vol. 12, No. 2.

Papp, Peggy (ed.) (1977), *Family Therapy: Full Length Case Studies*, New York: Gardner Press Inc.

Parad, Howard and Gerald Kaplan (1965), "A Framework for Studying Families in Crisis," in *Crisis Intervention: Selected Readings*, Howard Parad (ed.), New York: FSAA.

Parsons, T. and R.F. Bales (1955), *Family Socialization and Interaction Process*, Glencoe, IL.: Free Press.

Patterson, G.R., R.R. Reid, R.E. Jones, and A. Conger (1975), *A Social Learning Approach to Family Intervention*, Eugene, OR: Castalia Publishing Co.

Pillari, Vimala (1988), *Human Behavior in the Social Environment*, Pacific Grove, CA: Brooks/Cole.

Pittman, Frank (1989), *Private Lies: Infidelity and the Betrayal of Intimacy*, New York: Norton.

Pollak, Otto (1969), "Developmental Difficulties," in the *Family Dynamics and Female Sexual Delinquency*, Otto Pollak and Alfred Friedman (eds.), Palo Alto, CA: Science and Behavior Books.

Rapoport, Anatol (1968), "Forward," *Modern Systems Research for the Behavioral Scientist*, Walter Buckley (ed.), Chicago: Aldine.

Rapoport, Anatol (1956), "Homeostasis Reconsidered," *Toward a Unified Theory of Human Behavior*, Roy Grinker (ed.), New York: Basic Books.

Raybin, J.B. (1970), "The Curse—A Study in Family Communications" in *American Journal of Psychiatry*, Vol. 127.

Reusch, Jurgen (1956), "The Observer and the Observed: Human Communication Theory," in *Toward a Unified Theory of Human Behavior*, Roy Grinker, (ed.), New York: Basic Books.

Richardson, Ronald (1984), *Family Ties That Bind*, North Vancouver, B.C: Self-Counsel Press.

Rollins, N., J.P. Lord, E. Walsh, and G.R. Weil (1973), "Some Roles Children Play in Their Families: Scapegoat, Baby, Pet and Peacemaker," *Journal of the American Academy of Child Psychiatry*, No. 12.

Sager, Clifford (1983), *Treating the Remarried Family*, New York: Brunner-Mazel.

Satir, Virginia (1967), *Conjoint Family Therapy*, Palo Alto, CA: Science and Behavior Books Inc.

Scheflen, A.E. (1981), *Levels of Schizophrenia*, New York: Brunner-Mazel.

Schrodinger, Erwin (1968), "Order, Disorder and Entropy," *Modern Systems Research for the Behavioral Scientist*, Walter Buckley (ed.), Chicago: Aldine Publishing Co.

Schulman, Gerda (1973), "Treatment of Intergenerational Pathology," *Social Casework*, Vol. 54, No. 8.

Scherz, Francis H. (1971), "Maturational Crisis and Parent-Child Interaction," *Social Casework*, Vol. 52, No. 6.

Selvini-Palazzoli, M. (1978), *Paradox and Counterparadox*, New York: Jason Aronson.

Selye, H. (1974), *Stress Without Distress*, Toronto: McClelland and Stewart.

Skolnick, Arlene (1987), *The Intimate Environment: Exploring Marriage and the Family*, 4th ed. Boston: Little, Brown.

Skynner, A.C. Robin (1976), *Systems of Family and Marital Psychotherapy*, New York: Brunner-Mazel.

Sorokin, Pitirim A. (1947), *Society, Culture and Personality: Their Structure and Dynamics—A System of General Sociology*, New York: Harper and Brothers.

Spark, Geraldine (1974), "Grandparents and Intergenerational Family Therapy," *Family Process*, Vol. 13, No. 2.

Speck, R.V. and U. Rueveni (1969), "Network Therapy—A Developing Concept," *Family Process*, Vol. 8, No. 2.

Speck, Ross V. and Carolyn L. Attneave (1973), *Family Networks*, New York: Pantheon Books.

Speer, David C. (1970), "Family Systems: Morphostasis and Morphogenesis or Is Homeostasis Enough?" *Family Process*, Vol. 9, No. 3.

Stanton, M. Duncan, Thomas C. Todd and Assoc. (1982), *The Family Therapy of Drug Abuse and Addiction*, New York: Guilford Press.

Stein, Joan (1970), *The Family as a Unit of Study and Treatment*, Seattle, WA: University of Washington Press.

Stierlin, Helm (1977), *Psychoanalysis and Family Therapy*, New York: Jason Aronson Inc.

Stierlin, Helm (1981), "The Parents' Nazi Past and the Dialogue Between Generations," *Family Process*, Vol. 20, No. 4.

Stone, Elizabeth (1989), *Black Sheep and Kissing Cousins: How Our Stories Shape Us*, New York: Penguin.

Thomas, Alexander (1968), *Temperament and Behavior Disorders in Children*, New York: New York University Press.

Thomas, A. and S. Chess (1977), *Temperament and Development*, New York: Brunner-Mazel.

Toman, Walter (1969), *Family Constellation: Its Effects on Personality and Social Behavior*, 2nd ed. New York: Springer.

Visher, E.B. (1979), *Stepfamilies: A Guide to Working with Stepparents and Step-Children*, New York: Brunner-Mazel.

Wald, E. (1981), *The Remarried Family: Challenge and Promise*, New York: FSAA.

Wallerstein, Judith and Joan Kelly (1980), *Surviving the Breakup: How Children and Parents Cope with Divorce*, New York: Basic Books.

Watzlawick, Paul (1974), *Change: Principles of Problem Formation and Problem Resolution*, New York: Norton.

Watzlawick, Paul (1978), *The Language of Change: Elements of Therapeutic Communication*, New York: Basic Books.

Weakland, J. (1960), "The Double-Bind Hypothesis of Schizophrenia and Three-Party Interaction," *The Etiology of Schizophrenia*, Part VI, D.D. Jackson (ed.), New York: Basic Books.

Whitaker, C. (1975), "The Symptomatic Adolescent—An AWOL Family Member," *The Adolescent in Group and Family Therapy*, Max Sugar (ed.), New York: Brunner-Mazel.

Winer, Lillian R. (1971), "The Qualified Pronoun Count as a Measure of Change in Family Psychotherapy," *Family Process*, Vol. 10, No. 2.

Yorburg, Betty (1973), *The Changing Family*, New York: Columbia University Press.

Index

Absent members, in family therapy, 369-70
Adolescents, resistance to family therapy, 4-5
Adult children, parent/child relationship and, 204,211-65
Affairs, extramarital
primary relationship and, 348, 355-56,360
therapeutic difficulties with, 373-75
Aged parents, in therapy with adult children, 211-65,351
Agencies, sharing family information with, 370-71
Alcoholism, effect on family function, 4-5
Alliances
extrafamilial, 44-45
maladaptive, 44
therapist and, 44-45,76
Anxiety
caused by death, 53
in couples therapy, 162-63
debilitating effect, 268,271
emotional triangles and, 41-44
in families of alcoholics, 4-5
family change and, 272,273-74, 275,278,280,285
in individual therapy, 319
in parents, 72,106-107,110-11
reduction of, 276,278,283,340

Beginning phase therapy, 69-112
Birth order, sibling relationships and, 289

Caretaker role, 272,276
Case illustrations
adult child and parents, 214-65
children and parents, 79-112, 115-57
couples therapy, 164-97,212-13, 265-85,348-66
effects of therapists' background, 58-61
family losses, 133-57
family therapy with parents, 79-112
individual therapy, 324-44
middle phase therapy, 204-205, 265-85
professional family system, 65-66
relationship problems, 164-97, 212-13,265-85,348-66
sibling relationships, 290-91, 292-316
telephone contacts, 70-72
termination session, 348-66
Change, family. See family change
Change, individual. See individual change
Character disorders, family therapy and, 378
Children
differentiation process, 38-39
early attachment stage, 49
explaining needs to family, 140
focus on in therapy, 69-70
peer group influences, 31
perceptions of family behavior, 126,127
self-concept development, 38-39
separation stage, 49
validation needs, 50
vision for family, 130,131

see also adult children;
    parent/child relationship
Co-therapy teams, 377-78
Collusion, need for therapist to
    avoid, 18,76
Community resources, available to
    families, 24-25
Concurrent therapies, 372-73
Conflict, to maintain emotional
    distance, 8
Content issues, of family members,
    8, 75-76,78,291
Couples therapy, 159-97
    anxiety in, 162-63
    case illustrations, 164-97,212-13,
        265-85,348-66
    collusion avoidance in, 76
    defining the problem, 159,164-65,
        166-69
    examining the relationship,
        159-61,180,183-84,186,
        187-88,196-97
    extended families in, 270-271
    extramarital affairs in, 373-75
    family history taking, 169
    goals, 164
    interviewing, 165-66,177
    involvement of other family
        members, 180
    middle phase, 199-200,265-85
    past issues and, 180,191-92,193,
        195
    see also family therapy;
        relationships
Crisis intervention, in family
    therapy, 375
Criticism, control in family
    therapy, 6

Death
    family reactions to, 14,53,119,
        142,146,147-49,150,152,242
    friends reactions to, 168
Decision-making, family loyalty
    and, 51-52

Defense mechanisms
    in family members, 92,142
    in relationships,160-61,163
Desertion theme, 145
Detached "I" position, 61
Developmental changes. See family
    change
Developmental stages, of individuals
    and families, 31-32
Diabetic children, effects on family
    structure, 29
Differentiation process, 38-41

Ego boundaries, self-concept and,
    38-39
Emotional development, 39-40
    sex differences in, 50-51
Emotional distancing
    in marriage, 160-63
    parent/child relationship and,
        172-74
    in relationships, 12
    use of conflict to maintain, 8
Emotional triangles, in relationships,
    41-44,47
Emotional unfinished business. See
    unfinished business
Erickson's stage of trust, 38
Extended families
    as basic family structure, 16-17
    in couples therapy, 270-71
    effects on nuclear families, 12-13
    emotional impact, 16-17
    in middle phase therapy, 203,209,
        210-11
    unfinished business and, 200-201

Families
    alliances in, 44-45,76
    communication in, 46,114
    internal resources to help itself,
        28-29,65
    as multigenerational system,
        10-11,32-36

natural parents in, 30
need to define term, 18-19,30,
    116,125,127,129
relaxation to community, 24-25
sex differences in expectations
    for, 50-51
value system, 17-18
Families, extended. *See* extended
    families
Families, nuclear. *See* nuclear
    families
Family behavior
perceptions of children, 126,127
systems levels, 25, 26*il.*
Family change
anxiety caused by, 272,273-74,
    275,278,280,285
chronology of, 120-21
death and, 119
family vision for, 130,131,132,
    232
implementation of, 9-10,11-12
individual change and, 317
influence on family, 89-90,91-92,
    94-95,143-44,150,157
losses during, 272,273-77,275
as perceived by children, 122-23
resistance to, 3-4,8,67,77,206,
    301-302
sustaining of, 3-4,201
Family connectedness
importance of, 1-2
reconnection, 323-24
in siblings, 288-89,303,306,309,
    311,312,316
therapy and, 149,152,157
Family developmental stages
evolution of, 31-32
role of grandparents, 117-19
Family function
with alcoholic parent, 4-5
balance in, 53-54
family solidarity and, 4-5
historical aspects, 31
individual autonomy and, 4-5

workings of, 30-31
Family histories
in couples therapy, 164,169,
    179-81
in individual therapy, 317-19
in middle phase therapy, 210-11,
    216,218,219,220,227,253
relation to family problems,
    12-13,74,134,143-44,152
sibling relationships and, 288-89
Family losses
case illustration, 133-57
effects on family, 53,150,157
individual therapy and, 320
Family loyalty, 51-52
Family members
content issues of, 8,75-76,78,291
family response to problems, 2-3
Family relationships, 6-7,13-15,31,
    35
emotional safety in, 12
multigenerational patterns, 10-11
scapegoat process, 27
See also relationships
Family solidarity, family function
    and, 4-5
Family stories
challenging of, 163-64,325,337
connection of, 213
curiosity about, 206-207
individual therapy and, 318-19,
    320,323
influence on relationships, 11-12
influence on siblings, 291,294-95,
    314
as metaphors, 203
in middle phase therapy, 262,264
to maintain safety, 203-204
Family structure
changes in, 3-4,29
definition of, 16-17
development of, 30-31
multigenerational influences,
    10-11
Family systems, 23-54

changes in, 26-27
complexity of, 27-28
genogram role, 32-36
individual dysfunction within,
    29-30
organization of, 27-28
Family theory, 23-54
Family therapy
absent members during, 369-70
adult siblings in, 289
ambivalence toward, 4,77
assumptions guiding, 25-30
case illustrations with parents and
    children, 79-112,113-57,
    214-65
child involvement, 69-70
co-therapy, 377-78
concurrent therapies and, 372-73
contraindications for, 378-79
control by therapist, 6,7-8,81,
    142,155
crisis intervention in, 375
defensive reactions of family
    members, 92,114,142
ending a session, 130,133
family communication style, 46
first session, 69-112,113-14
focus on functional members,
    378-79
goals of, 19-20,43,292-93,379
individual differences and, 5-7,24
with individuals, 317-44
initial assessment, 73
introduction of new individuals,
    369-70
major systems involved, 57-68
with a member outside the home,
    371-72
as ongoing learning process, 28
with parents, 70,78-112
with parents and children, 113-57
physical setup for, 67-68
premature quitting of, 200,201
professional family system, 64-68
resources of family, 28-29,65

return for consultation, 347
safe environment for, 5-6,75-77,
    115-33,156
secrecy avoidance in, 367-69
session frequency, 376
sharing information with
    outsiders, 370-71
with siblings, 287-316
special therapeutic issues, 367-79
systems behavior in, 23-54
termination process, 345-66
therapists' background and, 57-64
therapists' limitations and, 61-62
use of client time, 375-76
values underlying, 17-19
whole family approach, 25-27,
    109-110,145,156
see also couples therapy;
    individual therapy; middle
    phase therapy
Family visits
adult children, 204
in middle phase therapy, 209-10
preparation for, 320
reactions to, 321
to rethink family story, 324,325
Family-of-origin
effects on marriage, 160
effects of own family on therapist,
    57-63
effects on relationships, 13-15,
    35-36,85,96,138-139,
    163-64,171-74,176-77,
    187-89,193
in middle phase therapy, 221,222,
    224,235-36
parent/child relationship and, 200
repositioning within, 209-210,320
therapeutic importance, 214-65
Feelings, control of, 44
First session, 69-112
goals of, 74-75
how to begin, 73-75
with parents and children, 113-14
stages of, 77

who should attend, 69-70
Foster homes, family therapy and 371-72
Fused-reactive stance, 40
Fusion (relationships), 41-44,47

Genograms
  case illustrations, 33,35
  in couples therapy, 165,170
  in family therapy, 34*il*.,74,77
  in individual therapy, 318
  multigenerational perspective of, 32-36
Grandparents, role in family development, 117-19

Histories, family. *See* family histories
Holocaust, long-term effects on families, 14,52,212-13,325, 344
Hospitals, family therapy in, 371-72
Hurt, defensive reactions to, 160-61

"I" position. *See* self issues
Indebtedness, to family, 51-52
Individual autonomy, family function and, 4-5
Individual change
  during course of therapy, 354
  effects on relationships, 162
  family reaction to, 317,320,364
Individual differences, therapists and, 5-6,24
Individual therapy, 317-44
  anxiety in, 319
  case illustrations, 324-44
  defined, 317-19
  distortion of experience, 321
  family histories in, 317-19
  family stories in, 318-19,319,320, 323
  goals of, 341-42

middle phase, 322-24
proactive phase, 322-23
problem areas, 319-21
repositioning in, 320,322-24,327, 330-31,333,343
unfinished business in, 318-19
Initial assessment, 73
Interviewing
  control by therapist, 142,155,223, 334
  ending a session, 130,133,240-41, 244-46
  first session, 74,165-66
  giving equal time, 177
  noninterference during, 229-30
  nonjudgemental approach, 196-97
  rooms for, 67-68
  safety in, 75-77,156,211
  see also case illustrations
Intimacy
  defined, 49-50
  in relationships, 49-51
Intraprofessional systems, therapists and, 67
Involved/detached "I" position, 61

Losses
  case illustration, 133-57
  family reactions to, 53,150,157
Loyalty, to family, 51-52

Marriage
  disappointments of, 160
  emotional distancing in, 160-63
  to one of similar emotional health, 40
  see also couples therapy; relationships
Men, performance goals of, 51
Middle phase therapy, 199-285
  adult focus of, 201
  aged parents in, 211-46
  case illustrations, 204-205, 212-13,214-65,265-85

difficulties of, 202
ending the middle phase, 246-65
extended family in, 210-11
family histories in, 210-11,216
frequency of sessions, 201-202
goals of, 202,287-88
going with the energy, 203-205
as learning experience, 202-203
new information in, 207
opposition in other family
    members, 205-206
practice principles, 203-11
proactive aspects, 199-201,
    206-207
process of, 199-211
repositioning in the family,
    209-210
research stance in, 206-207
self issues, 205-206,208-10
with siblings, 300
supporting the most functional,
    205-206
systems concepts in, 207-208
therapist as a consultant, 200
vision for family, 232
Mourning, family and, 53
Multigenerational family therapy,
    principles of, 1-20,30-54
Multigenerational influences, on
    family relationships, 10-11
Multigenerational maps. See
    genograms

Native-Indian families, problems
    with schools, 24
New individuals, introduction in
    therapy, 369-70
Nuclear families
    as basic family structure, 16
    extended family influences, 12-13
    in middle phase therapy, 203

Overfunction/underfunction
    reciprocity, 47-49

Parent/child relationship, 3-4,
    138-39,140
    with adult children, 211-65
    case illustrations, 79-112,115-33,
        211-65
    child as a confidante, 251,252-53
    death and, 14,53
    family-of-origin issues, 200
    future relationships and, 171-74,
        188-89
    sibling relationships and, 289
    in therapy, 6,69-72,78-79,113-15,
        157,200,268,271
Parents
    differentiation by children, 140,
        331
    in family therapy process, 74,
        78-112,115-57,214-65
    influence of unfinished business
        on children, 36-38
    vision for family, 132
    see also aged parents
Peer group, influence on children,
    31
Physical setup, for family therapy,
    67-68
Proactive stance, 39-40,134
    in individual therapy, 322-23
    in middle phase therapy, 199-201,
        206-207,211,246
Professional family system
    case illustration, 65-66
    in family therapy, 64-68
Projection process, parents to
    children, 37-38
Pseudoself stance. See reactive
    stance
Psychotics, family therapy and, 378
Purser/distancer dynamic, 48-49

Reactive stance, 39-40,134
    in individual therapy, 322-23
    in middle phase therapy, 211
Referral sources, 72-73

Relationship problems, 159-97
case illustration, 164-97
effects of change on, 162
family-of-origin influences,
163-64,171-74,176-77,
187-89,193
functional nature of, 161-63
need to define, 161-62
partners' attempts to resolve,
161-62
as a result of death, 168
Relationships
alliances in, 44-45
balance in, 47-49
changes in, 40-41
defense mechanisms in, 163
ego boundaries and, 39
emotional functioning in, 162
emotional triangles and, 41-44,47
expectations for, 159-60
fantasy making in, 160
intimacy in, 49-51
pursuer/distancer dynamic, 48-49
self issues and, 373-74
sex differences in expectations
for, 50-51
see also couples therapy; family
relationships; marriage
Repositioning
in individual therapy, 320,322-23
with parents, 327,330-31,333,343
in sibling relationships, 288

Safety, use of family stories to
maintain, 203-204
Safety in therapy, 5-6,156
with aged parents, 211
case illustration with children,
115-33
interviewing and, 75-77
with siblings, 292
Scapegoat process, 27
School counselors, 60-61
School systems, family therapy and,
24-25

Secrecy
in families, 101,291-92
need for therapist to avoid, 18,
367-69,374-75
Self-change, stages of, 208
Self-concept, development of,
38-41,42
Self issues
avoidance of, 373-74
in middle phase therapy, 205-206,
207-10
Self-questions, 76-77
Session frequency, in family
therapy, 376
Sex differences, in family
expectations, 50-51
Sibling relationships, 35,103,144,
152,157
adult siblings, 287-316
birth order effects, 289
case illustrations, 127,128,
287-316,290-91
content issues, 291
family connections and, 288-89
goals of therapy, 288-89
influence of family stories,
294-95,314
problem areas, 290-92
repositioning in, 288
secrets and, 291-92
in therapy, 103,152,157,287-316
unfinished business and, 288
Stories
need for, 77
see also family stories
Suicidal thoughts, in client, 141
Suicide, discussion in therapy,
100-101,110,135,141
Symptom relief, defined, 19-20
Systems concepts, in middle phase
therapy, 207-208
Systems levels, family behavior and,
25, 26*il.*

Teen-age mothers, 31-32
Telephone contacts, case illustration,
    70-72
Temperament, defined, 23-24
Termination session
    case illustration, 348-66
    formal evaluation session, 345-47
    raising future scenarios, 346-47
    readiness of client for, 345
    structure, 347-48
Therapists
    concurrent therapies and, 272-73
    confidence of clients in, 78
    consultants' role, 200,347-48,376
    control of session, 81,142,155
    crisis intervention by, 375
    detached stance of, 61,68,76,319
    family changes and, 89-90
    intraprofessional systems of, 67
    limitations of, 61-62
    need to know family, 1-2
    as overfunctioners, 58
    own family emotional system,
        57-64
    as pursuers, 48
    relationships with clients, 113-15,
        321
    secrecy avoidance, 367-69,374-75
    self-image of, 62

    sharing information with
        outsiders, 370-71
    triangle avoidance, 319
    unfinished business of, 8,58,63,
        64
    validation needs, 63-64
    values of, 17-19
    see also couples therapy; family
        therapy; individual therapy;
        middle phase therapy
Time allotments, in family therapy,
    375-76

Unfinished business, 36-38
    complements in partners, 163
    effects on relationships, 162
    of extended family members,
        200-201
    of individuals, 318-19
    multigenerational perspective,
        14-15,35,36
    of parents, 222-23
    of siblings, 288
    of therapist, 8,58,63,64
    validation, need for, 50,63-64,320
    value systems, effects on family
        therapy, 17-19
    videotaping, in family therapy,
        213-14,215,230,293

Women, relationship needs of, 51